RUN
to
FAILURE

ALSO BY ABRAHM LUSTGARTEN

China's Great Train: Beijing's Drive West and the Campaign to Remake Tibet

RUN
to
FAILURE

BP and the Making of the
Deepwater Horizon Disaster

ABRAHM LUSTGARTEN

W. W. NORTON & COMPANY
New York   London

For information about permission to reproduce selections from this book,
write to Permissions, W. W. Norton & Company, Inc.,
500 Fifth Avenue, New York, NY 10110

For information about special discounts for bulk purchases, please contact
W. W. Norton Special Sales at specialsales@wwnorton.com or 800-233-4830

Manufacturing by RR Donnelley, Harrisonburg
Book design by Helene Berinsky
Production manager: Anna Oler

Library of Congress Cataloging-in-Publication Data

Lustgarten, Abrahm.
Run to failure : BP and the making of the
Deepwater Horizon disaster / Abrahm Lustgarten. — 1st ed.
p. cm.
Includes bibliographical references and index.
ISBN 978-0-393-08162-6 (hardcover)
1. British Petroleum Company. 2. Petroleum industry and trade—
Moral and ethical aspects. 3. Oil spills—Environmental aspects—United States.
I. Title.
HD9571.9.B73L87 2012
363.11'9622338190916364—dc23

2011046141

W. W. Norton & Company, Inc.
500 Fifth Avenue, New York, N.Y. 10110
www.wwnorton.com

W. W. Norton & Company Ltd.
Castle House, 75/76 Wells Street, London W1T 3QT

1 2 3 4 5 6 7 8 9 0

For Jodie

Contents

PART THREE: *The Reformation*

Prologue

The burst of gas came from so deep within the bowels of the earth it may as well have come from another world. Thirteen thousand feet beneath the ocean's silty floor and the earth's crust and another five thousand feet underwater—a total depth farther than fourteen Empire State buildings stacked atop one another—hydrocarbons in the form of hot fluid saturated with dissolved methane seeped through the reinforced walls of a new oil well.

The well, an exploratory venture drilled by BP and called Macondo, was a three-mile-long tube of cement and steel that had been burrowed into the million-and-a-half-year-old rock in the weeks before. It was one of the industry's most important new efforts to find oil in the deep waters off the southern coast of the United States, and, while not the deepest, the Macondo was pushing the limits of drilling technology and risk.

This particular well had been a cursed project from the start. Miles above, where the sun skipped along the lapping waves of the Gulf of Mexico, the Macondo project's 126 oil workers had battled for weeks to control wild kicks of gas and to adapt to a series of setbacks doled out by this complicated and unpredictable well. Under stress and guided by conflicting mandates to drill quickly, drill safely, and drill cheaply, the workers had often made the wrong decisions. Now the Macondo was preparing to issue them one last challenge.

Inside the well, the gas, squeezed out of the earth by the natural pressure of the compressed rock and shoved upward by its own buoyancy, shot skyward at a pace that would bring it to the surface of the gulf in a matter of minutes. As it rose it expanded rapidly, the volume increasing the higher it got in the well, until the steel pipe and casing that channeled it upward could barely contain its explosive force.

On the ocean floor, the kick—as such a geologic burp is called in the oil industry—shot through the top of the well at the seafloor and continued upward through the mile-deep water in the long hose of steel called a riser pipe that connected the well to the surface. There, it slammed into the Deepwater Horizon drilling rig, a thirty-story structure with a footprint the size of an average Walmart Supercenter floating in the Gulf of Mexico. The rig was owned by a contractor, Transocean, and most of the crew on board were Transocean employees, all of whom were contracted to work for BP. With a burst like a canon, pent-up pressure from the oil and gas exploded from the twenty-one-inch pipe, which rose up out of the dark water. Bolts sheared off and valves were forced open. Drilling mud that had filled the well to cool the drill bit and balance the well pressure spewed across the deck of the rig, rushing against doors and spilling across stairways. With a roaring hiss, a cloud of natural gas began to envelop the rig.

The gas started at the drill floor, a small raised platform underneath the tower of a drilling derrick in the center of the Deepwater Horizon's main deck. The drill floor, one of the highest working floors on the structure, is where the drill pipe is managed and decisions are made about the fluids and pressure in the well. From there, the gas spread to the rig's main deck below and toward two subdecks.

On the drilling floor, the Deepwater's driller on duty, Dewey Revette, had been monitoring the well readings and watching for a kick, but he hadn't seen the signs—a strange but subtle fluctuation in well pipe pressure on multiple monitors. A few minutes earlier a sudden rise in pressure had broken a pump valve, and Revette had dispatched three of his crew to go belowdecks and fix it. When the blowout came, Revette, a driller named Stephen Curtis, and the rig's toolpusher, or drilling supervisor, Jason Anderson, scrambled to control the burst of gas. Anderson, cool-headed, had spent nine years working on the Deepwater Horizon and knew what to do. First, he diverted the spurting mud into a gas separator, thinking it would help capture the explosive materials from the messy mud. Then he triggered one of the emergency valves on the rig's blowout preventer, a three-hundred-ton piece of machinery lying on the gulf's floor meant to seal off the well in the case of a violent kick. But it was too late.

Two flights below, on the Deepwater Horizon's second deck, Mike Williams manned the rig's electronics shop, next to the engine room. There, in a steel box full of controls and monitors, he guided the platform's electrical systems and power. A few feet away, diesel turbines generated that power and spun the drill bits miles inside the earth. Suddenly, Williams heard a deafening whine as the revolutions of the engines increased. But the danger—an envelope of gas that ballooned from the top of the riser pipe on the drilling floor above—was invisible. Neither Williams nor anyone else on the rig except the small group that had scrambled to the drill deck had been told that the Macondo was blowing out.

The rig had an extensive network of sensors that were supposed to detect a combustible cloud of gas before it could reach the engines and the control room and issue a warning. Those alarms were meant to trigger a series of closing valves designed to keep the gas from burning up in the engines: one of the most important forms of protection in case of an accident. But the sensors didn't react, and the valves never shut. The gas saturated the air, turning the rig's engines' normal cooling and ventilation intake into a source of gaseous fuel. The motors sucked the fumes out of the air, screaming higher and faster, their pistons whipping back and forth furiously. Another critical safety backup, the blowout preventer that Anderson had already tried to trigger in order to cut off the well, also failed, meaning the gas cloud on the rig would only get bigger. By the time Williams realized what was unfolding, there was little he could do to change it. He ran toward a fortified steel exit door, but as he reached it, one of the engines exploded. The six-foot-tall plate of metal blew off its hinges, striking him midstride. Dazed and bleeding, he slowly picked himself up, only to be slammed back down again by a devastating second blast.

On the deck above Williams, the Deepwater Horizon's derrick was instantly engulfed in flames. The men on the drilling floor, including Jason Anderson, were killed quickly, but dozens of others were crushed or twisted or slashed by flying debris and were desperately crawling out of their own horrific emergencies, trying not to be entombed in an industrial grave. In his stateroom, Jimmy Harrell, Transocean's most senior supervisor on the rig, was temporarily blinded by flying insulation as the walls of his berth collapsed on him in the shower. On the second deck, Randy Ezell, the rig's senior toolpusher, was blown violently against the wall of his office and buried in debris.

Williams stumbled out toward a set of steel steps only to find that the walkway, which would have taken him up to the main deck, was missing. The engines were gone; the whole back of the rig was gone. Wiping away blood that blocked his vision, Williams sought another way. He heard a plea for help and stumbled over the body of an injured colleague. Above them a wall of black smoke drifted up from raging, seventy-five-foot flames. Williams couldn't carry the man. All he could do was try to save himself.

A short time later, desperate to escape the searing heat and giant cherry-balls of fire, Williams leapt off the railings into the black night, tumbling ninety feet into the roiling, burning, oil-streaked water of the Gulf of Mexico.

JEANNE PASCAL turned on her TV on April 21, 2010, just a few hours after the blast, to see a spindle of black smoke slithering into the sky from an oil platform on the oceanic expanse of the Gulf of Mexico. Right away she thought that it was a BP disaster unfolding on the screen. For a long while she sat transfixed on an overstuffed couch in her Seattle-area home, her feelings shifting from shock to anger. *God, they just don't learn*, she thought.

Pascal, a career Environmental Protection Agency (EPA) attorney only seven weeks into her retirement, knew as much as anyone in the federal government about BP, which had contracted the Deepwater Horizon rig to drill the Macondo well. And that morning, she understood in an instant what it would take others months to grasp: in BP's twenty-year quest to compete with the world's biggest oil companies, its managers had become deaf to risk and systematically gambled with safety at hundreds of facilities and with thousands of employees' lives.

At the EPA, Pascal's job had been to act as a behind-the-scenes babysitter for companies whose repeated violations or misconduct might disqualify them from billions of dollars in contracts and other benefits from the federal government. When they got in trouble, it was her job to guide them back toward being responsible and compliant companies. Over the years she'd persuaded hundreds of troubled energy, mining, and waste-disposal companies to quickly change their behavior. When she was first assigned to BP, in 1998, she thought that the company would be another routine assignment. But BP, it turned out, was in a league of its own.

For twelve years, she had watched the company flirt with one accident after another and struggle to correct its mistakes. On her watch BP had been fined hundreds of millions of dollars and charged with four federal crimes—more than any other oil company, in her experience—and had demonstrated what she described as a pattern of disregard for regulations and for the EPA. The company had repeatedly cut out key safety processes and let equipment languish to save a few thousand dollars at a time. It had taken risks at its wells in Alaska, on its platforms in the Caspian Sea, and at its refineries in Scotland. Undoubtedly, she thought, it must have done so in the Gulf of Mexico, too.

Across the United States but in Alaska in particular, there had been an inordinate number of warnings and many close calls, some of which could have turned into disasters. Equipment that handled explosive gases and volatile oils was left in poor repair, and the workers who tended these devices were pushed with excessive hours and unrealistic quotas and then rewarded with bonuses for helping the system limp along with minimal investment. BP's refinery business seemed no different. Four years earlier, an explosion at a refinery in Texas City, on the gulf coast, killed 15 workers and sent 180 people to hospitals. The common thread, Pascal thought, was one deeply woven into BP management culture—that preventative operations cost money. There was a corresponding belief that the chance of an accident was slim.

For a long time, Pascal thought something like the Deepwater Horizon disaster was imminent, and for years she had fought to prevent it. In late 2009, she warned officials in Washington and BP executives that the company's approach to safety and environmental issues was reckless. The implication was that another disaster was inevitable, and an environmental catastrophe likely.

PASCAL WASN'T the only one with concerns about BP. By early 2010 there was a growing contingent of legislators, government officials, former employees, and even executives at other oil companies who were increasingly nervous about how BP ran its operations. Some of them were actively working to prevent a disaster like the Deepwater Horizon explosion.

When the Macondo well was being drilled, several members of Congress demanded that BP Alaska's chief executive answer questions about the company's safety problems there, and openly questioned whether BP could be trusted with some of America's most important energy assets. BP, after all, operated the bulk of Alaska's oil fields and ran the Trans Alaska Pipeline, the single conduit ferrying some 8 percent of the nation's oil to the lower 48. The Department of Justice was still pursuing a civil case after past BP spills in Alaska, and at least one former senior investigator warned that another major accident was likely.

The state of Alaska was suing BP for negligence, and BP's probation officer there was weighing whether the company had violated its agreements to improve safety and operations. Meanwhile, the Department of Transportation had its eye on BP's pipeline management, and the Occupational Safety and Health Administration was about to levy tens of millions of dollars in fines for what it described as some of the most flagrant and willful violations of worker safety the agency's administrators had ever witnessed.

Inside the company itself, whistle-blowers were amassing in increasing numbers—an ombudsman's office set up by BP to handle such internal complaints had reviewed more than two hundred cases, including serious allegations that safety procedures had been disregarded and that hasty engineering was putting the company's facilities and operations at risk from Alaska to the Gulf of Mexico.

Even some of BP's own former management were weary, and in March—just four weeks before the blowout on the Deepwater Horizon—BP's safety and environment manager for the company's Gulf of Mexico operations resigned, claiming that the company wasn't paying enough attention to safety and environmental risks.

BP, in the gulf, should have been at the top of its game. It had extraordinary experience in deepwater drilling and in the Gulf of Mexico. While the Macondo endeavor was pushing the limits of the company's experience, few companies had spent more time exploring offshore than BP, or invested more in both leases to drill and the technology to drill.

Much of the criticism the company had endured related to aging infrastructure in BP oil fields that were past their prime. But the gulf was where the newest equipment and most sophisticated technology were being deployed, and it was there that BP had some of the best technical experts in the industry to implement them. The projects in the gulf were supposed to be different from some of BP's other endeavors. In the gulf, BP stood at the cusp of modern technology. This project was among the most important investments that BP, as a corporation, was making for the future.

Yet there appeared to be a sense of complacency. BP cut and pasted portions of its disaster plan from a website describing conditions halfway around the world. (The company called for the protection of walruses, which don't live in the gulf.) Both the company and the government regulators who oversaw the Macondo project rested on what they described as a thirty-year record of offshore drilling without major incident, even though there were plenty of examples to contradict that story.

Eighteen hours after Williams jumped overboard and a day after Pascal awoke to wall-to-wall television coverage of the disaster, the Deepwater Horizon, still burning atop an open sea, sank to the bottom of the gulf. Eleven people had burned to death or drowned. Seventeen people had been injured. A broken pipe with an opening the size of a basketball began spewing millions of gallons of oil into the water nearly a mile below the surface.

The world soaked up news about the accident, hungry to understand what it meant, and how devastating the oil spill was going to be for the gulf's environment. Immediately, important questions were raised about what had led to the accident: Why didn't the gas sensors and the blowout preventer function? Had BP cut corners in the cement job that was supposed to contain the high-pressure kick of gas out of the well? Why hadn't tests that every oil company routinely performs to guarantee the integrity of its well construction detected whatever cracks, gaps, or weaknesses had allowed the gas to seep out in the first place? And why, if the Macondo was permitted as an exploratory well, did BP follow procedures and make one decision after another that would normally only be applied to a production well, for which the risks were known and quantified? Was it about the money?

It would take many months to answer these questions. But right away Pascal, as well as several whistle-blowers and former investigators and oil industry executives who knew the company well, already understood that something larger was in play. These were people who had watched or worked with BP over the past fifteen to twenty years. While their perspectives and opinions varied, they agreed that there was something about BP that set it apart from the rest of the oil industry, something about it that seemed more eager, more hasty, and yet cavalier and even arrogant.

As they each reflected on the company's history in the context of what was unfolding in the Gulf of Mexico, they saw a pattern. The explosion and oil spill were not anomalies. The causes of the disaster didn't originate on the Deepwater Horizon rig in the days or weeks before the accident. In fact, the fall of dominoes that would set in motion one of the oil industry's most deadly disasters and worst environmental catastrophes began years before. The roots of the story of the Macondo failure concern corporate responsibility, business ethics, and leadership and go back at least two decades, to a point at which BP executives sought to redefine the company and reposition it as one of the great corporations of our time.

Because the series of missteps goes back so far, and was so well known by so many people—officials and company executives alike—the events that unfolded on the Deepwater Horizon in April 2010 were also predictable. Pascal, the Department of Justice, former employees at BP, all knew something like this might one day happen. Perhaps even the chief executives that led BP through its defining years—Sir John Browne and Tony Hayward—also knew that the strains they put on their company might one day lead to disaster. All of them had failed to prevent it. This is the story of why.

PART ONE

A New Dawn

1

THE RISE OF THE SUN KING

WHEN NEWS BROKE that John Browne would take over British Petroleum's worldwide exploration and production group—the part of the oil giant that actually produced oil—the analysts and investors who watched the industry had great expectations.

For anyone who held them, British Petroleum's shares had been a volatile investment. A chart of the company's stock price over time swooped and rose, bearing little resemblance to the steady and reliable climb of Exxon shares. Delivering shareholder value was by no means the only measure of a successful oil company; it may not have even been the most important one. But it's the one that mattered most on Wall Street, and it was becoming a driving force for British Petroleum's new, young management. Now John Browne was convincing investors that he was the man to do it.

Browne, then the chief financial officer at BP America, which was British Petroleum's North American division and represented more than half of the company's assets, already had a reputation as a shrewd numbers man. In 1984 he had taken the helm of British Petroleum's global finance group. Then, in 1986, he moved to Cleveland, where he became the CFO of the old John D. Rockefeller division, the Standard Oil Company of Ohio (Sohio), in which British Petroleum held a majority share. In 1987 British Petroleum took over Sohio completely and turned to Browne and Bob Horton, the man now in line to take the chief executive slot at British Petroleum, to transform it. When British Petroleum took over Sohio, renaming it BP America in 1987, it was awash in debt and failed exploration bids, with too many employees and too little promise. Together, Browne and Horton took a floundering and distracted operation losing a billion dollars a year, closed twenty plants, and set a path toward a half-billion-dollar profit. And while it was Horton who had earned the nickname "the Hatchet," it was Browne who had whittled the spreadsheets and made sense of BP America's financial outlook.

Now, in June 1989, as the summer heat and humidity fell upon the busy streets of New York, a group of those watchful British Petroleum investors and financial analysts were gathered in a private meeting to hear what Browne would do to the company's global exploration group, its most fundamental business unit. Browne had gathered the group in the Rainbow Room, on the sixty-fifth floor of the GE building at Rockefeller Center. The meeting was broadcast to London.

Browne's remarks were compelling and worrisome. On paper, British Petroleum had replaced its reserves—the amount of oil the company knew it could produce, but hadn't yet drilled for—faster than any other oil company in 1988, the previous year, and had enthusiastically touted its successes. In 1989 its production had dropped some, but historical cost profits—the figure relating revenue to the amount British Petroleum paid for its materials—was soaring. In that brief snapshot in time, British Petroleum looked to be as good a company as any. But Browne took a longer view and, flipping through the first few slides of data in his presentation, told the analysts the last thing any of them wanted to hear: that the way he looked at British Petroleum's assets, the company's reserves were actually down 94 percent over the past few decades. "This is dreadful," he began. "We're declining."

They were confusing comments, because almost every other picture the company put before its investors, including in the releases it sent to the media, was rosy. "What was said in those press releases was true, for the most part," says Tom Hamilton, who had just been promoted to head British Petroleum's international exploration efforts, and who had worked closely with Browne and Horton to reinvent the division in Cleveland. But the truth, in this case, was malleable. "There were some improvements in '89, but the record through the eighties had been weak in competitive and in absolute terms—especially in terms of booking new reserves," said Nick Butler, one of Browne's closest advisers. In fact, when profits were viewed not on a historical basis but in terms of replacement cost profits—the figure oil companies use relating revenue to the amount they would have to pay to acquire more oil to sell in the future—they had dropped in 1989. "John was thinking about the long-term competitive position of British Petroleum. The company had slipped down the industry ranking, and that needed to be reversed," Butler added.

Instead of plotting year-on-year growth, Browne and his team, in an effort to get the broadest panorama possible, had examined the company's key statistics over the last century, in five-year increments. The resulting line graph told a stunning story. In fact, in a single slide, British Petroleum's corporate biography was laid bare.

For fifty years, the company's oil assets in reserve steadily grew, becoming, by around 1960, a cache of some seventy billion barrels of oil. Then those assets began to decline. By 1989, even after several acquisitions and a decade of efforts to revitalize the company under its outgoing chairman, Peter Walters, British Petroleum's total reserves had dropped to just five billion barrels. Eighty-six percent of this total was in the United States or the UK, essentially what was left underground in Alaska and in the North Sea, both fields that Browne knew to be passing their peak and about to begin a steady drop-off in production. "I knew that BP controlled insufficient reserves and opportunities to secure its future," Browne later reflected. If British Petroleum continued to see itself as a company that made its money drilling for oil, it was on its way out of business. "BP had no option but to get its legacy sorted out, get faster on its feet, do more deals, and become more innovative."

The investors sat back to absorb the news. But its delivery was softened by the charm of the messenger, whose thoughts were somehow made more intellectual and more appealing to Americans by his easy temper and drawling British accent. Browne was a man who could be counted on to be blunt and honest. If you were betting your retirement on what he did, that was what you wanted. Browne was forty-one years old then, and he could scarcely have spent more of his life with British Petroleum if its engineers had grown him in a bottle.

When he was a child, Browne's father had worked for the company in the oil fields of southwestern Iran. In the 1950s the senior Browne had explored the field at Masjid-e-Suleiman, where William D'Arcy had first struck oil in 1908 and founded the Anglo-Persian Oil Company, which would become British Petroleum. John Browne junior—along with his mother, a Romanian who had survived Auschwitz—spent time in Iran during his boyhood. The young Browne had tagged along with his father to golf in a private club, and the family had lived in a prefabricated American-made home in a gated community with a heavily watered lawn and three full-time servants. It was a colonial existence if there ever was one. As a teen John had returned to England and had studied physics at Cambridge, his education paid for with a scholarship from British Petroleum. His professors thought he had the promise of a great intellectual and seemed disappointed when, upon finishing, he instead chose the more pedestrian path toward a career in business. Nonetheless, British Petroleum continued to pay. In 1969 the company sent him to Alaska's Prudhoe Bay, then a true oil frontier; oil had been struck there just one year earlier. Later, they moved him to New York, then back to England to learn the offshore business in the North Sea. In 1980 British Petroleum sent him to Stanford as a Sloan business fellow, and after he graduated, in 1984, Robert Horton, then in the role of British Petroleum's chief financial officer, promoted him to be the company's treasurer. His pedigree nearly complete, he later followed Horton to Sohio and Cleveland. Browne became the consummate company man, representing the interests of a corporation partly owned by the British government and never working another job.

Throughout, he was unwaveringly loyal, earning the trust of his superiors. Yet somehow he still managed to be the kind of guy whom his managers could rely on to think differently while appearing to preserve the status quo. When Browne was stationed in Alaska, he obeyed the mandate to find new oil, yet he insisted on finding new methods to do it, writing computer models, for instance, that improved accuracy and efficiency of exploration there. Horton, under whom Browne worked at BP America, and who would soon take over as British Petroleum's group chief executive in early 1990, had developed the utmost confidence in Browne after the two had worked closely in turning BP

America around. Horton's BP America turnaround was a practice run for what others, including Peter Walters, wanted for the entire company. Brown had become an integral part of that team. If he now wanted to upend the entire business, they trusted—based on his tutelage—that he was helping it grow. In fact, what Browne laid out that day in New York was an old trick he had learned from Horton back in Cleveland. "It's a matter of convincing people that however bad the news is, the end result is going to be better for them," Horton told the *New York Times* in 1988. "It's the art of generalship." It would eventually become a guiding human factor in Browne's tenure.

Browne was competitive. He wanted to experiment, as an executive, with the grandest opportunities he could imagine. British Petroleum should be the largest, most successful oil company in the world. But Exxon, which grew out of Rockefeller's old Standard Oil Company of New Jersey, had a virtually unassailable seat on that throne at the time, and British Petroleum was well behind Shell, the only viable European oil giant of the era. "If it was a secret, it was poorly kept that John wanted BP to be the largest UK oil company, and as long as Shell was sitting there with a UK presence, Shell was the target," said Hamilton. Shell, which had continued to book more and more reserves and thus didn't appear to share British Petroleum's problems of declining access to oil, scoffed at the idea of British Petroleum's ascendancy. Shell, Peter Walters told a reporter at the time, is "an enormously powerful company. We don't rate with Shell's financials overall. We are Avis to their Hertz."

To Browne the sentiment rang as complacent. He wished upon British Petroleum an appetite for risk. British Petroleum could overtake Shell and any other company it set its sights on, Browne believed. He may have overlooked the possibility that British Petroleum would have to be willing to gamble its safety net along the way. "It was a very hidebound company, an outgrowth of the British government, to some extent," says Ronald Freeman, a former head of oil and gas banking at Salomon Brothers, who in 1984 was assigned to fly to London and help orchestrate a large sale of the British government's ownership of British Petroleum. That's when Freeman met Browne, then the company's treasurer. "There were a lot of people at BP who had had long careers as civil servants in the British government," Freeman said. "It was a very hierarchical place, sort of stuffy. And that had to change. They had not found a way to replace reserves. They were not going to do so remaining hierarchical and stuffy. They had to get out there and compete." By 1989, after decades stationed on American soil, Browne had arrived at the belief that what his staid corporation needed most was a dose of ruthless and brave American entrepreneurship.

The problem that Browne saw was that the vast majority of British Petroleum's reserves and production at the time came from two aging fields, in the North Sea and Alaska's Prudhoe Bay. The company had managed to boost its reserves figures over the last couple of years, but that wasn't by discovering new oil, it was by technologically enhancing their ability to squeeze a little more product out of old wells, and then making an accounting adjustment that reflected how much of the oil was "recoverable" oil using the new methods. It was a patch job for the books, and a temporary solution, at best. Meanwhile, even if the company pumped more oil from those fields to increase production, that, too, was a game of diminishing returns. Browne expected production at Prudhoe Bay and the Alaskan fields to peak within the next two years and then begin a long, ten-year decline. By the turn of the century, he believed those wells would be almost dry. And so, Browne feared, unless BP could muster new reserves, in a new part of the world, and could muster the appetite for risk that he believed it would take to achieve that, his company's clock was ticking.

THE PUZZLE Browne sought to solve was bigger than BP and tied back to the oil crisis of 1973, when Egypt and Syria invaded Israel in the Yom Kippur War, and when the oil-producing nations, in protest, banded together in a cartel and refused to sell oil to the United States. Members of the Organization of Petroleum Exporting Companies (OPEC) launched a political war to wrest back control over the world's oil markets. The Western oil companies were kicked out of the Middle East, and OPEC tied a tourniquet on shipments of crude to U.S. refineries, sending a shockwave through the nation's markets and gasoline prices to record highs, and spurring a recession. One by one, OPEC nations nationalized their oil assets, blocking the world's largest oil companies from producing their oil, and in 1979, the Iranian revolution occurred.

British Petroleum had oil at the time in Kuwait, Abu Dhabi, and Libya, but its largest fields, by far, were in Iran.

Following British Petroleum's discovery of oil in southern Iran in 1908, the rich deposit had quickly become a pillar of the company's growth and identity, albeit a fragile one. Since the 1950s, British Petroleum had been clinging to life there, resisting an anti-imperialist tide and even working its connections with the CIA to pressure the overthrow of the Iranian government after Iran's prime minister at the time, Mohammad Mossadegh, seized British Petroleum's oil. "British agents began conspiring to overthrow Mossadegh soon after he nationalized the oil company," wrote Stephen Kinzer, in *All the Shah's Men*. "Immediately, the British asked President Truman for help." British Petroleum got a reprieve when the shah was installed at the West's behest. But it didn't last. By 1979 the shah's government was overturned by a furious Iranian public, and, with it, British Petroleum was sent packing.

"BP was the number one oil company in the Middle East. It was the first to commercialize Middle East production," says James Bamberg, a historian who has written extensively about British Petroleum. "So the loss of those reserves through nationalization was absolutely fundamental. It really posed huge challenges for the company. We must be talking about the vast majority of BP's crude oil."

It was a large part of the reason for the sharp decline on Browne's chart of reserves that he showed that day in New York, but it wasn't a problem that British Petroleum faced alone. All of the world's largest private oil companies lost access to prized reserves in the Middle East, Venezuela, and North Africa—at least 75 percent of the world's total supply of oil. While British Petroleum may have been hit the worst, the crisis forced deep reflection throughout the industry on how to survive, and it set off a survival-of-the-fittest competition to expand business and broaden sources of income. One way, according to the thinking that prevailed at the time, was to find security in becoming a global corporate conglomerate. The idea was that diverse and completely unrelated streams of revenue would help balance out the volatility of oil, which at the time seemed likely to remain so. So oil companies snatched up unrelated businesses, and British Petroleum, perhaps out of a sense of extra vulnerability, led the way, buying everything from a pet food maker to coal companies in the hopes that they would act as a shield against anything the market—or the OPEC cartel—could inflict on them. But almost ten years later, instead of providing a blanket of security, those extraneous companies had become an iron ball chained to the ankle of a company trying to clamber out of its own grave. British Petroleum had wound up a cumbersome and overly diverse corporation in need of focus and priorities.

Walters, who had by 1989 been a member of British Petroleum's board of directors since the oil embargo seventeen years earlier, had already begun cutting off the deadweight by the late 1980s, selling off parts of its chemical companies and then a copper mine interest in Australia. The hope was that the trunk would grow stronger and thicker as a result of cutting off the limbs. He got the company down near its core, and it was waiting for new leaders to build it back up again. Most of the task would fall to the new CEO, Horton, whose 1990 promotion was announced in late 1989; and the narrowed corporate focus would dictate that exploration and oil production pick up the slack. To a large extent, that job would fall to the man leading that one critically important division: John Browne.

Browne and Horton were taking over at a time of great tumult. In fact, the three years before Browne's transition had been a bit of a nightmare. First, in August 1987, Margaret Thatcher announced that the British government would sell off the 31 percent of British Petroleum that the government still owned, privatizing the company and putting a flood of shares on the market all at once. On October 10 the government arranged to sell 2.2 billion shares to the world's most prominent investment banks that underwrote the deal, including Salomon Brothers. But five days later, in a stroke of the worst kind of bad luck, the stock market imploded, registering the largest single-business-day losses in stock market history. Black Monday led to a 22 percent loss on Wall Street, and an 11 percent drop in the value of British Petroleum's shares—overnight. The Kuwaiti government seized the opportunity to snap up British Petroleum at a discount at precisely the moment American investors were gun-shy, buying a 22 percent stake.

Then, just two months before Browne's 1989 promotion to head of exploration and production, the *Exxon Valdez* tanker ran aground in Alaska, pouring millions of gallons of crude oil onto the shoreline of one of southwestern Alaska's most vital fisheries. That disaster seemed like Exxon's problem; but British Petroleum, as the largest managing shareholder in the Alyeska Pipeline Service Company, a corporation set up to run the single oil pipeline that winds eight hundred miles across Alaska from Prudhoe Bay to the tanker port in Valdez, was quickly proven woefully unprepared for the cleanup.

Besides the environmental calamity, the *Valdez* spill threatened to have other devastating consequences for the industry. It would change the way the public viewed the entire oil business, killing in an instant the political appetite for opening Alaska's Arctic National Wildlife Refuge (ANWR), the nineteen-million-acre North Slope wilderness tract just east of Prudhoe Bay, to drilling. ANWR was thought to hold vast deposits of oil that could replenish the industry's reserves, but distrust gripped the nation, and instead British Petroleum and the rest of the oil companies found themselves beginning an uphill political and environmental battle that would extend into the foreseeable future.

All of this weighed on Browne that June day in New York. There was, as Hamilton says, "a lot of concern about the lack of opportunity that we saw in the portfolio at the time." Browne faced a choice: he could keep his opinion private, and slowly work to shape a subtle turn of events behind the scenes and in the privacy of the boardrooms. Or he could shake things up—dramatically reset the stage in his first month on the job. He didn't have a road map, but he was beginning to form an intuitive sense of where he wanted to see both his division and British Petroleum go. To execute his vision, he needed the short-term invigoration brought by investor confidence and a booming stock price. At the same time, Browne—and British Petroleum—had to define a long-term plan. To do that, the company needed to turn itself around. And it had to start immediately. "The whole philosophy of the way we do business has to change," Browne would say a short time later. The investors gathered in the glass room towering above Manhattan's skyline listening to his pitch seemed inclined to have faith in a company led by executives capable of such blunt self-critique and self-invention. That day in June, they gave Browne the benefit of the doubt.

BROWNE WAS scarcely outside Rockefeller Center when he began making calls to staff members who could help him figure out what to do next. First on his list was Hamilton, whom he had always trusted to drop everything and work around the clock to turn his visions into reality. That's how it had been when they were together at Sohio, and that's how Browne wanted it now. On the phone, Hamilton was asked to come up with a scenario that reflected a new strategy, a calculation of the best chances for discovering new oil. Hamilton thought such a global assessment would take months. Instead, Browne gave him a few weeks.

"John's approach was you agree to a timeline—like, three months—and the next thing you knew John would have shortened that by about half," Hamilton said.

British Petroleum had drilling and exploration projects in thirty-one countries. Only thirteen of them were producing oil. More than half of the company's oil production came from Alaska's North Slope. Browne wanted a new class of oil discovery for British Petroleum—what the industry liked to call its "elephants," fields with a billion barrels or more of oil—and he was willing to make dramatic changes and cut some costs to get it.

Browne underscored a ground rule laid out by Walters: "there are no sacred cows." Walters had meant that in terms of planning British Petroleum's divestiture of distracting side businesses, but Browne applied it to whole oil fields, and even to the typical strategies that would normally guide an exploration business. It was to be a raw brainstorm. He wanted his staff to think differently, and to do that, they would have to get a little more comfortable with risk. The resulting intellectual exercises would begin to shape not only British Petroleum's immediate strategies for the future but Browne's long-term philosophy for how the company should be run. "We thought anything was possible," Hamilton said.

While Browne and his team sharpened their pencils and pored over data and world maps and filled whiteboards, other companies were doing much the same, in large part because many of the challenges British Petroleum faced were universal. The years between 1986 and 1989 marked a geopolitical transformation in the oil-consuming world and had been a do-or-die period for the entire industry. The Saudis flooded the market, believing they could profit by selling larger volumes of oil at lower prices. Oil prices had dropped to as low as $11.98 a barrel, and industry analysts called this period the Great Oil Depression. The new president of the United States, George H. W. Bush, had described it as "free fall" and a national security threat. Daniel Yergin referred to it as a realignment from ideological to economically driven priorities. An oil minister from the Middle East called it a "new realism."

By the end of 1989 Browne was picking up the pieces. The cultural shifts were big, but profits in oil, though increasing, were tenuous. The worldwide economy was headed toward a deep slump. While the cost for a barrel of oil had climbed to nearly $20, no one was confident it would last. In fact, Browne didn't think the industry could plan on a future above $15. "The danger arises when you think oil prices are going to get you out of a fix," he said. In late 1988 he had warned an audience at an oil and gas symposium in Houston that "long-range oil company planning must never again assume a quietly escalating price. . . . When the price does start up permanently, around the turn of the century, volatility is likely to continue, rather than diminish."

And while the big Western private oil companies—the ones not government-owned—were scrambling to find new oil to replace the reserves they produced each year, those new oil finds were in increasingly dangerous places or simply technologically challenging to get to. Even if they could be found, their harvest would cost astronomically more than oil in more accessible places. This exploration was being undertaken at the same time that oil prices couldn't be counted on to support the exploration; additionally, the world's most coveted supplies were politically inaccessible, and the best free-world producing fields were aging. It was the start of a paradigm shift and a new conversation that would ultimately evolve into questions about the sustainability of an oil economy. But in 1989, it simply meant it was nearly impossible to increase oil reserves and production—to visualize a future of growth for these companies—at a profit.

Browne and, by extension, his boss, Peter Walters, had to wrestle with fundamental questions that until the 1980s had tended to answer themselves: How can an oil company both satisfy the insatiable short-term demands of stock market investors, who provided an increasingly critical source of capital, and invest enough in long-term planning to be confident that the business would be sturdy twenty years from now? Publicly traded companies were all about profit, and dividends, in the moment. Shareholders tended to have little patience for delayed satisfaction. Yet patience, investment in operations, and long-range planning were what the oil business was supposed to be all about.

In the new post-embargo and post-nationalization era, some twenty-five companies controlled more than three-quarters of the world's oil, and almost all of them were nationally owned by governments in the Middle East or other oil-producing nations—companies like Saudi Arabia's Saudi Aramco and Venezuela's Pedevesa. The big private oil companies of the late 1980s—Exxon, Shell, British Petroleum, Amoco, and Phillips among them—controlled just a fraction of the world's oil. To help put things in perspective, a U.S. government analysis would later figure that while big oil nationals like Saudi Aramco had a reserve ratio of 173 years—meaning it would take them that long to run out of production without finding new oil—the big international private companies had a ratio of just 11 years.

It was a dramatically different picture from 1973, when the elite club of private international companies called the Seven Sisters dominated the global markets. Made up of the Rockefeller Standard Oil companies of New Jersey (which became Exxon) and New York (which became Mobil), plus Standard Oil of California, Gulf, Texaco, Shell, and British Petroleum, the Seven Sisters controlled some 85 percent of the world's known supply of oil and produced about 40 percent of global supply. But almost all of that oil—at least the oil that was believed to be recoverable using available technology—lay mostly in the giant reservoirs underlying Saudi Arabia, Kuwait, Iraq, Qatar, and Venezuela.

And so after being shut out of the OPEC nations, the majors went hunting for more discoveries of their own. They found them in Colombia and Vietnam and in new Alaskan fields and Indonesia, among other regions. These were the places oil could be pumped out of the ground easily and inexpensively, as in Saudi Arabia, where it costs as little as $2 a barrel to get oil from the earth to a refinery. Oil is cheap when it flows freely and purely out of the ground under pressure in large quantities. The deeper a company has to drill, or the more complicated the geology—or the politics—the more expensive the process gets. For British Petroleum, which for so long had drilled in its own backyard or in friendly U.S. territories, these were the places with the lowest possible additional risk. But together the reserves they added couldn't stack up to the amount of oil known to lie beneath Saudi Arabia alone.

While the free and independent producers of oil were on the hunt for new fields, the production of oil from the greatest reserves on the planet began to peak. In 1956, the geophysicist M. King Hubbert presented a now-famous paper to the American Petroleum Institute warning that the world's supply would soon decline; U.S. production might max out in the early 1970s, he said. The world's supply would peak by the end of the century. The realization that the Middle East might soon be out of capacity—not just the old Alaskan oil fields—sank in at about the same time that the world's demand for oil was skyrocketing. (Global oil demand dipped after 1979 for a few years but then continued its long-term growth trajectory.) In 1980, for the first time in history, the oil companies produced more oil than they discovered in new reserves. Whether the supply of oil was actually peaking or not, the oil companies' ability to produce it certainly was.

The idea that the world had started to run out of oil hastened an awareness among environmentalists, and even some politicians, that it was necessary to develop alternative sources of energy. With this, and long before the gravity of global warming settled into the mainstream, the importance of weaning the United States from its reliance on oil imports began to take root. In reality, however, the world wasn't going to run out of oil anytime soon. It was just going to get a lot harder, a lot riskier, and a lot more expensive to come by. It wasn't the end of oil, not yet. But it might very well have been the end of easy oil.

To find more, the oil companies would have to explore corners of the world that had until then been too unstable or too violent to consider, or simply too difficult to get to. Companies lusted after the resources underneath places like Nigeria and Sudan, countries imploding into a postcolonial inferno of violence and racial strife. They would soon put their souls on the block for deals with Russia; northeastern Siberian and Sakhalin Island were long known to hold bountiful reservoirs of hydrocarbons. And they began hiring teams of scientists and geologists to consider how much oil might lie deep beneath the ocean or beyond the polar ice cap, hoping that one day their engineers might invent the technology that would allow them to drill at depths not explored before. The Gulf of Mexico, for example, was promising but almost completely unexplored. In 1989, British Petroleum produced just eighteen thousand barrels per day there—a dribble.

If the oil wasn't to be discovered in some new place, then perhaps it would be uncovered in a new form. Unconventional oil supplies were sought after with increasing intensity. In Canada, pioneering companies were taking mud saturated with tar and melting it down to separate the particles of dirt from an oily resin called bitumen that could be refined into the crudest form of crude. The oil sands, as they are called, had been considered fringe resources in the 1960s but were attracting more interest by the late 1980s. In Colorado, Utah, and Wyoming, geologists had determined that the shale underlying the northern Green River Valley was also saturated in a basic form of hydrocarbons and that with extensive processing the rock could also be broken down and turned into oil. If the American West was mined for this shale, it could nearly match, in quantity, the oil coming from Saudi Arabia, according to some estimates. And, of course, the industry had begun to consider the importance of natural gas, a potentially valuable fuel that had long been discarded as a waste by-product when it burped up out of wells being drilled for oil and was burned, or flared, off but which was now making up an ever-larger portion of the oil industry's— and British Petroleum's—portfolio.

Each of these could significantly add to the world's supply of energy. But all of them were far more expensive than oil drilled for traditionally. Because the tar sands and oil shale in particular required so much mining and processing, they would also pose far greater risk to the environment. The choices represented distinct new paths, and following any one of them would require a mettle and fortitude for risk and innovation that only the greatest explorers had ever demonstrated. Not since the earliest days of its crude wells in the mountains of Persia had British Petroleum been one of those leaders.

With the protection it had enjoyed from the English government for much of the last eighty years, the company may not have been groomed to compete, and thus to innovate, the way that Exxon or

ARCO had in the mid-1980s. But the notion tapped squarely at the heart of John Browne's instincts. He was a New World sort of oilman, and liked to think of himself as an innovator. He always had.

In 1969, for example, when Browne was posted in Alaska, other young managers would spend their nights in Anchorage, leisurely pushing back water glasses of whiskey with the roustabouts. Browne remained holed up in a cheap room in the Anchorage Hotel, scratching algorithms on notebooks and writing primitive computer programs that would map British Petroleum's oil reservoirs digitally. After he maxed out the capabilities of whatever computers existed in Anchorage, he sought out a new, groundbreaking computer in Palo Alto, California, to continue his work. The computer filled an entire room. Later, in 1980, he would continue to foster this Silicon Valley strain of entrepreneurialism when he went to Stanford University and then connected with people like Andy Grove—a founder of Intel. Such influences only reinforced his notion that good business even at a traditional corporation would be enhanced by an entrepreneurial spirit of innovation and experimentation. It was in Browne's blood. It was the way he thought. And, as the man responsible for expanding British Petroleum's oil business in 1989, he brought this pedigree to the challenges he faced.

"He came to a company which was large and quite mature in an industry that was perceived to be mature," says Bamberg, the historian. "And entrepreneurship is very often associated with young, growing industries. It's quite hard to be a sort of dashing entrepreneur in a mature industry. It was unusual."

But innovation wouldn't be enough. John Browne was also quick to realize that the farther oil companies reached into the wilderness, new territories, the poles, and the oceans, the greater the risk to the environment. He would write that responsibility for environmental risk and producing energy were "inextricably linked." In his father's era, getting oil used to be a matter of finding a giant bubble deep underground and plugging a straw into it to catch whatever spurted out. Now companies would need to bend and turn their drill pipes, run them horizontally for miles, suck and coax out the oil, hydraulically fracture porous rock with gas, water, or chemicals to push the oil out, or go to underwater depths barely fathomed in the science fiction movies of the time. All of these stretched the capabilities of the current technology. The processes simply weren't safe enough, or practiced consistently enough, for anyone to know for sure that frontier wells could be drilled, or oil produced, as routinely as oil had been harvested in the past.

The complexities mounted relentlessly. Even as the technical risk increased, Browne saw—accurately—that after the *Valdez* disaster in Alaska, the industry would forever face a higher standard of both environmental and human safety in its drilling endeavors. "We were very aware of both our need to be safe, and to protect the environment," Browne wrote. His views were no doubt influenced by the times and the direction of the man he had worked under in Cleveland. In an interview in the fall of 1989, Robert Horton called environmental protection "the most important single issue in the coming decade." He added, "Any industrialist who ignores it does so at his peril." The rules had changed. With both citizens and governments more sensitive than ever to the ecological footprint of their extractive industries, the government approval needed for new exploration in the Gulf of Mexico, or in ANWR, would no longer be propelled by the government's need to encourage development of more energy supplies alone. Now that approval would also depend on oil companies' ability to convince government regulators that they could get the oil out of the ground cleanly, too.

That the environmental risks were poised for a stratospheric increase at almost the precise moment that the margin for error would close to a hairline was not lost on Browne. It was all the more reason why, he was sure, British Petroleum had few choices but to revise the rules of the game. "We must plan prudently for the future. The need for change is compelling," Browne said in late 1989. "The company in its present shape is the product of rapid global expansion and a strategy which has evolved over time. We face rising taxes, higher running costs and more onerous regulations worldwide. We are also aware that we must be leaders in responsible environmental protection and that there are lessons to be learned about promoting the health and safety of our workforce. All these factors are driving up costs and putting margins under severe pressure."

Even before he had settled on a plan, one thing was clear: the way out of the trap was through abandoning British Petroleum's historical affinity for safe and predictable operations and through taking some chances. Risks, in this new era, would be taken by all companies in different ways. Some would seek to emphasize one area, or one technology: deepwater drilling or oil sands or gas. Others, like Exxon, would grow so large that their sheer size made them impervious to geopolitical strife or market instability. In terms of Browne's personal success and the survival of the great company he worked for, the stakes had never been higher. But he was also sharp enough to recognize an opportunity in the high risks. If British Petroleum could figure out this next piece of the puzzle fastest; if it could get there, and get there first; if it could do it efficiently enough to turn a profit, especially while the price of oil languished—the payoff would be huge. The question was, Could he do it cheaper, safer, and better?

IT TOOK THREE MONTHS for Hamilton to help Browne come up with a strategy. "I had forty-two offices in eighteen time zones," Hamilton says. "I'd spend a bunch of my week on an airplane, Saturday and Sunday in the Middle East, get back and have a meeting with John, go home, dump my suitcase and repack it to go again." He assembled a team of thirty-five engineers and began analyzing the world's oil basins for new prospects, trying to get a sense of the total playing field and a stark evaluation of the properties British Petroleum already owned.

British Petroleum had reams of historical data on the Middle East and was allowed back in to those countries to update its studies and create a new inventory of the world's supplies. That global inventory, perhaps the best accounting of all the known oil in existence, gave British Petroleum a picture of where the competition stood, and what the best possible upside to new exploration could still be. Hamilton's team also took a cold look at British Petroleum's existing projects. Hamilton quickly saw a slew of foreign drilling partnerships that, while each turned a healthy net profit, sucked company talent and resources and would never add up to a sizable enough whole. The problem was that for years British Petroleum had preferred to play its investments safe—like buying a mutual fund instead of an individual stock—and the result was that there was too little to gain. The fields in Indonesia were a per-

fect example. The country split the oil produced with the foreign companies that drilled for it 50-50. Then British Petroleum had diluted the
opportunity in its remaining 50 percent cut by bringing in three other
oil production partners to share the risk. It meant that a 100-million-
barrel oil field had been reduced to just 12 million barrels of potential
production for British Petroleum.

If Browne wanted bold declarations, Hamilton was prepared to
give them to him: dump Indonesia and any other slow-growing oil
field, even if it was making a profit. That would clear up resources to go
and pursue newer, bigger fields or press into countries that had so far
locked the oil industry out. It was the start of a new era of exploration,
partnerships, and new priorities for British Petroleum. As it turned
out, the housecleaning was exhilarating.

"It was one of the most exciting times—the sorts of times that
come along with the sort of world change that was going along with
the collapse of the Soviet Union and a company that was in the process
of remaking itself," says Hamilton. "If that couldn't get your adrenaline
going, then there wasn't much that could."

By Browne and Hamilton's calculations, there were 1,300 "recognized sedimentary basins" in the world likely to contain oil. By 1989,
only 300 of them remained unexplored. Increasingly, Browne believed
that British Petroleum should abandon fields it had held onto but
which yielded only lukewarm profits or had never been drilled and
focus instead on new drives to target these last untested geological
regions. The statistics were in favor of the company's finding good-
sized fields. If history was any measure, half of the basins would yield
some sort of oil field, and one in twelve of those would be the elephants
that could make or break British Petroleum's future. That meant that
somewhere, perhaps in the most unreachable or violent regions on
the planet, there were still some thirteen elephants out there for the
hunting. Finding them would become Hamilton's focus, and the core
of John Browne's redesign of British Petroleum's exploration and oil
production business.

On September 14, 1989, Browne announced a plan that news
reports called "shocking for its boldness." The exploration and production group that he headed would shed as many nonproducing or
declining assets as possible, cut jobs, reorganize the group's manage-

ment, and do whatever it took to find more oil. The upheaval was to have the effect of recalibrating British Petroleum's performance goals toward the "medium to long term." "The rapid growth of the business in the past three years has prompted us to examine our current shape to make sure it keeps us competitive in a harsher business climate," Browne said. "Performance this year was less than we believe to be adequate. Something had to be done."

For starters, he promised his division would immediately save some $150 million a year in operating costs and would cut 1,700 jobs: 280 in Houston, 470 in London, and the rest in Scotland. Most of Browne's exploration division would move out of Britannic House, in London's financial district, to a more modest office building in the suburbs. Browne shuffled the cumbersome exploration and production unit into three new operating companies—a North American group, a frontier and international group, and a European group—plus a new exploration technology division and a natural gas group.

The moves would streamline the exploration and production part of the organization and simplify the management structure at the same time that Horton, the incoming CEO, would continue to streamline the global corporation and rest increasingly on E&P for growth. "In essence we are significantly re-directing the company. We are putting in place simpler, less costly managerial structures and an organization that more accurately matches the future geographical spread of our business and the right mix of people and skills in the right place." The goals were broad: "We will create a business that is stronger, more sharply motivated, less complex and costly, better at achieving profit from existing assets and able to provide, through exploration, for the renewal of business into the next decade and the next century," he said.

To meet these goals, Browne would follow Hamilton's guidance and back out of existing lackluster production projects, trimming as much inefficiency as he could find. He called an immediate halt to onshore exploration across the continental United States and sold a grab bag of the company's assets around the world to a Dallas-based oil company called Oryx for $1.3 billion. The Oryx sale disposed of British Petroleum's leases and projects in Dubai, Gabon, parts of Ecuador, Colombia, parts of Indonesia, and a big chunk of the North Sea, severing the company from an astounding 367 million barrels of its reserves. The properties sold to Oryx amounted to 80 percent of British Petroleum fields at the time, according to a report by United Press International, but only 20 percent of the company's production, clearly illustrating the sort of chaff Browne saw anchoring the company globally and that he hoped to eliminate.

Everything was aimed at narrowing the company's focus and proceeding with a few well-informed bets. "We are reducing our scatter-gun approach. This is a high-risk, high-reward strategy," Horton said in October 1989. That meant turning the focus to new exploration to replace the company's global assets that Browne had just gutted. Once again, Browne turned to Hamilton. "It was getting back to the heritage of the company to sort of be a pioneer in many areas of the world again," Hamilton said. "To say it was challenging was a bit of an understatement." The most important aspect of Browne's evolving strategy was to breathe some life into the company's "frontier" exploration plan with the expectation that the risk would be a portal through which British Petroleum would find its new identity. "He wanted to pull them into the big leagues," Freeman said. "He wanted to decentralize BP. He wanted to make it cutting-edge. And he definitely wanted to increase its proved producing reserves and make it one of the majors."

The company would invest large amounts of capital in new exploration. In September British Petroleum said it would begin by focusing on exploration in Vietnam, off the coast of Scotland, and, increasingly, in the deep waters of the Gulf of Mexico. Hamilton was still on the prowl for new areas, too, and when the Berlin Wall crumbled in November 1989 he pounced on the opportunity to chisel a foothold for British Petroleum in the USSR. "It is vital that we explore more aggressively but selectively for new reserves," Browne said. "We have conducted a very thorough analysis of the world's unexplored basins. Many are in areas which, until recently, were inaccessible to the oil majors."

But even with fresh growth there was no escaping the fact that with such a lopsided dependence on the North Sea and Prudhoe Bay—old fields in decline—maintaining the status quo there was as important as finding new oil elsewhere. That meant that the real emphasis would be on gaining efficiency. In fact, while a newfound appetite for

risk defined the company's frontier exploration, Browne's mandate
was far from a blank check. Throughout every piece of his strategy
there was an overarching ethos of controlling costs. Here, Exxon
had set the standard. The company had boiled all of its investments,
measures, revenues, and trajectories down to the simplest possible
metric that revolved around producing oil: net income per barrel.
It squarely put everything Exxon did in the context not just of revenues, but of revenues directly related to the company's production
and reserves, and thus to its potential for the future as an oil company.
Where British Petroleum may have allowed a big production year
in Egypt to offset an expensive pipeline rehabilitation in Alaska, or
an acquisition of another oil company to puff up its annual revenues
on a general basis, Exxon made sure that each specific business segment was performing well in its own right, effectively locking every
dollar the company made directly to the activity or barrel of oil that
made the income possible. Browne seized upon the model, pushing to
define British Petroleum's new exploits in terms of per-barrel profits
as well. It meant that Alaska had to operate efficiently in the context
of Alaska alone, not just in the context of contributing to a global pot
of profits. "The drive was to drive that down to something as good as
or better than Exxon's net income per barrel," says Hamilton. "That
sweeps up almost everything you do—the capital you spend, the costs
you create—so it was a heck of a challenge to try and run your business
so you didn't run yourself off the rails when it came to that sort of a
measurement."

In the background of everything British Petroleum did going forward, there would be an emphasis on cutting costs and finding more
efficiency. Strict standards were set for an expected rate of return on
all assets, and costs would be controlled ruthlessly. "Cash and management resources have to be targeted," Browne told London's *Sunday
Times* that October. "Volume and price are uncontrollable. The only
controllable variable is costs."

That statement, and Browne's goals in this regard, would come to
define a generation or more in which British Petroleum rigorously
sought to reduce costs. Browne wanted British Petroleum to be lean
and mean; cutting off the fat could give the company a fighting chance

at becoming a real global competitor. In the fall of 1989, it made sense to both the company's managers and to its shareholders. But what Browne didn't necessarily see was that a cutting-based strategy's roots would extend into the very foundation that he was so meticulously building, insidiously splitting and expanding the cracks. It would happen so slowly that for a long time nobody in senior management noticed what was happening.

2

THE WHISTLE-BLOWER

WHILE BROWNE and his team raced out from the starting blocks to execute their newly conceived plan, a powerful undercurrent continued to tug at the industry and at British Petroleum's hopes for the future. In Alaska, the *Exxon Valdez* spill hadn't gone away. It had gotten worse.

By the fall of 1989, nearly eleven million gallons of oil were spread out along twelve hundred miles of rocky coastline of Prince William Sound, puddled in tidal pools, lapping at the hulls of fishing boats, and coating shorebirds with goop. Even the floating ice breaking off the end of the Columbia Glacier was stained black. Months after the March spill, cleanup crews were still spraying millions of gallons of toxic chemical solvents in hopes that they could break up the oil and disperse it, in diluted form, into the environment. It was being called one of the greatest environmental catastrophes in history, and it had everyone's attention, from the president of the United States to the workers who made the oil companies tick. It was a game changer, and already it threatened to derail Browne's plans for British Petroleum's future.

The previous March 23, the *Exxon Valdez* had pulled away from the tanker terminal in Valdez, Alaska, with a full cargo of 53 million gallons of oil bound for Long Beach, California. It charted its way through the Valdez Narrows without incident, as some 8,700 tankers had done before, and out into the shipping lanes of the sound, toward the Pacific Ocean. The ship was on autopilot, and its captain was asleep in his berth. Then, just before midnight, a deck watch sighting for icebergs spotted a coastal warning light on the Bligh Reef. To the deck watch's surprise, it was off the wrong side of the bow. Alarms were sounded and rudders cranked to turn the 987-foot-long supertanker around, but it was too late. At 12:04 the crew felt the ship shudder and then bump along as it ground into the jagged reef. Eight of its eleven cargo holds were splayed open as the hull ruptured against the rocks, sending millions of gallons of oil spewing instantly into the sound.

Then, for the better part of a day, nothing happened. John Browne, who happened to be in Alaska, was huddled in his cot at Prudhoe Bay's base camp on the coastline some eight hundred miles north when his general manager, George Nelson, woke him up at 5:00 a.m. "We've got a message. There's some oil seeping around Valdez," Nelson told him. "But no one seems to be doing anything."

"*Get* someone to do something," Browne shot back, climbing out of bed. Since the spill happened near the terminus of the Trans Alaska pipeline—the single conduit for oil from Alaska's North Slope to the tanker port in the south—it was the consortium that owned the pipeline, not Exxon, that was supposed to lead an emergency response in Valdez. The pipeline was jointly owned by the companies with an interest in the oil it transported, mainly Exxon, ARCO, and British Petroleum, and run through a corporation called the Alyeska Pipeline Service Company. British Petroleum, as the largest shareholder, managed Alyeska and operated the line. George Nelson was both a British Petroleum executive and the president of Alyeska at the time. When the *Exxon Valdez* spill happened, Alyeska didn't have a formal plan in place to deal with it, and so by extension, it was British Petroleum that was dropping the ball.

Critical equipment for the response lay buried underneath mounds of snow in the port of Valdez, and an emergency response barge kept on call for just such an event had never been loaded with booms and other equipment. Oil gushed from the ship and gurgled to the surface, where it spread in a thin sheen across waters teeming with whales and halibut and king crabs, and there was virtually no initial response. In the immediate aftermath, no booms were set out to collect the oil, and no cleanup crews were mobilized. It would take Alyeska's response barge fourteen hours to reach the wreckage. John Browne, departing for Anchorage later that morning, diverted British Petroleum's private jet for a flyby of the port and, upon seeing the tanker, was dismayed: "It was a chilling sight," he wrote in his 2010 memoir, *Beyond Business*. "Oil was flowing out from a gaping hole in its side to form a massive, shadowy slick. Dark oil stretched as far as the eye could see. It seemed as if very little was happening. By then I had expected the response boats would be in the water trying to contain the spill."

The *Valdez* accident changed the rules. Overnight, it attuned Americans to the risks of energy production and the fallacies of the industry's safety claims. And it reoriented the industry toward its responsibilities to the public, and not just to the task of getting oil. The accident was the clarion call that many of the world's big oil CEOs would learn from. It eventually changed Exxon's core values. Going forward, Exxon would learn to manage its risk and safety operations with a militaristic control and total conformity among its 104,000 global employees, setting an international example of good management.

Although the accident shaped Browne's critical thinking about a new level of environmental responsibility for the oil companies that he had spoken about in New York in June 1989, British Petroleum would struggle to set the same sort of standard. Browne was keen to understand the philosophical impact the *Valdez* disaster would have on his plans for British Petroleum's future, and he said all the right things. But he seemed blind to his own company's role. The Alaska Oil Spill Commission would eventually say that the entire *Valdez* spill could have been cleaned up in a matter of a few days, had Alyeska been prepared to respond swiftly to the emergency. Response from Alyeska was "unexpectedly slow and woefully inadequate. . . . Wide gaps between regulations or professional postures and the reality of oil transportation in Prince William Sound invited disaster," the commission's final report said. "With a well-prepared contingency plan . . . the disaster . . . could have been far less serious." It was only after watching Alyeska do virtually nothing that Exxon jumped in to manage the cleanup itself. Still, Browne lamented that Exxon had set the low bar by which British Petroleum would now be judged. In essence, he blamed Exxon for giving big oil, and British Petroleum, a bad name.

Browne wasn't the British Petroleum executive responsible at the time for the cleanup in Alaska, but he understood who was supposed to be in charge. He never reflected, at least not publicly, on the fact that while the accident was Exxon's, British Petroleum bore a chunk of the responsibility for what unfolded in Alaska that summer of 1989. British Petroleum's apparent hope was that any problems the company faced would remain in the background while its executives focused on the higher priorities of increasing reserves and profits. Browne's bold June 1989 presentation in New York, and his public restructuring efforts that followed, seemed to be the exception to his silence.

In Alaska, the company might have been able to continue under the radar unnoticed if it weren't for the depth of the problems wrought by the Exxon spill, compounded by the persistent noisemaking about pollution and mismanagement from a tenacious bulldog of a man named Chuck Hamel. Since 1982, Hamel, an entrepreneur with close ties to the oil industry, had been waging a righteous war against Exxon and the Alyeska consortium. He had grown up in a blue-collar family in Connecticut, studied in Paris, and served in the army in Europe during the Korean War. When he returned to the States, he worked as a congressional aide, first as a student staffer for then-majority leader Lyndon Johnson and later as chief of staff for several senators, including Alaska senator Mike Gravel. Hamel learned to work the halls of the Hill and to deal in egos and power as well as hard goods: with connections and a nose for business, he became a prolific trader, finding a niche as a middleman who brokered and shipped commodities like wheat and corn around the world. The wealthier he got, the more he became interested in oil speculation. First, he bought up a bunch of leases on Alaska's North Slope. He lobbied heavily for oil development in Alaska and used his connections in Washington to urge support for the construction of the Trans Alaska Pipeline in the 1970s. Then, in 1980, he invested millions in a company that would transport North Slope oil at a discount on independent tankers through the Panama Canal to the refineries in the Gulf of Mexico. The smaller ships obviated the need to use the industry's pipeline across the Panama isthmus and allowed him to undercut Exxon's prices.

For a short time, Hamel lived large. The consummate business innovator, he relished his success and bought vacation homes in Florida and Sun Valley, Idaho. Then suddenly and to Hamel's great surprise his oil, bought straight from the pipeline terminal in Valdez, turned out to be mixed with water. When his buyers found out, the business sank faster than a steel anchor. Hamel was furious. The Alyeska companies, he believed, had conspired to contaminate the oil they put in his tankers and preserve their monopoly on both the shipping and the interocean transport of Alaska's oil. (A state hearing board would later find that the company did not intentionally contaminate the oil.) "They denied the truth, and apparently hoped that I would forget about my business, the damage to my credibility and reputation, and my lost income," says Hamel. "I could not do that."

Most people, faced with a fight against three of the most powerful corporations in the world, would stand down. But Hamel didn't. Instead, he made retribution against the industry a personal mission. He left his home in a Washington, D.C., suburb and flew to Alaska, rented a shabby hotel room in Valdez, and set out to prove his case. Slowly, word spread—from the bar stools at a dive called the Pipeline Club to the fish cleaning company down from the pier—and Alyeska employees began to show up at the strangest hours. In the middle of the night, they would flock to his room, where, with window shades drawn, and among stacks of records and notebooks, he would listen as clandestine visitors ratted out the company they worked for. Soon, he heard what he had come for: allegations that Alyeska had covered up its records showing that the oil given to him for transport did indeed contain water before he received it. Alyeska's files were fixed to show that the shipments were pure. Hamel brought his complaint before the Alaska Public Utilities Commission, and several Alyeska employees testified that they had doctored the company's records. But the allegedly doctored records were nowhere to be found, and even after those testimonies and all the interviews, Hamel found himself long on talk and short on proof—at least proof good enough to convince the commission. Alyeska dismissed his claims as conspiratorial, and the commission ruled in Alyeska's favor.

Hamel was about to pack his bags when he began to hear concerns of a different sort altogether. The phone continued to ring day and night. The workers kept coming, feeding him a fire hose of confidential information. They alleged that the consortium had dumped toxic sludge into the Valdez Arm, the narrow waterway that leads inland toward the Port of Valdez. They said that there were leaks along the pipeline that went unreported; that vast quantities of carcinogenic emissions were being vented willfully into the air from Alyeska facilities. The informants painted a picture of systematic safety management lapses and a pattern of gross water and air pollution along the Trans Alaska Pipeline. They showed him logs of falsified water quality tests Alyeska had sent to the Environmental Protection Agency.

This was not his beef. And Hamel, a guy with oil interests who suddenly found himself filing away complaints about the environment, had to choose whether or not he cared. "The more I heard, the angrier I got," he says. "It was as if the environmental regulations of the United States did not even apply north of the Canadian border: no regulators, no oversight, no enforcement—nothing. I realized that I was not the only victim of the dishonesty of the oil industry in Alaska—we were all victims, and no one was doing anything about it. We were living in a conspiracy of silence waiting for an environmental disaster to occur."

In 1985, Hamel took his information public, mounting a campaign to—in his words—save the Alaskan wild and stop the criminal practices of British Petroleum, Exxon, ARCO, and the rest of the oil companies there. There was no disputing that Hamel had a very large axe to grind. And indeed, he gleefully exposed every complaint he heard about British Petroleum, hassling the company with each whistle-blower's accusations. Many of the allegations he brought forward were found to be accurate. He revealed, for example, that when a smokestack incinerator on an Alyeska facility had broken down, Alyeska had continued to use the facility anyway, pretending for a decade that it was still working. The incinerator was meant to make toxic gases safe by burning them off. Without it, the company simply ran the pollutants through the pipe and into the air. He uncovered similar problems with emissions from the port's water treatment facility. "They knew there were problems with everything," says Rick Steiner, at the time a member of the Marine Advisory Board at the University of Alaska. "But they thought they could skate through it, and, until Chuck Hamel came along, that's pretty much the way it happened."

The more Hamel learned, and the more he pushed, the more the safety and environmental concerns began to consume him. As they did, he says his vengeance faded, and an overriding sense of public justice began to take over.

He brought the workers' concerns to Congress, to Alaskan officials, to the EPA, and to any reporter who would listen. For the most part, they feigned interest but did little. Yet the more complaints Hamel brought, the harder British Petroleum and Exxon tried to silence him. The industry steadfastly disputed his claims and attacked his credibility. They took his passion and his penchant for hyperbole and used it to dismiss his accusations as exaggerations made by a slighted competitor hell-bent on revenge. Alyeska published brochures discrediting him, and its executives gave public lectures in which they said that Hamel didn't really care about the environment, and that he just wanted a payoff. "I was treated as a kook," says Hamel. "The Alyeska public relations campaign was working. Few newspapers would print the facts. Few regulators would even listen. There was a profound skepticism everywhere that the oil industry would knowingly pollute the environment and harm their own employees in Alaska."

One of the issues he took up concerned reports that Alyeska had dismantled its oil spill response program, leaving no way to clean up if there were a catastrophic leak. He brought the allegations to the EPA, and to Alaska's Department of Environmental Conservation, which did little. "My voice of alarm was sort of in the wilderness," he says. And then, just as he was beginning to capture the attention of a congressional committee with claims that an environmental catastrophe was inevitable, the *Valdez* tanker ran aground. It thrust Hamel into the spotlight, and the issues he had been begging people to listen to days before became the government's highest priority.

IN FEBRUARY 1990, Alyeska decided it wanted to talk. The consortium had a new president, Jim Hermiller, an executive on loan from British Petroleum. Hermiller invited Hamel to fly to Alaska to map out a plan to deal with the safety issues and, Hamel hoped, take a more proactive stance. Hamel made the trip, arriving on a blustery late winter day. But half an hour before the meeting, Alyeska canceled. The company told an intermediary, the University of Alaska's Steiner, simply that there would be no discussion—no rescheduling, no explanation. It seemed suspicious to Hamel and Steiner that Hermiller would bring Hamel all the way to Alaska just to cancel, but there was little he could do.

Steiner met Hamel anyway, that night, in the lounge of the Captain Cook, a prominent downtown hotel named after the British explorer who first discovered the Bering Strait and the Alaskan coast. Over drinks at the bar, the two men were quietly discussing the *Valdez* fiasco when a woman interrupted them. She was young, blond, voluptuous, and dressed in the sort of silky blouse that seemed out of place on Anchorage's subzero winter nights. They brushed her off, but a few minutes later, she was back, flighty and flirty. She seemed to be propositioning them. "I joked to Rick that I was too old for her. But seriously, she was bothering us so much that we couldn't communicate," says Hamel. "So we left."

A few days later Hamel was boarding his flight back to Washington when he recognized the woman from the bar loading her bag into the overhead compartment next to him. In an awkward conversation, the woman introduced herself as Ricki Jacobson and handed him a business card for a company called EcoLit, a law firm specializing in ecological litigation. She told him that she was a researcher and that she had come to Anchorage hoping to get interviews for a case but that the meetings hadn't come through. She was worried for her job and had kids to take care of. One of her children, tragically, had recently died. Hamel, who had connections in Anchorage and was interested in environmental concerns, offered to help her, and the two exchanged phone numbers before they parted.

A few weeks later, Hamel got a call from Jacobson in Washington. She wanted to know if he would meet her boss, a Dr. Wayne Jenkins. Jenkins, the director of EcoLit, said he had resources that might help Hamel in his fight against the oil companies. Hamel was intrigued but skeptical. "I still don't understand, who are you guys?" he asked, in a subsequent phone call with Jenkins. "Who *are* you?"

"EcoLit is a group of people backed by this foundation to do research preparatory for litigation," Jenkins told Hamel.

His instincts might have made him cautious, but Hamel wanted it to be true. He was tired, and he was nearly broke. The fight against Alyeska had lasted eight years and was taking its toll. It had tested his marriage with constant distraction and defined a time when he could have been starting another business and saving for retirement. Hamel had gained weight; his wispy locks of hair had long ago turned white. His stature had assumed a slight stoop. EcoLit was like a white knight appearing out of the darkness. "Here is someone with a big-time law firm who would defend the whistle-blowers and take over," Hamel later recalled thinking.

I was so relieved for Chuck," said his wife, Kathy, a sweet and proper woman who had steadfastly supported her husband's crusade. "There is just so much that one person can do."

Shortly after their conversation, Wayne Jenkins went to Hamel's home in Alexandria, Virginia, a pleasant four-story brick townhouse overlooking the Potomac. At the door Hamel met a well-built man with an oval face, beady eyes, and close-cropped hair, the kind of guy who would look natural in a varsity letter jacket. The men exchanged greetings and Hamel went into his kitchen to get coffee, shouting small talk from there.

Left alone, Jenkins pursued his true agenda. He darted to Hamel's office, a small, undecorated box off the main living area, and began rifling through Hamel's records. He found crates of files and flipped through them, his thumb running over the labeled manila tabs until he saw something he recognized. Then he thrust his fist indiscriminately into the crate, grabbing a bunch of paper, and stuffed the wad of files into his bag. Next, he checked the fax machine, where he found a series of yellow Post-its with phone numbers of sources stuck to the side. "Patti Epler, Dan Lawn, Rick Steiner, Ricki Ott," he read out loud from one of the Post-its, capturing his own voice in a hidden microphone and recording images of the phone numbers with a tiny hidden spy camera.

Suddenly Hamel was in the doorway. "Did you bring that thing for Kathy?" he asked, referring to something Jenkins had mentioned he'd bring his wife, and oblivious to what had happened.

"I sure did," Jenkins replied smoothly. "I was just standing here talking to myself."

Their conversation continued seamlessly, Hamel never noticing anything amiss. They discussed the nature of the issues that Hamel had been learning about from the workers at Alyeska and the potential for a lawsuit against the company. The men agreed to work together.

EcoLit would set up an office in a nondescript concrete building about a mile away, on Jefferson Davis Highway. They would meet there soon to discuss the next steps.

Jenkins, of course, was not who he said he was. EcoLit was a sham, set up by a private spy and security firm called Wackenhut. Jenkins was an alias for Wayne Black, a private agent for the firm contracted by Hermiller and Alyeska's security team to try to reveal Hamel's whistle-blower sources inside the company. Black had a reputation, among those who knew him, for being aggressive, even threatening. His staff complained that they feared for their safety; that he could be retaliatory and exact retribution. Black had sent Jacobson, a naïve and inexperienced investigator, to Anchorage in the hopes that she would lure Hamel back to her hotel room and tape their conversation. "I was so scared," Jacobson would later say about her mission to Anchorage and the mysterious man she was taking orders from. "I didn't know what was real."

"Black told Ricki to do whatever it takes," her lawyer, Michael Lozoff, says. "Clearly that meant seduction." Now, in Alexandria, Black had taken on the case himself, determined to report back to Hermiller and Alyeska which of their workers had been complaining about the company's safety record in Valdez, and to provide the goods that would finally shut Hamel up.

Until the *Valdez* accident, Hamel had been an annoying but tolerable thorn in the side of the oil companies. But with the attention the oil spill brought, Hamel's actions now threatened to cost them money on a grand scale. British Petroleum, in particular, had placed great hopes on expanding its Alaskan operations into ANWR. As the largest and least developed wilderness area in the United States, ANWR had long been a flashpoint for opposition from environmentalists. It is widely believed to be completely untouched—the last frontier for both explorers and the oil industry's geologists. In fact, British Petroleum, in a test project with Chevron, had already drilled a well there in 1985. The results are a closely kept secret, never made public and guarded under extraordinary security in British Petroleum's offices, but they led the company to say publicly that they believed they could produce a million barrels of oil a day there. In the context of John Browne's down-to-the-studs renovation of global exploration strategy, ANWR represented an easy, cheap, and accessible bonanza. ANWR's development by the oil companies, however, was dependent then, as it is today, upon the industry's being able to convince Congress that they could drill safely, without their exploration having a detrimental effect on the pristine land and sensitive wildlife that thrived there. It had been a tough sell to begin with. The *Valdez* spill made it harder. And if Hamel's stories about the oil industry's habitual recklessness began to cut through the industry's rhetoric about safe drilling and a "new era" of environmental stewardship, it was possible that the plans to develop ANWR would be shut down for good.

In his public comments John Browne spoke about a company with a newfound awareness of the importance of environmental responsibility—the kind of company that would identify the problems, fix them, and set a fresh example for how an oil company would operate. But his managers in Alaska, at least while they were on loan for Alyeska, seemed to care far more about shutting Hamel up than they did about fixing the environmental problems that Hamel raised. The directive seemed clear: Hamel had to be stopped. Alyeska saw the information that Hamel obtained and leaked to the press as stolen company property. "I felt that we had a right and an obligation to attempt to find who was stealing our documents, to retrieve those documents, and to take appropriate legal action against the individual who did it," says Pat Wellington, Alyeska's director of corporate security at the time, when asked by a documentary filmmaker why it was okay to rifle through Hamel's personal files. Alyeska continued to allege that Hamel was motivated by the hopes of a multi-million-dollar settlement with the company. If Hamel sold the whistle-blowers' tips for a profit, they believed, it would prove that he wasn't acting out of concern for the environment, or workers' safety, and it would become a crime. Alyeska wanted the names of Hamel's informants, but it also assigned Wackenhut to Hamel to catch him taking the money. If they could do that, they might do better than silence Hamel. They might even send him to jail.

Hamel met the man he still knew as Wayne Jenkins at EcoLit's sparse new offices in Alexandria. At the doorway, he was met by another scantily clad, long-legged secretary wearing stiletto heels, a short skirt, and a halter top. Jenkins joked that he had had to move her up from the company's offices in Florida; that's how they dressed down there. He seemed to be pining for some sort of admiration from Hamel. Once, he conspicuously complained that his vegetarian meal had upset his stomach, as if it were necessary to be a vegetarian to identify with Hamel's concern for the environment in Alaska. A federal investigator would later describe Wackenhut's EcoLit ruse as "almost a keystone cops kind of operation." Comic or inept as they may seem in hindsight, there was a relentless focus to Jenkins's efforts. He needed to prove that Hamel was an extortionist.

At the office, the two men sat at adjacent desks, and Jenkins wasn't subtle. "Speaking of commitment, I have some spending money here, and we might as well start our relationship here today." He took his feet off the desk, reached into his pocket, and tossed a stack of bills across the desk at Hamel.

"Whoa . . . how come you've got cash?" Hamel asked, taken aback.

"It's just easier for different things," Jenkins replied. "I can write you a check if you want, if you hate cash." He chuckled. "But that's real cash. That's two thousand dollars in real *you-nighted-stayts* currency there," he added, in a mocking Texas drawl.

Hamel was uncomfortable with the gesture. He pushed his chair back a couple of inches, as if the paper notes were poisoned. "You guys don't operate with cash, do you?" he asked. The money sat untouched on the table. "I can't touch this until I give you the documents," he said.

The conversation was recorded by a microphone that a Wackenhut operative had installed in the ventilation duct above Hamel's head. They had used a child's remote-control dune buggy to put it in place. A low-grade black-and-white video was recorded by a tiny hidden camera that whirred away inside the speaker of a boom box that sat on the desk.

"Take it now and give me the documents tomorrow," Jenkins said, insistent.

Hamel refused similar entreaties three or four more times. Finally, he picked up the wad of cash and dropped it back in front of Jenkins.

"I want you to have those documents before you engage me as a consultant because I don't want it ever said that I sold the documents," says Hamel. "I didn't. I'm not selling the documents. Those documents were given to me. . . . I'd let you have them when I feel comfortable . . . with who you guys [are]—that you [aren't] going to give them back to Alyeska."

Jenkins began to feel his catch slipping through the net. "It's between us," he said. "If I give you this cash, you're not going to be on our books."

"No," Hamel said finally. "I *have* to be on the books."

A few days later, in a last-ditch effort, Jenkins sent his long-legged assistant, Sherree Rich, to Hamel's house, where she recorded a one-sided statement telling an aghast and now pissed-off Hamel that she was stopping by to deliver "the two thousand dollars for the documents that you gave us." Hamel's dog, a fluffy apricot poodle named Muffin, went nuts, sensing the high-pitched ring of the wire Rich wore underneath her clothes. "I got them for nothing, and you guys get them for nothing," he said.

That might have been the end of it. A few days later EcoLit's Alexandria office mysteriously disappeared. The lease was under a false corporate name and the rent was never paid. Hamel never heard from Jenkins again. But then one afternoon Hamel's phone rang. A guy on the other end identified himself as Gus Castillo. He warned Hamel that the man he knew as Wayne Jenkins was actually Wayne Black, and that Black had been hired by Alyeska's shareholders, including British Petroleum and Exxon, to spy on Hamel. Castillo was paranoid and full of conspiracies and seemed to be overtaken by an extreme and irrational fear that he was in danger. He flew to Virginia to meet with the Hamels, and he told them that Black and a man named Richard Lund, an electronics and surveillance expert who also went to work for Wackenhut, were hunting him. Hamel flew him to Seattle, where he holed up with Kathy Hamel in a house nearby that she had inherited from her parents. There Castillo described the Wackenhut operation and gave the Hamels a list of names of employees who had been involved in the case. He told them that Lund in particular was dangerous—that he was infamous for having shot someone and then inserted his fingers into the guy's bullet wound to force him to talk, an account that would later be repeated in court by several other witnesses. Lund, it turned out, was a national expert on wiretapping and worked as a hired gun to train U.S. government agents in countersurveillance. A Wackenhut employee, when asked in court whether Lund was someone to be afraid of, said: "He was very secretive, very creepy. I wouldn't want to run into him in a dark alley." Another witness had similar views. "He had no conscience at all," said Anna Contreras, a former U.S. Customs agent and another Wackenhut employee who worked for Black. "Everybody was scared of Rick Lund."

In fact, both Lund and Black had reputations for being dangerous or intimidating. When Lund pressed for wiretapping of people only peripherally related to Hamel, Contreras warned her boss he was breaking the law. Then she tried to quit the Hamel case because she thought Black and Wackenhut had crossed the line. Black had her fired, and, in a moment that made her fear for her safety, cornered her at her desk as she was packing her things. "You better not mess with me," he told her. "You don't know who I am."

At the Hamels' Washington State home, as he told the Hamels about the case, Castillo sat rigidly on the couch. An old hunting shotgun lay on the floor by his feet and a semiautomatic pistol sat in a folded newspaper on his lap. Each time a car went by on the quiet suburban street, he jumped up and peered through the blinds. "Gus was terrified for his own life," says Kathy Hamel. "He knew what Black and Lund could do. I was terrified for Chuck."

Hamel, not sure where to turn, brought the events to the attention of Congress. A couple of staff members from the office of the House Interior and Insular Affairs Committee—now called the Natural Resources Committee—who had been following the events in Valdez, started poking into Hamel's story. "We became more and more aware that this was an even more extensive operation than even Chuck had thought," said Linda Chase, chief counsel for investigations at the committee at the time, in an interview with Court TV for a 2004 documentary about Hamel's case. His trash had been stolen and rifled through by people hired by Alyeska. Wackenhut had obtained Hamel's phone records and tracked his calls; ran background checks on his sources in Alaska; and even ran a credit profile on a bartender who regularly served Hamel in the hopes of leveraging him to dish dirt. When one of the papers Black had stolen from Hamel's office in that early meeting turned out to have the name of an Alyeska employee, Robert Scott, in the return address, Scott was immediately fired. Alyeska's human resources department resisted the firing, finding no cause, but a committee run by Hermiller overruled that department and got rid of Scott anyway.

In Virginia, Hamel's phone was tapped, and a small camper van parked down the street monitored his calls for months. Then congressional staffers got a tip that truly provoked the ire of the government: the Wackenhut investigation didn't stop with surveillance of Hamel and his contacts; rather, it had targeted the chair of the committee, California Democrat George Miller. "Naturally that gets your attention when you are a member of the congressional staff and somebody's going after a congressman," said Linda Chase. "You know that is something you *have* to investigate." Spying on Hamel, as distasteful and illegal as it was, was one thing. Threatening the security of a sitting member of the U.S. Congress was another. Hermiller, Alyeska, and Wackenhut had kicked the hornet's nest.

Within weeks the committee had hauled Wackenhut, Black, Lund, and the executives of Alyeska and the big oil companies up to the Hill for a public flogging. The Wackenhut scandal, as it quickly became known, made its way into the newspapers. The companies that owned Alyeska, including Exxon and British Petroleum, said that the Wackenhut job was the initiative of Alyeska's security director, Wellington, and that they had stopped the investigation in a matter of hours when they first learned it was going on. "Within two hours we vanished. Eco-Lit vanished. Dr. Jenkins vanished. Everyone vanished," Black told the Court TV reporter. But Alyeska, with Hermiller at the head, shares an Anchorage office address with BP, and later Exxon executives would testify that they knew about the plan six months earlier.

Black and Lund both refused to testify, exercising their right to avoid self-incrimination. Years after the case closed, they remained unapologetic. "I am more concerned about the environment than he was. Chuck Hamel is an oilman," Black said, defiant in the Court TV documentary. "I'm very happy with our investigation. I would do it the same way again . . . I would do it tomorrow." Four women from Black's team, however, did testify about the details of their operation, including Anna Contreras and Ricki Jacobson. "I told him [Hamel] that—and this is really horrible—one of my children had died," Jacobson confessed to Congress, detailing her early meetings and lies to Hamel. "I thought I was in above my head." The Wackenhut women became known in the newspapers as "Chuckie's Angels" and made up the cornerstone of Hamel's case. Hamel, too, testified. Sitting beside his lawyer, Washington attorney Billie Pirner Garde, he read a flowery statement celebrating his martyrdom as much as his cause: "Their 'kill the messenger approach' backfired," Hamel told the committee, referring to Alyeska. "The harder Alyeska tried to discredit me publicly, the more their employees came to me with information privately."

What neither Hamel nor British Petroleum knew then was that the workers would continue to use Hamel as their conduit for complaints against the company for many years to come. They would do it because he was willing to listen, because the issues he had warned about in Valdez were signs of larger, more persistent cancers growing not just in Alyeska's but in British Petroleum's operations elsewhere, and because the Wackenhut case had proven to the workers beyond a doubt that their own supervisors, executives, and safety managers couldn't be trusted to keep them safe.

3

THE FIRST OFFENSE

WHAT THE OIL INDUSTRY refers to as Alaska's "North Slope" is actually an expansive coastal plain stretching hundreds of miles north from the shoulders of the Brooks Range, Alaska's northernmost ring of high peaks, until it descends almost imperceptibly into the icy waters of the Beaufort Sea and the Arctic Ocean. Its name is a more technically than visually accurate description. The slope loses altitude along the way, but the change is so gradual that the barren landscape appears nearly flat—so flat, in fact, that the rushing torrents of mineral-rich glacier water flowing out of the mountains wind indecisively around ever-changing oxbows and push their gravel beds whimsically from one side to another, forming circuitous braids of stone piles. The river appears so broad and shallow that it can seem like the water is about to spill over the banks and spread across the table-flat tundra.

It was here that British Petroleum had been branching out around the edges of its most productive historical field—Prudhoe Bay—for more oil.

The tundra is arctic permafrost. It is topped by tough tufts of grasses that look inviting and meadowlike from a distance but are spindly and stubborn underfoot. The earth here is filled with pockets of water and frozen solid for two thousand feet down. Most of it hasn't thawed for more than ten thousand years, but at the topmost layer, the mud thaws in the warmth of the summer sun and softens into a sucking morass of delicate earth. Its subtle undulations are filled with the water from melting snow, which spreads into hundreds of thousands of shallow pools a few feet deep. On a calm day, the placid water mirrors the hazeless sapphire sky and popcorn clouds, turning the horizon from a finite line into a subtle fade where earth blends into sky.

In this fragile land polar bears venture forth for summer food, some of the nation's largest caribou herds migrate, and shore birds breed before traveling thousands of miles south to the Gulf of Mexico. The landscape has become an iconic symbol for Americans of all the wild places that were never preserved and have thus been lost. It is their most pristine natural habitat; one of the last great wild places. As such, the slope and ANWR—the still-underdeveloped region to the east of Prudhoe Bay—have become a focal point for the nation's concerns about industrial impact upon nature and thus a sort of rampart for threatened environments across the continent. The place's outsized meaning has turned into a political burden for lawmakers across the country and has made the balance of preservation and development more complicated in Alaska.

In the midst of the slope's delicate ecosystem, midway across Alaska's northern shoreline, at least eight different drilling fields had been developed by the mid-1990s. The slope had become a vast industrial complex consisting of thousands of miles of pipelines and roads connecting well pads—several acres where multiple wells had been drilled in a systematic grouping—to giant turbine houses and the compressor plants that capture the oil and natural gas and squeeze it under pressure into the pipelines. From the compressor stations, gas is routed back into the field, where it will again be pumped underground for disposal. The oil is sent on its eight-hundred-mile trip south over the Brooks Range, through boreal forest, across the Chugach Mountains, and finally to the ice-free terminal port across the bay from the town of Valdez. At the time, British Petroleum ran roughly half the fields, the largest being Prudhoe Bay, once one of the twenty biggest reservoirs of oil in the world. The Atlantic Richfield Company also owned half of the Prudhoe Bay field, and Conoco operated fields nearby. Companies like Exxon and Chevron held an investment stake in the oil there but left it to the others to get it out of the ground.

By the time the slope reaches the coast, the subtle fade of earth into sky is nearly complete. Here the ocean laps gently at the sandy shore without waves or any of the drama typical of a great body of water encountering a coast, in part because the perennial sea ice on the horizon breaks the waves, and in part because the water is only several feet deep. Imagine that gradual descent of the slope from the mountains continuing, submerged, stretching just as subtly out under the ocean, until it finally drops off the continental shelf some forty miles from shore. Two miles out, the water is in many places only fifteen feet deep.

To drill for oil off this coastline, BP has dredged and moved the earth enough to pile mounds of seafloor above the water's surface and create small, man-made islands. Between them the soil has been scraped together, like the ridges a child molds with sand on a beach, into long causeways that connect the roads of the slope to these newly engineered coastal islands of the Arctic.

British Petroleum discovered oil off this northern shoreline in 1978 and began drilling in 1985. It was the world's first continuously producing offshore arctic drilling venture. The first field to be developed was Endicott, and within a year it would become the North Slope's third most productive drilling field, producing some 115,000 barrels of oil a day. The Endicott field and Endicott Island sit ten miles east of Prudhoe Bay, about two miles offshore, connected by one of the island causeways. From October to June the ice solidifies around the small, man-made island, turning the open waters into a solid sheet. And for those long, cold months, oil workers can traverse the frozen permafrost and then the ice over the open ocean in giant tractors rolling on bulbous, treadless inner tubes that disperse the vehicle's weight and travel softly over the fragile ground and ice. Most of the time, however, the trucks still use the causeway.

Endicott Island, an expanse of forty-five acres, was built to handle seventy wells, most of them drilled by a two-hundred-foot-tall derrick owned by a contractor named Doyon and unremarkably named Rig 15. The drill rig is like a power tool, a specialized piece of equipment that gets moved from one target location to another. It drills holes into the earth and constructs each well site before leaving it to go on with another. Once the drilling is finished and a well begins pumping oil, the site is marked by a stack of pipes and valves, six to twelve feet tall, that jut out of the ground like faucet knobs and are housed inside a small metal shack.

The island has an infirmary, its own oil processing center, a fire station, and sleeping quarters big enough to shelter 150 workers. The mess hall was renowned for bountiful smorgasbords of fruit and meats and vegetables flown in from points south. If there was one luxury to toiling in this outpost, it was an endless supply of free food. But business got so bad in the early 1990s that British Petroleum, in an across-the-board-effort to shave costs, started taking away even those simple luxuries, right down to the ice cream machines. The company, despite John Browne's newly defined strategy, hadn't found a way out of the rut, and neither had the rest of the industry. The Alaskan wells, not just British Petroleum's but ARCO's and Exxon's, were pumping oil like mad. But crude prices trundled along the market's floor, rarely breaking the $20 mark and once dipping to about $15—a far cry from the $30–$35 a barrel that was normal in the early 1980s. The companies found themselves in survival mode. Nothing was going right. ANWR, where British Petroleum held some pre-refuge drilling rights and placed hope for the future of the company, remained politically untenable, since the *Valdez* spill had shattered the environmental reputation of Alaskan drillers. A federal ban on oil exports, a vestige of the oil crisis–induced fears of the 1970s, meant that even though there was a glut of oil on the American West Coast, the companies couldn't ship crude to ports in Asia. At least ARCO and Amoco had refineries on the West Coast. British Petroleum's oil had to go by tanker all the way to Panama, then by pipeline across Central America to the Gulf of Mexico, where another tanker could take it up to the company's refineries on the gulf coast. It was expensive. Some thought it was crippling the business.

Everyone cut jobs in those years. But by late 1992 no Alaskan operator had cut more workers loose than British Petroleum, which slashed a quarter of its 1,600-person North Slope workforce as part of a global plan to eliminate 11,500 jobs. The company sent pipe fitters packing, fired welders, terminated engineers and accountants. It was costing more to run British Petroleum's myriad businesses, and to drill and produce oil in Alaska and around the world, than British Petroleum had been able to make selling oil, and in 1992 the company found itself mired in debt. After first-quarter earnings plummeted 82 percent, the company posted its first loss ever. Its chairman and CEO—and John Browne's mentor—Robert "the Hatchet" Horton, was immediately toppled, replaced by the company's chief operating officer, David Simon, who became the third CEO to serve British Petroleum in as many years. Perhaps Simon, a thirty-year company veteran who was less brash than Horton and brought a stronger financial backing, could keep the company on track.

If there was a single coherent message of the day, it was to save money any way possible. Simon set out to cut $1 billion in expenses, the layoffs being the first step. Since heading exploration, Browne had so far been successful in saving costs, turning some North Sea operations from a loss to a profit in his first few years. Now he put the company's Alaska division on notice: if it wanted to drill more wells, it would need to finance that exploration with savings from its own budget. The pressure mounted to keep draconian budgets on track, from British Petroleum's management to contractors to individual pipeline inspectors and mechanics out in the field trying to meet their quotas.

The cost cuts and anemic budgets could explain all sorts of ugly stresses on British Petroleum's operations in Alaska in the early 1990s. They are also widely believed to be the reason why, beginning in 1993, employees for the British Petroleum contractor drilling wells on Endicott Island stopped trucking most of their hazardous waste away over the man-made causeways for legitimate disposal down south and started getting rid of it on their own, right there on the island.

Drilling through thousands of feet of rock produces a veritable toxic smoothie of chemicals and solvents, ranging from benzene to antifreeze. There's the drilling mud, consisting of all the dirt and rock and some solvents that are displaced by the actual spinning drill bit as it carves a hole four miles into the earth. And then there are all sorts of other lubricants and oils and machine cleaners and chemicals used on any drill site. There are exemptions and allowances in the regulations for some of the waste to be disposed of locally at the well site. Included are the drilling muds and the mix that directly results from the drilling process, which are exempted from environmental regulation. But the really bad stuff—toxic wastes that are known to kill sea life and cause cancer in people, and which can contaminate an entire tank of drinking water with a single drop—is required by federal law to be shipped off to a designated disposal site. There, it is supposed to be treated or injected underground in specialized and highly regulated disposal wells that are crafted to store waste in bedrock vaults thousands of feet below the surface.

British Petroleum and its contractor's waste from Endicott Island should have been trucked back over the causeway and south into the Prudhoe Bay field, where it could be considered for disposal there or trucked further, for five hundred miles along the Dalton Highway and over the crest of the Brooks Range to a suitable disposal site somewhere in the Alaskan heartland. It was an expensive process, and Doyon management knew well that every dime they spent on disposal meant there was one dime less in British Petroleum's budget for its contractors. Doyon relied on British Petroleum for 80 percent of its business.

On Rig 15, the toolpushers worked in virtual secrecy. Their site lay shrouded in an apron of corrugated steel panels meant to shield them from the blistering winds and driving ice of the Arctic. But the enclosure also made them invisible to anyone, including supervisors or regulators, outside the rig's footprint. And behind that veil of privacy, starting in 1993, the workers connected a waste pipe to a valve that led back into the ground and started illegally injecting its toxic waste into the empty space inside the oil well.

When a well is drilled, it is constructed like a telescope of successively smaller pipes stretching down a mile or more toward the earth's core. In the first section, a hole of roughly nine and a half inches in diameter is drilled some four thousand feet down, into the center of which is lowered a steel pipe, called a surface casing. Cement is poured around the pipe and, with the steel, serves as a barrier, holding back layers of mud and rock and gravel and protecting the earth and freshwater aquifers from oil and other contaminants. Once that surface casing is in place, the process is repeated farther down, to maybe eight thousand feet, with a second, deeper and narrower hole, perhaps five inches in diameter. Intermediate casing is installed in the deeper hole and is run all the way back to the surface, creating concentric rings of steel pipe and leaving an empty space, called an annulus, between the two casings, in the first four thousand feet.

Rig 15's toolpushers were supposed to be filling that annulus with the mud and tailings taken out of the well bore, but the opportunity for the company to bury the more harmful materials in all that empty space instead of shipping it overland for proper disposal proved irresistible. Behind the rig's windscreen, the workers were instructed not to use the tailings but instead to fill the annulus with lead-laden toxic waste oil and solvents, including paint and paint thinner containing methylene chloride, naphthalene, toluene, and benzene, all carcinogens.

The dumping went on for at least two years, during which time the workers grew gradually more concerned about what they were doing. They complained to Doyon managers that the fumes from the solvents they were injecting were noxious and severe. Some of them began to wear respirators for protection. Meanwhile, British Petroleum records showed that while federally regulated toxic waste was being produced and shipped from other drilling sites on Alaska's North Slope on a regular basis, very few shipments had been made from Endicott Island for years. Had the company not noticed?

Then, on January 15, 1995, one Doyon toolpusher had had enough. A foreman ordered him to inject another 23 barrels—or 966 gallons— of oil and solvents down into the well. The worker told a forklift driver who told a supervisor that he refused to do the injection. He probably understood that the annulus isn't completely sealed off from the environment. The fluids dumped into the well could be pushed down as far as 4,500 feet and then out into the earth, and forced into cracks and caverns in the ground, where they could possibly spread into freshwater aquifers. It was as good as pouring the contaminants out over the tundra. Worse, the dumping was a serious crime—a felony offense that could send him to jail.

The next morning, January 16, the Doyon crew dumped the waste into the well anyway. The Doyon supervisor would later say that he relayed the worker's concerns about illegal disposal and the dangers of the materials directly to British Petroleum drilling supervisors. The company told him that it approved the injection of the chemicals because they would help "freeze protect" the well, a process wherein chemicals are relied upon to keep a well from cracking as it runs through deep layers of arctic permafrost. Records, however, show that the toxic concoction of waste wasn't being used for freeze protection at new wells on Endicott Island; in those locations British Petroleum used the fluids legitimately designed for that process. It appeared that British Petroleum was using the freeze-protection process to conceal its illegal disposal of the additional material.

Seven and a half months later, the Doyon worker who raised the initial concerns took his complaints directly to British Petroleum's management, sending a boulder crashing down the hillside of British Petroleum's operations. Management, having been explicitly told about the dumping, couldn't ignore the concerns, and the complaint triggered a high-level internal review that concluded that the injections had indeed occurred and were illegal. But the company waited two weeks before it alerted federal authorities—a delay that was a violation of federal law. It wasn't until September 13 that management placed a phone call to the National Response Center, the federal government's hotline for environmental accidents. The call would lead to a criminal investigation and, later, felony charges against the company, setting off a series of negotiations and scrutiny that persisted for more than a decade. While the dumping case was eventually closed, the underlying issues it raised between British Petroleum and the U.S. government were never resolved.

IN THE MIDST of this unfolding crime, British Petroleum's top leadership endured another shakeup: Simon would become chairman of the board, but he was no longer CEO. In June 1995, at the age of forty-seven, John Browne became the youngest chief executive in British Petroleum's history. Through Browne's own hard work redefining the company's exploration strategy, and the surgical reshaping of the other business units that his predecessor, David Simon, had excelled at as CEO, British Petroleum had risen from the dead. Its finances were far more sound than in the late 1980s and early 1990s, its management more efficient, and its assets trimmed down to the essentials. In the six short years since the fateful investors' meeting—some of the toughest years the industry had ever endured—British Petroleum's executives had managed to wrap their arms around the giant fraying bundle of loose threads, extraneous businesses, and tangled interests that the company had become since the 1970s.

Browne played an important part in that process. As head of the company's exploration unit, he had already transformed British Petroleum from a "two-pipeline" company, with near-total dependence on Alaska and the North Sea for its oil, into a company with viable production coming from places like Vietnam, Colombia, and Azerbaijan. At the same time he had streamlined British Petroleum, pulling out of dozens of countries with dismal oil production. Along the way, he cut lifting costs—the money it takes to get the oil out of the ground—and increased profits. Promoting him to the CEO role was a vote of confidence from British Petroleum's board that the changes Browne had brought to exploration and production were responsible, at least in part, for the company's growth. It also reflected their belief that Browne's approach of unemotionally axing costs, aggressively pursuing new development, and reducing long-standing operations to their maximum efficiency was the right philosophy to guide British Petroleum into the future.

The world, however, still knew little of John Browne. And what was known could make him seem odd. "In many ways he wasn't a Texas oilman. But he was also not even a European oilman," says Carola Hoyos, a writer for the *Financial Times* who covered Browne for years. When Browne was seen in public, it was often with his mother, whom he even moved to live with him in Ohio in the late 1980s. Browne was an opera buff and an arts buff who had British Petroleum's corporate lobby festooned with oil paintings. "He had very refined taste. He enjoyed fine wine, and he enjoyed his cigars."

One night, recalls Ronald Freeman, the banker who worked closely with and befriended Browne, "John called me up in my office and said, 'Ron, would you and Helen'—my dear wife—'like to come out,' such-and-such an evening. 'Oh, sure, John, that's very kind of you. What are we doing?' He named the opera. 'Are—will you be accompanied?' 'Yeah. I'll bring my mother with me.' So John and his mother, a Romanian lady about four-ten, and Helen and I went to the opera together. No other CEO—and I've known them all in my long career—has ever invited me to come with his mother to the opera. John was definitely different in that regard."

Browne's inseparability from his mother stoked tabloid headlines like "BP, Mother and Me," in the London papers, and incessant curiosity and rumors about his private life. He was never seen to date, had never been married, and had no children or other relatives. His life revolved around his mother, and the company he had just been handed the reins to manage. "He was absolutely and completely devoted to that company," said Matthew Gwyther, the editor of *Management Today* magazine. "Almost married to it, if you like."

Perhaps because of that, Browne was also seen inside the business community as a leader with impeccable business acumen and unmatched commitment and intensity. In a seminal profile of Browne in the *Financial Times*, a boyhood friend described Browne as an intellectual powerhouse, and always questioning: "The teacher would say 'this is the formula,' and John would ask 'why'?" Years later, in the oil business, colleagues and competitors similarly regarded him as highly intelligent and ambitious. He was soft-spoken but thoughtful. And though often nearly inaudibly muttered, his statements were forceful for their intellectual heft and the confidence with which they were delivered. Colleagues describe him as having a powerful presence that earned adoration from the public and automatic respect among his employees. "When John entered a room you knew the boss was there," said one former executive who worked closely with him. "You felt it." He pushed his employees with the surety of an Ivy League professor, peering over his wire-rimmed glasses in silent judgment, his large head atop narrow shoulders and a slight frame. "I asked people to challenge the status quo and look for a better way to achieve objectives," he would later write. And his objectives were often expressed as convincingly as if they were already fact.

In British Petroleum, Browne inherited a trim and fit business. But it remained a very average one. As one publication put it at the time, British Petroleum had become an international corporation, but it hadn't figured out how to be a global corporation. It still spent more to find its oil, and more to replace its reserves, than almost any other oil company in the world. And it still struggled to compete with the great oil companies of the day, Shell and Exxon, and had only recently surpassed Mobil and Texaco in profits. Without the breadth, wealth, and diversity of those companies, it stood little chance of weathering the volatile and inhospitable storms that had repeatedly swamped the oil industry in past years and likely would again. Browne didn't shy from the company's reality and instead seemed to view himself as its savior. "There had been a yearning desire for leadership in BP. . . . The company needed purpose and values," he wrote. "BP was stuck as a 'middleweight insular company.' It was either up, or out."

But while Browne was emboldened, even invigorated, by the challenge he faced, it couldn't have come at a more difficult time. Not only was the oil business still climbing out of a deep financial depression, but Exxon's devastating *Valdez* spill still hung heavy in the hearts of environmentalists and politicians, and Lee Raymond, Exxon's CEO, seemed to scrape at the open wound as he stubbornly refuted environmental concerns and continued to fight the case in court. It had been four years since the United States had finished its short war in Iraq, but the country remained traumatized by the searing images of smoking, environmentally catastrophic, booby-trapped oil wells in Kuwait, and angry mobs shouting "blood for oil" on the streets of Washington remained ingrained in the public consciousness. Industry executives lamented that an oil company conjured images of a "big fat greedy guy with a cigar and dirty fingernails counting his money."

Browne was unabashed about his intentions to transform British Petroleum into a global oil industry leader. He also had a loftier moral goal. Browne hoped to respond to the industry's critics by turning British Petroleum into the antithesis of Big Oil, and to singlehandedly change the public's perception of the oil business. "The industry was now measured by its weakest member, the one with the worst reputation," he wrote, referring to Exxon's environmental record at the time. He began to say things that no oil executive had ever said: that the oil industry should consider environmental sustainability, and that oil companies could, and should, take steps to address climate change. He disparaged the oil industry of the past as profiteering and environmentally selfish, as if just saying so was enough to distance him from it, and as if simply pledging a moral high road would earn him immunity from public skepticism. He also often spoke as if the problems associated with the industry were entirely separate from British Petroleum, and as if his company would do no such things. He pledged to bring the message home; to affect the culture inside British Petroleum's operations.

Among Browne's favorite issues was the need to enhance both worker safety and environmental protections in his company's operations, and he acknowledged the pressure the public scrutiny put on British Petroleum, especially in Alaska. "We had to ensure that there were no deviations and that our operation was perfect in terms of the law. This changed the way we did business in Alaska."

However, Browne never publicly acknowledged the criminal environmental scandal simultaneously unfolding at his operations on Endicott Island, and he seemed surprised when the backlash over *Valdez* and Big Oil persisted. In December 1995, when President Bill Clinton vetoed a bill that would open ANWR to drilling, killing one of British Petroleum's great hopes for new oil discoveries in Alaska, Browne was embittered. "No amount of argument would support our case," he wrote. "We soon realized that this was not about reason. This was about emotion. We were an oil company and we were being portrayed as wanting to damage a beautiful place with blowing grass, wild flowers and an abundance of wildlife for the sake of short-term profits. We simply could not be trusted."

He seemed to have forgotten about Chuck Hamel and the Wackenhut scandal, and not to have understood the significance of the Endicott case that was then unfolding. It was the public, he seemed to be saying, that was misinformed. The public, he thought, had failed to take British Petroleum's word. He seems not to have considered that British Petroleum, and the entire industry, for that matter, had not yet earned the public's trust.

That tightrope walk between reformation and running a disciplined traditional oil business would come to define many of the challenges facing British Petroleum for the next fifteen years. And all the good intentions in the world wouldn't mean much if that business didn't survive. Such was the realization that Browne was reaching by the end of 1996, and it meant that he needed to direct some effort not just to sprucing up the company's image but to transforming the business of British Petroleum itself.

It was a confusing time. Oil prices remained near record lows—around $15 per barrel—and the United States was drowning in supply. Adventurous foreign exploits were proving how risky and uncertain the oil business would be in an age in which diminishing reserves forced companies to search farther and harder for crude. British Petroleum's Colombia project was unsettled by terrorism and political strife, and places like Nigeria were too corrupt to deal with. British Petroleum had done well in securing access to a sliver of Russia's vast resources after the fall of the Berlin Wall, and by winning rights to drill in former Soviet states such as Azerbaijan. Those regions were unpredictable, however. It was the beginning of the post–peak-oil era, a time during which risk, whether geopolitical or environmental, would have to be undertaken because all the easy oil was gone.

Browne saw the industry's leading companies treading water, not sure which way to swim, or who to lock arms with in order to stay afloat. He believed that a wave of consolidation was coming; that mergers would sort out the strong from the weak. And British Petroleum's situation was no different. It was no longer failing, but it wasn't going anywhere, either. And the landscape was changing unpredictably. Globalization was coming to define the world's markets, yet the emergence of India, China, and Russia as powerful, permanent players wasn't accepted as a permanent trend, he wrote in his memoir. The Internet was still fledgling and experimental. "I would be at the helm of BP during a period when across the globe in almost every industry, in every aspect of life, it would seem as if the patterns of the past were being scrambled."

Certain circumstances, however, were clear. A company like Exxon, with more than six billion barrels in reserves and oil production in more than a dozen countries, had the diversity to withstand the spikes and troughs of the market and stay buoyant. British Petroleum had paid down its debt by $1 billion a year, boosted profits by $2 billion a year, and dramatically cut spending. And yet it still did not have the size or stability to compete. Chosen as CEO in large part for his magical abilities to squeeze out more earnings with less capital, Browne forecast that over ten years he could grow the company's production by a million barrels a day, nearly doubling it. But even that, Browne was increasingly convinced, wouldn't be enough. Browne, it seemed, had maxed out the company's potential for organic growth. That, according to the Salomon oil banker who had now worked with Browne for more than a decade, left just one more place to look for oil. "Oil companies have two choices," Freeman says. They can find the barrels in the ground or they could find the barrels on Wall Street. There's no other place."

In September 1996 Browne met with British Petroleum's board of directors at the Four Seasons Hotel in downtown Berlin and presented a daring plan to buy his way to the top of the industry. He left Germany the next day with permission to shop for a merger, embarking on the path toward one of the most ambitious growth plans any business had ever seen, and one that would eventually transform not just British Petroleum and Browne's career but the entire industry.

AT THE SAME TIME, however, Browne remained fixated on the notion that the oil industry—and all of industry, for that matter—could be reframed as sustainable and environmentally responsible. Fascination with the issue divided his time. On May 19, 1997, he went to Stanford University to deliver an address that would serve as a turning point for both the oil industry and the business world. In it, he blamed the oil business for the stratospheric rise in greenhouse gas emissions, and said that those emissions might be causing global warming. "The time to consider the policy dimensions of climate change is not when the link between greenhouse gases and climate change is conclusively proven," he said, "but when the possibility cannot be discounted and is taken seriously by the society of which we are part."

Exxon had made a business of funding studies that debunked climate change and denying its threat in every way. Browne was the first oilman to acknowledge that climate change was real, and his speech set an example for how global businesses can be engaged in addressing it. In a few words he changed history, cementing his role as a leading thinker in management, and rebranded his struggling oil company into a global environmental leader. "He wanted to identify himself as the anti–Lee Raymond, the anti-Exxon," said Freeman. "He did not want to be stuck in the oil patch. He said that oil fell short as a source of energy for human society. He wanted to be out there beyond oil. And he took a lot of criticism for it. He identified himself with the climate movement, with the green movement, the alternative energy movement."

The new stance provoked his peers, angered competitors at Exxon, and caused him to become further estranged from the good old boy culture that was so much of the oil business. "The American Petroleum Institute said that I had left the church," Browne said with a laugh in a TV interview around the time of his speech. "What it has done is also given us a seat at the table while people are talking about what to do with global warming."

Plenty of people, though—including many within British Petroleum—questioned whether Browne was sitting at the right table. They wanted him to focus on making British Petroleum bigger and operating it as the best oil company it could be. Browne's attention was divided, and his environmental sympathies began to clash with British Petroleum's own interests and its ability to move within the industry. His first merger attempt, with Mobil, fell apart, and the industry seemed to relish his slip. "The whole thing about climate change earned it the enmity of its peers," says Derek Brower, a longtime oil analyst and editor of the *Petroleum Economist*. "Shell, Chevron, Exxon, they've all been happy to see BP suffer, because BP especially under Browne sounded so sanctimonious."

Browne shrugged off the criticism. And perhaps buoyed by the rush that came with setting himself apart from the industry so publicly, he instead wheeled his attention back to making British Petroleum bigger. In 1998 Browne set his sights on Amoco, also known as the old Standard Oil Company of Indiana, another old Rockefeller company and one of the largest and most storied oil brands in the United States. The refining business was at its lowest point in decades, gasoline was being sold at clearance prices, and oil remained around $14 a barrel. Amoco had huge natural gas assets, significant oil reserves, and two of the largest U.S. refineries. It had technological strength and sophisticated engineers exploring for oil in the Gulf of Mexico, and it had more than nine thousand retail gas stations that complemented those British Petroleum already owned. Yet Amoco had been floundering. It had spent the decade investing billions in new wells without discovering new oil, and had been spurned by several foreign governments in countries in which it had hoped to invest. Amoco was weak. Merged with British Petroleum, it would become the world's third largest publicly traded oil company and the number one producer of oil and gas in the United States.

To Browne and British Petroleum's board, the takeover was an obvious opportunity. The merger would at first be presented as a joining of equals, and BP Amoco would be formed. But Browne exerted his muscle in the transaction from the moment it began, finishing with his insistence on reaching an accord with Amoco's CEO, Larry Fuller, at 5:00 a.m. on a Saturday morning while Fuller was at a private family home celebrating the birth of his granddaughter. British Petroleum insiders say no one on either side held illusions that this was a merger of equals, and in fact, within twenty-four months Amoco's name would be discarded. To make the consolidation work, Browne would eventually fire 16,000 Amoco employees and cut more than $4 billion in operating costs and $10 billion in assets from the merged companies. It was the start of the kind of ruthless stripping of resources that earned John Browne the nickname "Neutron John" in some press reports and would make British Petroleum stock soar, but which would inevitably threaten its workers in Alaska, Texas, and the gulf.

The deal, signed on New Year's Eve in 1998, was valued at $61 billion and at the time was the largest corporate merger in history. Conveniently, it would mask an astounding fall in British Petroleum's profits in 1998, but that was just one aspect of its elegance; in another show of his Stanford business school colors and the Silicon Valley playbook, Browne paid for Amoco with BP stock. And the deal sailed through government approval. "Put the two together," Browne said in the merger announcement, and "you have a world class set of assets."

It was a tremendous victory for Browne, establishing British Petroleum overnight as Britain's largest corporation and raising Browne's status so that he stood nearly shoulder to shoulder with Exxon's chairman, Lee Raymond. Instantly, British Petroleum gained the sort of stability and breadth that Browne had thought was so badly needed in 1996. Its capitalization was edging toward Exxon's, and its oil reserves were now greater, ranking British Petroleum's access to oil second in the world, behind Shell's.

Combined with his brave stance on climate change and his profundity in bringing American-style management to Britain, the merger solidified Browne's celebrity status in the business world. London's *Financial Times*, in an astoundingly flattering and extensive 1997 profile, had already likened him to Louis the XIV, the Sun King, bestowing a nickname that would stick, though it tended to be used both flatteringly and in jest. In mid-1998 Sir John was awarded a life peerage to become Lord Browne of Madingley. And he became a sought-after speaker at Davos. Having again commanded the public eye, Browne reveled in the spotlight. "BP was the star of the show," says the *Petroleum Economist*'s Brower. "John Browne was the main attraction at every conference he went to. That's who people came out to see, a larger-than-life character. John Browne certainly considered that his place was at the table beside Clinton and Putin and so on, and for a while it was."

After British Petroleum merged with Amoco, the industry raced to consolidate. Before the deal was even done, in December 1998 Exxon announced it intended to snatch up Mobil, for $81 billion, proposing to reunite two more old Standard Oil companies and create the largest company in the world. Other potential industry mergers began to take shape as well. But as the companies grew, the underlying business climate continued to worsen. The oil business was as bad off as it had ever been, and what few small companies remained found themselves in exactly the predicament that Browne had feared British Petroleum would get in back in 1996: adrift with sails too small to catch any wind.

As if addicted to the adrenaline rush that came with his meteoric rise in stature and influence, Browne set his sights even higher. Never mind that the Amoco merger had added tens of thousands of employees and hundreds of operations and needed to be carefully integrated into the colossal British Petroleum corporation. And never mind that most mergers, largely because of the difficulties of synthesizing disparate groups, fail. Browne still wanted to be the biggest. So when the chief executives of ARCO called him to test the waters of another merger less than a month after the Amoco deal had closed, Browne bit hard. ARCO, too, was hemorrhaging money. But the company brought to the table nearly everything Browne was still missing for his perfect composition. ARCO had two refineries on the West Coast—refineries that already processed British Petroleum's oil from Alaska. ARCO was a leader in offshore drilling in both the Gulf of Mexico and the North Sea; and it had extensive natural gas projects in Southeast Asia, where British Petroleum was already active. Most importantly, it owned the other half of the North Slope's oil, presenting a unique opportunity to consolidate the companies' Alaskan properties and find the sort of efficiency that Browne had become famous for pursuing. ARCO also had some eighteen thousand employees and thousands of facilities in both Alaska and around the world.

Browne, according to reports, indulged in grandiose visions of where another merger could lead British Petroleum. While the Amoco deal had briefly made BP the second largest oil company in the world, and the largest U.S. producer of oil, Exxon's proposed merger with Mobil promised to put Exxon squarely back on top. If BP Amoco bought ARCO, the combined company would again lead in America and run a close second to an Exxon Mobil worldwide. That would leave Shell vulnerable to a BP buyout, and a hypothetical BP-Shell could then overtake Exxon as the largest company in the world. Mission accomplished. Exxon's deal was eventually approved by federal officials in November 1999. To complete his vision, Browne needed the ARCO deal to go through, too.

It wasn't as sure a thing as Browne had hoped. Each of the mergers had drawn scrutiny from federal trade officials, and this last one promised to be the most complicated. One by one, the industry's mergers were reuniting the old Standard Oil Trust, the ultimate monopoly that had inspired the U.S. government to keep companies from having total control over an industry and suffocating competition. In 1890 Congress passed the Sherman Antitrust Act, and in 1911 the act was used to break up the Rockefeller oil empire into thirty-four separate companies. Two of the largest companies, Standard Oil Company of New Jersey and Standard Oil Company of New York, having become Exxon and Mobil, respectively, had now been brought back together. British Petroleum, which had already bought out the old Standard Oil of Ohio group in the late 1980s, and then Amoco, the old Standard Oil of Indiana, was now attempting to reunite a third company with Rockefeller roots. ARCO's heritage was tied to the old Atlantic Petroleum Storage Company.

The prospect of BP Amoco buying up ARCO was raising antitrust resistance anew, in large part because it would put the vast majority of North Slope oil under one company. The state of Alaska warned that competition in the state would be stifled, that the merger would lead to higher unemployment, and that inevitably it would just bring about further cutbacks that could affect safety and environmental protection.

"The potential impacts . . . are major," said Alaska's attorney general, Bruce Botelho, referring to the merger. The Federal Trade Commission (as well as Exxon) sued to stop the merger, and Alaska's governor, Tony Knowles, threw himself into the mix in the hopes of mediating an arrangement that would work. But there was little doubt that further cost pressures on Alaska's operations were in store. "We can only do this by creating greater efficiencies, reducing costs, and increasing our financial strength by combining our organizations," James Palmer, then head of external affairs for BP Exploration Alaska, the company's Alaska unit, told state legislators. Kevin Meyers, ARCO Alaska's president at the time, confirmed their fears. "Clearly this acquisition will bring short-term pain—there's no doubt to that," he said. "But it is also the key to a better future."

The question nagging at many Alaskans who protested the merger was, Better for whom? The antitrust confrontation began to hinge not only on questions about how competition might be squelched but on how consolidation and cost cuts would ultimately affect safety and environmental protection. Even before the ARCO deal was proposed, concerns were arising in Alaska that cuts and years of belt-tightening were taking a toll on both British Petroleum and ARCO's equipment on the slope and on its safe operation. The old issues of Chuck Hamel and BP's slope workers persisted. In hearings on the merger held the previous June before a committee of Alaska state legislators, oil field workers, contracting companies, and public interest groups testified that cost shaving in the past had already led to poor pipeline maintenance and high unemployment. "Downsizing will result in less self-monitoring of compliance with environmental standards," Kay Brown, director of the Alaska Conservation Alliance, told the committee.

The issues of morality and public trust that Browne had spoken so much about in the early 1990s, and the question of corporate culture and character, had come full circle to intersect with Browne's expansion plans in Alaska, leaving the negotiations in a fragile state. At this point, neither the state nor federal opposition to the merger was taking into account the charges being leveled against BP for illegal chemical dumping. A protracted exposé of that issue could amount to more than a slap on the wrist; it could derail Browne's entire plan for his company. The last thing he needed was for some small environmental crime in Alaska, like the Endicott Island case, to interrupt his trajectory. To finish the ARCO deal, Browne needed Endicott to go away.

ONE DAY in late 1998 the phone rang in Jeanne Pascal's office at the EPA building on Sixth Street in downtown Seattle. It was a lawyer for BP Alaska. The company wanted to talk.

As a senior attorney for the agency, Pascal specialized in what the government calls "debarment" cases for the Northwest, the mountain states, and Alaska. If a company commits fraud or breaks the law too many times it can be debarred, or stripped of its government contracts. Certain environmental crimes, like a violation of the Clean Water Act or of the Clean Air Act, automatically lead to a government ban, at least for the facility where the violation occurred. But the feds—people like Pascal—have a lot of discretion, and they can be lenient, or they can decide to ban an entire company from all government contracts in the United States. Pascal worked with senior managers to rehabilitate the corporation as a good citizen deserving of government contracts and benefits.

BP hadn't yet been convicted of a crime, but the Department of Justice was about to charge its Alaska division with illegally dumping hazardous waste. Doyon Drilling had already pled guilty to fifteen counts of violating the federal Oil Pollution Act, and three Doyon employees had been convicted; one of them would do time behind bars. At the time is was the Amoco merger that was under way—Browne hadn't yet gotten to ARCO—and British Petroleum hoped to head off the uncertain risk that an eventual debarment case would bring by coming to Pascal and reaching a settlement as quickly as possible. A ban on government contracts or prohibition against new drilling rights was the kind of bad news that could tank a company's stock price and ruin a merger. It would be far better to deal with known consequences that to operate under a persistent shadow of government scrutiny.

Debarment might not seem like much of a threat to BP, but its business was inextricably interwoven with the federal government. "It was very worrisome," said one senior executive, describing the concern at the time. "We felt very responsible and followed the deferred debarment very closely and rigorously. The company took it extremely seriously—the possibility that we could lose the contracts." More than half of the company's reserves of oil and a fifth of its gas still came from the United States, and each of its leases, whether in Prudhoe Bay or the Gulf of Mexico, is a form of government contract. It was unlikely that the leases would get canceled on the spot, but BP wouldn't be able to buy new ones. Besides the leases, British Petroleum was one of the largest suppliers of fuel to the U.S. military, and received more than $1 billion a year in contracts. It also ran pipelines both in the United States and abroad, and received various forms of subsidies or tax breaks for everything from refining to exploration. Each of these is critical to BP's business, but as British Petroleum entered its season of acquisitions, nothing seemed more important than having the best record possible with which to woo Federal Trade Commission approval.

Sometime soon after the call, Chris Phillips, a senior vice president for operations at BP Alaska, and Carol Dinkins, an attorney representing the company, flew to Seattle, where they met with Pascal at the Fairmont Hotel to plead their case in person. In the plush conference room BP executives reserved for such meetings, Phillips fiercely defended the company, telling Pascal that the Endicott dumping crime was the fault of BP's contractor, Doyon, and insisting that BP management was not complicit in giving the orders for disposal. After all, Phillips pointed out to Pascal, the Doyon case was already closed. But BP hadn't alerted the feds to the dumping even after it had begun to address the problem itself, Pascal reminded them, and while the delay might seem like a bureaucratic sticking point, it was in fact a serious crime. BP was willing to own up to it, Phillips told her, but they wanted a clean settlement with the government, and they didn't want the negotiations to drag on too long.

Pascal cared less about getting a strong conviction than she did about how the debarment process could be used to make BP a safer company in the future. Short and rotund, with carefully coiffed hair and a residual southern charm that poked through the rugged individualism that had brought her to the Pacific Northwest, Pascal, 49, was an affable woman. Her easy, motherly demeanor could hide her acute sense of justice and lead you to forget that she would decide the fate of a $300 billion London-based corporation. Pascal was born in a speck of a town in northern Mississippi, where, she says, "nothing's happened but a train wreck," and later, raised in Tennessee. Her family had education and means—her father was a radiologist. But her youth was colored by the ugly racial tensions of the South in the 1950s, which occasionally touched her own household. She was nine, she recalls, sitting on the front porch at her best friend's house, when the girl—a white Baptist—said: "My momma says as long as you aren't a coon, a kike, a con, or a Catholic, you're okay." Pascal, whose family was Catholic, wrestled with this for a moment. "Does that mean it's not okay to be friends?"

The influences of injustice stacked up until she could use them to shape her own sense of moral clarity. She was disturbed by the closed-mindedness and ignorance she found in the South, and by people's improvident approach to the environment. Eventually, she found direction by contrasting herself to the things she hated, in a world that seemed to her to be defined by prejudice and carelessness. One day when she was thirteen, her brother Greg took her on a joyride in the family's motorboat on the Tennessee River, where they kept a summer cabin. He swilled beer as he drove, tossing the cans out into the current. Pascal shouted at him to stop. "Oh, jam it," Greg told her. When the two pulled up dockside at a general store so Greg could buy more beer, Pascal left him there and drove off alone. "I'll be back when I find every can," she yelled. She returned to the dock to pick him up hours later with a bag full of trash.

It isn't clear how Pascal acquired these feelings. Her parents were never idealistic about the environment. They took a practical approach to the utility of natural resources, seeing them as a form of wealth that should be selectively spent to build the conveniences they all enjoyed, and believing that they shouldn't be wasted. Her brother's littering that day struck her as arrogant and dissonant. The feelings stuck. As she got older, outrage became her compass. "I really started thinking about the stupidity and absurdity of discrimination, and how the people in the South seemed not to care at all about the environment, either. So I decided if I was going to make a difference at all, I needed to go to a place that was more enlightened," she said, describing her gradual orientation toward working in law. She got her law degree from the University of Memphis. When she graduated, she was twenty-eight, Jimmy Carter was president, and the Eagles were a pop music sensation. Pascal, in search of bigger minds and a broader experience, drove west.

In Washington State, she got hired as a young lawyer in the Snohomish County prosecutor's office, north of Seattle. It was good work for a time. She sharpened her skills prosecuting small-town criminals and married a sheriff's deputy, Dallas Swank. But she had ambitions of dealing with bigger issues on a bigger stage, and so she doggedly pursued a job with the EPA. For a year, she mailed weekly letters to the agency's local director, until, on March 21, 1984, she got a job as an assistant regional counsel, focusing on water and environmental enforcement. "I'm absolutely positive the guy hired me to get me off his back," she says. "I actually put the memo of hiring into a scrapbook."

The work's appeal wore off quickly. Pascal grew frustrated with and cynical about the futility of environmental enforcement. It wasn't that the laws weren't effective; they were. But traditional environmental enforcement placed everything in black-and-white terms: when a concern came to her desk, there was little the government could do to affect how a company operated until it actually violated a regulation or caused an accident. How a company attempted to comply with those regulations was none of the government's business. Even after a violation, there might be a cash fine or penalty, but that was the end of it. Pascal longed for a mechanism that would change a company's habits and bring about reform. To make matters worse, she found the bureaucracy of the federal government to be an abyss. "It was an archaic system," she said. Decisions that she thought could easily be made or finalized inside the EPA instead were run through managers in the Justice Department or the Interior Department, severing lines of accountability and adding endless illogical delays that often consumed more than a year per case.

So when Pascal was invited, in 1991, to help launch the EPA's new debarment office, it was a chance to take an entirely different tack. The debarment office was expanded and formalized during the Reagan administration as a tool to guarantee that taxpayers weren't being cheated by corrupt private contractors. The Department of Defense had had a debarment group since the early 1980s. In 1989, the EPA, realizing that big industry seemed to pose as much of an environmental threat as a threat of fraud, began to think it could make good use of the law, too. Its goal, however, wasn't just to police the corporations. Rather it was to use moments of legal vulnerability to reach mutual agreements that would force a company to rehabilitate itself and keep out of trouble. In fact, by definition, debarment wasn't meant to be punitive. Instead it capitalized on a moment of leverage to increase oversight and shape a company into something closer to the government's ideal mold: an economic stimulant that complied with the law and worked to minimize its footprint on the environment. "It was a very effective tool to bring about compliance from people that have federal grants, and it was just lying dormant," Pascal says.

By the time she was assigned to the BP case in 1998, Pascal had handled at least six hundred EPA cases against large and small companies, usually juggling a caseload of twenty-five to fifty at a time. In almost all of those cases, the system worked beautifully. The government and a company would sign a contractual agreement laying out probation-like terms of behavior that all but guaranteed compliance with environmental laws. Until the period ended, the company was suspended from any new government contracts: guilty until proven innocent. Companies were usually eager to satisfy the agreement and demonstrate that they met all the benchmarks along the way. Eventually the sanctions were lifted. In Pascal's experience, most companies complied quickly and in good faith—the fastest path back to normal business. It didn't seem as if BP would be much different.

As expected, on September 23, 1999, lawyers for BP Exploration Alaska pleaded guilty to one felony count of illegally disposing of hazardous waste. The plea was to a lesser charge than Doyon had admitted to but a compromise that Department of Justice officials welcomed because it set out a plan for greater environmental sensitivity at all of BP Amoco's U.S. operations. The company agreed to pay $22 million in fines and costs associated with the plea, including establishing a new environmental management program for the U.S. For BP Amoco, the plea couldn't have come at a more critical time. The Amoco merger had been approved but now the ARCO acquisition was in jeopardy, and debarment would almost certainly present an insurmountable obstacle to the merger. BP escaped the federal environmental crimes charges that would have automatically triggered debarment, but the conviction still meant that the EPA would formally open a discretionary debarment case, a broader form of sanctions that the EPA could choose, subjectively based on the company's general conduct, which placed BP Amoco and its pending merger with ARCO at Pascal's mercy.

Pascal, in large part because the company had sought her out first, was prepared to give BP the benefit of the doubt. Phillips, the executive the company put forward to work with her, was known as a slick corporate politician. He had been transferred to Alaska only months before from BP's natural gas developments in Indonesia. But he also conveyed a candid Texas charm that made him seem genuine. Pascal wasn't naïve, but she did maintain an underlying faith that people were good; that they said what they meant and meant what they said. She understood that BP Amoco, like any big oil company, relied on thousands of contractors. If the company said it suffered because of poor decisions made by a couple of rogue toolpushers, she was inclined to believe them.

But when she started to poke around, she ran into problems. For one, Doyon's celebrated CEO, Morris Thompson, who had chaired the Bureau of Indian Affairs under the Nixon administration, insisted that his company had been told by BP to get rid of the waste. "BP always had a company man on the drilling rig," Pascal recalls him telling her, "and that BP drilling guy was directing the contractor to dump hazardous waste down the well."

Another prominent Doyon executive, Randy Ruedrich, who would later serve on Alaska's Oil and Gas Conservation Commission with Sarah Palin and head the state's Republican Party, also insisted, in an interview, that he had discussed the practices with British Petroleum executives long before the dumping was made public.

It turned into Doyon's word against British Petroleum's, and since the Justice Department had already settled its case, Pascal, too, moved toward an agreement. She pushed to build on the promises of the criminal plea agreement and earned concessions that would ensure not only that environmental concerns were better managed in the future but that BP's workers and contractors had open lines of communication to raise concerns that might prevent another Endicott Island situation. In January 2000, the parties reached a final compliance agreement—a contract that laid out a lengthy set of management changes and obligations aimed at establishing "a revised corporate attitude" at BP Amoco's Alaska operation.

In exchange for not being debarred, BP Amoco agreed not to pun-
ish employees who reported environmental concerns and said it would
spend $15 million on an environmental management program for
its operations in Alaska, Texas, and the gulf. It promised to establish
direct lines of management authority and to put the group responsible
for health, safety, and environmental concerns in a position to report
directly to the president of the company—a bit of organizational architecture that Pascal considered essential to avoiding, in the future, the
conflicting accounts of who knew what, and delays in response. In this
way, top executives couldn't avoid hearing about serious safety concerns, and when they did, they would be accountable. The EPA identified this as one of the most important things BP could do to reform its
safety culture in Alaska.

It wasn't the only capitulation BP Amoco made to preserve its business that spring. On April 14, 2000, the Federal Trade Commission
finally approved the company's takeover of ARCO. To win over regulators, and to settle Exxon's suit to block the deal, Browne had to give
up much of what he wanted in the merger in the first place: almost all
of ARCO's North Slope assets would be sold to Phillips Petroleum,
effectively splitting the Alaska portion of the deal in two. Phillips and
Exxon would both retain roughly 36 percent of the North Slope assets.
BP Amoco, with the remaining share, would also remain the sole operator of the oil fields, running them for the two other companies. There
was no mention in reports from those final negotiations of the compliance agreement BP Amoco had nearly simultaneously reached with
the EPA, but making the felony go away certainly didn't hurt.

The Endicott compliance agreement was to last five years, expiring
on January 31, 2005. For Pascal, the dumping case paled in seriousness
compared to some of the other crimes she had pursued against industrial companies in her career. But however routine this one case might
have seemed at the time, it was the first in a string of British Petroleum
dots that would be connected over many years. And while the agreement seemed to dwell mostly on mundane management issues, in signing it, British Petroleum—now called BP Amoco-ARCO—had set the
ground rules for how the company should behave and be judged in the
United States for the next decade.

4

A SLIPPERY SLOPE

MARC KOVAC is built like a compressed spring. He has blue eyes, short-cropped brown hair, a straight, thin nose, and the kind of square, muscled jaw that makes you think he is about to chew you out. He is short, boxy, broad-shouldered, and thick-chested—built like a competitive wrestler. His incisive stare is the first clue that this man harbors an acute, almost obsessive affinity for highly technical engineering detail, and that he has a razor-sharp memory for the most obscure facts, from the type of artificial fishing fly that is most effective on the Sagavanirk-tok River in June to the compression threshold of the natural gas being run through a section of pipeline.

Kovac lives with his wife, Shannon, in a white-shingled ranch house in Seward, Alaska, near the head of Resurrection Bay. It's a small town, 130 miles south of Anchorage on the eastern flanks of Kenai Fjords National Park—the kind of place where black bears tipping garbage cans are more mischievous than the town teens, and neighbors know each other's business. In his spare time, Kovac takes his boat out into the sound to fish for halibut. Every four weeks, like many workers on Alaska's North Slope, he packs a modest duffel bag full of jumpsuits and turtlenecks and steel-toed boots and hops a puddle jumper over the southern edge of the Alaska Range to Anchorage. There he boards a private BP-owned 727 for the flight 620 miles north to Deadhorse, the tiny labor outpost in Prudhoe Bay that serves as base camp for all the drilling there. Kovac will work here for a two-week shift, as a mechanic and a welder, then go home and repeat the cycle two weeks later.

He shares this lifestyle with thousands of workers who stream in from as far away as Newfoundland, Michigan, and Seattle to the wretched cold of this lonely outpost near the top of the world. These are the globe-trotting, migrant, specialized experts that the oil industry relies upon to keep its operations going: mechanics, radiation testers, fracturing technicians, roustabouts, mud engineers, and truck drivers. They spend half their lives in repose with family, tending to chores, mowing lawns, and enjoying long weekends. And then they dart off to spend fourteen straight eighteen-hour days in dangerous jobs. On the slope, they fight fatigue and arctic winds and stomp through snowdrifts to inspect a pipeline for cracks or drown in the din of ballroom-size compressor engines while peering into a bird's nest of valves and dials in one of the facilities that moves the oil. They sleep in prefabricated "man camps," lonely dormitories stocked with free food and televisions and Ping-Pong tables, then board an old school bus to be ferried back out to the site again the next day. The camps are like a giant engine in constant revolution, with workers landing at the airport as others depart, and those on the night shift heading for bed shortly after those on the morning shift pack out.

Kovac has been on this sort of schedule since his first job here, as a mechanic, in 1971. He keenly recalls the days when the field was new, full of hope and promise, and its equipment gleamed in the summer sun. He was always a British Petroleum man, but in those days the company ran just a fraction of the slope. It was before John Browne's ARCO acquisition went through and the company's workers, along with all their disparate facilities spread over hundreds of square miles, were combined into a single organization; before BP had sold off a chunk of the wells to Phillips Petroleum to satisfy the antitrust concerns of the feds. And it was before he had joined United Steelworkers, attaching himself to a national union that gave him the voice to be heard in this sea of big industry and big money. He was proud, then, to work for a company like British Petroleum. The pay was good—it still is—and Kovac enjoyed a sense of purpose, knowing that his work helped to fuel the country and allowed his state of Alaska to thrive.

But between 1995 and 2000 he had begun to see a subtle squeeze put on the slope's operations, the effect, he believed, of John Browne's efforts to reduce the company's expenses. From the start of Browne's tenure, he had mandated severe cuts. He had scarcely finished erasing 1,700 jobs in 1990 when he asked his managers to find $750 million in budget reductions across the company. In Alaska, more than one thousand British Petroleum jobs had been lost between 1992 and 1999, and several thousand more if British Petroleum's contractors' layoffs and ARCO's pre-takeover layoffs were counted. For at least six years, British Petroleum's maintenance crews had been pushed to do more with less. Now, all the acquisitions had to be shoehorned into his strict paradigm for efficiency and net revenue per barrel, too. But in Alaska and at every other aging British Petroleum property, managers faced a paradoxical task: make more money on a per-barrel basis even while the number of barrels produced is decreasing, daily operating costs remain more or less constant, and the equipment needed to do it requires more maintenance and larger investments. The trends were pointing in opposite directions. Browne's management acknowledged this paradox with a concession: instead of trying to produce more oil at lower cost, in Alaska management should focus on maintaining "lifting costs," or trying to produce the same amount of oil at the same cost.

Preservation of the status quo was proving to be a challenge, however. There are only so many ways to save money in Alaska. Either the costs are fixed—as with royalties (where the government sets a percentage fee on production) or food—or spending cuts would affect the profits of another company British Petroleum owned a couple links down the food chain. The new vertically integrated style of supermajor—one of the world's largest publicly traded oil companies—was likely to own not only the division that produced the oil but the pipeline subsidiary that charged to transport it, the shipping vessels that brought it overseas, and the refineries that turned it into gasoline. "We would say, 'Why not try to reduce the tankerage costs [referring to the shipping charges],' and they would say, 'Well, that is off the table,'" said one union representative in Prudhoe Bay, presumably because a British Petroleum company runs the shipping, too. "The same thing with the pipelines," he added. "BP owns 40 percent." Cuts in any of those budgets would effectively be carved out of BP's profits from other divisions. That left maintenance and inspections as the fungible items in the balance sheet of Prudhoe Bay production. The company was always directed to spend what was "needed," and Browne, in keeping with his philosophical emphasis on environmental protection, continued to emphasize that safety was a priority. But "needed" became subjective, and it was left to the troops to use their own judgment in figuring out how to satisfy their boss and the realities of the field at the same time.

Browne never hesitated to demand the impossible. But he didn't like to get his boots dirty solving operational-level problems himself. In fact, he didn't think that he should. A critical component of Browne's original reorganization of BP's exploration and production group in 1989, and then the rest of the company after he had become CEO, was a simplifying and flattening of the organization with an aim to reduce internal negotiations, cut costs, outsource more, and leave responsibility in the hands of local managers. For a long time BP operated under what Browne called a matrix organizational structure, in which authority was fragmented and responsibilities for decisions lay in a consensus between the various business groups interested in the outcome. Browne thought the architecture was cumbersome and expensive. "We devised a new decentralized organization that abandoned the matrix and gave real authority to managers who ran the business units," Browne wrote. "We pushed decision making and resource control down to the individual managers of these units. This was not simply a re-shuffling of the cards, as many company reorganizations might appear to outsiders. It was a move that would radically change the way people thought about and actually did business." It was the fashionable management philosophy of the day—part of the thinking that Browne had picked up at Stanford, and under the influence of McKinsey and the other consulting houses that he increasingly relied upon.

It also happened to be a quantitative way of viewing a massive corporation, and it seemed a match for Browne's personality. One side effect was that it threatened to divorce top-tier executives from the nitty-gritty details of operating complicated industrial processes. It also forced the operators to make decisions that defied their best judgment. Worse, it would tempt some to commit fraud.

BP Alaska's executives had puzzled over how to hit their aggressively tighter targets for a decade now, and Kovac was beginning to see the effects of their decisions. The workers were fewer and the hours longer. He worked on a maintenance crew, and the backlog of tasks and dates that rolled off the old dot-matrix printer was growing lengthier by the day. Tasks that a pipeline inspector used to complete every three months now happened maybe once a year. The change was almost imperceptible. Just as his hair had begun to gray and his thick workman's hands had wrinkled, he could see the sheen wearing off the equipment and the pipelines on the slope. Then the subtle shift passed some sort of threshold, and he and his fellow workers found themselves in trouble. Equipment they knew was critical to safety was degrading in a way that only their trained eyes and daily contact could detect. Yet when they brought the problems to their supervisors they were ignored, or fixes were scheduled and then never completed. Some of the machinery meant to save lives—fire and gas detectors, shutoff valves to stop a leak—was growing obsolete. Mechanics like Kovac could keep an old chunk of steel running for decades with the right pampering and a little bit of money, but they couldn't machine essential, highly technical replacement components from scratch.

If Kovac's growing unease was about aesthetics, he could accept that the oil field was passing its prime and should be managed into decline. But this wasn't about keeping the production field pretty. This was equipment that carried highly flammable or highly toxic substances under enormous pressure through systems that were becoming so unreliable they might not be able to contain what was inside them. A wrench banged into a fragile pressurized pipe in the wrong way could kill a man. In the previous two years a handful of spills and two deadly accidents had already been blamed on faulty equipment. Guys like Kovac were at the front lines of a complex and expensive global operation, one that British Petroleum spent tens of millions of dollars maintaining each year. They were the canaries. And, in 1999, sensing that John Browne's sustained pressures to keep saving money was dissolving the fabric of reliability and safety that made the slope tick, the canaries began to take flight.

BRITISH PETROLEUM had come to Alaska in 1959 in a pioneering mood, following on an early south Alaskan oil discovery by a company called Richfield Oil (which would later merge to become Atlantic Richfield), and chasing rumors that the Inupiat people in the far north had found oil seeps on the open tundra. It was just months after Alaska had become the forty-ninth state, and the company bought up a bushel of leases along the northern flanks of the Brooks Range, beside the U.S. Navy's 35,000-acre petroleum reserve. Geologists studying the area recognized a series of anticlines—bell-shaped layers of rock deep inside the earth that can trap rising oil beneath them—similar to those that underlie the Zagros Mountains in Iran, which had proven bountiful. They had high hopes, but the competition was stiff. When the government auctioned off more drilling leases above the prime areas, in 1964, British Petroleum lost out. ARCO won the right to drill squarely on top of the geologic dome. British Petroleum bought up everything it could around the perimeter. By early 1968, according to John Browne's memoir, British Petroleum had drilled more than eight dry wells and spent more than $30 million trying. It turned out that the area British Petroleum's geologist had thought was most promising, a fold of deep rock the company called the Coleville prospect, didn't contain oil. The company was calling it quits.

Then, a few months later, ARCO, along with Humble Oil (later bought by Exxon), drilled the Prudhoe Bay State Number 1 well in the heart of an area they called the Prudhoe Bay prospect, striking oil. Another good well was soon drilled nearby. British Petroleum hastily canceled its retreat and, by March 1969, ten years after it had arrived on the North Slope, struck its own Alaskan oil. A frenzy began. Prudhoe Bay was then believed to hold some ten billion barrels of oil, the largest discovery in North America. And by luck, much of it would turn out to lie in the geological perimeter bought up by British Petroleum.

It was at the start of this frenzy that John Browne, as a young petroleum engineer just out of Cambridge, was sent to Anchorage. "The North Slope was vast, beautiful, and very special," he wrote about his first impressions. "More so than I could ever have imagined." The oil companies, Browne observed with fascination, were quick to mark their presence. A dock was built on the shore of Prudhoe Bay, roads were laid, base camps erected, and an airport constructed, all for the import of people and supplies on a grand scale. The matériel, including the giant drilling rigs—like the one Doyon used on Endicott Island—had to be shipped by freighter in the ice-free months of summer through the Bering Strait and around Point Barrow to the Beaufort Sea. "The race was on to develop the discoveries, get the oil to market, and find more oil," Browne recalled. Along the way, the slope was transformed into a new sort of Wild West. "I saw people fishing using the dynamite employed in geophysics. They were just exploding the fish out of the water. I saw others writing obscene words in the permafrost, like some sort of polar graffiti, with a Caterpillar tractor." Limited regulation and no oversight, Browne wrote, "gave us the feeling that we could write the rules . . . arrogance prevailed."

It wasn't until 1977 that North Slope oil began to gush in earnest. The OPEC embargo had pushed Americans to find their own sources of oil, and it eroded environmental fears and political opposition to the construction of the Trans Alaska Pipeline. When Alyeska came on line, and North Slope producers had a cost-effective way to ship crude to the rest of the world, Alaskan oil came of age. Alaskan oil threw a lifeline to British Petroleum. By 1977, just after the company was exiled from its most valuable properties across Africa and the Middle East, it began producing more than one million barrels of oil a day from the North Slope. And it elevated British Petroleum's Alaska operations to arguably the most important slot in the company. As in any new field, the company poured billions into the facilities and networks to harvest the oil, prepare it, and ship it. It had thousands of well pads connected by steel pipes, each carefully constructed to sit on joists above the permafrost that would both protect the environment and keep the equipment from sinking into the earth. It built giant compressor stations the size of General Motors factories, and huge industrial gathering centers where dozens of networks of pipelines met in a single large stream to be cleaned up and shipped south. Each of these facilities were state-of-the-art in their heyday, great examples of advanced technology applied on one of the wildest frontiers of the oil industry.

British Petroleum, though, only owned the oil in half of the Prudhoe Bay field, and shared interests with Exxon, Phillips, and other investors in other portions of the North Slope. On the eastern side of Prudhoe Bay, where ARCO held the drilling rights, ARCO maintained its own, nearly mirror-image, network of development. And that's how it would remain until British Petroleum bought ARCO in 2000.

At the peak of production in Alaska, in 1988, British Petroleum's various drilling fields on the North Slope contributed 55 percent of the company's global oil production and represented more than half of the company's global oil reserves. That year 51 percent of British Petroleum's exploration profits—and 24 percent of the company's global profits over all divisions—stemmed from its oil business in Alaska. The Alaskan operations, for a time, represented British Petroleum's best technological ambitions, its strongest science, its most adaptive infrastructure management, and its most innovative drilling. As the focal point for the company's growth and innovation, it also became the portal through which any rising British Petroleum executive would have to pass—the quintessential training ground. John Browne himself had worked there in the late 1960s, of course, before again managing its operations as head of the exploration and production unit from 1989 to 1995. At any point in time, Alaska's management was made up of rising executives the company sent to its most important drilling region—individuals the company felt had great promise and would one day assume corporate responsibilities far beyond the arctic north.

The outsized importance of Alaska to British Petroleum's global operations meant that what happened there could fairly be viewed as reflecting the company's deepest core management values being tele-graphed from London. What happened in Alaska was closely watched by the company's top executives, and issues unfolding there could be seen as predictors for the sort of decisions and leadership that would soon spread out to other divisions and would affect operations around the world.

NOWHERE WITHIN the organization was the effect of Browne's bud-get mandates more insidious than in its pipeline maintenance pro-gram. The pipelines, arguably the most critical pieces of infrastructure in the business, are in a constant process of corrosion and decay. Snow, rain, and mud wear on the metal day and night. On the inside, the con-stant flow of chemicals, hydrocarbons, and gas relentlessly eat away at the steel walls. There is no way to stop it—the science is in controlling the process enough to make the pipelines last as long as possible, and in predicting when they are approaching failure. British Petroleum employs an entire Corrosion, Inspection and Chemicals (CIC) department and, with contractors specializing in corrosion monitoring, hundreds of people to prevent a pipeline failure.

In the mid-1990s, a man referred to here as Ryan Crannis was one of those contractors. (Crannis wouldn't allow his real name to be used because he feared that being identified would result in his never finding employment in Alaska again.) He worked for a contracting company called CPI Alaska, which handled facility and pipeline engineering inspections on the slope, and he reported to a team leader named Richard Woollam, a sophisticated engineer and a bull of a man known for crude tactics and an intimidating management style. Woollam was the guy British Petroleum relied on to tame the corrosion dragon. He designed a chemical mixture to be injected into the pipelines that would inhibit the decay, and he ran the testing and surveillance program—at a budget of nearly $40 million a year—meant to monitor its progress. Woollam reported to a tough-minded British field manager named John Manzoni, a rising star in Browne's constellation of future leaders at the company who had also followed the Sloan business school track at Stanford and would eventually be entrusted to guide Browne's merger process with Amoco. (For a short time, at the end of his tenure in Alaska, Manzoni worked beneath Tony Hayward, a talented, baby-faced young Brit who had also once worked in Alaska and become the director of the company's global exploration business in August 1997.) Woollam's team, under Manzoni, was charged with preserving the pipelines. Instead, Crannis says, the group was constantly pressured to save costs. And, invisibly to anyone outside of the CIC group, in the latter half of the decade, Woollam's plan, and with it the CIC program, had begun to buckle.

As the oil field got older, not only did the equipment need more maintenance, but the wells produced less oil. After a well had produced for some time, and the natural flow of oil tapered, water and gas would be pumped underground to enhance the recovery of more oil. Eventually, more water came up than crude. The water and gas, though, flow at higher velocities, with more damage to the pipe. The effect was that as the field matured, more damaging material ran through the pipelines, and the rate of corrosion accelerated.

Woollam had promised he could limit the corrosion to no more than 2 millimeters each year, a measured loss that could extend the lifeline of the equipment for years with careful maintenance. The problem was that the budget was dictated from the top of the corporation, and it depended on Woollam hitting his mark. But the less oil produced, the more the pipe corroded, and the harder it became to hit that target figure. Crannis's job was to measure the pipeline wall thickness at random points, especially at joints and seams, where the corrosion was most common, and report back on the effectiveness of the program. He quickly found out that the program as designed wouldn't work. "The data on my area of responsibility was demonstrating that two millimeters a year was neither practical nor realistic," Crannis says. "The corrosion rates were far in excess of that. It turned out to be a miserable failure. And in the area I was responsible for, we started raising the flag and saying this isn't working—corrosion rates are very high."

The inspection budget with which the work was done dropped from about $3 million a year in 1985 to under $950,000 in 1997. "It was draconian cuts," Crannis says. When he got to the point at which he didn't think he could sustain his program, Crannis wrote to Woollam, asking which part of the program he should eliminate. "I never got a written response, but I was given a verbal response that basically said, 'Well, you are the expert, that's why we hired you. So you decide what to cut.'"

Crannis was now in an impossible situation, unable to use anything close to what he considered to be sound judgment. And then, one day, he was asked to make a presentation to Manzoni, senior management, and about fifty members of the maintenance teams. The meeting was held at the Prudhoe Bay base center. Crannis showed a couple of slides that detailed corrosion rates and pipeline thickness. They told the story on their own. "I said it's your prerogative but you need to recognize that you are substantially increasing the risk level. So rather than cutting our budgets you need to fund a greater level of inspection. Otherwise this problem is going to get away from us," he warned.

When he finished, to the surprise of many people in the room, Manzoni was unsympathetic. "Stop your whingeing," he told him, in front of the group. "It's not productive."

Woollam, however, bore the responsibility for making the program function, and to Crannis, he seemed to grow anxious. British Petroleum emails from the time show pipelines were in bad repair and getting worse. One risk was that sediment collecting inside the pipelines could speed decay, but the company hadn't tested its main lines for sediment in years. "The main concern is . . . the quantities of solids which are laying [*sic*] in the bottom is [*sic*] entirely unknown," Woollam acknowledged in a 1997 email. In a preceding email, Kip Sprague, a corrosion manager for British Petroleum, detailed some seventy locations with substantial corrosion, some with less than 50 percent of their walls remaining, or "corroded almost the entire length."

According to Crannis's account, he began to get pressure to manipulate the data by intentionally diluting it with good inspection results. If an inspector has a flow line, with, say, fifty data points indicating serious corrosion, and he measures those points using ultrasonic technology every three months, after several visits he arrives at an average number representing the rate of corrosion. Crannis was asked to measure corrosion rates for points along the line that were not expected to corrode—say, a safe section of elevated line in a dry location. "When you are running a program you try to hit the high-risk areas first," Crannis says. "So they were playing those games and we had some very contentious meetings where some of us argued that this was not a responsible way to go about it." When those minimal corrosion rates were later averaged into the larger data set, they lowered the overall corrosion rate for the field, allowing the corrosion group, and British Petroleum, to justify their program.

Meanwhile, Manzoni had taken a keen interest in Crannis's findings. He would stop by Crannis's office to chat privately, and by Crannis's recollection, Manzoni told him that despite the dismissive comments in the meeting, he valued Crannis's blunt assessment. Crannis found the visits awkward but eventually came to think they were good. As he saw it, one of two things would result: Manzoni would either wake up executive management to the seriousness of the problems and then throw some money at it "or say we don't give a damn and we are just going to continue on this path."

"What I didn't plan on was that there was a third option: to just get himself transferred out of there [so] it wasn't his problem anymore," Crannis says. In 1998 Manzoni was transferred out of Alaska to Houston, a promotion that brought him closer into John Browne's fold.

"Nobody wants a major incident under their watch. So he basically dodged the bullet," Crannis says.

Woollam had been promoted to manage the entire CIC program in the late 1990s, and by 1999 he was calling his own tough shots. The budget pressure that year only got worse. "We will not be getting any relief on the budget," Woollam wrote in an email to his corrosion managers on June 2, 1999, about the need to control corrosion in lines that carry produced water (PW), a form of well waste. "They all think that PW inhibition is the right thing to do, but, no one is prepared to let loose the purse string . . . ugly, I'm afraid."

Since the corrosion program is about controlling the rate of decline, a reasonable or responsible program can be extended over time, or deferred, with an only incremental increase in risk. Woollam no doubt knew this. But delaying doesn't make those maintenance expenses go away, it just piles them atop other scheduled maintenance projects in the future, thus ruining a safe, five-year plan merely to save money in the moment. It becomes an imperative, then, to double down two years later to catch up. It's not altogether different from a homeowner taking out a risky second loan on property that increased in value; British Petroleum borrowed against its future in the form of savings from deferred maintenance. But it was acquiring a risky sort of invisible debt, and it would need to make sure it could afford to pay it all back when the bills came due.

Two days later, on June 4, Woollam ordered his team to discontinue the use of the most effective chemical treatment altogether. Another manager warned, in an email, that it meant "the PW system may be subject to increased corrosion activity and fouling." A plan was set to let the remaining supply of corrosion inhibitors run through the pipe until they were gone. They would last two more days. They would not be replaced.

The email announcing that decision so shocked one disgruntled manager that he forwarded it to colleagues inside British Petroleum with this snide editorial: "Here's one for our HSE files," he wrote, referring to British Petroleum's Health, Safety and Environment program. "We'll see if this is a 'safe' way to do business."

In fact, many of BP's managers were not naïve about the effects of their decisions, and they debated the ramifications of curtailing the corrosion program. Four days later, on June 8, a member of the corrosion management team wrote to Woollam and others that "much of the system is in poor condition" and that, without the chemicals, British Petroleum should expect to start replacing the pipelines by 2001. "It will shorten the life of the system, resulting in either abandonment or expensive repair/replacement . . . the longer the corrosion continues at the uncontrolled rate, the harder it will be to arrest it and achieve satisfactory life of the equipment." On June 9, the Prudhoe Bay operations manager wrote back, copying the entire team. "Thanks for the warning. Is this the right thing to do? Does this place the line integrity in jeopardy in the short term and give us a risk of a spill near term?"

Woollam would have known as much as anyone that the company would have to come back to these pipelines with more vigor in the future or pay the price. But in that year, 1999, the budget target could be hit. It didn't hurt that Prudhoe Bay managers received a generous pay bonus for hitting their budget goals. They'd deal with the consequences later.

There is no sign that Browne ever knew about the decision to mortgage the future of the pipelines in Prudhoe Bay, and it's unclear how high up the chain of command that critical compromise was relayed. British Petroleum's chief executive for western North American operations at the time, Bob Malone, hadn't been told, either. Yet the workers had tried repeatedly to ring alarms about what was taking place to the president of British Petroleum Alaska, and to their managers. "That's the way that upper management maintains plausible deniability," Crannis said. "The truth is, at least at Manzoni's level, they were very much aware of the condition of the pipe. The corporate culture that British Petroleum has operated in, I can tell you that naysayers aren't welcome. They don't want to have bad news."

In the view of Marc Kovac and the other maintenance and pipeline workers on the slope, Woollam's corrosion compromise was just one example of the unfolding disintegration of precaution and prudence. Elsewhere key safety infrastructure was falling apart. Crews complained that louvers designed to close and trap leaking gas to prevent an explosion failed a majority of the time, seals on oil pumps were leaking, old welds on holding tanks were rusting through. All the while, the crews that were supposed to be out fixing them were getting smaller and smaller. Those who remained worked harder and for longer hours, often approaching dangerous tasks in a state of exhaustion.

IF BRITISH PETROLEUM'S midlevel executives wouldn't listen to the concerns on the slope, the workers would have to go over their heads. In early 1999, having grown frustrated by the degradation they were witnessing, Marc Kovac rallied seventy-seven workers to stand up to the company, and the group sent a letter directly to John Browne.

"Dear Sir," it began, "We are writing this correspondence because we consider impending staffing cuts to represent a safety imperative." In the boldest of terms, the letter laid out critical management concerns that should have gotten Browne's attention, including the allegation that his executives had been withholding bad news from London in order to make him happy. "Anything we say either stays at this level or gets filtered on the way up to a version of 'can-do sir'. . . . We want to remove deniability. You and others in management cannot say, 'we didn't know things were that bad. No one told us.'

". . . Our feedback is ignored because it doesn't support the pre-ordained agenda. When will the body count, capital destruction and loss of production be enough to halt this dead-end course? Your front-line management and supervision will continue to cut as long as you direct and sanction it, right up to the precipice of disaster and over. There will be a short near-term savings realized at the cost of a huge near-future loss," the workers warned.

"We are doing all we can. We are talking. Are you listening?"

John Browne never replied. A few months later, he announced through a meeting with financial analysts in London that he would lop an additional $4 billion off British Petroleum's spending worldwide. More than half of it would come from the business segments that search for and produce oil, called "upstream," including Alaska. Most of the rest would be taken from the refining and marketing segments, or "downstream." The news was devastating to the workers on the slope.

In 1999, the greater Prudhoe Bay area oil fields produced 451 million barrels of oil. It was far from the field's peak, in 1988, of 743 million barrels, but still removed from what geologists expected to be a steady, ten-year dwindling until the fields there ran out of oil altogether. Already, the oil had lasted thirty years—far longer than John Browne or anyone at British Petroleum had expected. When Kovac started the job, Alaskans were told the oil would last until the late 1980s. In 1989, Browne himself had given the field little more than a decade. Now British Petroleum's management thought the slope would sustain a profitable level of oil production until sometime around 2008.

British Petroleum faced a unique and difficult challenge in Alaska. "We're using equipment that was designed to be thrown away in 1987," Kovac says. The equipment was designed to last through its useful life but not necessarily further, and the budget was allocated to match that plan. After two decades in the exquisitely harsh weather of the deep North, the thousands of miles of pipelines and the hundreds of facilities there were beginning to show their wear. "These pipelines are shot. Some of them have hundreds of patches on them. Some were meant to be temporary," Kovac adds. But their function was as indispensible as ever: British Petroleum still earned more than a quarter of its annual profits from ongoing production from Alaska and expected it to remain important even as it ramped up exploration in Asia and the Gulf of Mexico.

But no one expected it to last forever.

Since production had peaked, Prudhoe Bay was on the equivalent of Hospice care. No one knew how long the fields would take to die, but while they were on their way, there was little motivation to invest in their long-term operation. Browne didn't want to spend a dollar more than was needed to produce Alaskan oil up to the day it petered out. "It's a philosophy of all the oil companies, once you are in the field and operating, you operate it to the point where it is no longer profitable to you," Kovac says, "and then you leave—you sell it. But when you leave you won't leave one dollar on the table, you take all the pipe, you don't leave one piece of good equipment, it's all worn out." Yet in this case British Petroleum had the delicate task of constantly recalculating its plans to accommodate the slope's unexpectedly enduring vitality.

5

SAVING THE WORLD

AFTER THE ARCO MERGER was approved in March 2000, it became clear that Browne would need to bring order to an otherwise chaotic chain of developments. On July 24, standing at a podium in front of BP Amoco's office building near downtown Los Angeles with Bob Malone, BP's new head of West Coast operations, Browne announced he was dropping the Amoco name and changing the BP brand entirely. In an effort to "greatly strengthen the sense of identity and common purpose," British Petroleum, he said, would now go simply by the initials "BP." The company was changing its slogan to "Beyond Petroleum," a phrase that emerged from a $200 million focus-group-tested rebranding effort. The change emphasized Browne's vision of a forward-looking company with a footing in all sorts of climate-friendly energy sources, not just oil. With that, Malone ordered ropes holding a large curtain across the top of the office building to be released, and the veil fell away to reveal a bright new Helios logo. BP would no longer be known by the old green shield emblazoned with the letters *B* and *P*. The Helios, with its lively green shoots radiating from a blazing dot of yellow, like a sunflower, was an optimistic proclamation of allegiance to solar power and renewable energy. "They have nailed their colors very firmly to the environmental mast," said Patrick Barrow, managing director of the Public Relations Consultants Association at the time.

The new brand announced that day was accompanied by an ad blitz across the United States that seemed intended to draw attention away from the company's core oil and gas operations. "We believe in alternative energy, like solar power and cappuccino," one ad read.

All the while, BP continued to invest more in its fossil fuel business than ever before. "BP really had a sense of selling itself that was unusual in the oil industry. They're really good at talking about the future," says Joseph Pratt, a professor of history at the University of Houston and the author of *Prelude to a Merger: A History of the Amoco Corporation from 1973 to 1998*. People in the world wanted to hear, at that point, that oil companies could be environmentally cleaner and better, and that they could help instead of harm the environment. Browne played to that expertly. "Without a doubt in forty years inside the oil industry, BP was the smoothest-talking oil company I've ever seen."

Rebranding and proactive climate talk alone, of course, couldn't address the fundamental challenges of integrating such huge and unwieldy companies, and in fact, it risked becoming a distraction. Even while the concerns about worker safety and the oil field in Prudhoe Bay rose to the surface in Alaska, Browne struggled to bring order to his new, big company. In addition to the Amoco and ARCO mergers, Browne had bought five other smaller companies. Almost overnight, BP had become the sole operator for the vast majority of North Slope oil (and part owner, after the forced Phillips sale dictated by the merger approval), again becoming the largest oil producer in the United States and the third largest oil non-government-owned company in the world. BP also took over Amoco's refineries, including the Texas City plant, one of the largest in the world, and the most productive in the United States. In five years the market value of BP had quadrupled. It was exactly the stature Browne had set his targets on eleven years earlier. BP, from 1998 through the two mergers, was "a company that was really moving around the world," says Pratt. "They were really taking competition by the throat, and really standing out."

The growth, however, brought with it burdens and culture clashes. BP suddenly had some 110,000 global employees, many performing similar jobs in redundant offices. The various groups desperately needed to be slimmed down and combined, their employees integrated so that they felt a part of the same team. Their disparate ways of doing things—including maintenance in the Arctic—had to be coordinated and synchronized to build a stronger whole.

It was an oversized challenge. From the start Browne approached the mergers as congenial, and seemed to believe that he could just stack the other companies' attributes on top of British Petroleum's, and that the cumulative effect would be a stronger corporation. But there was no strong overarching British Petroleum culture to define how the new company would operate. Browne seemed to want to absorb the good while ignoring the baggage and the new responsibilities his acquisitions introduced. Amoco, for example, had an aging U.S. refinery infrastructure that desperately needed updating. Browne showed little interest in that operational task and focused instead on trying to absorb Amoco's financial assets and revenues. He tried to take the best from both British Petroleum and Amoco, for example, and integrate them, expecting to preserve those cultural strengths, in large part by leaving Amoco the way it was.

Except he didn't leave it the way it was. He cut costs. And in doing so, he changed what Amoco was and eroded the very asset he had hoped to absorb. "So they created something that hadn't existed yet, but they didn't make it BP other than by name or financial accounting," says John Hofmeister, then CEO of Shell. "There was a sense among us [the major oil companies] that they didn't really know what they were doing. It felt like a crowd milling about, with the mergers all coming so thick and fast, there was a sense of constant motion."

As it turned out, the cultures of Amoco, ARCO, and BP didn't necessarily mix. BP was seen as aloof and foreign, while the Americans prided themselves on engineering bonafides and rigorous discipline. Years after the merger, workers in a company mess hall were still likely to identify themselves as being from Amoco, ARCO, or BP. Browne seemed not to recognize that these divisions led to poor communication in the company's lower ranks and eroded safety and maintenance in places like Alaska. "Between breadth and depth there's only so much management time in a day, so much management attention," said Freeman, the Salomon partner. "Growth creates challenges to management. There is no question." BP's sudden breadth, plus the ancillary issues of climate, environment, and the rebranding of BP, began to push that limit.

IN JANUARY 2001, Chuck Hamel received a letter from a group of BP workers on Alaska's North Slope. It had been years since the Alyeska lawsuits had wrapped up and since Hamel had waded into the midst of the whistle-blower issues. But the workers, having tried to raise their concerns to management, and sensing that conditions were beginning to spiral out of control, didn't know who else to turn to. In the hopes that Hamel would make their grievances public, they detailed the dangers on the slope.

"Our workplace environment has significantly deteriorated to the point that many of us are now afraid for our very lives," they wrote. "We no longer have the ability to respond to emergencies in a timely enough manner to prevent escalation of events. We can no longer close the valves that must be closed to isolate blowouts or major leaks, quickly enough. Our emergency response plan now is just to 'run for our lives.'

". . . All of these concerns have been expressed time and time again to BP management. . . . We have been ignored, disregarded and harassed as a result," the letter continued. "We feel that a major catastrophe is imminent."

More documents and complaints gushed forth, and they got more and more specific, painting a disturbing picture of the effect John Browne's earliest "efficiency" initiatives were having on the company's operations. The alarm systems meant to warn workers of a possible explosion or fire were breaking down, were often bypassed, and were difficult to repair. BP had procrastinated, deferring the fix, for years. The workers alleged BP was lying to federal authorities and wasn't fulfilling the obligations of its conviction agreement after the Endicott Island dumping case. One worker said that he had watched BP managers go out into the field themselves one night and grease up the safety valves so that they would work correctly during an inspection from federal probation authorities the next day. Once, an oil well that was out of compliance was permanently shut down just before the inspection because managers knew it would fail flagrantly. The list went on.

Then, in late February, the Alaska State Department of Environmental Conservation—the state agency that regulates the oil and gas industry—conducted a field test of the safety valves on the pipeline at G Pad, a drilling site at which dozens of oil wells are connected through a web of pipes into a central flow line that runs off to the big facilities. The pipes at G Pad carry oil and gas and a brew of toxic waste products, and in the event of a rupture, the surface safety valves are supposed to close them down. In an oil spill, the valves are designed to prevent widespread carpeting of the wild tundra with poisonous hydrocarbons. In a gas leak, they can prevent a monumental explosion that would likely kill anyone nearby. But during the trial runs, nine out of thirty valves failed to close. At two other pads, at least 10 percent of the valves tested failed. Despite the fact that workers had been warning about the valves for more than a year, BP's head of Prudhoe Bay area operations at the time, Neil McCleary, called the tests "anomalous."

The workers' concerns, and even the dramatic test failures, percolated quietly. In Seattle, Jeanne Pascal knew little of the worker's complaints even though she had just signed the debarment compliance agreement with BP over Endicott Island. If she had known, she might have immediately concluded that BP was not honoring its promise to take extraordinary measures to guarantee environmental compliance in Alaska or, perhaps, anywhere else. "I was more interested in the implementation of the environmental management system," Pascal says, "which was where I thought the rubber was going to meet the road. I hadn't heard anything at all about corrosion, or retaliation, or safety valves."

She would also have been dismayed to learn that employees were not able to get management's attention with their health, safety, and environmental concerns—a key stipulation of the company's agreement with the government. But in the first annual report she received from British Petroleum's Chris Phillips, he assured her that everything was proceeding smoothly. "Everything was glowing. 'We are doing all these superb things. We are changing the culture,' he told us," Pascal recalls. And so she remained unaware of the depth of the problems.

Chuck Hamel, it seemed, was the only one willing to do something. And he found an executive within BP who he believed might help. In 1996 BP had put Bob Malone in Anchorage to manage the Alyeska Pipeline Company. Malone and Hamel had worked together in those years over ongoing issues on the pipeline and the Valdez port, ultimately addressing many of the issues that previous Alyeska presidents had resisted. And though the relationship was always contentious, Malone and Hamel had developed a mutual respect, seeing each other as honest and well-intentioned while acknowledging their differences. "Theirs is an odd relationship," a writer for the *Anchorage Daily News* once observed. "Malone and Hamel greeted [each other] with a brotherly hug like opposing football captains wishing each other well before the big game." Malone had shown a genuine interest in working with Hamel in those years. Since then, Malone had risen to corporate vice president and regional head of the company's North American operations, based in Los Angeles.

Bob Malone was a frank and gregarious Texan who brought a waft of cultural fresh air to BP. He had started out as a metallurgical engineer, and then had worked as a mining executive for Kennecott Copper, which was bought by the old Standard Oil of Ohio and folded into British Petroleum when it acquired Sohio. In 1989, as BP shed its extraneous companies, including Kennecott, it held on to Malone, sending him to the MIT Sloan School of Management, then to Alyeska, and then back to BP in Los Angeles. Malone had a knack for putting people at ease. He could assume a slick public face and was an expert negotiator. He was the kind of guy who lived by the rule of keeping your friends close and your enemies closer, always believing that engagement and dialogue would lead to more predictability, and ultimately more results, than defensiveness and posturing. Malone was recognized as a capable manager with sharp insight and a vision of the endgame.

In 2001, before the grumbling in Alaska could fester any further, Malone agreed that it should be stopped. Hamel had managed to get a story about the broken safety valves into the *Wall Street Journal*. And the George W. Bush administration was preparing another try at opening the ANWR. In March 2001 his Interior secretary, Gale Norton, had visited Prudhoe Bay herself. Whether John Browne took the time to see it or not, Malone knew that a fresh public fight over safety and the environment in Alaska—while BP was still on probation for the Endicott Island conviction, and with the ANWR again on the table—would serve no one. That summer he quietly ordered BP Alaska's president at the time, Richard Campbell, to conduct an internal review of the workers' allegations—to find out whether they were true, and if so, to fix the problems.

To manage the review process, BP Alaska assembled a robust, independent team that included industry experts from the lower forty-eight and BP executives from Houston. Kovac, as a representative of United Steelworkers, was included. So was Chris Phillips, vice president for operations in Alaska and Jeanne Pascal's liaison. Curiously, BP hired Billie Pirner Garde—the woman who represented Chuck Hamel during the Wackenhut case, who was later retained by Malone—and added an independent consultant from New Hampshire, Paul Flaherty, as an arbitrator between workers and executives.

For seven weeks during July and August, the panel interviewed 250 BP field workers and 50 additional contractor employees working throughout Prudhoe Bay. The resulting review of the company's "operational integrity" presented a diplomatically worded but damning indictment of BP's operations in Alaska, portraying many aspects of Prudhoe Bay's safety and maintenance programs as in disarray, riddled with "unacceptable" lapses. It found that there was no comprehensive system for tracking ongoing maintenance concerns across all operations and said that the backlog of issues awaiting attention was growing. It said that the company was having difficulty meeting its own safety requirements, as well as government regulations, because its inspection and maintenance had fallen behind. Valves meant to shut down gas and oil leaks hadn't been tested. Corrosion monitoring had fallen behind schedule. A critical water system needed to extinguish a fire had been shut down—and not fixed—for six months.

Even when the company had been warned about specific lapses, it had failed to act. In October 1999 a contract service company provided BP Alaska management with a notebook of deficiency reports related to the twenty-five-year-old fire and gas detection system. "These reported deficiencies have not been systematically verified, evaluated, nor, if appropriate, corrected," the review found. "The technicians responsible for maintaining the systems are very concerned about continuing degradation of reliability," it continued, finding that the venting systems meant to clear out poisonous and flammable gases didn't always work and that the Halon system relied on to suppress a fire before it led to a catastrophic explosion—where a cloud of chemical gas is spread to interfere with combustion at the molecular level—also might not be effective. In one of the slope's largest facilities, that system was leaking an estimated fifty pounds of Halon compounds, which are highly toxic, each day. "The team strongly recommends upgrading the fire and gas systems."

The valves essential to controlling a spill and an explosion were in no better shape. Even where they were deemed capable of sealing off a leak, the review team found that the valves would not operate automatically and would need to be shut by hand; already short-staffed teams would be expected to race around some of the most dangerous facilities in the moments before an impending disaster hand-cranking knobs to close the valves that could eventually save the entire plant. Even then, the engineers weren't confident the valves would withstand the pressure exerted on them. "It is a significant problem and under certain circumstances may pose a potential hazard," the report said.

Unambiguously, the report concluded that overzealous cost cutting had led to the deterioration of the facilities. A concentration on lifting costs, it said, "has resulted in significant pressure on operating and maintenance budgets over the past decade." It continued: "Budgets have been cut too deeply and . . . management's top priority is controlling costs in order to achieve short-term budget targets and not safety, regulatory compliance or delivering long term operational integrity."

The most critical aspect of the operational integrity review didn't concern the condition of specific equipment. Rather, the report identified a cancer in BP's corporate management. "There is a fundamental lack of trust of all levels of management," the review team concluded. They found that the mistrust and poor communication "stems from a long progression of decisions, actions and inactions over the last five to ten years." In that time BP Alaska's management had taken "corrective" measures that were "not deemed sufficient." They had made promises and failed to keep them, and they had made decisions that flew in the face of the long-term sustainability of safe operations. All the while they had continued to focus disproportionately on cutting costs.

Moreover, the report said that many of the problems could be linked to a high turnover rate among management at BP Alaska—a direct result of BP's long-standing policy of using Alaska as a training ground for its rising stars. "The tenure of key managers has been too short to develop, implement and assess the impact of management initiatives," the review stated. "Assigned actions are not always time-specific and follow through is lacking . . . programs initiated in previous years are often abandoned when the manager is transferred."

In the end, the authors of the report found BP Alaska to be "an organization that does not clearly assign accountability for delivery of operational excellence or operational integrity." They concluded, "There is a disconnect between Greater Prudhoe Bay management's stated commitment to safety and the perception of that commitment at the operator level. Many workers believe, based on actions taken, that achieving short-term budget targets is GPB management's first priority." It was the first stark acknowledgment from inside the company that BP faced a corrosive cultural challenge that could stand in the way of wrangling its vast workforce and keeping its operations under control. In commissioning the report, Bob Malone had demonstrated what seemed to be a genuine commitment, from the corporation's executive management, to address it proactively and properly.

Pascal was told about the review and its findings by Phillips; and she was told that the gripes that prompted it had more to do with a couple of union reps angling for leverage in their contracts than it did with genuine safety concerns. Phillips convinced her that the review process was an example of the company's proactiveness—evidence of management's virtue rather than its failures—and she believed him.

It remained to be seen whether the report would lead to real change. Distrust was so pervasive that workers found it difficult to take the company's assurances at face value. Instead, they saw another set of promises and an obfuscation of the core problem. "They consider it a smokescreen to facilitate concealment of the most egregious of the unsafe components of the facilities," Hamel wrote to the United States probation officer in Anchorage in December 2001.

Kovac and the other field workers felt that the clock just kept ticking. They kept reporting for work, every day, as human fire detectors, as mechanics, handling equipment they knew could blow at any moment. And they continued to do it knowing that the foundation they stood on for safety had been slowly eroding, year after year after year. They had little choice. There are few jobs in Alaska outside the oil business. And in the oil business, there are few jobs outside BP. The company runs the show, hires the contractors, operates the fields, and even manages the pipeline. Cross BP, and you've crossed an entire industry.

ON AUGUST 15, 2002, Don Shugak reported to work for a night shift in Prudhoe Bay. Shugak, a native Alaskan known for generously volunteering on health and welfare issues in his spare time, was fifty-one years old. He was a devoutly religious man who donated his time to charity for Alaska's native people and who could often be found in town performing Christian folk songs on his acoustic guitar. He worked the same two-week schedule as Kovac—for $80,000 a year—but as a well pad operator. That short late-summer night was his first on the slope, and it was going to be a doozy. Shugak was responsible for three separate sixty-acre drilling pads, with at least a hundred oil wells to check for leaks, pressure problems, and any other sign of trouble. It was going to be a rushed job. With the time he was given, Shugak could spend less than five minutes at each site, scarcely enough to give a well a good look over. Some wells would need adjustment, and some sites would need to be checked twice. The union boys called it "mopping up."

That night, mopping up meant bringing a handful of wells that had been temporarily closed down back online. Checking his list, Shugak stopped his white Ford double-cab pickup at the Number 22 well on A Pad, about nine miles west of Deadhorse. A-22 had been drilled in 1982 and had been producing almost continuously since 1984. As with a lot of the oil wells in Prudhoe Bay, though, there wasn't enough natural pressure to force the oil out, so BP injected gas at high pressure back into the well to help force the oil out. Still, A-22 experienced a string of problems containing the gas.

Two weeks earlier, on August 1, the outer structure of the well had been found to contain gas at over 1,000 pounds of pressure, nearly twice what state records had shown for the last reading of that well, and a sign that somehow the gas inside the well core—the innermost of the concentric circles of steel that make up a well—had leaked into the outer space, or annulus, risking a blowout. The data could have been interpreted as a warning of a fault in the structure of the oil well itself, but on August 5 the well was restarted anyway, in part because BP engineers misinterpreted the high pressure as a sign that the structure was airtight rather than taking it as a sign that something deep inside it was actually leaking gas. Records show there was never any analysis done to determine the source of the gas under pressure.

On August 9, the well was again shut down, and soon after, a leaking flow line was discovered. On August 14 the company again found high pressure in the well; it was bled off by a technician. BP's safety and engineering policies don't allow high pressure in a well annulus, but earlier on the morning of the fifteenth, BP's well integrity engineer granted a verbal waiver, allowing the well—which produced eleven thousand gallons of oil a day—to be restarted. Once it was restarted, the plan was to check it regularly and shut it down seventy-two hours later if signs still pointed to a need for further work.

BP wanted every drop of oil it could get. Every hour the well wasn't pumping equated to thousands of dollars in lost revenue. Each well's production figured into Alaska's net revenue per barrel—John Browne's cherished metric—and then on to the company's global calculation of the same. If A-22 were kept offline, it would stunt some production statistic somewhere and undermine the case for keeping Prudhoe Bay itself an operating oil field. There was simply no wiggle room. On August 15, Shugak fixed a couple of details on the production equipment, and at 9:37 p.m. he restarted the well.

He might have stayed to check on its progress, but the demanding schedule for his evening routine forced him to race on to the next site. Besides, there were no meters at A-22 to measure the annulus pressure, and Shugak hadn't been issued the tools to read it even if he had wanted. It wasn't until 2:00 a.m., two hours after the sun had finally dipped below the arctic horizon, that Shugak went back to the well to check its progress. He pulled the truck up to a few feet short of the well house enclosure and hopped out to take a look.

Inside A-22, the pressure had built rapidly. The force on the outer annulus had reached more than 1,900 pounds of pressure per square inch, far greater than the well could sustain. Seventeen feet underground, the pressure burst through the steel and cement enclosure, releasing a rocket of pent-up gas into the earth at about the same time that Shugak approached the building. It shot up the outside of the well and out into the night, popping the wooden planks on the floor of the well house loose and sending gravel scattering. Within seconds, the two-story corrugated steel box of a well house had filled with concentrated methane gas. Still, Shugak saw no outward signs of trouble.

He reached for the door handle with his right hand and pulled. It's difficult to know exactly what happened next. One theory is that the gas reached the filament in the single light bulb that dangled from a wire on the ceiling. Or, one of the skittering stones—maybe the metal door itself—struck a steel pipe and, like flint, released a spark. The next thing Shugak knew he was lying against his truck. Flames darted into the sky some forty feet above the well house. His ears rang with a high-pitched scream, and his legs didn't work.

He didn't realize that the truck's tires had been blown off, that flames had enveloped the cab and shot out of the rear window and were approaching the gas tank, or that the man-sized crater in the side panel was from the force of his own body, airborne, hitting steel. He thought he had work to do, and he tried to move. "I started crawling two and three inches at a time with my elbows," Shugak says. He tried rolling, but his legs, like those of rag dolls, got tangled up. The heat was searing. He made it fifty feet. "God, you've got to help me!" Shugak shouted into the night.

Then he felt the fabric of his jumpsuit tighten around his neck and chest as an unseen hand grabbed at his clothing from the back, and suddenly he was sliding backward over the ground, away from the flames. Within minutes, more help arrived as the flames at A-22 shone like a signal flare in the bleak night of the tundra. The workers who pulled him from the scene lifted him into the bed of another pickup and sped away. "I didn't even feel like I was hurt. I didn't feel anything," Shugak later told a reporter from the *Anchorage Daily News*. "I just knew that nothing was working the way it was supposed to." He heard talking, in hurried, hushed tones, and then he slipped into unconsciousness.

Shugak awoke two weeks later in the burn unit at Harborview Medical Center in Seattle. He had been flown by air ambulance to Anchorage and, within a day, by jet to Washington. More than 15 percent of his body, including the roof of his mouth, had been badly burned. His face was blackened and melted, his right ear burnt down like barbecued meat. The same with his back, and his right hand—his strumming hand. His knees were badly injured, and two vertebrae were compressed from the force of the impact against his truck. Both of his thighs had been snapped—a pin held his right femur together and three screws bound his left. It was a difficult year for BP Alaska: not the first accident, and it wouldn't be the last. But Shugak was one man. A-22 was just one well. It could have been worse.

IN LONDON that fall John Browne had other problems to deal with. The mergers had left him with a new set of financial and production challenges that required his undivided attention. They had also left BP saddled with debt. For years, BP had overextended itself compared to the other oil companies. It was one reason the company's stock price was often more volatile than the stock of stalwarts like Exxon; more risk attracted Wall Street for its potential reward, but it could also make investors skittish. Rather than reduce its debt, however—the company normally kept a debt-to-capital ratio of about 37 percent, while 25 percent was an industry norm—it borrowed more to fuel the growth of the late 1990s. "We are quite prepared to let the debt ratio go up for a period of time to take advantage of acquisitions," Browne told a reporter for the oil industry news group Platts in 1988.

Fadel Gheit, a prominent oil industry financial analyst with Oppenheimer, in Toronto, says BP kept a debt ratio "at least 10 percentage points higher than normal" during the time of the mergers. "BP has historically maintained higher debt levels and debt ratios than its peers. It believed that debt is the cheapest source of capital," he added. "U.S. majors, Exxon and Chevron, believe in low debt, or even no debt, and investors seem to like that."

Browne countered by promising Wall Street that he could continue to deliver growth in BP's core business—oil—in ways that other companies could not. "BP was promising its shareholders 3 percent growth at the same time it promised to go beyond petroleum," says Derek Brower. "Exxon never got into that. They say, 'We are an oil company, we are big, this is what we do.'" The markets were excited by Browne's razzle-dazzle forecasts, and he leveraged his reputation and his record to reassure them. Investors loved what they heard.

By late 2001, however, in the midst of the mergers, the branding, the speeches about climate change, Browne strained to keep his promises. Even as workers in places like Alaska were beginning to see signs of breakdowns in their own facilities in the oil field, analysts watching Browne's every move at the global level grew concerned about his control over the company. "He made promises he couldn't keep," said Shell's John Hofmeister. "He set expectations that couldn't be delivered because he didn't build the systems and the process that would enable him to deliver them." It began in September 2002, when Browne, after spending eight months reiterating confidence in his ambitious production goals, had to restate BP's production targets, the equivalent of sounding a Defcon warning siren on the trading floors. Then, just a month later, he repeated the misstep, again undershooting his targets. This was disappointing on two levels. Not only was Browne not producing enough oil, but the inaccurate forecasts raised questions about whether he knew what he was doing. "BP had to restate its production targets three times in a row," says Hoyos, "which gave the impression that John Browne wasn't really on top of things."

Inside the corporation, the mergers were still wreaking logistical havoc. The ARCO deal in Alaska had begun before Amoco had even finished. In the midst of the transition BP Alaska was led by three different executives: John Manzoni, who was pulled out in 1998 to lead BP's transition with Amoco; Richard Campbell, who retired in 2001; and Steve Marshall. Thus Alaska lost much of any institutional knowledge that Manzoni had gathered about the corrosion program and the cost pressures there, and it had suffered from inconsistent leadership ever since. BP thrice severed the chain of command that would communicate production capabilities—and risks—from Alaska back to London. The effect of the turnover may have been made worse by the fact that Browne wasn't known to take criticism in stride. "At the same time," Hoyos says, "we were hearing that [Browne] wasn't an easy person to approach. He'd had all this glory. And you would think that his head of exploration or production, and others, would approach him and say, 'Look, these targets are unrealistic. We are not going to be able to make these targets.'"

An erosion of confidence in BP began to spread throughout the financial markets, right up to some of Browne's closest financial partners. "All of a sudden the emperor had no clothes—or at least had no socks," says Ron Freeman. "And he was starting to miss his numbers. At this point do you, as a banker, call him up and say, 'What's going on?'"

6

A WAKE-UP CALL

JEANNE PASCAL returned to work after the Christmas holiday, in January 2004, to a rude awakening. The BP case, by her estimation, had been going well. That is to say, the company seemed to be complying with its agreement, and she hadn't been too concerned, or too engaged, for several years. She brought to bear several understandings that tended to favor BP: She expected that it would take a long time before an ethos of environmental responsibility was prevalent in every aspect of BP's operations, and she wasn't surprised to run into a couple of bumps along the way. Secondly, she had seen labor unions exaggerate and overact, instilling in her a skepticism about union complaints. So when BP's Chris Phillips told her that a couple of the company's problems amounted to personnel gripes and backhanded labor contract negotiations, she sympathized, and understood.

Pascal had worked with hundreds of corporations. She was familiar with the risks inherent in dealing with big industry and had few illusions about corporations' ability to perform to an environmental standard of perfection. Her concerns were always more about a company's intentions and progress than with achieving a totally incident-clean record. And in her experience, companies' intentions were less often nefarious and usually focused on getting on with business in the most expeditious, and legal, way possible. That meant complying with environmental laws, and in cases where that obligation had already been broken, it meant doing their penance and putting the issue in the past as briskly as possible. Just as companies were eager to settle in the first place, they were usually eager to prove their compliance with their settlement agreement. Then and only then would they earn a clean slate from the federal government. That's the way debarment law worked. Why should BP be any different?

It didn't hurt that for three years, while Pascal juggled such a large EPA caseload that she could barely keep up with what BP may or may not have been doing to correct its errors, Phillips and BP Alaska president Steve Marshall had gone out of their way to sell her on the company's progress. Twice Marshall came to Seattle, meeting with Pascal personally in the Fairmont conference room to explain how BP had improved its employee relations and was rigorously monitoring safety issues. Pascal, having spent most of her career on cases outside of the oil industry, had a steep learning curve. Only once she more fully grasped the technical details and the terminology of the oil industry would she be able to make sense of the records and complaints that came to her desk. Like any sophisticated entity steeped in public relations, BP sought to sculpt her experience in its own mold by educating her first.

A few years earlier the company had invited Pascal on a company-sponsored junket to the greater Prudhoe Bay area. Along with a group of state and federal regulators and politicians, she took the company's 727 flight from Anchorage to the North Slope. It was August, and when they stepped off the airplane in Deadhorse, it was snowing heavily. The group was bused through the tightly controlled security gates that control access to the operating area—a minor shock to federal authorities, since the North Slope is publicly owned land—and then some twenty miles up north to the seashore, and across the causeway to Endicott Island.

Pascal had conflicting but dramatic first impressions. She found the landscape serene and ethereal, an "ice desert," with moisture rising out of the ground in curiously beautiful geometric configurations of hoar frost. She was amazed by the size and scope of the massive facilities and the endless tangle of pipelines: "Pretty much the entire shoreline of the Arctic was locked up." But she found the slope littered with everything from garbage to metal scraps and discarded industrial debris. Couldn't they have at least cleaned it up? "They were sloppy," she said. "They knew all these regulators were coming. Oil and gas operations are not the cleanest operations in the world."

She spent several nights in the living quarters at Endicott, where she had to pull tight the heavy darkening shades to block out the constant glow of industrial fluorescent lights that flooded the island. Nothing could block out the vibrating thrum of machinery. In the daytime, she was shown the best parts of the facilities. She was fascinated to learn how carefully the pipelines, and sometimes buildings, were propped up on stilts to protect the permafrost underneath and keep the structures from sinking into the softening earth. Whatever negative effect the trash had on her was assuaged by the excitement of being there and the fantastic detail of the operations. She questioned a few superficial things, but she went home assured, once again, that BP was fulfilling its promises.

That judgment was sustained in the years that followed in part because Phillips seemed to flood her and the EPA with confessional accounts of every little spill. According to the plea agreement with the Department of Justice, BP wouldn't be punished for minor environmental violations during its probation as long as the company reported the incidents to authorities. Pascal received almost weekly accounts of minor accidents: a dozen gallons of antifreeze tipped here, a diesel drip there. She believed that she was being amply informed about everything that happened in Alaska without having to spend her own overallocated time investigating.

By mid-2003, Steve Marshall was pressing Pascal and the EPA for early dismissal of their case. The compliance agreement was scheduled to expire at the end of January 2005. The company thought it had demonstrated enough goodwill to be released early on good behavior. Pascal didn't see much of a problem. She thought BP had earned it, and it would help clear her caseload. She would review the material and make a decision after the New Year.

Then, shortly after she returned to the office from vacation, Pascal got a phone call that would change everything. It was Marc Kovac, calling under an imperative of secrecy. The *Anchorage Daily News* had run an article saying that the EPA was about to let BP off the hook. Kovac was concerned that without the government's hammer hanging over BP's head, any progress he and the workers had made toward fixing the conditions on the slope would be undone. "There are awful things happening on this oil field," Kovac told her.

Pascal had never before talked with Kovac or any of the workers on the slope. She says she had heard about the operational review but hadn't seen it herself, instead relying on Phillips's explanation that it was evidence that BP was fixing every problem it could identify. Kovac told her about the facilities in which he was working near the shore of the Arctic Ocean, the very sites Pascal had visited on her tour. He explained that the facilities didn't have a working fire alarm system, even though they processed flammable materials. He told her that a closer glance at the pipeline insulation that looked so tidy from the roadway would show that in many places it was saturated with water, and that the pipes were rusting away at an alarming rate. And he explained a part of what Crannis, the corrosion manager, had told him: that while BP's records showed the pipelines were in reasonable shape, the numbers had been manipulated through Richard Woollam's methods. Finally, Kovac said that workers who complained about the problems had been fired. He warned her that a leak or, worse, an explosion, could happen any day. "I'm scared for my life," he implored her. "If you have a case against BP Alaska you don't want to let them go."

Kovac was referring to the ticking clock the EPA and the Department of Justice had in Alaska. There were twelve months left until the compliance agreement, and BP's probation, expired. Once that happened, the agencies would lose jurisdiction over BP unless another crime was committed. Though it may have violated the company's probation and debarment agreement, there was no clear crime in delaying maintenance or shrugging off workers' complaints that would justify a separate prosecution after January 31, 2005. So if she were to do anything, she would have to get a handle on what was happening on the slope and build a case for action by then.

Indeed, Kovac's call wasn't the first clue. Pascal had caught worrisome rumblings in a letter she received from an Alaskan official a few days before. In it, the state environmental regulator responsible for the slope, Ernesta Ballard, charged that BP's behavior on the slope was reckless, and suggested that the company had violated its settlement agreement with the EPA. She listed a couple of examples: in 2003 the company failed to report a six-thousand-gallon oil spill until after it had begun cleaning it up; and after the explosion at A-22 burned and maimed Don Shugak, the company had tried to blame the accident on him, even though a state investigation found that BP had not managed the well's problems properly or equipped Shugak with the right gear to measure the well's pressure. In her letter to Pascal, Ballard expressed concerns about letting BP out of its agreement early—and said that at the time she was considering more criminal charges against BP. Pascal found the news from Ballard surprising. For example, Pascal had spoken with Phillips at length about the Shugak case, only to be told that the unfortunate accident was due to operator error. She hadn't had time to read through all of the state investigation reports on that case, and she began to realize that Phillips had misinformed her. She began to learn about all that had happened—with Hamel, with Kovac—and it was overwhelming. She had dozens of other cases that consumed her in Seattle, and BP was allotted just a sliver of her time.

Suddenly, the Alaska situation seemed to snowball, demanding more and more of her attention. After Kovac's call, Pascal's phone kept ringing. It was as if Chuck Hamel had put a diversion in the dyke of complaints and sent the flow rushing off toward her. To some degree he had. She heard from union guys on the slope—Bill Burkett, a BP production operator, and Glen Trimmer, a lead BP operator at Gathering Center 3, one of the large plants where the pipelines congregate. And she learned that after the Shugak case, one worker, Rob Brian, who had been vocal about changes in safety precautions after the accident, was fired. It seemed like exactly the sort of retaliatory treatment of workers that she had spent months trying to address in the 2000 compliance agreement. She wanted the Health, Safety and Environment division to report directly to senior executives precisely so that these sorts of things wouldn't happen. In her view it was the fundamental building block for a safe corporate culture in the future. Without it, no workers would report problems on the slope, and there would be no way BP would be a safe company, then or twenty years from then.

Once Kovac linked up with Pascal, the workers turned a fire hose of information on the government. They detailed problems, then sent her documents and internal company emails to support their claims. They told her that they were working in a death zone, and that it was inevitable that something horrible was going to happen. Though they wouldn't be made public for years, Pascal saw some of the emails from Woollam's CIC group, lamenting the shutoff of corrosion prevention measures. And she began to grasp, for the first time, how John Browne's corporate emphasis on trimming costs had led to more than just the cutting of extraneous fat; that it had continued into the muscle of the organization. She was stunned by the information, and by the volume of it.

"It was a floodgate. I'd had whistle-blowers come forth before, like one or two, maybe three. I've never had thirty-five to forty people come before me," she said. Suddenly, the BP case was unlike any of the other cases she had handled. And she was furious. Increasingly, it appeared to her that BP had deliberately misled her and had violated its compliance agreement with the federal government. "I tend to take people at face value," she said. "After witnesses came forward and told me that what was really going on was 180 degrees different from what BP told me was going on, I realized that they lied."

Overnight it transformed Pascal from a regulator who had been a sort of advocate for the company's way of dealing with its problems in Alaska to one of its most rabid opponents. She became obsessed, and focused on BP with more and more of her time. She would check their records herself and investigate the claims whistle-blowers were making. She felt betrayed, and business had become personal. "I realized that I had been managed—that these lovely, delightful people had been hired by BP to manage me, and that I had been so easily manageable. One of the hardest moments of my life with BP was realizing that I had swallowed their line: hook, line, and sinker." Instantly, the prospect of early termination of BP's agreement with the EPA was off the table. But Pascal wondered if she needed to go further. Had BP violated the terms of its compliance agreement?

Debarment law is clear on this point. A debarment agreement itself is a sort of second chance in that it maps a pathway toward compliance and allows time for a company to reach it in good faith, in exchange for deferring the ultimate sanctions in the government's quiver. "It is often chemotherapy for the cancer," says Robert Meunier, the former EPA debarment official who wrote the regulations in 1981, under the Reagan administration. "It says we are going to make you put all these things in place, we are giving you the opportunity as a company . . . this is your last chance to survive." But if the program didn't have sharp enough teeth to bite down when it was forced to, the whole system would be meaningless. From the earliest designs it was understood that a violation of a debarment compliance agreement had to be met with swift, decisive action. "God help you if you don't comply with this," Meunier says. "You might go home on a murder charge, but you will go to prison on contempt. The worst possible hell can break loose." But to conclude that BP was in violation, Pascal would need more than workers' accounts. She would need proof.

The BP case, for Pascal, was suddenly about more than bringing a company into environmental compliance; it was about restoring her authority and her reputation. Maybe, on some level, she even thought it was about restoring the EPA's authority to control what happens in the oil fields.

DON SHUGAK'S ACCIDENT could have been a turning point for BP. It could have been the moment when the company slowed down, examined the cause of the explosion, and recognized a pattern in the integrity of its operations. It managers might have said then that BP would not be a Russian roulette sort of organization, where operations hung on crossed fingers that the next contractor didn't screw up, or the next pipe didn't rupture, or the explosion didn't happen on today's watch.

That's what Exxon did after the *Valdez* spill. In 1989 and 1990, Exxon confronted a string of serious problems that, in the space of a few months, began to make the company look like one of the most reckless and irresponsible industrial outfits there could be. The day before Christmas, in 1989, an explosion at an Exxon chemical plant in Baton Rouge, Louisiana, killed a worker. Then, less than a week later, its pipeline in Bayonne, New Jersey, sprang a leak and sent 567,000 gallons of heating oil into the Arthur Kill waterway separating Staten Island, New York, from New Jersey. Critics howled then that intense competition and industry cost cutting were forcing all the oil companies to cut corners.

Exxon could have taken these events in stride and plowed forward with its normal way of doing things. Instead, the company was quick to recognize after those disasters that there was no more room for chance in a business as critical as the oil business. "Exxon answered very aggressively, 'This will not keep happening,'" says Joseph Pratt. "Then they set up systems and pursued them over a long period." Some people in the company called it a "moral imperative." It wasn't that Exxon got warm and fuzzy or was overly concerned with the public good and preventing pollution—it wasn't. But the company's leadership, namely its chief executives, Lawrence Rawl and, later, Lee Raymond, realized that the success of Exxon's business depended on being predictable and stable. Raymond in particular saw that absolute safety for its workers, and a clean environmental record, equated to reliability and consistency in the eyes of both shareholders and regulators. Raymond redoubled his focus on operational integrity, understanding that many of the things that are intrinsic to excellent operations and safety are the same kind of things needed for efficiency in overall operations. The more efficient Exxon was, the more profitable it would be. It was the same end that Browne chased, but by entirely different means.

By 1992, Exxon introduced its Operations Integrity Management System (OIMS), "a full-scale, top-to-bottom review of our operations," according to Rex Tillerson, later the company's CEO, that led to a set of prescribed actions that "guide every operating decision we make." The goal was to institute a rigid set of standards that translated across every Exxon division in every country, and to make everyone from the senior management down to the delivery people accountable for it. Raymond was famous for keeping obsessive tabs on his employees and remaining personally involved in OIMS implementation. If a truck driver in Jakarta twisted his ankle, the news was said to make it to Raymond's desk in Texas. OIMS deemphasized reliance on safety equipment and placed more importance on safety systems and communication. It established eleven core elements, from risk assessment to construction to maintenance, and attached a guiding principal to each one, followed by a detailed system for evaluating adherence. "It is our common global language for safety and accountability," Tillerson says. Simply put, it was rules, rules, rules, plus the transparency to observe how they were implemented.

Exxon insiders describe the process as having neutralized the emotion and the ego that can go with managing complaints, risk, and budget stress by focusing more objectively on a common end goal—to run a safe and profitable corporation—and relying on a team to do it. Raymond coached that team, and everybody knew he was militant about it. The employees, in his system, were the company's first line of defense. The thinking was that if they weren't at risk, the corporation wouldn't be at risk. In the years following the implementation of OIMS, the number of lost man-hours due to injuries—a standard industrial statistic for safely—dropped steadily, as did the number of fatalities and the number of spills. The company has not had a serious catastrophic failure or environmental disaster since. To learn, and evolve, from its mistakes, Exxon established a company-wide database, with details of more than ten thousand incidents. The data can be sorted and constructed to help identify common themes and weaknesses or to spot early trends, such as a rash of small pipe failures, for example.

BP said it wanted many of the same things. It produced reams of documents advertising a commitment to sound operations and insisted that safety was a priority. No oil executive spoke more publicly and more often than John Browne about the importance of environmental responsibility and safety. He was unquestionably a leader in expressing such rhetoric. His words should have trickled down to operations. BP's safety manual stresses that an employee is empowered to shut down an operation if he thinks it is unsafe. And the company's leaders maintained that the policy worked. "I have not had an employee tell me that they were concerned to raise a safety issue," said Bob Malone, "or an employee tell me they would not hesitate stopping or shutting down an operation they thought was unsafe."

Employees at BP say they have never been convinced of those priorities. Managers inside the company say that it was unlikely, in practice, that an employee would act to stop or shut down an operation. "The question before BP is the question that was before Exxon," Pratt says. Somehow, though, the answer was proving less attainable. BP didn't have as strong an engineering emphasis as Exxon, Pratt says. In place of it, BP focused on amorphous goals like being "green" and on maximizing profitability. The example BP led by—a constant emphasis on saving money and bonuses for doing it—made operational rigor a tougher sell to its employees.

Instead of cultivating an environment where workers not only felt safe in voicing concerns but felt obligated to do so, by 2004, there was a long list of confrontational disagreements between BP and its workforce. Not only did BP workers distrust their managers' intentions and motivations, but they made dozens of allegations that individuals had been punished or fired for bringing their concerns forward. "BP does not have a culture that values that frontline input as the last line of defense," said one consultant who worked closely with the company's executives to shape its safety policies. "It has the best of intentions, but a real blind spot about how decisions get made that affect risk."

Exxon, on the other hand, not only encouraged candid interaction with its laborers but incentivized its employees to say something. When they did, they got a free gas card to fill their tank. The idea was to impart a sense of responsibility, right down to the hourly contractors. "It's not you versus us. It's us for the company, and each one of us has the obligation to do our part and make sure that the integrity of the operations is as good as it's going to be, and that goes from the lowest-level employee up through the refining department and up beyond that," said one Exxon employee who worked closely with the implementation of the OIMS system. "It's a common culture and common obligation and we all have an obligation to make it work."

Even as BP worked to build a brand and a reputation as the most environmentally progressive oil company in the world, it was Exxon's operation plan that quickly became a model of operational integrity in an era of stricter regulatory oversight and greater expectations for environmental responsibility. Even contingents of BP's management were quick to see its value. When Bob Malone, as head of Alyeska pipelines, squared off against Chuck Hamel in the mid-1990s and faced a never-ending barrage of serious maintenance and environmental risks with the pipeline in Valdez, he thought that replicating Exxon's system would help get the pipeline company back on track. He quickly created the Alyeska Integrity Management System (AIMS), in Exxon's model, and he thought then that BP could use something similar across all of its operations. He personally tried to bring that discipline to the company. But it never quite took hold.

BP, as an organization, may have been resistant to a rigorously prescribed approach to operational safety in part because of a philosophical thread that ran through its corporate culture, emphasizing aspirational goals rather than strict rules. Generations of executives in BP relied on principles-based management, where broad philosophical boundaries of behavior may be set but there is wide leeway for nuance and creativity inside those boundaries to achieve an end by a variety of means. Executives set the tone—like "Beyond Petroleum"—and operational managers figure out how to implement it. American industrial companies, on the other hand, were, as one senior BP manager put it, more "Napoleonic," with every aspect of every procedure codified and dictated from the top, meaning the boundaries of accepted behavior are more narrowly defined and uniform. In the case of Exxon, for example, this resulted in more consistency but less creativity.

People from both companies described it as a subtle split between British and American business culture that in the oil industry was becoming a chasm. To some in BP's senior management, American culture was one of rules and bureaucracy that hamstrung creative problem solving and seemed to assume that people couldn't handle the intellectual responsibility that came with true freedom of management. BP's executives placed great trust in the abilities, diligence, and vigilance of their management. "The key culture clash really is just an engineer's approach to the world versus more of a professor's approach," Pratt says, "where I have big ideas, and we're going to mull over the ideas. And we'll fit in the practical issues as we go along." In a sense, they seemed to think they didn't need rules; they already knew, and would stay within the bounds of, what was right. Exxon's operations plan was as good an example as any of the sort of compulsively overprescribed approach that the Brits despised.

It's just a theory, picked up by keen observers close to the company. But if the theory holds, then it raises a question: What happens when someone unaccustomed to working outside the prescriptive environment is plopped down inside a principles-based corporate culture with all its broad freedoms? That is essentially what happened at BP in the United States after 1998, as it tacked on tens of thousands of employees who came from generations of the American oil business and were used to being told what to do. And it leads to another critical question that BP company executives would be asking themselves for many years: Were their employees still good enough to be entrusted to work within BP principles, or did the mergers in the United States dilute that culture and weaken BP's very DNA?

PASCAL, for her part, remained concerned with questions about BP's leadership: were all Steve Marshall's assurances of a fresh era of responsive management at BP's Alaska division a bunch of hot air? She needed to burrow to the bottom of the worker complaints, but she was a lawyer, not an investigator, and the debarment office was not an investigative office. The first logical step seemed to be to ask BP to square its rhetoric with the allegations the workers were laying out before her. In May, having privately collected as much documentation as she could, Pascal relayed Kovac's and the other workers' complaints to BP management. And she demanded, under the authority of the compliance agreement, that the company launch an internal investigation and compile a report based on its findings. Had the workers truly been threatened for speaking up about unsafe conditions? Were data about pipeline corrosion really being manhandled until they could be used as proof the system was safe? "I told them to do the report or I would debar them," she says.

BP Alaska hired Vinson & Elkins, the noted international law firm based in Houston that specializes, among other things, in serving the energy industry. Vinson & Elkins had represented Enron in 2001, and had been accused then of whitewashing internal Enron investigations that could have unveiled that company's problems. In Alaska, BP's inquiry would be led by Carol Dinkins, head of environmental litigation at the firm, who had previously worked at the U.S. Department of Justice as a deputy attorney general and as head of the agency's environment and natural resources division. By June, the Vinson & Elkins team had begun reviewing the documents sent to them by Pascal and Kovac, and by July, it conducted the first of several rounds of interviews with workers in Prudhoe Bay.

The attorneys interviewed more than forty workers and at first seemed more interested in a shakedown than an investigation. "They had been up there for thirty nanoseconds when the workers started calling me and saying that the attorneys from Vinson and Elkins were

up there asking questions and were more interested in who was talking to me than in what was going on," Pascal says. But they quickly
found some truth in the complaints. BP's contractors, the lawyers
established, were under enormous pressure to hit various quotas and
statistical targets, including achieving a very low rate of injury or environment incidents, or "recordables," as the industry calls them. In
some cases, the contractor would truck injured workers to offsite medical locations so that their incidents would not be tallied in BP's database or be relayed to the U.S. Department of Labor. In other cases,
there were blatant threats. One team, the contractors who worked
with Crannis's corrosion group, was warned, when it resisted staff cuts
and budget pressures in the corrosion and inspection program, that
the entire crew could be replaced if they didn't fall in line. Another
employee was warned that he could have been fired for raising his environment and safety concerns.

Many of the stories seemed to trace back to Richard Woollam, the
corrosion program manager, and one example explored by the investigating attorneys helped show how poor communication among BP
Alaska's top management had led to mayhem. Sometime in 2001,
the company's corrosion department had decided to cut the staff
that checks coupons, or small tabs of metal placed inside a pipeline
as a sort of litmus test for corrosion rates along the pipelines. Coupon-pulling work is the most dangerous and demanding of any within
the corrosion and inspection program. It requires workers to handle
sensitive equipment on pipes under thousands of pounds of pressure,
often while perched on a ladder somewhere out in the blowing wind
and drifting snow. But the coupons are essential to understanding how
quickly, and how severely, the pipelines may be breaking down from
the inside out. They are critical to the company's efforts to maintain
Prudhoe Bay and prevent a spill. Woollam, believing that less oil production necessitated fewer coupons in the pipelines, ordered BP's
contractor to cut its coupon-pulling staff by 25 percent, a move that
would save BP $250,000.

The dictate was met with outrage from some of the program's
supervisors, including a manager for one of the contracting companies
that BP hired to do the work, Mark Petersen. Workers had been given
more and more responsibility as part of previous rounds of layoffs and

cost cuts; now they filed their own data, shipped their own materials, visited more test sites over a broader area, and drove more than four hours a day. Even if there were roughly 20 percent fewer coupons in use than a few years earlier, Petersen lamented, the staff's work was substantially greater. "I'm sure Richard [Woollam] is smart enough to know these facts, but they don't help to bolster his case so he chooses not to use them," he wrote.

When another request made its way to Woollam for more inspectors in the months after the staff cuts, Woollam shot back angrily: "I am struggling to understand why [the contractor] thinks the response will be anything other than 'NO!' or even 'HELL, NO!' and therefore why we are being pestered with these requests."

Petersen's objections, however, and those of others, went unheeded. In February 2002, BP's contractor grudgingly made the changes. "I will make any changes you feel are warranted," the supervisor overseeing the coupon program, Larry Burgess, wrote to Woollam. At least one manager who resisted the transition was "run off" the slope. The program was cut, worker shifts jumped to seventeen-hour days. The backlog of inspection points ballooned.

Later emails show that senior BP management didn't just want compliance. They wanted enthusiasm. "We need to get commitment . . . to make this successful, versus doing what we request and expressing doubt," a senior BP team leader wrote to Woollam in 2003, after still more cuts.

When field manager Maureen Johnson was preparing for a site visit of the slope in 2004, Woollam told his staff they'd better be ready to sing from the same page. In particular, he seemed concerned that workers would rat out the company for not being open to criticism and not allowing them to speak out. "We need the very best HSE performance possible on this trip," he wrote, and directly ordered any staff that Johnson interviewed to "say that they know they can, and do[,] report all HSE concerns."

Kovac didn't work in the corrosion division, but its offices were nearby, and he had heard enough gripes and fears from the men who did to understand that they felt increasingly at risk. Despite the mantra of reporting all problems, the workers were too afraid of Woollam to make another complaint themselves. So in early 2003, Kovac filed his own formal complaint on their behalf. He accused BP of operating under a program of "run to failure," allowing the facilities to wind down their lifespan with minimal investment in maintenance. And he said that workers were not being outfitted with the right equipment, such as pressure monitors, to do their jobs safely. He warned that spills and injuries were inevitable.

Kovac's letter enraged management. "Dan wants somebody fired over this," Burgess said at the time, referring to his boss, the manager of the coupon-pulling program. The group went on a manhunt for the people who had complained to Kovac.

The Vinson & Elkins attorneys were horrified by the tone of communications they uncovered and the disorder that it had appeared to seed in the Prudhoe Bay operations. When they presented their findings to BP's executives in Alaska in late August, their critique was damning on a cultural level. The report confirmed that workers "experience an unintended chilling effect" and faced harassment for raising safety and environmental concerns. Intense pressure to achieve spending targets and other statistical goals effectively coerced managers into making poor decisions.

The report was highly critical of Richard Woollam, blaming him as an "aggressive manager whose approach can be summed up [by] the term . . . 'extreme performance management.'" Woollam's behavior had the side effect of encouraging managers to "drive reporting underground." Woollam, the report said, had earned the moniker "King Richard" on the slope, and the CIC program was his "kingdom."

"We found evidence of managers forcing the adoption of decisions made by Mr. Woollam regardless of their reservations over them and line worker complaints about them, largely because of Mr. Woollam's overbearing management style, which does not countenance debate and open discussion," the report stated. "His pressure on contractor management to hit performance metrics . . . creates an environment where fear of retaliation and intimidation could and did occur. . . . If the number of HSE incidents is treated as just another metric, and a manager like Mr. Woollam demands that metric be met and is intolerant of situations where it is not met, there is inevitably a pressure not to report incidents," read the report, marked privileged and confidential.

Vinson & Elkins highlighted BP's stated policy, which, like Exxon's, requires that every single safety or environmental incident be reported to management, and then explained why it wasn't working. "BPXA [BP Exploration Alaska]'s goal is certainly laudable, but can cause problems in the hands of an aggressive manager like Richard Woollam, who pushes contractors very hard to hit performance metrics and threatens contract loss on a regular basis. The inherent tension between '100% reporting' and 'zero incidents' requires a manager who is able to reduce that tension . . . instead Mr. Woollam exacerbated this tension."

But the report went soft when it came to the potentially criminal allegations raised against BP: that the company was manipulating the corrosion test data and allowing the pipelines to deteriorate while risking a catastrophic spill that could kill workers and shut down oil production in the Arctic. "Our investigation did not uncover any evidence to suggest that such falsification was actually occurring," it said. Instead, it blamed the allegations and heightened fear on workers' misunderstandings, and said that they did not understand how the corrosion program was supposed to work. One by one, it systematically dismissed all of their substantive complaints as rumors infecting the work camps. Among the complaints it dismissed were allegations that corrosion-monitoring coupons were placed in safe spots in the pipeline and that pipelines ranked *F* for failure were not being repaired. It said that a climate of mistrust allowed workers to believe every negative tale, and blamed Marc Kovac for spreading disinformation.

The report concluded that Prudhoe Bay's corrosion program was technically excellent and that its maintenance was under control. "Nothing we learned in our investigation suggests that the field is, as a general matter, unsafe or prone to catastrophic failure," it said. "It does not appear that the allegations regarding fraud in the corrosion program are correct." The conclusion—filed by a law firm that is no stranger to liability and was then under siege for having contributed to Enron's defrauding of its workers and investors—came with an odd disclaimer: "We are not technically qualified to evaluate the adequacy or timing of repair decisions. . . . Our review in no way reached the level of detail that would be obtained by a comprehensive audit of the corrosion program's data system." It recommended that BP undertake a separate technical review to truly evaluate the corrosion program.

In the end Vinson & Elkins determined that if BP was guilty of anything, it was poor communication with its workers. The report implied that with bolstered worker confidence, many of the technical complaints would evaporate. If BP would only educate its workforce, the report implied, employees would come to see that their complaints were in fact minor. Despite its criticism of Woollam, it remained equivocal about the extent to which he should shoulder blame. The report recommended that Woollam be removed from management, mostly because he had bullied too many of his staff and wasn't a congenial guy. It didn't say anything about the failures of the corrosion program, or how Woollam might be responsible. In a way, the report exculpated him—making clear that he never explicitly told workers not to report incidents—and meted out praise. It described his technical skills as excellent, and said his approach to controlling costs and corrosion were highly effective for BP. "We want to emphasize that it was not Mr. Woollam's . . . intent to intimidate or retaliate against any employee raising HSE concerns." The results were mixed messages for BP's executives. Was "extreme performance management," after all, what John Browne and others in London wanted, because it served BP best? Or not?

THE FINDINGS were presented to Jeanne Pascal and her team at another meeting at the Seattle Fairmont in October 2004. Steve Marshall was present, as was Carol Dinkins, and several other managers closely involved in the issues addressed in the report. At the end, they asked: "So what do you think about the report?"

"What do I think?" responded one of Pascal's staff, incredulously. "I think it's the same as a reporter, after the sinking of the *Titanic*, asking if it was true that the ship hit an iceberg and sank last night, and the White Star Lines said, 'It's against our policy to hit icebergs.' "

"It was a whitewash," said Pascal. "It was bullshit."

In fact, documents show that at the precise time the Vinson & Elkins report was under way, cuts were being made that seem to contradict some of the report's findings and statements. For instance, the Vinson & Elkins attorneys report that in an August 24, 2004, interview, Richard Woollam told them that rather than cut costs, he had been increasing expenditures in the CIC program; total spending had actually jumped $8 million in 2003. That statement didn't seem to represent the entire picture. A series of documents and private email exchanges between Woollam and other senior BP Alaska personnel from September 2003 shows the team was still trying to reduce costs, the exact opposite of what the report states. On September 8, according to the emails, Woollam was given forty-eight hours to cut more than 2 percent from his budget. "I want to see what it will take in terms of actions and risks and mitigations to those risks to reduce your LE [lower estimate] by 1 million bucks by Wednesday morning," wrote Woollam's boss. Until the cuts could be found in the program itself, they would be taken from managers' salaries.

Internal documents show that Woollam's team analyzed several options to win back the money and preserve their pay, including cutting back on the scope of inspections and corrosion control. BP had already considered cuts to inspections, chemical use, and external corrosion protections in 2002. A budget document lays out some of the potential ramifications at the time, including a 30 percent increase in corrosion rates, waning confidence among BP's corporate partners (namely Exxon) in Prudhoe Bay, and concern over the response of Alaska state regulators.

Eventually, the team arrived at their number, but not unanimously. "Nancy [Faust, BP's manager of maintenance and reliability in Alaska] was not in favor of the cut but felt we had to do it based upon pressure and Steve [Marshall]'s comments," a CIC team leader wrote to Woollam on September 10, 2003. "She was clear that she would not allow program cuts without being directed . . . to do so, and is sensitive to news of this cut getting out to the workforce which would undoubtedly cause HSE concerns."

Internal documents show that one budget item on the chopping block in 2004 was the company's smart pigging program. Smart pigging is the process whereby a small robot is sent through the pipelines to clean them and test their integrity. It was estimated that cutting the program would save another $250,000 a year. Also being considered were a 17 percent reduction in inspections, for a savings of $1.4 million; and a 17 percent reduction in the use of chemicals to prevent corrosion, for $1.6 million in savings. At the bottom of the list was a small item that would take a big toll on corporate morale: a cut of all Sunday barbecues, the company's fun run, and, finally, all "discretionary spend on materials that are absolutely not required to produce electricity or maintain safety." BP, which earned $285 billion in 2004, would remove televisions and cable channels from staff barracks to pocket an additional $20,000 in budget savings.

THE WORKERS had convinced Pascal that an accident on the slope was inevitable. "I just didn't know when," she says. "I didn't know if it was going to be an explosion, [or] a catastrophic leak that would be devastating." And she also believed their accounts of fraud and abuse. The allegations alone weren't enough to find the company in violation of its probation, however. Though despicable to her, the blacklisting and punishment, even after being documented in an internal report like the Vinson & Elkins paper, weren't actionable unless the Department of Labor first ruled there was wrongdoing. The more serious allegation, that the company was hiding information from regulators about the safety of its pipelines and equipment, and the correlated charge that spills that had occurred were the result of gross negligence in maintenance, would also need to be substantiated with a higher standard of proof.

After the Vinson & Elkins report, Pascal didn't think BP would investigate the issues vigorously on its own. To take matters further, she'd need to get government investigators involved, and she had just two months left to do it. Pascal turned to the EPA's Criminal Investigation Division in Seattle.

At first, she was stonewalled. The division's special agent in charge (SAC), Don Sims, seemed uninterested. "He wouldn't budge," Pascal says. "He would say, 'You don't tell me what to do. I'm the special agent in charge. I make that determination, not you.'" Sims eventually sent an investigator from the FBI up to Prudhoe Bay to check out the claims, but the agent, who was described by people close to the investigation as "expressively gay," had a "personality conflict" with the workers on the slope, and they told him nothing. "He couldn't investigate his way out of a paper bag," Pascal says. After that trip, according to Pascal, Sims told her he considered the employee allegations of poor maintenance unfounded. The agent hadn't found anything that could be knitted into a prosecution. He didn't think there was a case.

It was a tough time to prosecute an oil company. The George W. Bush White House discouraged the EPA from taking bold action. Sims, by many accounts, was a politically savvy and ambitious employee. Furthermore, BP in particular had a lot of leverage on the U.S. government. With nearly one hundred thousand employees now spread over about one hundred countries, it controlled a significant portion of the U.S.'s non-OPEC supply of oil. Specifically, it supplied nearly 12 percent of fuel to the U.S. military—which was freshly engaged in Iraq and still waging war in Afghanistan—for which it was paid more than $1 billion annually in taxpayer dollars. By some accounts, nearly 80 percent of the critical war-support jet fuel came from BP. The company also was the largest shareholder in, and the operator of, the Baku–Tbilisi–Ceyhan Pipeline, perhaps the most important free-world supply of gas from the Caspian Sea and former Soviet states, through Georgia. BP had taken the bold step of jumping into the Iraq situation, agreeing early on to process and ship Iraqi oil during the war. It was often rumored that in exchange for some of that access, and for the United States' tacit protection of BP's global interests, Tony Blair agreed to support the American coalition in the Persian Gulf.

In short, BPs interests were heavily intertwined with U.S. national security interests, and here a couple of inspectors from a small government bureaucracy in Seattle were trying to wrestle it under control. If there were times when BP began to feel unmanageable to Pascal, it was almost understandable. But the question that roused her was this: If the U.S. government couldn't do anything to stop them, who could? Was BP simply too big to control?

Pascal pressed her case on the U.S. Department of Justice directly. She met with Tim Burgess, the U.S. Attorney in Alaska, at the end of 2004. "I said I had documents which showed the pipelines were in bad shape and that sooner or later there was going to be some kind of a failure," Pascal said. Burgess rebuffed her on the basis of the fact that the federal government didn't have jurisdiction to interfere with oil and gas infrastructure unless a crime had been committed or an accident had already happened. It was a Catch-22. Though the evidence for concern was compelling, environmental laws are written to be responsive, not proactive. If the big punitive stick of a felony threat isn't enough to deter malpractice, the government doesn't have the authority to go onto BP property and force it to change its own routines. And the government can't prosecute until a law is believed to be broken.

Debarment itself also has to be triggered by a crime. The debarment office's jurisdiction would end the moment the compliance agreement over the previous criminal conviction expired. Pascal had run up against the boundaries of regulatory oversight. In the end the government simply had to wait for something worse to happen, and hope that it happened before the debarment group was off the case.

On January 31, 2005, the compliance agreement over the Endicott Island dumping case expired. BP's probation agreement was up. The company was released from its responsibilities to the EPA, and Pascal's responsibilities for overseeing their activities on the slope came to an end. "Our laws don't create any barriers, any limits, on their ability to keep operating," says David Uhlmann, the former head of the environmental crimes division at the Department of Justice. "As soon as they have cleaned up whatever mess they have made, they are off the hook, simple as that." There is no legal mechanism to address a repeat offender; Pascal couldn't do anything more to correct the worsening safety conditions in Alaska unless BP broke the law again. "I explored that with all kinds of people and I couldn't find a jurisdictional way in, other than to let it happen," Pascal said. "So we had to wait."

PART TWO

Crisis Years

7

DANGER AT THE PLANT

MARCH 23, 2005, began as a quiet morning on the grounds of BP's largest refinery in Texas City, Texas, at least in the northwest corner of the twelve-hundred-acre, fenced-in facility, where some of the most delicate parts of the gasoline-making process took place. The morning shift change was as monotonous as ever. The light of dawn drowned the glow of thousands of incandescent orange lights illuminating the piping systems and cooling stations and smokestacks of the refinery. Hundreds of workers spilled silently through the security gates on Fifth Avenue, under coils of razor wire. Dressed in royal blue jump-suits, white hard hats, and steel-toed boots, they filed past similarly uniformed workers on their way home. Among those entering were David Leining, a BP construction supervisor; Eugene White; and Linda and James Rowe—employees who worked for, or would be meet-ing with, a contractor on-site, JE Merit.

The refinery was divided into a grid of streets, with alphabetical avenues running east-west. Leining and the others turned right as they passed through the refinery's entrance, and walked down Avenue F for the length of several city blocks, toward their offices in a group of trail-ers on an otherwise empty concrete lot adjacent to the isomerization unit. The "isom," as it was called, was one of more than thirty separate process units at the refinery, and was itself a large square industrial site with four separate facilities over several acres abutting the south side of Avenue F. At the isom facilities, mediocre-grade hydrocarbons are upgraded into higher-octane blends of fuels that can then be mixed into gasoline. One unit removes sulfur. Another runs a molecular catalyst on the fuel. A third recovers vapor. The fourth, called a raffinate splitter tower, is a skinny metal silo, 13 feet wide and 164 feet tall, in which rough hydrocarbons are boiled so that the lighter molecular segments can separate out into a vapor and rise to the top, where they are gathered as distilled high-octane gasoline.

The raffinate splitter tower sat in the southeast corner of the isom unit, diagonal to the lot where the JE Merit workers were sited, nestled in a bird's nest of pipes that connect all the different isom facilities. Next to the splitter, a small concrete shack housed a satellite control room—the only manned building on the isom block. From there, a small crew of one or two men communicated with a central control center in a different part of the refinery a few blocks away. On the isom block, feeder pipes ran from the raffinate splitter tower past the control room and then west, to another antiquated tower in the northwest corner of the isom block called the blowdown drum, where overflow flammable liquids were routed in case of an emergency. The blowdown drum was less than 150 feet from the trailer with the JE Merit crew.

The office trailers weren't supposed to be there—their placement violated safety standards, and BP had never completed a risk assessment of their location. But siting its contract workers there was one of the ways BP made use of extra square footage inside its fence line.

The trailer closest to the blowdown drum was a double-wide, prefabricated mobile home office, with a wooden frame and corrugated metal walls. Inside, a long hallway divided eleven offices and conference rooms, the closest one to the blowdown drum being in the northeast corner of the building. The JE Merit team stationed there had nothing to do with the isom unit. They were assigned to work on a different fuel upgrading facility entirely, called an ultracracker, located on a block across the road. The double-wide offices were simply a base out of which the contractors managed that project. And so that morning the Rowes, White, and the other JE Merit workers had no idea what was taking place in the isom's raffinate splitter tower facility a couple hundred feet away. For them, the day started off as routine.

Next door, at the isom, run by BP technicians, the routine also appeared normal. The whole plant hummed and thrummed—enough so that its constant work could be sensed in the bones of a clerk all the way across town. Yet the splitter tower was quiet. For four weeks the isom's raffinate facility had been idled for regular maintenance, its boilers shut down and no liquid run through its network of hoses and cisterns and chimneys.

That morning it was in the process of being restarted. Slowly, the raw hydrocarbons were being circulated through its complex veins, and the machinery was coming back to life. This is the most dangerous time in a refinery: not when it's up and running, but when it is being restarted, because the fuel is being heated and pressure is changing and everything is unstable and in transition. During a reboot, no one who is not directly involved in the operation would want to be nearby. Normal practice is to put the area around it on heightened alert and evacuate nonessential workers. But that morning, even though more than seven hundred people had attended the daily 7:00 a.m. safety meeting, no one had mentioned that a reboot of the isom was under way, and nobody in the JE Merit trailer, or anywhere else nearby, had noticed.

WHEN THE REFINERY was built, in 1934, it was one of the most complex and state of the art fuel-making facilities in the world, and one of the largest. It covers twelve hundred acres, nearly one and a half times the size of New York's Central Park. Its thirty facilities can accept almost half a million barrels of oil a day and produce auto fuel, jet fuel, and diesel, as well as chemical feedstocks to supply the nation's manufacturing. Mainly, they process some eleven million gallons of gasoline a day. In 2005 that was the equivalent of 3 percent of the nation's gasoline, an extraordinary amount to come from one company and one facility. It was also one of the most important links in the American energy supply chain. When problems arose at Texas City, it could send the retail price at the pump as far away as Boston skipping by a couple of cents a gallon.

The refinery sits forty-five miles south of Houston, across the bay from the town of Galveston, on the shore of the Gulf of Mexico. Texas City is a hyperindustrial town existing almost solely off the refining and chemical industries. Besides the BP plant, there are smaller refineries, owned by Marathon and Valero. There is a shipping port, and supertankers arriving from Valdez or Qatar dock directly at Texas City to unload their crude. It was on one of these docks, in 1947, that Texas City's first industrial disaster unfolded. An ocean tanker exploded and 581 people were killed. Ever since, the entire city, with roughly 44,000 residents, has learned to live with toxic emissions sensors and explosion shelters and the knowledge that, every day, the people who go to work in the petroleum industry risk not coming home alive.

A refinery works a lot like a distillery, except that it's for hydrocarbons, not booze. And one of the most critical distillation processes happens in the raffinate splitter tower. Like the sweet fermented mash being turned into whiskey, the crude oil is heated, in this case to 720 degrees Fahrenheit, bringing the oil to a boil and turning the crude liquid into a vapor that makes it easier to separate out the "fractions," or myriad types of fuel within. The longer the hydrocarbon chain, the hotter the temperature at which the fluid will boil, and the lighter the resulting fuel. As they vaporize, the hydrocarbons are run through a pipe into the splitter's distillate tower, which looks a lot like a giant oboe standing on its end, except with hoses and pipes extending out of it where the air holes and valves would be on an instrument. The vapors rise toward the top. As they rise they cool, condensing into liquid droplets, which get caught by trays at various heights. The molecular chains for the heavy fuels cool first, turning into liquid on trays near the bottom of the tower. These fuels are used for chemical feedstock or blended into gasoline later on. As the hydrocarbons get lighter, they settle out farther up the tower; diesels are slightly more buoyant, then naphtha, a midrange flammable fluid, then kerosene, which lands about halfway up. Near the top, maybe a hundred feet up, the lightest and simplest hydrocarbon settles: gasoline. Then the gasoline is passed on for further refining.

BP bought the Texas City refinery when it bought Amoco in 1998. It was one of the central properties traded in the deal, and control of the facility was transferred on December 31, 1998. Overnight, the refinery became one of BP's most significant assets. It was also one of the company's most troubled, in large part because little had been improved there in the seventy years since it was built.

Even before the merger, the plant was showing wear. Not only did it continue to rely on the fifty-year-old technology of blowdown drums to prevent an explosion, but the various metal valves and wheels and stacks were turning from a shiny tin hue to an amber rust. In places, bolts and rivets were so decayed they sheared off; in others, holes had worn straight through sheet metal or iron plates. Below valve handles and elbows, brown, oxidized streaks and stains marked the deposit of decaying metal.

Lots of things at the refinery were past their functional prime, but there was no better example than the blowdown drums, the critical overflow safety mechanisms that had been installed as a safety backup when the refinery was built. For a facility that exists to boil volatile liquid hydrocarbons under pressure, nothing is more important than having an effective escape route for those hydrocarbons if the refinery units overfill or leak. The drums are a crude solution. They work like a chimney, capturing excess fluid and gas and shooting the heavier gas up a tall stack and releasing it into the open air at 115 feet, a height that is supposed to disperse it safely and keep it from settling back down near any potential source of ignition close to the ground. Over time, technology for disposing of excess hydrocarbons had improved. By the 1970s, refineries were relying on flares, a sort of pilot light at the top of the stack that ignites any excess fumes and burns them off in a controlled flame. This way, the vapors are disposed of before there is a chance of the stuff collecting in a confined place or blowing up. "A flare is more efficient and safer than a blowdown drum," says T. J. Aulds, the editor of the *Galveston Daily News*, a Texas City native who has been reporting on the refinery for nearly two decades. "There were several blowdown stacks within the refinery that were this old technology. I mean, long after a lot of other folks say, 'We're not using those any-more,' B.P. still was using them."

The blowdown drums at Texas City should have been replaced with flare systems—or at least updated—as early as 1977. That's when the refinery's written safety standards were revised to ban the installation of new blowdown drums and require that any old drums eventually be modified with either a flare or a vapor recovery system to keep the fuel from venting straight into the atmosphere. In 1992, with little equipment having been upgraded and after several close calls, the U.S. Occupational Safety and Health Administration (OSHA) ordered the refinery, still under Amoco management, to replace its blowdown drums because the agency viewed them as exceedingly dangerous. Amoco, in a settlement, won an exception to the order, and OSHA backed off. Afterward, the risk only seemed to increase. Five times in 1994 and 1995, the blowdown drums filled with flammable gases and overflowed, allowing a volatile vapor cloud to fill the surrounding area. These were serious incidents: alarms were sounded and evacuations triggered, and emergency crews leapt into action. The tiniest spark could have caused a catastrophic disaster. In each case, however, nothing happened. On October 4, 1998, a blowdown stack at the refinery caught fire, but again, there was no explosion.

By the time BP bought the plant, Texas City was notorious as an aging money pit that Amoco, perhaps because of its own gradual financial weakening, had let languish for years. Everyone in the industry knew that the site needed work, and that the work would be expensive. BP seemed undecided about how to handle it.

"They knew exactly what they were buying with Amoco . . . because there were a couple of assets that were just beautiful, and you thought, Gosh, [Browne's] got the vision," says the *Financial Times*'s Carola Hoyos, who covered the BP Amoco merger. Besides the Texas City refinery, the merger brought instantaneous, surging growth to BP. It gave BP a broader retail gas station footprint, locked its dominant position in California, and gave the company a strong position in the U.S. fuels market, or the "downstream" segment. Suddenly BP had a reliable vertically integrated outlet—meaning it controlled the drilling for oil, refining of oil, and retail gas stations—for its North American production in both Alaska and, increasingly, the Gulf of Mexico. While the press lauded the move as brilliant, there was still the question of how to incorporate Texas City. "On the other hand, there were some assets that they didn't develop for a while, where you thought, Why are you sitting on them?" Hoyos adds.

Refining is a brutally competitive business, and a tough one to make much money in. Every refinery goes through the same process. It buys its oil at the same market rate, and in the end sells its product for more or less the same price. The key to profit lies in working the margins. BP was expanding its production in the Gulf of Mexico, but in 1998 the oil being shipped to Texas City was, for the most part, coming from thousands of miles away, burdening the operation with significant transportation costs while other gulf coast refiners processed crude from nearby Texas and California and, to a lesser extent, the gulf. In this sense Texas City was at a fundamental business disadvantage, in a segment of the industry already known for anemic profits. Added to that burden was its need for an infusion of investment to fix its aging infrastructure.

At first, BP thought it would flip the refinery to another buyer, unloading the liability altogether, but a deal never materialized, and BP grew resigned to integrating it into the corporation. Yet neither Browne nor anyone else seemed to plan for the special rehabilitative needs the refinery presented. Instead, Texas City fell into the same rubric as every other BP operation, and off the bat, the facility most famously in need of heavy investment found itself instead working to cut back.

As in Prudhoe Bay, the 25 percent across-the-company cost cuts that Browne had ordered in 1999 were just the beginning. In addition, $1.4 billion had to be cut from the refining and marketing group alone. According to the facility's written business plan at the time, still heavier cuts seemed to be "the only major opportunity to capture advantage."

In fact, according to internal BP documents, it was not just the size of the cuts that was essential but the speed with which they were to be implemented. Among the ways in which the refinery's manager sought to catch up was to "continually and aggressively drive costs out of the system at an accelerated pace relative to other refiners." Goals were set to bump profits and boost return on capital from 7 percent in 1999 to 20 percent in 2005. The refinery's managers, having already cut costs by 17 percent, aimed to scrape together another 10 percent in savings from the facility's annual expenses by 2001. They would make it happen by firing staff and "by driving unnecessary costs from turnaround work lists": that is, they would eliminate as many steps and redundancies as possible from maintenance processes like restarting the isomerization unit. As it had done in Alaska, management would whittle right down to the tiniest details to save money that, in the multi-billion-dollar scope of BP's operations, amounted to pennies. They would cut inspectors and maintenance workers by the dozens to save just over $1 million. Eliminating safety calendars saved $40,000. Not buying new safety shoes for employees saved $50,000. Cutting back on rewards for safety performance saved $75,000. In 2002, all of those cuts together equaled the amount of money BP brought in from seventeen seconds of operation.

In 2002 John Browne delegated oversight of these refining budget goals and of BP's worldwide refining and marketing business to John Manzoni, the tight-lipped and tough field manager who had presided over some of the corrosion program cuts in Alaska. Manzoni's colleagues said that he brought to his work the same confidence and brutish intensity he had once shown on the rugby field. He had come up through the company fast, and, they said, it had made him arrogant. According to Tom Hamilton, John Browne's former international exploration hand, Manzoni was one of the guys who "thought a bit more of themselves than maybe they should have when they came into that job. He didn't have an easy connection with the operating level workforce."

However, Manzoni had proven capable of slashing costs in Alaska and had helped to bend BP Alaska's square budget into Browne's round box six years earlier. He continued to impress when Browne brought him down to Houston to orchestrate the merging of the Amoco assets into BP. Manzoni was one of Browne's "turtles"—named, reportedly by Browne, for the Teenage Mutant Ninja Turtles who were valiant and devoted fighters in the service of their sensei. Browne's turtles were being groomed to take over the role of chief executive. The next test for Manzoni, as head of refining, was to see how he could handle the downstream side of the business.

Manzoni didn't manage day-to-day operations in Texas City, but he had three tiers of management underneath him that did, and each of these managers was eager to please. It was hard to imagine replacing Texas City's blowdown drums in such a repressive budget climate, but at one point, the plant's operators tried. The drums had suffered yet another severe fire in January 2000 but continued to function. When a flare system was being installed in one of the refinery's facilities in 2002, plant operators debated undertaking work that would equip the ailing blowdown drum at the isom with a flare. "We need to decide if we want to spend $150M now to save more money later on," one plant manager wrote to his superiors, using the Roman numeral for "thousand." The response was swift and decisive: "CAPEX [the budget for capital expenditures] is very tight. Bank $150k savings now."

A couple of hours later, a more senior manager, George Carter, concurred, as if to say the question should never have been asked in the first place: "Bank the savings in 99.999% of cases."

In 2002 BP tapped Don Parus to manage the company's south Houston operations, which included several chemical plants and the Texas City refinery's operations. Parus had a master's degree in chemical engineering from Northwestern and a business degree from DePaul University, and had spent more than twenty years in the oil business for Amoco. He knew the downstream oil business as well as anyone. He was well liked and, his staff said, well intentioned. He had spent thirteen years at the Whiting refinery in Ohio—now owned by BP—and nearly a dozen years in other posts. Parus went to Texas in April for a series of long meetings and briefings with the manager he was replacing. Safety and the condition of the company's assets were seen as acceptable and never mentioned as a concern.

When he arrived on the job, however, Parus began to form his own opinions before he had even passed through the entrance gate. The refinery appeared "run down" and "decayed" and hadn't been painted, he recalled; it looked decrepit compared to how he remembered it from a visit ten years earlier. These were superficial but telling impressions, and the more layers he peeled back, the more problems he found. The roofs hadn't been repaired. The offices were dilapidated. Everywhere he looked, the infrastructure was "in complete decline."

Almost immediately, Parus began examining the refinery's reliability. He found that Texas City had had more than eighty hydrocarbon releases in the previous two years. He commissioned a study, in August 2002, that warned of "serious concerns about the potential for a major site incident," and he documented overdue inspections and reliability issues, including faulty instruments—findings the report described as "urgent and far reaching." To Parus it was increasingly clear that the refinery would not be able to operate safely for much longer. His report said that Texas City needed a "major overhaul of the basics," and he requested $235 million in increased maintenance spending.

Another consultant determined, in October 2002, that the refinery's integrity and reliability issues were "clearly linked to the reduction in maintenance spend[ing] over the last decade," and that capital spending had been reduced by 84 percent since 1992. Maintenance spending over that same time had been cut by 41 percent.

Over the next two years, Parus tried to whip the refinery back into shape and get the message that Texas City was in trouble out to the rest of the company. "Cost cutting efforts have intervened with the group's work to get things right," stated a 2003 report he commissioned. "Usually reliability improvements are cut." Another report described the condition of Texas City's infrastructure and assets as "poor," and said maintenance spending was limited by a "checkbook mentality." Parus was backed up by a company-wide review by BP auditors in London that found that thirty-five business units around the world suffered from a host of safety problems, including "widespread tolerance of non-compliance" with basic safety and environmental rules and "lack of leadership competence and understanding." In 2000 a series of fires and accidents had rocked BP's largest refinery, in Grangemouth, Scotland, and scathing investigation reports blamed the company for overzealous cost cutting, poor attention to risk management, and not training its workers properly.

Parus, using these examples, convinced BP's executives to invest more money in Texas City's maintenance in 2003, and he launched a multiyear plan to rehabilitate key infrastructure. But even as he began that work, a conflicting edict from London ordered still more cuts. Texas City, a manager wrote in an email, was drawing 18 percent of the company's refining safety budget while only producing 15 percent of its refining profits. The site wasn't pulling its weight, and another $30 million in cuts and $140 million in profits would need to be found. In an email to BP staff about the efforts to upgrade Texas City's maintenance program, Dennis Link, a Texas City plant manager, wrote that the "key message" was that the refinery "is NOT delivering on profitability vs. % of capital investment. This is part of our 'sense of urgency.'"

Parus's plans to invest heavily in maintenance went nowhere. The harder he fought, the more he was held at a standstill by a wall of organizational bureaucracy. One glaring problem was that even though he was the senior operations manager, he didn't have the authority to make critical budget decisions. He was responsible for safety and day-to-day operations, but he didn't control spending. The purse strings were held instead by a separate business unit leader. The "account-abilities were unclear and disputed," he later told BP's attorneys. Any changes Parus proposed had to be approved by at least one separate office. It was a vestige of BP's diffused matrix management structure—where, rather than a strict hierarchy, employees were grouped according to their skill sets or which projects they were assigned to and could wind up reporting to several managers at the same time. Parus ran operations for both the chemicals group and the refining group. But each of those groups had its own business unit leader who dictated the budget. To spend more money, the business units had to agree on their overall changes and, almost by committee, convince Parus's boss, Pat Gower, before anything could get done. It was never clear whether Gower fully conveyed the urgency of Parus's findings to more senior executives. Throughout the organization, Parus and other managers were hampered by a lack of communication and the resulting difficulty of conveying, to Manzoni and Browne, the severity of Texas City's problems.

Mike Hoffman, the only other manager between Gower and Manzoni in the refining segment's hierarchy, seemed unable to swing the pendulum of underinvestment back in the right direction. In late 2002 Hoffman directed his staff to try to figure out, as he put it, "how . . . [South Houston had] gotten into such a poor state." Hoffman, one of his staff wrote in an email, "is concerned that the top level in London need to understand the consequences of their orders." The email referred to Browne's flat-rate order to slash costs. "In '99 our 'cut by 25%' . . . seems to have been taken literally."

"There were a number of reports coming up to as high as the board level that indicated serious problems throughout the BP system," says Don Holmstrom, lead investigator at the U.S. Chemical Safety and Hazard Investigation Board, who would later investigate the refinery.

Parus thought the problems in communication and prioritization, at least in Texas, were due to a cultural rift between Amoco, where his career had begun, and BP. Amoco, he said, "had a set of principles and philosophies. I think BP was just different." After the merger, BP upended the network of health, safety, and environmental systems that Amoco had in place at Texas City, discarding the groups that ran them and instead addressing concerns on a case-by-case basis. "BP is decentralized, with a central group monitoring the numbers," Parus said. "Amoco was less focused on the numbers—it was more people-oriented." Others thought that the problems in Texas City and Alaska were more likely reflections of John Browne's own personal priorities. He had become an international celebrity CEO, and he enjoyed it. Statesmanship, big deals, and big thoughts— and all of the kudos and magazine articles that went with it—were more interesting and gratifying to him than getting his hands dirty with the particulars. People who knew Browne said the precision and exacting attention to operational detail bored him; that making sure the company ran safely, and that there were channels of communication, bored him. At the same time, Browne was clear, opinionated, and forceful about the priorities he did set, mainly financial ones. His own bias, then, intentionally perhaps, was against operational issues. That, plus his famous displeasure with being questioned or crossed, made it difficult for him to hear the message from the front lines of his army.

"There wasn't much of a dialogue," says Hoyos, the *Financial Times* writer. "It was quite difficult for people . . . beneath him to be able to go to him and say, 'Look, I know you want these cost cuttings, and I know in the current situation it's very important. And refining has always been the black sheep because it doesn't bring in as much money. But there's certain things we have to do on a daily basis to, say, stay safe.'" A senior BP executive involved in the Texas City issues put it this way: "To have an operating culture you have to have people who know about operating, they have to be valued, you have to have the right kinds of authority and you have to have the right metrics to encourage improvements.

"It's been a struggle," the executive continued. "It is just very difficult to explain what you are trying to do in the business. Especially if you are increasing spending: I'm not going to make more this quarter, but I have to increase spending in order to have a long-term viable business. That's hard. I was just always explaining or trying to explain

what we were trying to do in a language that is not purely financial."
It didn't help that Manzoni rarely visited Texas City. Though it was,
in addition to being BP's largest, by many measures the most complex refinery in the world, he preferred to manage it from his office
in London.

In 2004 the constellation of facilities known as "BP South Houston" was dissolved and Don Parus was left to run only the Texas City
refinery, where he was also granted full budget and operational authority. By then, the cost pressures and degradation he had begun to identify earlier were common knowledge, and the refinery was beginning to
unravel. The number of uncontained releases and spills, a major indicator of both environmental risk and the risk of an explosion, jumped
from 399 in 2002 to 607 in 2004. In March 2004 a furnace pipe outlet ruptured, causing a fire that cost the refinery $30 million in dam-
ages. An investigation report found that the outlet was supposed to
have been checked the year before but had not been. The omission was
never reported. "The incentives used in this workplace may encourage
hiding mistakes," the report said. "Bad news is not encouraged."

A few months later, in September, a pipe flange under hazardous
pressure was opened by three workers performing routine maintenance, and it burst, killing two of the men and severely burning
another with scalding water and steam. The system had none of the
standard equipment, valves, or checks in place that could have averted
the accident. "It was typical for them to experience a fire every week,
on average," says Mike Sawyer, an independent process safety consultant who worked on several BP cases. "A fire every week is a warning
sign that something is critically wrong at the facility."

For the first time since taking the job, Parus, distraught by the
deaths on his watch, asked for a record of historical fatalities at the
plant. He was alarmed by the response: in thirty years, twenty-three
workers had been killed, one almost every sixteen months. They were
more than statistics to the plant's veterans, those who had spent
decades working in the refinery business in Texas.

Dave Leining, one of the workers in the JE Merit mobile office
trailer, remembered many of them. "I recall a guy slipping off a tank,
the top of a roof one time, and falling. And I think a guy crawled into
a tire that had nitrogen in it and died. I know there was, a couple guys

years before that at the coker, they were doing welding on the bottom of the drum and the thing just burst into flames and burnt one or two of them and one of them died," he said.

"I know there was a pipe fitter fell off, he leaned over a scaffold and the guardrail on the scaffold was loose and he fell about thirty, forty feet and died. A guy worked a steam trap and got splashed with hot steam and he died from that," he continued. Both of Leining's grandfathers worked for refiners in Texas City. His father had worked for Amoco before it was swallowed by BP. His brother, brother-in-law, and sister all work at the Texas City refinery.

"Another guy got electrocuted working on the switch gear. He went around to the back side and got the wrong box and got tangled up in the wire and he got electrocuted. I played softball with him for years. A lot of those guys that, you know, I knew the majority of them."

Parus, angry, frustrated, and newly educated, knew something needed to be done. In October 2004 he flew to London to make his case directly to Manzoni. The two had met the previous July, and Parus had warned him that the tasks he faced at the refinery were overwhelming. At the time, Manzoni said nothing, and Parus regretted that he had complained.

This time there was a frank and heated meeting. Manzoni, Hoffman, and Parus discussed Texas City's safety record and the company's tolerance of risk. Parus, heavy with emotion, showed Manzoni five PowerPoint slides, the first bluntly titled "Texas City is not a safe place to work." He laid out the statistics—not just the deaths, but thirty-two OSHA-recorded injuries in 2004 and three near-fatalities in 2003. Then he showed Manzoni the pictures of the men who had died. Israel Trevino was twenty-six years old. His wife was expecting their first baby the month he was killed. Leonard Moore Jr., a gruff, thirty-nine-year-old rodeo cowboy, had three kids and had grown up with Amoco and BP: his father had worked for the company for thirty years.

Parus "portrayed to them that there was a huge cultural issue at TXC [Texas City] on safety," one of the lawyers who later interviewed him wrote in the company's internal report. "He thought he delivered the message and he believed that Mr. Manzoni and Mr. Hoffman got the message."

By 2005, the sustained starvation of Texas City's maintenance programs and operations made the refinery an even more dangerous place to work. David Senko managed operations for JE Merit, the contractor stationed in the double-wide by the isom. JE Merit, a subsidiary of the global technical services firm Jacobs Engineering, was one of the world's largest engineering and construction firms, similar to Halliburton's former subsidiary, KBR. BP was JE Merit's largest client, and Senko was an operations manager who oversaw turnaround projects at refineries. He had 750 staff working in the Texas City refinery and countless others at various other refineries.

Texas City, according to Senko, stood out. "I saw right away that the refinery was not in prime shape, put it that way. Rotted-out columns supporting a pipe rack. In some cases, the steel was rotted out completely and hanging there. So it wasn't serving any support," he says. "But those things don't have to be like that. It's just like exercising and eating right as you grow older. There's ways to extend your longevity." When he went to work at Conoco's plants, or Exxon's, the facilities were "gold plated."

In the fall of 2004, shortly after he arrived at the refinery, Senko was driving across the site when he passed a BP crew working on maintenance of a heat exchanger. The exchanger is a large tower that uses hot steam or oil to control the temperature of the products running through the refinery. At its core, installed like a peg in a board near the base of a silo, is a tube bundle that has to be periodically replaced. It's about three feet wide and twenty feet long and it weighs several tons. The crew was trying to get the bundle out of its casing and couldn't get it to budge. They hooked up a string of webbing to the hitch of a big truck used to haul coking waste and, with staff standing up on scaffolding around the bundle, began yanking on it with the full force of the truck's diesel engine.

"It was crazy, just crazy," Senko says in disbelief. "This truck was getting a running start and the wheels were spinning, making black marks on the sidewalk, and then they back up again, put slack in the cable, and *ktsscchh*." Eventually the exchanger slid out, falling twelve feet to the ground and impaling a concrete slab with a deafening crash.

Senko called his crew. "Stay clear from here," he ordered. "You don't want to be a part of this ruckus." He was disturbed by the scene. Instead of reporting it as an incident with severe consequences, the BP workers stood next to it for a photo "like it's a prized swordfish they just caught. They think it's cool."

Don Parus was hearing similar stories, not only about the state of equipment but the judgment of managers running the facilities. By the tenor of the complaints, it seemed as if the plant was approaching some sort of threshold. "Something's really wrong," one worker wrote. "We're tying it together by the seat of our pants. Pre-startup safety reviews here are non-existent. It's a paper exercise. We are not doing the right thing."

"What does it take for us to get into action?" another asked. "Does it take a serious incident like the [March 2004] fire or a fatality? We've had lots of serious near-misses. Big chunks of concrete falling. Bolts on the RHU [residual hydrotreating unit] that fell 60 feet. We've had people overcome with H2S [hydrogen sulfide] fumes—they got dizzy and passed out. But they woke up. So soon it was right back to business as usual."

Changing the course of maintenance, safety, and reliability at Texas City was like steering an oil tanker in a U-turn. It was going to take some time. Parus seemed to have gotten Manzoni's attention, but now he needed to document the specific failings at the plant and understand the extent to which worker confidence had eroded. In November, consultants for the Telos Group began interviewing workers about their attitudes and concerns working at the plant. The group had been hired to assemble a dossier Parus could deliver to Pat Gower and eventually to Hoffman and Manzoni. The idea was to collect the opinions of some eleven hundred workers. Such a document, if it bore out more of the same findings, would help underscore the urgent sentiment Parus had expressed and justify his plans for heavier investment and a higher prioritization of safety.

The message he got from the Telos Group was alarming to him, even after the months he had spent hashing out the details of the refinery's poor repair. The plant's employees, even supervisors and superintendents, were uniformly frustrated and worried. According to one mechanic, "We tell them what goes down in the trenches and they say, 'You don't do that.' They call all of it Risk Management. They tell us, 'Every accident can be prevented.' But how *can* you when you have to work in conditions you know aren't safe but you have absolutely no control over it?" The units, another man reported, referring to the separate process sections at the refinery, are routinely "run to failure," as scheduled maintenance is deferred to massage the books and meet budget targets. "We do not walk the talk."

The report warned Parus of "an exceptional degree of fear of catastrophic incidents at Texas City." Workers complained of a "culture of casual compliance" and said that rules and best practices were routinely violated in order to cut corners. They noted that everything from abandoned asbestos to piping integrity issues had been ignored. They said that worker training was poor and that the maintenance turnarounds, the stopping and restarting of equipment, was often recklessly done. They said that every time management got concerned, it issued new policies to emphasize safety and wrote a bunch of reports, all to no effect.

One of the most trenchant messages was that BP didn't care enough about the individuals who made the company tick. Workers at Texas City ranked what they believed the priorities of the refinery were at the time. Number one on their list: making money. Number two: cost and budget. At the very bottom—dead last—was "people."

Parus, at least, cared greatly about the people in his plant, and it looked as if this might be the guy who could get things to change. The workers, however, warned that his success, and their safety, would depend on a commitment from BP's top executives, and some longevity in the leadership at Texas City. Not only was Manzoni a relative stranger at the plant, but Texas City had been run by six different business unit managers in the last seven years. "We have never seen an organization with such a history of leadership changes in such a short period of time," one of the consultants wrote in the Telos review. The turnover, as in Alaska, led managers to collect short-term bonuses for hitting spending targets and put off major projects because they would almost certainly not be around long enough to be rewarded for their successes, or to suffer the consequences of their failures. The dysfunc-

tion also served to further separate BP's executives from the operations. "The people who have the most influence over the decisions that
determine the safety and integrity management of a particular site are
almost always the most distanced from those conditions," the report
said. "Unless managed, the result is blindness for the senior-most level
on the site as well as those above the site."

Even though his superiors had paid lip service to the notion that
the refinery needed to be improved, without the direct engagement
of high-level management, Parus was never able to get the money.
According to the Telos report, "There is a strong sense that the commitment shown by Don Parus and others is undermined by the lack of
resources to address severe hazards that persist."

One supervisor estimated that by January 2005 Texas City was
$500 million in the hole. That's how much it would cost to catch the
refinery up on all the issues that had already been identified as risks.
"We don't see a plan to sustain what we need and what's going to be
improved. We have warning signs every year. How long until the asset
begins to deteriorate from lack of investment?" he asked. "This place
is set up for a catastrophic failure."

On February 15, 2005, Parus made a presentation on the status of
his efforts to improve reliability at the plant and to incorporate the
Telos findings and learn from them. To his bitter disappointment,
Mike Hoffman didn't come to the meeting. Instead, Parus drove to
Houston that same day to present a small part of the Telos summary
to Hoffman and Gower in person. Hoffman didn't read the report,
according to statements Parus later made to a BP attorney. Instead,
he "wanted a dialogue." Sometime that winter, Parus received an order
from Pat Gower by email: cut yet another 25 percent from his 2005
budget. Parus was livid. "I exhausted every avenue I had to get the
funds," he would later tell BP's investigators. "And it remained a 'no.'"
In a final plea, he sent Gower a list of everything he would need to cut,
hoping that seeing the itemized casualties on the page might change
his boss's mind. Still, he didn't receive the money.

On February 20, a company safety manager wrote in an email, "I
truly believe we are on the verge of something bigger happening."
Three weeks later, a fresh BP business plan document for the compa-

ny's Health Safety Security and Environment group again drew a dark line, predicting: "TCS kills someone in the next 12–18 months."

"That message didn't seem to go to the top, and that was a very, very important disconnect," says Hoyos. She thought that the disintegration of management at Texas City was an early sign that John Browne's reign was troubled. "And once that disconnect happens, it becomes much more difficult for a CEO to run a company."

For Senko's crew, the fear and the frustration were palpable, and it was getting to the point where they couldn't do their job. Senko's site manager, Morris King, was threatening to walk off the job. King, a JE Merit contractor, thought the BP supervisors were riding his crew about "slips, trips and falls"—badgering them for not holding the handrails or not buckling a seatbelt—while ignoring huge operational risks every day. Senko bided his time, knowing JE Merit would complete its job on the Texas City refinery site in a matter of weeks. "I said, 'Morris, focus on the task at hand. Just disregard this. Soon we'll be off to somewhere else.'"

Then, about ten days later, on or about March 20, Senko was at his office in Houston for meetings when he got a call from his project safety manager at the Texas City job, Eugene White. There were lots of loyal, capable people on Senko's staff, but White was the best. He was meticulous, diligent, and thorough. "Everybody was his son and daughter," Senko said. "That's how he acted. He was very conscientious. And he took pride in a safe work environment for his people." JE Merit had just completed one of its safest years ever—even in the midst of this ailing refinery—and it was White who had made it happen.

"Dave, I've had enough," White said. "I'm quitting. I just wanted to tell you first." Now two of Senko's most senior managers each had a foot out the door. Senko walked out of his meeting and got into his car, still talking to White.

"No, you're not quitting," he said. "Just stay right there. I'll give you a call when I get to the gate." The forty-mile drive down I-45 had never felt so slow, but half an hour later, Senko was parked and inside the refinery's fence, where he met White in an open space out on the pad so White could blow off some steam.

"I can't take this any longer," White said. "I'm gonna go back to

North Carolina. Be with my family. I'm tired of this environment. I'm tired of bein' badgered, second-guessed."

Senko thought JE Merit would be finished and off the site by the first week in April. Then he'd transfer White, Morris, and everyone else off to a fresh new assignment. White could have his pick—he could take an easy tour somewhere back east if he wanted. Senko pleaded with him to stay. "Eugene, just hang in there," Senko said. "We have two weeks left."

ON MARCH 23, White was carrying out his morning routine, writing a monthly detailed memo to Senko on JE Merit safety statistics. Not only was he unaware that the raffinate splitter was being restarted, but neither he nor anyone else at the plant had any way of knowing how wrong things had gone the night before.

To restart the isom system, the raffinate splitter tower gets filled with a few feet of raffinate, the heavy hydrocarbons that need to be boiled and distilled to turn into various grades of fuel. There were at least five people on the job: a set of board operators who are technical experts and man the computers and instrument readings from inside a control room, and a set of lead operators who are more senior, and who roam the site, both inside the control room and out and who also juggle other refinery responsibilities. Finally, a BP supervisor oversees those groups. At 2:15 a.m., BP's night-shift lead operator in the satellite control room, Steven Adams, opened the valves and began introducing raffinate into the splitter tower. At the base of the tower, a gauge showed the level of the filling liquid and transmitted the information back to the control room. But the gauge—the only one on the entire tower—only read the liquid level up to nine feet. If the tower were filled beyond that, the liquid line would rise invisibly behind the solid wall of metal, and no one would know.

Normally, a level of 6.5 feet of fluid is maintained in the tower. But during a restart, the crew had the habit of breaking this rule and allowing the raffinate to rise above the 9-foot line out of fear that if the levels dropped too low during the reboot process, it could damage the unit's furnace. At 3:09 a.m., as the liquid hit the 8-foot mark, a high-level alarm sounded in the control room, but Adams let the fluid continue to rise, having been told by his supervisor to ignore alarms because there wasn't enough time to check them anyway. By 3:30 the level indicator showed that liquid had filled the bottom 9 feet of the tower, and, about 20 minutes later, the feed was stopped. Neither Adams nor the board operator on duty at the time could know exactly how high the liquid was, but later estimates put it at about 13 feet, significantly greater than the crew would have expected. The process was nearly done. At 5:00 a.m. Adams updated the night board operator in the control room about his progress. Adams left his shift about an hour early.

The day lead operator who replaced him, Scott Yerrell, arrived at about 6:00 a.m., groggy and ragged from too much work. It was his thirtieth day in a row working a twelve-hour shift. Since Adams had already left, Yerrell checked the night book for notes on where the isom process had left off. Adams had written just one line: "Isom brought in some raff to unit to pack raff with." It said nothing about how high the liquid level was and offered no instructions about how to route the liquid feed through the system when the startup resumed. At 7:15 a.m. the isom's supervisor—who oversees the operators—arrived to take the day shift, more than an hour late. Obviously, he had missed his briefing from the night shift altogether.

At 9:51 a.m., the fresh set of day-shift operators resumed the startup and again began circulating the hydrocarbon feed into the splitter tower, unaware that it had already been overfilled. Because the 9-foot level, and the only gauge to measure it, had long been surpassed, there was no indication of how high the volatile fluids were. A second warning alarm some ways up the tower failed to go off.

Normally, the board operator would begin to regulate the liquid level using an automatic control valve, a yellow-painted steel hand wheel on one of the pipes leading from the isom, sending some of the fluid to a storage tank. But the board operator in the control room that morning had conflicting instructions on where to route the liquid, and so the valve was left closed, blocking the flow of liquid from the tower. It was at about this time that the burners were lit on the furnace, and the grossly overfilled column of low-grade volatile fuel inside the splitter tower began to heat up.

A few moments before 11:00 a.m., the day supervisor, Scott Yerrell, got an urgent phone call about a family medical emergency. He left the refinery in the middle of the isom restart process, and no experienced supervisor was assigned to replace him. This was the sort of staffing redundancy that Gower had weeded out of the organization in 1999, and on March 23 it left a single junior control board operator without supervision running three separate operating units, including the isom, by himself.

That control board operator didn't have a lot to go on, either. The control panel wasn't configured to warn of danger. It didn't show flows into and out of the unit on the same screen, and it didn't calculate the total quantity of liquid in the tower—the most obvious and basic information that can help an operator use common sense. So he watched a single indicator for the isom that told him the level of raffinate was at 8.4 feet and falling. But that indicator hadn't been calibrated. Inside the tower, unbeknownst to anyone at the plant, raffinate continued to flood in, reaching 98 feet—fifteen times the safe level—shortly before noon. As the furnaces burned the fluid inside, the tower continued to heat up, and the level of raffinate continued to rise, topping 100 feet, and then approaching 130.

There were still, at that point, no signs of trouble inside the control room. The tower's indicator told the board operator that the fluid was at just eight feet. And to others outside the control room, there were no indications that anything was taking place at all out on the plant's grounds. The JE Merit crews took off for the lunch tent, where several managers took turns congratulating them for making it through the previous month without a lost man-hour—meaning no injuries. This luncheon had been planned to celebrate JE Merit's exemplary safety record.

At 12:41 p.m. an alarm went off inside the control room as the rising liquid in the raffinate tower compressed the remaining gases at the top. The fluids had reached 148 feet. Responding to the alarm, but having no idea that the tower contained more than 8 feet of liquid, the operators opened an emergency vent valve, controlled by a chain, to release gases into the emergency overflow system. Because they couldn't understand the source of the mounting pressure, they also turned off the two burners in the furnace, believing that this would reduce the gases. Only then did they get concerned about the lack of fluid flow out of the tower. Manually, they opened a release valve at the bottom of the tower to remove some of the liquid and send it to storage tanks. They did not sound an area alarm that would have alerted the workers in the trailers. The liquid they let flow out was scalding hot, and as it passed through a heat exchanger it transferred its warmth to an adjacent pipe, raising the temperature of the fluids still flowing into the tower by another 141 degrees.

It was 1:00 p.m. The JE Merit crews returned from lunch and settled into the double-wide trailer for a normal afternoon of business. In the hallway, a yellow banner with a commitment statement to operational safety had been strung up by grommets, and dozens of signatures were scrawled in blue and black permanent marker. "We, the project team," the banner read, "do hereby commit ourselves to the team by making sure we have a safe project."

White was in one office, probably taking care of paperwork. In another meeting room, at the corner of the double-wide, Dave Leining had shown up for a late-stage project planning session. James Rowe was returning to his office after having had lunch with his wife, Linda. She had just walked over to give him back his eyeglasses, which he had left at the mess tent. And shortly after 1:00 p.m., Kim Smith, an accountant in an office across the lot, stopped by and rapped on the door. She had some bills to get paid, and, rather than wait for someone to stop by and sign the invoices, she had brought them over herself.

About a hundred feet from the double-wide, the hot feed liquid inside the tower started to boil and swell. Like a frothing pot on the stove, the tower full of boiling fuel filled the remaining space at the top and began spilling into a vapor line that runs out the top of the tower and down the side. The weight of the fluid sitting in the full, 145-foot-tall relief line exerted enormous pressure on the emergency release valves at the bottom. At 1:14 p.m. the three emergency valves at the base of the raffinate tower popped open, and nearly 52,000 gallons of fuel shot through the lines toward the isom unit's blowdown drum across the yard. The fluids rushed into the drum, an upside-down funnel with a long stem, or chimney, reaching 150 feet into the air. All the while, the high-level alarm on the raffinate tower never went off, and neither the operators nor the crews in the trailers were ever alerted.

A blowdown drum is like a large cistern, and it is meant simply to catch and hold excess fluid. Its stem serves to distract and release any vapors that come off the fluid held down below. The blowdown drum on the isom lot, however, was far too small for the raffinate tower it was paired with, and so when the fuel flowed into the drum, it quickly filled it. Within minutes, the fuel shot from the top of the stem like a geyser, spraying hot liquid fuel into the open air. "The equivalent of nearly a tanker truck of hot gasoline fell to the ground," according to reports, a boiling, toxic rain. The spilled gasoline pooled around the base of the drum and vaporized in wavy clouds of fumes that spread outward.

8

A TRAGEDY

INSIDE THE JE MERIT TRAILER, the focus that afternoon turned to putting the finishing touches on the contractor's construction job. Leining and six other men were meeting in Morris King's office, in the northeast corner of the double-wide, to discuss punch-list items on their worksheet. It was the closest office in the trailer to the blow-down drum in the northwest corner of the isom block—about 130 feet away. The men talked, unaware of what was taking place outside. Leining sat in a chair with his back to the door, addressing the group. It was wrap-up time. The team had painting left to do, scaffolds to tear down, a patch of insulation to repair, and other odd jobs. "Just some details, not much, you know," says Leining. "Putting identification on pipelines, and little bitty stuff, didn't amount to nothing." The meeting wouldn't last more than thirty minutes.

Outside, twenty-five feet away from the blowdown drum, two men sat in an idling pickup truck. As the spreading cloud of volatile vapor reached them, the pistons of the truck's diesel engine sucked the fuel from the air. The engine revved, overwhelmed with fuel, as if its driver had stomped on the gas pedal and wouldn't let up. Faster and faster, the RPMs increased until the engine whined and the truck began to vibrate, rocking violently from side to side. The men inside tried to shut off the engine, but cutting off the fuel line made no difference to an engine absorbing fuel straight out of the air. Unable to control the truck, its occupants popped open their doors and fled.

Inside the trailer, Leining and the others heard a loud bang that Leining said "sounded like the tailgate on a dump truck." It was a puzzling sound, they thought. The site work was finished, and no one should be delivering more dirt. For a few moments, the men in the trailer carried on their conversation. Then there was a second loud bang. The truck's engine had backfired, sending a short blast of flame from its tailpipe and igniting the cloud of gas that hung on the site.

Leining, unable to explain the second sound in his mind, stood up inside the office and reached for the doorknob. As he did, the ignition quickly consumed all the oxygen in the huge cloud of vapor. For a split second it was quiet. To witnesses, it seemed as if the cloud contracted, Then the ignition rebounded. As the temperature of the gas increased, the gas expanded exponentially, sending a shock wave, like an invisible fist, straight toward Leining and the JE Merit work trailer.

Leining, in midstride, heading for the door, was swept off his feet and slammed to the ground by the shock of the explosion. Then the sound overwhelmed him, like a jet airplane landing, its twin engines thrust full-throttle in reverse, only worse, much worse. Everything around him seemed to levitate. Papers, staplers, and the trash can swirled through the air. Dirt, gravel, and splinters packed into the spaces in his ears. He felt a sudden and tremendous pain. "It was just a real steady, steady constant pressure that was squashing me sideways," he says. Around him, the walls of the trailer disintegrated into tiny pieces, disappearing in a cloud of debris. "I was just trying to hold on and stay calm just so, you know—you hope that it won't last much longer, but then it got black. Total black."

Leining isn't sure what happened to him next. "I don't think I really blacked out. It got real peaceful but it was still black, and then you could kind of see little figurines moving around in the distance," he says. "But it was real peaceful, real black, no pain, no nothing. And so then I started saying a few prayers, wanted the Lord to save me and all that kind of stuff."

Then, in a rush that took his breath away, the searing pain returned. And with it, racing up behind the blast of hot air that had decimated the trailer, a ball of fire that raked the pile of rubble and retreated, like a broom sweeping. The splinters and the papers burst into flame and the trailer was on fire. Leining tried to get a sense of his surroundings. He lay on his right side, buried in a sea of debris from his ribcage down. His right arm stuck out from the mess, but he was lying awkwardly on top of it and couldn't budge it. Jack Skufca, a BP employee, was sprawled across his knees. Then a filing cabinet was piled on top of them, and a desk, and a bunch of busted-up boards and lumber. Leining could see his foot. It was at an odd angle to his knee; his entire leg was wrapped like a pretzel. Somewhere nearby he could hear more explosions, one after another. It was a war zone.

At the city's emergency dispatch center, the switchboard lit up.

"Texas City 9-11 state your emergency," a dispatcher answered.

"A plant just blew up, oh my god, oh my god," a frantic woman shouted.

And across BP's radios the call was no less panicked. "It's the isom! The isom!"

Leining had two radios on his belt, one for talking with his crew and the other for communicating with the refining staff. He tried to reach for one. His left arm was free. He whispered into the radio a plea for help. There was no click, no static, and no reply. The radio was dead.

EVA ROWE was in a gas station, forty-five minutes outside Texas City along Highway 146, when she caught news of the blast. It was playing on a television behind the counter, lodged between the cigarettes and the lottery tickets. The pictures were unrecognizable. News helicopters circled around billowing black smoke that rose from a big, charred scar on the ground. It was like a campfire had been burned on a concrete driveway, except the charcoal smudge stretched for hundreds of yards. The challenge was to understand the scale. When she looked closely she could make out the frames of whole buildings, and remnants of cars. Her heart leapt into her throat. Where were her parents?

Rowe lived in Hornbeck, Louisiana, 211 miles northeast of Texas City, and she was headed to the refinery to spend Good Friday, and then Easter, with her parents. She was twenty, a pretty, spunky girl with a bit of Lynyrd Skynyrd flair. Life for her still revolved around her parents. She would fish with her father and travel with her mother—to see the giant sequoias in California, or Arlington National Cemetery in Washington. The Rowes had raised Eva in Hornbeck; her house was two doors away from her parents', though the Rowes had been staying at the home of her aunt's sister-in-law while they worked at the refinery. Her parents were Eva's best friends. "I tried to call my mom on her cell phone and she didn't answer," she says. "My mother always answers her cell phone. And at that moment, I knew that something really terrible had happened."

The explosion shook the town and sent it flying into action. The blast had whipped across Fifth Avenue South, across the baseball fields at Bremond Park, and down Twenty-third Street, and it had shattered the windows in Wallace Christian's home three-quarters of a mile away. At the Texas City Tavern, a quarter-mile from the BP plant, William Hudson was knocked off his barstool. The ceiling tiles peeled off inside a grocery store across town. Houses rattled in Galveston, five miles across the bay. And at the police station, Chief Ed Lucas told the *Galveston County News* his first thought was "that one of the fire trucks had been driven into the building." The city's alarm sirens went off, and at the high school, the kids were shepherded out of classrooms and into bomb shelters—the way they had drilled for so many times. The hospitals in Texas City and Galveston dispatched their Life Flight helicopters long before they knew whether they would be needed. At the plant, workers fled in all directions. They skipped the magnetic strip swipes at the gate, hopped fences, ran through the auto gates—whatever they could do to get away from the refinery. On the way they passed emergency medical technicians racing toward the scene.

After a few minutes the smoke began to clear on the isom site and Leining could see a row of cars and trucks parked by the trailer—the source of at least some of the explosions he continued to hear. The vehicles were all in flames, and one by one their gas tanks caught fire and blew up. Ralph Dean, an engineer, was stabbing at them with the prongs of a forklift, heroically trying to clear them out of the way so fire trucks could get to the isom. In the trailer, hot cinders were swirling now, falling on Leining's neck and face. He tried the radio again. This time, it worked.

"This is Dave Leining. Help us."

"Who is this?" came the reply.

"We're over here in Morris King's office on the northeast corner, the [JE Merit] trailer," Leining repeated.

"You can't be," the voice came back. "There's nothing left."

"I'm telling you this is where we are, we're here stuck in the trailer. This trailer here's on fire. We need to get somebody over here to put some water on it."

It might have been another twenty-five minutes that passed before Leining felt a spray of water. Dean was one of the first people to reach the scene. His wife, Alisa, and his father-in-law, Larry Thomas, were in the trailer. The men worked toward Leining from the east, because the parts of the trailer closest to the isom had mostly been cleared by the force of the blast. Leining lay in the westernmost corner, piled where the debris caught. He watched as they pulled the other victims from the debris. They found Morris King, who had complained to Senko about the job just a month earlier, still in his chair slumped forward over his desk, or at least what remained of it. Larry Thomas, a project superintendent, was lying on the floor, dead. Ed McKenna, Leining would later hear, survived the blast but got blown completely out of the trailer and was lying in the middle of the street.

When the EMTs finally got to Leining, they had to pull Skufca off first. Skufca was alive, but he could barely talk. His sternum was cracked, and the splintered bone had sliced an artery. The rescue crews didn't know it on the scene, but he was fading quickly, his breath was labored, and his body cavity was filling with blood.

Finally, they began to pull the debris off Leining. When they got to him, he was conscious and talkative. He tried to stand up, and two men pulled him by his armpits to his feet. Leining, a big bear of a man who prided himself on his physical strength, couldn't hold his own weight. He couldn't feel his legs. "I was cut to pieces," he said. His right ankle was torn nearly clear off. His left ankle was also broken. And he had sustained numerous other injuries. The rescuers laid him down on a stretcher and an EMT came over to take his vitals. "We got to get him a lifeline and get him to John Sealy," the man shouted, referring to the critical care unit at the University of Texas Medical Branch in Galveston. Leining was flown there by helicopter.

WHEN EVA ROWE got to town she went directly to her aunt's sister-in-law's house. The flames from the refinery were still shooting into the sky at about the roofline of the houses, and news helicopters circled overhead. On the television, emergency contact numbers ran across the bottom in a banner, and Eva dialed every one. Lots of people were missing, she was told. Nobody could say, yet, what had happened to her parents. She raced next door to her father's friend's home. He also worked at the plant. When he opened the door and saw Eva standing there, he collapsed to the floor. "He had been looking for them since the explosion," she says. "He was so sorry that he couldn't find my parents. So then I knew."

DAVID SENKO was visiting another BP refinery in Carson City, California, about thirteen miles from downtown Los Angeles, on March 23. He had flown there that morning, on an emergency mission of sorts, in large part because that was the place where he believed the safety situation had deteriorated to the most critical level. Like Texas City, Carson—one of the largest refineries in California—had had problems. Between 1999 and 2002, the refinery had had nearly perfect regulatory compliance. It reported no tank problems and made virtually no repairs. The record was so clean that inspectors for the state of California got suspicious. Initially when they tried to enter the refinery, BP locked them out and forced a judge to rule on their access. When they finally won access, they discovered tanker seals with tears nearly two feet long, fuel tank roofs with gaps, and pervasive leaks in all sorts of holding equipment. There were enough major defects to lead to thousands of violations. "They had been sending us reports that showed 99 percent compliance, and we found about 80 percent noncompliance," said Joseph Panasiti, a lawyer with the South Coast Air Quality Management District, the state agency with oversight of the refinery. "Production was put ahead of any kind of environmental compliance." The state sued the refinery for falsifying its inspection records and for extensive air quality violations. BP settled the case in 2004 for $100 million.

When Senko got to Carson, it didn't look as if much had changed. As he walked the site that Wednesday morning, he found his JE Merit crew working deep in trenches full of gasoline vapors and with no clear exit. "It was the worst construction workplace I've ever seen in my life, anywhere in the world," Senko says. The stench of hydrocarbons was so strong it was difficult to breathe. Potential sources of ignition were everywhere: metal tools lying in a heap, running vehicles, "hot work," or welding. The workers didn't wear any sort of protection, and if there was a fire, they couldn't get out. Senko was furious. "I shut the whole job down," he says. "It was deplorable. And I was so mad at my guys for not pushin' back and refusing to work in that condition that I was ready to fire every one of 'em."

This is how lives are lost in the oil business, he thought. Senko was so angry he didn't know where to begin. He paused to collect his thoughts before confronting BP's on-site managers. He wanted a list of names of those responsible, and he wanted them fired. He strode off angrily to the foreman's trailer to give him an earful. It was shortly after 11:30 a.m., California time. Before he reached the trailer, his cell phone rang.

"Dave, where are you?" It was Senko's wife, calling from the University of Houston, where she worked. She had caught the first news reports of the refinery blast on the television in the university cafeteria. She panicked about her husband's whereabouts, having forgotten that he had flown to Los Angeles that morning. "There's been a big explosion. It looks pretty bad. It's on TV," she told him. There was no information yet about what was on fire, or how the explosion had happened. The television just showed a large black ball of smoke rising above Texas City.

"When you get home, tape the news coverage for me," Senko said to her. He ended the call, eager to reach someone who could tell him what was going on. *Well, it's an explosion*, he thought to himself. *Explosions happen all the time at different places.*

Within seconds—before he could place a call—his phone was ringing again. This time it was his boss, Walt Lisiewski, a vice president of JE Merit's parent company, Jacobs Engineering. Lisiewski was in a car, racing from Houston to Texas City. He could see the smoke from the highway, thirty miles out. He didn't know the Texas City job well, and he sounded rushed and panicked. "Dave, I need a list of all the people in the trailer," he barked. He didn't offer any information; he assumed Senko already knew what had happened.

"Where was the explosion?" Senko asked him. But Lisiewski, too, didn't have any information. He cut Senko short. He just needed the names.

At first Senko, stunned, was caught off guard. "We had eighty-four projects ongoing. A couple of big ones. We have a lot of trailers." And Lisiewski needed a list of all the people in *the* trailer? Then, in an instant, the possibilities became clear. The double-wide trailer was an office hub, the largest on the Texas City site. But Senko couldn't offer a straightforward answer. There were people who were normally there, and then there were other workers there at various times: some for meetings, others who'd come just to get a drawing copied or pick up a purchase order. "I'll need to hang up, make a list of the people that I think were in there, given the conditions, and call you back," Senko told him. "I just can't spout 'em off. I mean, that's fifty people."

The two conversations had taken place in less than a minute, and Senko was still in the dark about the magnitude of the explosion. Then the phone rang a third time, with a call from another construction manager at Texas City. "Dave, this is bad," he said. "This is very bad. It's a big explosion at the isomerization unit." The enormity of the situation began to sink in as Senko realized that this was exactly where JE Merit had the greatest number of people.

"Is there anything else you know about it?" he asked, desperate for information.

"There's gonna be fatalities," the manager said. "I think there's four already."

The hair rose on Senko's neck and arms, and a chill ran through him. He had never handled a situation that had grown this serious this fast. Without a word to anyone, Senko walked off the Carson refinery site, jumped in his rental car, and raced towards LAX, still on his phone.

Along the way, he started calling his managers at the isom site. First, he dialed Morris King, the manager of the ultracracker job, on his cell phone. The call went straight to voicemail. Then he called his project superintendent, Larry Thomas. And then Eugene White, the site safety manager. "Those guys always answered," Senko said. But on this day, none of them did. Senko's gut twisted and his mind raced as the lack of news unleashed a nightmare scenario in his mind.

"I got scared," Senko says. "I'm—that doesn't even describe my feeling. I felt helpless. I felt like I needed to be there right then."

Senko was angry that he was stuck in California and angry at the time it would take him to get home. And he was angry about the irony of his having come to attend to what he believed were emergency conditions at the Carson refinery when the explosion rocked Texas City. Senko was wracked with guilt. The explosion happened on a Wednesday—the one day each week he always went to Texas City for the safety luncheon with his crew. He would have been in the trailer.

As he sat in the terminal waiting for his flight, he watched CNN and saw images of the Texas City site for the first time. It was a scene of total devastation. The unthinkable had happened. Except that it shouldn't have been unthinkable at all. The most notoriously dangerous refinery in the United States met exactly the fate that was predicted not only by its own manager, Don Parus, but in years of generalizations and complaints from workers in Texas city, in Alaska, and across the nation in other BP operations.

SENKO LANDED in Houston at 11:00 that night. Despite his instinct to drive straight to the refinery, Lisiewski asked him to go home and try to get a couple of hours' rest. Thursday would be a long day. At home, Senko made himself a stiff drink and watched the news footage. On the TV he saw Don Parus, dressed in a blue BP jumpsuit, his thinning hair slicked back and blond mustache neatly trimmed, solemnly telling a gaggle of reporters that "words cannot express what I'm feeling right now, and what the people of Texas City are also feeling." Parus explained that fourteen people had lost their lives in the fire. Senko knew Parus to be straight-talking and serious about safety at the plant. He looked distraught, and struggled to find the strength to enunciate the words he struggled to utter. It was how Senko himself felt, and when he tried to sleep, he couldn't. At 4:00 a.m. he got up, showered, dressed, and went to the temporary command center that BP had set up at the Texas City refinery.

The center was chaos when he got there. Nearly a day after the blast, nobody had a final count for how many people had died, and dozens were still missing. At 4:30 that morning Eva Rowe had called Jacobs Engineering's corporate offices, asking after her parents. Later that morning, the message was dispatched back from Senko's group at the command center: they had not been found alive. Eva should report to a convention center where people were gathering the next morning for more information. The hunt continued.

Ambulances had taken more than 180 people away from the refinery. Since the workers had evacuated in such desperate haste, they hadn't swiped their pass cards, and the personnel accounting system that tracks who is on- and off-site broke down completely. Senko was still trying to put together a list of who might have been in the double -wide and near the isom operations. But BP had taken complete control of the site, Senko says—no non-company personnel, including contractors, were allowed back in.

The day flew by. Although the body count wasn't final, Senko was the manager who had suffered the greatest losses. Throughout the day, he had almost no interaction with BP management at all, and no one, not Don Parus or anyone else, ever stopped by the JE Merit room in the command center to offer condolences.

Early that morning, BP executives had begun to arrive. John Manzoni was departing for a family skiing vacation when he heard about the refinery. Manzoni, who had a reputation for working tirelessly in Browne's regime, always seemed to be canceling vacations on BP's account. This one was important—time with his two daughters had been rare in recent years, and he was loath to drop his plans. When Manzoni received an email from a friend that morning advising him to go to Texas, he later shot back a curt, almost hostile reply: "We spent the day there—at the cost of a precious day of my leave." It was a human remark in the context of Manzoni's fast-paced personal life, but with bodies splayed across a facility that he was responsible for, it seemed reckless and callous. The comments only seemed to further distance Manzoni from the workers at the company and underscore the coldhearted image of a corporate management disengaged from the blood and tears being shed by workers to make BP tick.

John Browne was the opposite: he wanted to come and his attorneys advised him not to. When the explosion occurred, John Browne was in California at an Intel board meeting. He wanted to go to Texas immediately, but the company's lawyers thought there was little he could do to change the situation. They warned that a visit would thrust him into the spotlight in a situation that could only damage his reputation, and that he might just get in the way. Browne, however, insisted, and by 3:00 a.m. on March 24, he was in Texas City.

But if Browne was as full of emotion as his colleagues say, it didn't show in the press conference he held in Texas City later that afternoon. He was sympathetic, but cool and collected. The news conference was at the city hall. BP's press spokesman stepped to the podium and, as if he were introducing visiting royalty, said: "Mr. Browne has spent the morning visiting our site, talking to the people, learning about the incident, and lending support. He has now agreed to spend a few minutes with you. This is John Browne, our group chief executive."

Browne, wearing a tailored gray suit and an evergreen tie, addressed the crowd from his chair. His hair was carefully combed back and his trademark glasses perched low on his nose. His dapper appearance stood in stark contrast to the weary refinery staff and reporters who had spent the last twenty hours at the refinery site. Browne read slowly from a prepared statement. "Yesterday was a dark day in BP's history," he began. "All of us at BP are very deeply saddened by the loss of life and injury suffered by so many people. I've been with BP for a very long time now—thirty-eight years—and it is the worst tragedy that I've known."

In fact, it was the worst industrial disaster in the United States in decades, and the worst accident in Texas City since the oil tanker blew up at the docks in 1947, killing 581 people.

"What I would say to the families is this," Browne continued. "When something like this happens lots of things are broken. The future is broken. And the past is different from the future. BP can't mend that. Because that is something very human, and something very individual. What we can do, though, is bring our resources to bear to help in whatever way we can do it to make the future feel a bit better. To make tomorrow better than yesterday. . . . BP fully intends to do that. That's what we do."

IT TOOK FORTY hours for JE Merit and BP to account for everybody after the blast, and it wasn't until Friday that the Galveston County chief medical examiner, Stephen Pustilnik, was able to announce who had died. In the meantime, the companies had set up a meeting and information area—separate and away from the incident command center at the refinery—for friends and the families of the victims at the Doyle Center, a large conference space on Fifth Avenue North, a couple of blocks from the refinery, toward the center of town. Senko was designated by JE Merit to be the company's public liaison.

For nearly two days after the blast, officials and family members knew that at least fourteen people had been killed. But there was still widespread confusion over who those victims were. The counts for men and women produced by the refinery didn't square with the names of the dead that city officials had collected. Making matters worse, fifteen people were unaccounted for—one more than the county coroner had at the hospital. Some 180 people had also been treated for injuries, and seven people remained in critical condition.

Senko had the unenviable job of comforting families while withholding what little he knew. The names of the victims couldn't be given to the public or to the families until the coroner had been able to formally identify the bodies. And the coroner wouldn't begin the identification process until officials could square the counts of the victims.

At the Doyle Center, the waiting families each grasped on to the discrepancy in the numbers and held out hope that the fifteenth missing person would be theirs, and that the person would be found alive. "I can't describe the atmosphere, what took place in that Doyle Center. All these people, hopeful, I don't think any of them knew for sure," Senko says. The families each sat around a large, round banquet table, "hoping and praying as hard as they could that it was going to be their loved one that's the fifteenth." Then, sometime on Friday afternoon, the rumors spread that officials had identified a fifteenth victim. Eventually Senko had to tell them the news.

At that point every single family at the Doyle Center knew that their loved one had almost certainly died in the explosion. Only then did the coroner begin to formally identify the bodies. The progress was painstaking and excruciating. JE Merit kept a fleet of vans at the Doyle Center, and each time the coroner, working across town, determined the identity of a body, he would call for the family members to be brought to the hospital. One by one, the families were called out of the crowd, loaded into the vans, and driven five miles to Mainland Hospital to identify the body of a parent, a husband, a wife, or a child. With the help of security reinforcements hired by JE Merit and BP, they fought through throngs of journalists and photographers, and billboard lawyers trying to hock their services.

Eva Rowe was the last person called. She would have to identify her parents' remains. Their bodies had been so badly burned that Eva had to supply the coroner with detailed medical history—for instance, about surgeries her parents had had—in order for him to identify them. When he asked Eva to make the final confirmation, she couldn't do it. "Everybody else had left already," she says. "And I told him I didn't want to. So I gave a DNA sample, and they confirmed everything from there."

For the most part, BP appeared stunned into silence. Senko does not recall that John Browne, John Manzoni, or Mike Hoffman ever visited the Doyle Center or interacted with the families there. In a room full of hundreds of people, Senko remembers a single representative from BP, a manager named Stephen Morris. Morris sat with his head down at a table by himself in the middle of the room, everyone milling around him. "He didn't say a word to anybody that I saw," says Senko. "Didn't say a word to me. I didn't approach him, either. I didn't have any words. I didn't have any good words."

BP representatives did work their way through town, eventually sending community outreach teams to residents' homes in the weeks after the blast and stationing human resources teams at the hospitals. But in the first days they didn't make an impression. In fact, says Senko, reflecting on those days with the victims' families, "I don't recall anybody from BP ever expressing any condolences, accepting any blame or any of that." The company's inaction was especially hard for him to comprehend because he took the tragedy personally.

The grounds of the refinery where the isomerization unit had once stood were unrecognizable, a heap of blackened, twisted steel arched over the scorched skeletons of vehicles. Where the trailers had once stood, a mess of pipes and rails stuck at odd angles into the air. When Dave Leining awoke in his hospital bed and saw the images of the refinery on television, he thought the cameras were filming the wrong place. "Them stupid reporters, they're taking pictures of the coker," he told his wife. The coker unit, where residual fuel is broken down into a gas, is always black and charred. She turned to him. "You think that's the coker?"

Eleven of the dead were on Senko's crew, including Eugene White, and the losses tortured him. No matter how he thought about it, he came back to the senselessness of it all. It was true, there had been no warning of the isom reboot; and there had been serious safety lapses. But why were the trailers located so close to that equipment in the first place? The JE Merit team had nothing to do with the isomerization unit; and the job had almost been finished. Senko had held many of his workers at the Texas City site for a few extra days even though he hadn't needed them, just in case something came up. "They weren't even working," he said. "I just was holding them in case I needed them during startup in the next week."

The loss of White, in particular, less than a week after Senko had worked so hard to persuade him not to go home to North Carolina and to finish up the job in Texas, was haunting. Years later, Senko still held on to a final 12:30 p.m. email White had sent him. White had stayed behind and missed the safety luncheon so that he could deliver Senko a promised report of the team's safety stats. "I can't get rid of it," he says, replaying the scene in his head. "He punched that button [sent the email] for *me* and then zipped down to the lunch tent to be a part of the ceremony. That was a tough one, because he wasn't there for Jacobs. He wasn't there for BP. He was there just because I asked him to be there."

In later conversations, Senko eulogized each of the people he had lost. He thought about Morris King, his project manager, and Ryan Rodriguez, his electrical superintendent, who was twenty-eight years old and had his whole life ahead of him. Art Ramos survived as a medic in the worst years of the Vietnam War only to die in Texas City. Senko still spoke about James and Linda Rowe in the present. "They're still in love. Man and woman that traveled together and worked together." Lorena Cruz-Alexander, Susan Taylor, Glenn Bolton, and Larry

Thomas were all dead, as were four other contractors working with BP who didn't work for Senko: Larry Linsenbardt, Rafael Herrera, Daniel Hogan, and Jimmy Hunnings. Most perplexing to Senko was the loss of Kim Smith, who had run by the JE Merit trailer to pick up an invoice. "To my knowledge, that was her first and last visit," Senko says. "And I don't know why that happens. I was spared—and she wasn't. I was there all the time. She was there once."

More than a week after the accident, Senko was finally allowed back on the grounds of the isom. He was picking through the debris where the double-wide trailer had stood when his foot hit a white dome of plastic. He picked it up. It was one of the hardhats his crew wore for protection on the site, and it was crushed. One side was caved in, and the edges had melted into a solid ball of plastic. Senko kept the hardhat, stowing it away on a shelf in his garage at home, and he kept the item he came upon next as well.

Lying under a pile of broken wood and debris was the yellow edge of the safety banner that had been hanging in the hallway the morning of March 23. It was in tatters, but some of it survived. Each person on the project had signed the banner in black permanent marker, and Senko held the sheet of plastic fabric in his hands and read the names. In places, holes had burned through, and charred black rings spread from them, obscuring the signatures. One entire side of the banner had burned clear off. Senko fought back tears. For the most part, he observed, the names that were legible were those of the workers who had survived the blast. None of the names of those who had died were still on the banner.

AT FIRST, in the months after the blast, BP resisted the inevitable judgments and conclusions about the conditions at the Texas City refinery. The company's president of North American operations, Ross Pillari, announced that the blast had been caused by operator error, and said it would never have happened if not for the mistakes of a few individuals. "The core issue here is people not following procedures," Pillari said. Don Parus was placed on leave. Steven Adams, the night lead operator, and Scott Yerrell, the supervisor, were fired, along with four other employees.

BP, as it had so many times in Alaska, in Grangemouth, and else-where, conducted its own internal investigation. It put its chief oper-ating officer for U.S. fuels at the time, John Mogford, in charge of it. The findings were made available in December 2005. The report also pointed the finger at the refinery's employees, blaming them for not using the equipment properly and for killing their innocent col-leagues. "Failure to take emergency action resulted in loss of contain-ment that preceded the explosion," the report stated. "These were indicative of a failure to follow many established policies and proce-dures. . . . It is not clear why those aware of the process upset failed to sound a warning."

The report continued, "The team found no evidence of anyone con-sciously or intentionally taking actions or decisions that put others at risk." In a statement that must have mystified people like Don Parus, who had been shouting from the rooftop about the problems at his refinery for years, the Mogford report stated, "Given the poor vertical communication and performance management process, there was nei-ther adequate early warning system of problems, nor any independent means of understanding the deteriorating standards at the plant." It was as if BP management had never heard of any of the repeated pleas for help and funding in the years before the isom accident.

Faced with the blame for the incident, the operators who filled the ill-fated raffinate tower erupted in anger and frustration. How could they be blamed for equipment that not only didn't work, but that had been designated for repairs and never fixed? The alarms meant to warn them when the liquids were overfilled never sounded. The gauge in their control room showing the fuel level registered a *drop* in flu-ids even while the fluids were rising. "They tried to put the blame on lower-level workers and make them scapegoats," the regional director of the United Steelworkers, Gary Beevers, told the *Houston Chronicle*. The six employees who were fired after the blast—the ones manning the raffinate startup and their supervisor—sued BP for libel and wrong-ful dismissal. They eventually settled for an undisclosed sum.

The company was called out on its attempt to avoid responsibil-ity by its workers, the press, and the federal government, which lam-basted its executives for not assuming blame. While it was quick to investigate and transparent with its findings, BP's report never asked who had hired the "irresponsible" workers. Who had trained them? Who had managed them? And did BP executives really believe, as the lack of any other explanation would suggest, that these hourly workers had made key decisions such as where to site the JE Merit trailer on the refinery property? An editorial in the *Houston Chronicle* said that BP was "going through the motions" and shirking accountability. It gave the company an "A for effort, F for a grade."

Texas City could have been John Browne's *Exxon Valdez*. But it was not—at least not in the sense that the company would learn, and begin to address the root causes leading to the disaster. In fact, the Texas City disaster laid bare a sort of learning disability on the part of John Browne and BP's senior executives. The company had had the refinery blast at its massive facility in Grangemouth a few years before, following three separate other occasions on which massive leaks and over-flows led to fires and shutdowns in large portions of the plant. Those incidents were similar to the Texas City accident—and the buildup of circumstances that preceded it—except that by some stroke of luck they didn't culminate in any loss of life.

After Grangemouth, too, there was an investigation, as was the case after every BP incident, and a major report was issued by Scottish officials. The report, issued in 2003, said that BP had become dissoci-ated from its own process safety management and displayed inatten-tion to detail that could reap a company-crippling, deadly disaster. It laid out a set of suggestions that, had they been implemented in BP's global operations, would almost certainly have helped prevent the accident at Texas City, if not others. Yet little happened, even while John Browne consistently preached about safety and environmental care. To many, it was beginning to seem that he couldn't square his rhetoric with reality.

On March 24, the day after the Texas City accident, when Browne was asked about this pattern and the previous string of incidents at the Texas refinery, he was obstinate in his reluctance to connect the dots. It had not been an accident waiting to happen, he said. "There is no stone left unturned . . . there is no limit to the amount of the activity that we have taken in Texas City to make it a very safe plant and it is a very safe plant. I think these events are unrelated," he said. "There have been a few, and we regret each one."

He continued, "These tragic incidents have taken place, but behind that the safety record for this refinery has improved considerably. In fact the OSHA recordable incident rate has come down by a factor of four over the last three years. So the safety-first culture is definitely there. . . . We don't produce day-to-day, just to make a quick buck irresponsibly, we just don't do that sort of thing."

Yet when the Mogford report was released, parts of it were so similar to the reports issued after the previous investigations that for some, it was difficult to remember which incident was being written about. "The working environment had eroded to one characterized by resistance to change and lacking [sic] of trust, motivation and a sense of purpose. . . . Process safety, operations performance and systemic risk reduction priorities had not been set and consistently reinforced," the Texas City report read.

A *Houston Chronicle* investigation at the time found that BP had far more worker deaths at its refineries in the United States than any other company, and not just in Texas City. They happened in Whiting, Indiana, and in Washington, too. There had been seven fatal accidents since 2000, and the company was responsible for more than a quarter of all the refinery deaths in the United States. BP had ten times more fatalities at its plants than Exxon, its closest rival.

"They should've learned some major lessons. And they are very slow in learning their lessons. BP hasn't quite put it together yet," said Jordan Barab, deputy assistant secretary of labor at OSHA. "They profess to be very interested in safety. They want to be leaders in process safety management. They're having a little trouble translating that down to the ground."

Certainly, BP made efforts to underscore its commitment to safety, and neither Browne nor anyone else in management explicitly shunned its importance. Yet given one more opportunity, they again showed no signs of making safety and environmental controls a high enough priority at the company's oldest and riskiest properties. As more and more incidents occurred, attention turned from what BP promised to be doing to what it didn't do and didn't say. It became harder and harder, staring at the masterpiece that John Browne was painting, to ignore what wasn't there: a rigorous intent to evaluate the risks inherent in this dangerous business and to take every possible precaution to anticipate and prevent deadly and environmentally catastrophic accidents.

FOR JEANNE PASCAL, the Texas City disaster and the response to it laid bare an awful truth about BP: that the problems she was documenting in BP's Alaskan operations were not unique to that operating group, and that the issues there were symptoms of a disease that had spread throughout the entire BP system—nationally, perhaps even globally. The night after the explosion at the refinery, in her home outside Seattle, Pascal had broken down in tears. The blast should have been averted, she told her husband, Dallas Swank. "She was fairly certain that when the dust settled they were going to find out that this was due to lack of maintenance and all the same things happening in Alaska," he said.

As information was gradually released, Pascal saw similarities between her experience and what had happened in Texas. Workers and managers at the Texas City plant had been raising alarms eerily similar to those she was hearing in Alaska. The blowdown drum maintenance in Texas had been explicitly deferred in almost exactly the same way that BP Alaska's executives kept putting off replacement of the fire and gas detection systems and holding back on pipeline corrosion treatments. When workers in the Texas refinery reported injuries and safety concerns, they too were met with retaliation by the company. Finally, workers in Texas also used the phrase Pascal repeatedly heard from Marc Kovac to describe what was happening to the company's pipelines and equipment on the North Slope: "run to failure."

She found the parallels deeply discouraging. In Alaska she had affected little change, and even after internal investigations such as the Vinson & Elkins report, things seemed only to deteriorate further. Just as 1,200 Texas workers had warned Don Parus in 2004, Kovac, Pascal, and others worried that a spill or an explosion in Alaska was inevitable. Was a Texas City–like blast in Alaska the sort of event it would take to get BP Alaska in line?

Later that summer, Pascal emailed Kovac: "If a catastrophe has to occur to get others to belly up to the plate, it's regretful, but it may be necessary before real change will take place. In the meantime, keep on trucking. I think this is win-able—the issue is at what cost."

IN TEXAS, in mid-2005, the conversation was turning to a more literal sort of cost. The workers, for their part, believed that BP should pay, and they sued. The families of people killed or injured filed 1,300 law-suits. In all, 4,000 claims were made against the company, and, with $2.1 billion set aside, BP began systematically settling them. Some of the settlements were high-profile, making it into the local papers, and others were not. Some never even made it to lawyers because BP began seeking out victims and their families preemptively, offering sums of money in exchange for a signed waiver that often not only released the company from any future liability but bound the workers and their families to silence. It was standard BP practice, and common through-out the oil industry, causing critics to characterize the settlements as hush money. Soon, the silence would be bought from nearly everyone with anything damaging to say about the company.

Neither the cost of the silence nor the damage to the refinery would do much to slow the growth of the BP profit machine. When the company issued its annual report three and a half months after the explosion, it devoted just one paragraph in five hundred pages to the Texas City tragedy; and it claimed that the event wouldn't make a dent in BP's profits for the coming year. "BP has finalized or is in the process of negotiating settlements in respect of fatalities and personal injury claims arising from the incident," the financial filing states. "BP cur-rently expects that the total amount of these settlements will not be material to the results of operations or financial position for the year 2005."

BP had $285 billion in revenue in 2004 and $17 billion in prof-its. The Texas City refinery had been transformed from money-pit for the company into one of the corporation's most profitable units, contributing nearly $1 billion to the bottom line that year. "It appears they are taking their moral standards from the balance sheet, which has become the soul of this corporation," Rob Ammons, an attorney representing some of the blast victims, told the *Houston Chronicle*. "BP says this is only going to affect them for one quarter. But the victims and the neighbors and the taxpayers in this community have to live with this damage for the rest of their lives."

Years earlier, BP managers had established, in general terms, the cost of an industrial accident to the company and the value of each BP worker who might be at risk. A slide presentation from an internal BP workshop on risk analysis used a crude fairy-tale analogy, likening the company's own decisions about whether to institute safe and environmentally sound processes to the Three Little Pigs' decision about whether to build a house of straw or of brick. The brick might be more sensible, but it was also more expensive, and would only protect against a rare, unlikely scenario. "The big bad wolf blows with the frequency of once per piggy lifetime. . . . If the wolf blows down the house, the piggy is gobbled. . . . A piggy considers it's worth $1000 to save its bacon," the BP risk analysis document said. The implication was that some degree of process safety risk was acceptable, since it balanced the cost with the probability of an accident.

In November 2000, shortly after taking over the Texas City plant from Amoco, Robert Mancini, one of BP's Health, Safety and Environment representatives, conducted a "fire and explosion" risk assessment for the company's refineries that in hindsight seemed to show that the company knew exactly what sorts of consequences it was toying with in Texas City. "An immediate motivation for this study was the desire to find a risk basis that could be used to set priorities for performing external process safety audits," the report said. The report set out the "expected value" of certain risks, with the aim of figuring out what the company could afford.

For the isomerization unit, for example, the assessment stated that the cost of the risk to its properties and workers spread out over the number of years it would take for an accident to happen was about ten thousand dollars a year. If taken literally by plant managers, that meant it would be cheaper to take the risk than it would be to invest more than ten thousand dollars in maintenance of operations per year. It quantified people, too—not just the facilities—by calculating how many workers would be in close proximity to operating units. To flesh out its scenarios, BP set a price tag of $10 million on each employee's head.

Even within BP, the measure raised eyebrows. "COST OF A

HUMAN LIFE. BP embraced the principle that these costs can be specified for the purposes of cost benefit analysis," Mancini wrote to a group of BP managers in an email. "Amoco was generally unwilling to take this step. This is more a cultural issue than a technical one, but one that will have to be addressed."

WITH ITS COSTS so clearly estimated, BP sought to settle its accounts after the refinery explosion. It began mailing checks to the homes of the fifteen workers who had died. When the letter arrived in Eva Rowe's mailbox five weeks after the blast, she wasn't sure what to expect. She hadn't heard so much as a word from BP since the accident—not from the community relations team that was supposed to visit and console the victims' families or anyone else. She was angry and hurt. "My life ended that day," she told reporters at the time. "I feel like they murdered my mother and father." Couldn't someone at the company at least have picked up the phone and acknowledged her loss?

Rowe tore open the envelope. It looked like a form letter. Or at least, if it were written to her, it wasn't penned by someone who cared very much what he or she was writing. "Dear Ms. Rowe. . . . On behalf of BP America, Inc. and our employees, I want to extend our sincere condolences on the death of your loved one, James." She wondered whether her father's name had been inserted into a blank. She kept reading, an incredulous anger beginning to well up inside her. "The explosion and fire on March 23 was a tragedy, and we are very sorry for the enormous consequences it has had on you and your family. . . . enclosed is a check for $25,000." She got all the way to the end and didn't see it: where was her mother's name? Had they forgotten her? "This sucks," she said aloud.

The letter was signed not by any senior member of management but by the human resources director, and it left a phone number for Eva to call if she had any questions. *Five weeks and nobody from BP can pick up the phone?* The letter was attached to an oddly chilling receipt, as if Rowe could use it in filing her taxes: "Invoice date: 4/28/05 . . . payment to family member of Texas City."

Soon after, BP came with its settlement offer. The $25,000 check was just to tide her over. BP had been paying out undisclosed sums to all the families, generally understood to be somewhere in the $10 million-a-head range that the risk analysis had laid out. "To receive that, I had to sign a confidentiality agreement saying I would never talk about anything I knew that happened there ever again in my life," Eva says. BP wasn't even offering Rowe $20 million. It wanted to pay a little less. Rowe has never disclosed the amount. "Call it a two-for-one deal," she says wryly.

It was never about the money, though. "People had already signed settlements and confidentiality agreements that they would never speak about what happened, to any media, or speak against BP. And I knew that was something that I would never do, that I would never sign something to say that I wasn't allowed to say how I feel about them or the accident," Rowe says.

"BP knew the risks they were taking and they did nothing," she says. "They were small repairs that would've cost their company a hundred thousand dollars for a flare system that would've prevented the explosion. They didn't do that."

By November 2005 she was the only one left out of the fourteen families who hadn't accepted a settlement with BP. Some of the others had signed simply because the negotiations took so long, with no income coming from the family member who had died; they needed the money to pay bills. At first Rowe hated the idea of suing BP. It wasn't how she thought. Then she resolved to fight. "I realized, we have to know what happened," she says. "And if we just take a settlement, and sign a piece of paper, we'll never know, and nobody else will ever know it, either." She planned to meet John Browne and his global corporation in front of a jury.

9

CODE BLACK

On July 8, 2005, three and a half months after the Texas City blast, Hurricane Dennis swept across the Gulf of Mexico. The storm battered the platforms floating in the middle of the gulf with 140-mph winds and 60-foot waves. Several thousand workers stationed on 350 rigs across the gulf had been evacuated. When the clouds cleared, BP's newest and most important venture, the monstrous but still incomplete Thunder Horse platform, appeared to be sinking.

Thunder Horse was the world's largest semi-submersible offshore oil platform, offering the acreage of three football fields, its broad, flat deck sitting some twenty stories above the water. It had two derricks, capable of drilling—and producing—twenty-three wells from the same floating station. It represented the latest in offshore drilling technology, where a platform floats atop four large towers, connected underwater by pontoons, like the skids on a helicopter. Technically, the floating facilities are marine vessels, ships that can sail into position. There, the ship's towers and pontoons are flooded with water to partially sink it until ninety feet of it is below the surface. This allows enough stability for it to handle the open waters of the North Sea and the deep Gulf of Mexico. While the accidents at Texas City and in Prudhoe Bay and their attendant problems could be blamed on outdated operations, Thunder Horse represented the latest investment and most modern efforts by BP to aggressively expand its operations.

The rig was designed to drill in the deepest waters being explored at the time. Thunder Horse was supposed to withstand a 100-year hurricane event. BP, in a joint venture with Exxon, had spent $1 billion to build it, and it was a veritable floating factory, complete with the largest floating power station in the world, capable of generating enough electricity to run 80,000 homes. Daily, Thunder Horse was expected to pump 250,000 barrels of oil and 200 billion cubic feet of natural gas, an amount that would double BP's production in the gulf and roughly equal the company's production from the North Slope.

Wall Street couldn't wait for Thunder Horse to come online, and the company's executives, even while writing off billions in expenses from Texas City, built expectations that the new platform would yield enough profits to put BP back on track. Projects like Thunder Horse were meant to be the company's savior. When BP committed to an explicit strategy of underinvestment in what it called its legacy assets—the aging oil field in Alaska and refineries like Texas City—it was so that the company could invest more efficiently in new technology and fresh exploration and expand BP's opportunities in places like Russia and Azerbaijan and, most importantly, far beneath the world's oceans. That's what Browne had laid out in 1989 and had channeled BP's resources to ever since.

Since 2000, while BP aggressively cut budgets in Alaska and Texas City, it simultaneously invested $50 billion in exploration, as much as half of it targeted on the Gulf of Mexico. In 2005 alone, right after Don Parus was denied a maintenance increase of a few hundred thousand dollars that he argued would save lives at Texas City, BP spent more than $10 billion on exploration, a big chunk of it developing the Thunder Horse field, about 150 miles southeast of New Orleans. The gulf was fast becoming the vanguard of the world's oil development fields—for every oil company. And yet it was universally characterized as one of the most difficult and most complicated. The deepwater deposits increasingly targeted were high-pressure, high-temperature oil fields unlike anything the industry's top-notch geologists had ever seen before. And in the gulf BP would deploy its most technologically advanced and modern systems to tap into those deposits in new ways.

"There were many technology gaps to fill when we started out, and we've pushed beyond existing limits on many fronts," noted an article in one of BP's corporate publications. "The result is a world-class engineering achievement, a pioneering step akin to those needed in the past to open up the North Sea or the North Slope of Alaska, which will be of benefit to BP's future deepwater projects and to the wider industry." BP put all its chips down on these projects and enjoyed one success after another in fields the U.S. Department of the Interior classified as "deep water," meaning in depths of more than 1,000 feet. It had begun pumping a field it called Pompano in 2,200 feet of water just southeast of the mouth of the Mississippi River in 1994. By 1999 BP was farther east and deeper, pumping 60,000 barrels of oil a day in 3,200 feet of water from a development called the Marlin field, 125 miles off the coast of New Orleans. And in January 2005 it reached first oil on the western side of New Orleans, about 100 miles south of Grand Isle, Louisiana, in a moderately deep field it called Mad Dog, in 4,400 feet of water. By the company's estimates, as much as half of its global exploration budget was being poured into the gulf. Even as conditions at Texas City worsened, deepwater exploration was booming. "It was a marvelous time" for the offshore oil industry in the Gulf of Mexico, BP's chief of offshore development, David Eyton, told an offshore technology conference in early 2005. Deepwater drilling in the gulf, he said, was "a comparatively high-risk, high-reward arena, and not a place for the fainthearted." Rarely, he added, had BP experienced "such an exciting period of concentrated production growth."

It wasn't just BP. The industry's progress was heady, and as the efforts got increasingly aggressive, the federal regulatory agency charged with overseeing the progress and keeping it in check, the Minerals Management Service (MMS), was equally enthusiastic. A report from the MMS had called 2005 "an exciting year for exploration." Deepwater wells were producing twenty times what a shallow-water well was yielding. Ninety-four new gulf wells had been drilled by the industry in 2004, thirty-six of them in deep water. More wells had been drilled in water depths exceeding 7,500 feet than ever before, and fifteen of those exploratory wells had struck oil.

In ten years, production had increased fivefold. By March 2005, there were 107 deepwater wells producing nearly a million barrels of oil a day. The gulf had come to supply nearly a quarter of the nation's domestically produced oil, and deepwater offshore drilling, whether in the Gulf of Mexico or Brazil or off the coast of Africa, was fast becoming the promise of the future for the entire oil industry. Industry experts estimated that within a decade, half of the world's new production would come from deepwater wells. It was exciting to think that so much of that lay in U.S. territory.

In the Gulf of Mexico, BP seized the lead. It snatched up leases faster than any other oil company, setting a course toward becoming not only the largest leaseholder in the gulf but the largest producer; and it had three promising new high-profile fields expected to come online in 2006 that could rival the promise of the ANWR. As gulf drilling became the epicenter of BP's operations, it began to take the mantle from Alaska as the company's primary and most important training ground. When John Browne was a young engineer, he was sent to Alaska to cut his teeth in a real exploratory oil field. Future executives—Browne's Turtles, including Tony Hayward—would have to prove themselves in the gulf.

To the extent that there was any thought given within BP to the strains being experienced on the polar ends of North American operations, in Alaska and Texas, it was understood that those operations were troubled because they were old and undermaintained. Perhaps there was even a sense that they were being sacrificed so that the company could afford to expand in places like the gulf. There was little comprehension that, whatever the disease plaguing those operations was, it might also affect the company's newest and slickest operations. And there was also little acknowledgment that what they were doing—drilling deeper and deeper into previously inaccessible reaches beneath the ocean—came with inherent new risks of its own.

Yet there were signs. In 2000 the Minerals Management Service had warned in an environmental impact study that accidents in the Gulf of Mexico were not uncommon. Blowouts, where underground pressure bursts through an oil well's structure and spews oil or gas uncontrollably, had occurred about 151 times over the past twenty-five years in the gulf, or once every two months. The MMS said that in a worst-case scenario if a well blew out underwater it might not be controllable. The study was a review of operations for Shell, not BP, but its findings applied to all drillers and served as a strategy document for allowing drilling to go deeper into the gulf. "Blowouts can occur during any phase of development," the report warned. "Blowouts occur when improperly balanced well pressures result in sudden, uncontrolled releases of fluids from a wellhead or wellbore. . . . . Of particular concern is the ability to stop well control loss once it begins, thus limiting the size of a spill. Regaining well control in deep water may be a problem since it could require the operator to cap and control well flow at the seabed in great water depths and could require simultaneous fire-fighting efforts at the surface. . . . In the event that a subsea blowout occurs, the intervention that would most likely be employed to regain control of the well would be the drilling of a relief well. If the outer casing strings are breached, the likelihood of a successful surface intervention would be minimal."

BP had had several brushes with fate in the gulf already. In August 2002, during a drilling operation, a well suddenly began spewing mud, gas, and oil uncontrollably. The rig was abandoned, and the diverter system capturing the flow caught fire, burning for hours before it was brought under control. Then, just three months later, another rig was evacuated after a faulty cement barrier inside the well's casing gave way. Gas blew out for eight days, and the well had to be cut off before the situation was brought under control.

The close calls even raised questions about whether BP was pushing too hard, too fast. In his 2005 conference presentation, Eyton struck a tone of caution. "If we've learned anything so far about the deep water, it is that it contains surprises," he said, and he lamented that perhaps BP was being so aggressive it might not be able to absorb the lessons from experiences gained along the way. "We find ourselves developing systems for 10,000 feet of water before the lessons of working in 6,000 feet of water are fully learned and identified." Eyton's team, by his own account, was constantly under pressure to go farther, faster, and the pressure came from the company's exploration business. A possible source was that group's chief executive, Tony Hayward, a relatively young and highly ambitious Turtle with an eye on refocusing BP away from issues like climate change and "green-washing"—Browne's relentless efforts to recast BP the oil company as an environmental steward—and back on its fundamental strength of producing oil.

In this context, Thunder Horse was an extraordinary gamble and a technological leap that needed to pay off. At 2005 oil prices, it would earn the company more than $18 million a day in revenues, producing nearly as much as the entire North Slope of Alaska combined. But the project was late, and BP had promised its investors that it would have Thunder Horse operating by the end of the year.

On the morning of July 11, the world awoke to images of BP's golden egg listing precariously in the aftermath of the hurricane; one of the platform's four towering pontoons was nearly completely submerged. The deck and all the enormous industrial facilities atop it were tilted at more than twenty degrees, dipping one end into the waves of the gulf. It was a stunning and disturbing site. Newspapers called it BP's "leaning tower."

Most rigs in the gulf were built to sustain a Category 2 storm. Thunder Horse was built to handle 147-mph winds and 100-foot waves—a Category 4. It was supposed to be far sturdier than most oil rigs. And Hurricane Dennis, for all its might, had scarcely nicked the heart of the drilling waters. Virtually none of the other drilling facilities in the gulf had sustained any damage at all. So what had gone wrong on Thunder Horse?

BP raced to right the rig and to save it. Engineers pumped water out of the enormous legs of the platform, delicately adjusting to keep the teetering 55,900-ton mass from toppling over. Divers and submarines were sent down to inspect the hull, in the expectation of finding gashes or other damage, perhaps where floating or loose debris had been rammed into it by the currents of the storm. But no damage was found.

At a July 26 news conference to announce BP's second-quarter earnings, Browne told analysts that Thunder Horse wouldn't start producing oil anytime soon, certainly not in 2005. Tony Hayward explained that the hull and the pontoons that supported it had been flooded. The flooding had damaged cabling and electronic instruments and wiring throughout the platform. "There is no damage to the subsea equipment, there is no damage to hull or pontoon . . . there does not appear to be any structural damage," he said. But if there was no obvious damage that had caused the rig to flood, then what had gone wrong? Hayward did not describe the discoveries that explained the flooding, and the cause of the near-disaster appeared to be a mystery.

Three months later, on October 25, the company and the U.S. government confirmed that the near-sinking had had little to do with the hurricane at all. "It was not storm-related, but was caused by a design weakness," Browne was quoted as saying in news reports. Thunder Horse was the victim of a series of straightforward assembly errors, followed by lack of emergency planning and preparedness. Alarms sounded and were ignored, equipment wasn't checked, and backup systems weren't in place.

First, when the crew learned that they would evacuate to prepare for Hurricane Dennis on July 8, they isolated and closed the valves that control the flow of seawater in and out of the pontoon base to keep the platform level and stable. Power to the valves was cut off so that they could not reopen. But as they evacuated, multiple alarms on Thunder Horse sounded, and instruments indicated that more than eighty of those valves were moving, meaning there was enough residual power on the rig to allow the valves to open anyway, and for water to pass through them. The alarms were ignored.

In the days that followed, water rushed into and out of ballast tanks on the rig's pontoons, sending the platform listing precariously to the starboard side and then, just hours later, all the way back to the port side. Check valves in the bilge—valves that only allow fluids to move in one direction—would have helped shed some of the water, but an MMS investigation found that the engineers building the ship had installed them backward. Instead of shedding water, the system took on 15,000 metric tons of it, almost enough to drag the entire vessel underwater.

When the water rushed into the manned corridors of the rig, it slapped up against plastic seals that surround cables and electrical wiring as they go through the bulkhead, a wall that has to remain watertight. The seals failed in large numbers, allowing water to flood through the bulkhead. The investigation found that these seals also were improperly installed.

There are standard inspections and processes that could have mitigated each of these problems, but they weren't performed, according to the government report. No one had noticed that the ballast valves couldn't be completely closed; BP had skipped what's called a hazards operability review, a standard test to consider the worst-case scenario, and no standard operating procedures were ever developed to shut the system down. When the ill-fated cable seals were installed in the bulkhead, no one ever visually inspected them, as is recommended practice. Thunder Horse was also designed to have a remote monitoring system that could allow the ballasts and the flooding problems to be controlled from Houston, but the system was not completed in the shipyard, and it hadn't been finished once the rig was put out to sea. Any one of these processes might have stopped the cascade of events that nearly sank the rig.

Just months after the refinery blast, while investigators still sifted through the wreckage in Texas City, BP had suffered another serious and very public setback. Repairing Thunder Horse would cost some $240 million. The company's stock dropped, and investor confidence was rattled. To those watching closely, it seemed that no aspect of BP's business was immune to risk. "Having always seemed so competent when compared with its arch-rival Shell in recent years," wrote London's *Daily Telegraph*, on October 29, 2005, "it must have been galling for Lord Browne of Madingley to now admit that Thunder Horse, the world's largest oil platform based in the company's main profit centre, and a key part of BP's growth strategy to boot, will not be operational until the second half of next year."

The Thunder Horse incident was a different kind of accident for BP. It seemed to have more to do with haste than budgets, and the company's advocates were quick to say that this debacle had nothing in common with the explosion at Texas City. Nonetheless, the question of whether some deeper management deficiency might underlie both incidents was raised. The budget pressures that caused the corner-cutting at Texas City and stoked the rush to get Thunder Horse up and running hadn't gone away, and BP took a onetime charge of $2 billion in 2005 as a result of those two disasters—not counting lawsuits and legal payouts.

ON MARCH 2, 2006, in the pitch-black predawn of Alaska's early spring, a BP field worker and his manager raced out by truck to check on a report they had received of a strong stench of hydrocarbons along the access road paralleling a major oil transit line.

The line, coming from the far western end of the Prudhoe Bay drilling area, transports as much as 70,000 barrels of crude oil each day from Gathering Center 2—a processing facility at which gas and water are removed to separate pure oil—toward the start of the Trans Alaska Pipeline. Along the way it connects with pipelines coming from each of the field's five other gathering centers, and flows through a juncture point called Skid 50 and down into the first facility along the Trans Alaska Pipeline, called Pump Station 1. From there oil is shipped south to Valdez.

The transit line had already shown some signs of wear. In 1998 a corrosion test had been conducted by a "pig," a robotic bullet-shaped device full of electronic sensors that is run through the line to measure the pipe metal's thickness. The pig had found that in some places the pipe walls had already lost 30 to 50 percent of their thickness. As a result, a section of pipe attached to the line had been "de-rated," meaning that it had failed to pass the test for normal operations and that oil would only be allowed to run through it under lower pressure. No more pigging analysis was conducted, though the state recommends that it be done every two years, and then, in 2005, a series of external inspections found that the line seemed to be corroding much faster than in the past. Six specific vulnerable locations were identified. One of them was near where the two men now scoured the snow for a leak.

The men drove slowly, raking the snow banks with a bright spotlight, looking for signs of trouble. When they, too, detected the sweet, sharp smell of spilt oil, they stopped. But in the darkness they couldn't see anything unusual. One of the men got out of the truck and approached the pipeline, climbing up over the drifts of blowing snow until he stood on top of them. He found a black hole, a snow cave melting away under a steady flow of dark liquid. It was oil. Backing away, afraid the snow might collapse under him, he called in a "code black" to headquarters at 5:58 a.m.

John Browne was in London when an urgent call came through from Alaska. He took the call in his office. "We've got a leak," the voice on the other end said, according to Browne's account in his memoir.

"Where?" he asked.

"Gathering Center 2 . . . we don't think it's much."

Perhaps Browne knew then that whether the leak turned out to be large or small, after what BP had been through in the past twelve months, he would fall under increasing pressure to explain what was

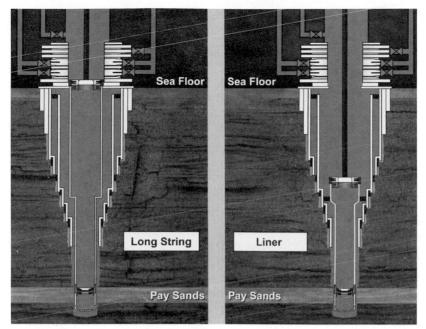

One of BP's critical mistakes in drilling the Macondo well was the choice of a single string casing design—which has fewer protective barriers—over a liner, pictured here. Combined with other factors, the decision contributed to the company's blowout in the gulf. *TrialGraphix*

Lord John Browne, the CEO of BP from 1995 to 2007 who led the company through a slew of mergers and aggressive cost cutting, stands in the entrance to the House of Lords on March 10, 2009, in London. *Getty Images*

BP's "crown jewels" are its oil fields on Alaska's North Slope. Production there peaked in about 1998 and has been in decline ever since. Its equipment has been steadily degrading. *Abrahm Lustgarten*

At its peak, the Alyeska Pipeline, completed in 1977, ran some two million barrels of oil a day from the drilling fields more than 800 miles south to the shipping terminal in Valdez. It is owned by a joint venture but operated by BP. *Abrahm Lustgarten*

A former oilman, Chuck Hamel became an outspoken critic of BP in the early 1990s when whistle-blowers on the North Slope began sending him confidential documents proving that the company wasn't maintaining its facilities. *Abrahm Lustgarten*

To stop Hamel's work, BP employed the Wackenhut security firm, staffed by former CIA and FBI operatives, to spy on him, in what famously became known as the Wackenhut scandal. *Abrahm Lustgarten*

As a senior debarment attorney at the U.S. Environmental Protection Agency, Jeanne Pascal was assigned to work with BP in 1998 after the company's first environmental crime conviction. Twelve years and three criminal plea bargains later, the EPA has not been able to reach an agreement with BP mandating tighter environmental safeguards and worker safety improvements. *Abrahm Lustgarten*

BP mechanic and welder and Steel-workers Union representative Marc Kovac has been outspoken about safety and maintenance issues in Alaska. "BP has always focused more on policy and behavior of the workers than on fixing the danger, and that's what we are trying to change," Kovac said. *Abrahm Lustgarten*

As the EPA's special agent in charge of the government's criminal investigation into BP Alaska after the company's 2006 spill, Scott West believed he would be able to build a criminal case against the company's executives. Then the case was abruptly settled. *Abrahm Lustgarten*

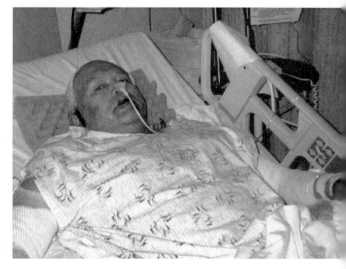

In 2002, Don Shugak was inspecting a BP oil well when a bubble of gas escaped from a faulty casing and blew up in his face. Shugak broke many bones, was badly burned, and spent weeks in a coma after being flown to a Seattle hospital. *Don and Kendra Shugak*

BP blamed the accident on Shugak's error, but it was later revealed that the company had covered up an investigation that found problems inside the well. Shugak, who now lives in Anchorage, signed an agreement never to talk about his accident in exchange for a settlement with the company. *Don and Kendra Shugak*

Before a 2005 blast killed 15 workers and injured 170, an internal BP report had said that workers at the Texas City plant had "an exceptional degree of fear." One worker had died at the plant about every eighteen months for the previous thirty years. In 2002, the company decided not to upgrade key safety equipment in order to save $150,000. *Abrahm Lustgarten*

David Senko managed a team for a BP contractor, Jacobs Engineering. He lost eleven members of his crew in the Texas City blast. "BP pleaded guilty to criminal charges," he said. "But the company didn't commit any crimes. It's the people that work there that committed the crimes. There's been no accountability. Not a single person bottom to top has suffered any kind of consequence." *Abrahm Lustgarten*

Eva Rowe was in a convenience store when she learned from news reports that the Texas City refinery had exploded. Both of her parents were killed in the blast. The company sent her one letter and a check for $25,000. "I want to extend our sincere condolences on the death of your loved one, James," the letter stated. It made no mention of her mother, Linda. *Abrahm Lustgarten*

Thunder Horse, a semi-submersible platform owned by BP and one of the company's most important ventures, nearly sank in 2005. *U.S. Coast Guard*

Mike Thuerich works for a BP contractor named Mistras, choosing inspection locations along the pipelines. "They would say, 'We want you to do equal to or more inspections than you did last year, but you're getting ten percent less for it. You figure out how to do it,'" Theurich said about the budget pressures. "And when you're pickin' five or ten locations on a line that's miles and miles long to inspect, it's kinda like a crapshoot." *Abrahm Lustgarten*

A blowout on April 20, 2010, led to an explosion and the sinking of Deepwater Horizon, killing eleven oil workers. *U.S. Coast Guard*

Brett Cocales (*left*), a drilling engineer for BP from the Deepwater Horizon rig, swears in at the joint investigation hearing, August 27, 2010. *U.S. Coast Guard*

Doug Suttles (*right*), then BP's chief operating officer in North America, answers questions from the media during a press briefing held in Port Fourchon, Louisiana, June 1, 2010. Suttles was previously the president of BP Alaska, where he dealt with safety complaints from workers and an aging pipeline system. *U.S. Coast Guard*

Mike Williams, a Transocean chief engineer technician, testifies at the Deepwater Horizon joint investigation hearing, July 23, 2010, about his experience near the engine room of the Deepwater Horizon when it exploded on April 20. *U.S. Coast Guard*

BP chief executive Tony Hayward is sworn in before the House Oversight and Investigations Subcommittee for a hearing on "The Role Of BP In The Deepwater Horizon Explosion And Oil Spill," June 17, 2010, in Washington, D.C. *Getty Images*

beginning to look like a pattern of problems in his company. The vise had been tightening. After Texas City, the federal government had launched a two-pronged investigation: into environmental crimes associated with the release of toxins from the blast, and into safety violations (the latter was conducted by OSHA). Then Thunder Horse almost sank. And now this. "I could see problems brewing," Browne wrote in his memoir. "It was bad not only for the environment, but for the company's reputation. This was completely unacceptable." Browne, after all, had tried to convince the company and the public at each turn that BP was not the sort of company that placed speed or profits over safety and environmental responsibility, and that the company always did the right thing.

"Overreact," Browne ordered the Alaskan crew.

In the daylight that illuminated the scene two hours later, BP's emergency spill response crews found three acres of blackness shimmering in the snow. "We had a lake of oil out there that was over three feet deep," said Kovac, "rippling in forty-below weather." The fears that had been expressed to Richard Woollam when he slashed the budget of the pipeline corrosion prevention program years earlier had now come true. A hole the size of a dime had worn through in the pipe. The oil dripped steadily into the snow. Thousands of barrels a day had seeped out this way for some time, melting the arctic snow underneath the pipeline and then spreading outward like black blood against the whiteness of Alaska's still-frozen spring. It wasn't clear how long it had been going on.

BP employs a leak detection system on its pipeline, required under Alaskan regulations. It's a sophisticated setup, with the pipeline divided into segments for the purpose of taking measurements, and a computer mathematically calculating the volume passing into, and then out of, a section of line in a twenty-four-hour period to make sure the volumes match up. If less oil flows out of a pipeline than was measured flowing in, alarms begin to go off, increasing in urgency depending on the size of the discrepancy detected by the flow sensors.

In the seven days before the spill was found, the alarms on the oil transit line had gone off at least four separate times. But each time, because the system had grown so quirky and unreliable that it was difficult to read, the alarms were repeatedly "interpreted as an error" by

BP operators, according to the company's incident report. And each time, rather than dispatching an inspection crew to check the line, the operators manning the detection system reset the computer and remained in the heated, sheltered comfort of their control room. No alarms sounded at all on March 1 or 2. The leak would later be estimated at 212,000 gallons of oil. It was the largest in the history of drilling on Alaska's sensitive North Slope.

It took months to clean it up. Crews in white hazmat jumpers stepped thigh-deep through the snow to scoop the polluted slush with shovels, vacuum it up in big hoses, and then bulldoze the tainted snow away with giant land-moving equipment until there was nothing left. Fortunately, the spill had happened before the spring thaw. The oil sat cradled in the layers of ice and snow protecting the earth, freshwater streams, and lakes of the area in summer. "Two hundred thousand gallons is nothing to be sneezed at," said Scott West, an EPA criminal investigator who flew up from Seattle to inspect the scene. Had it been midsummer, with the way the water in the region drains across the landscape into the Beaufort Sea, "two hundred thousand gallons would have been an environmental and ecological disaster."

Browne, though, while he seemed keenly aware of the mounting public pressure on his company to correct its mistakes, was evidently disconnected from the actual operational details that had allowed his company's facilities to deteriorate to such a degree. He ordered an urgent inspection of all the field's lines and said the entire transit line would need to be replaced. "Twenty-nine years of testing, improved processes, leak detection systems and alarms, and yet it had happened," he wrote in his memoir. "Why did our system not detect a leak of this magnitude?" He also wondered, given the scope of the pipeline inspection operations in Alaska, why the corrosion had accelerated so rapidly.

WAS BROWNE unaware of the difficult decisions his employees were forced to make in the field operations as they strived to meet the financial directives he delivered from his offices in London? He certainly seemed not to understand the cost pressures he exerted on BP's business units, or what they in turn did to meet his objectives. In 1997 Richard Woollam had pushed BP Alaska's corrosion program to the brink of failure in order to meet budget objectives that originated with John Browne. And in 2005, just months before the pipeline spill, internal BP emails show that the CIC group, at a time when it might have been reinvesting to make up for the compromises it had accepted earlier, continued to wrestle with similar challenges. (In January 2005, Woollam had been transferred out of Alaska to a nonmanagerial position in Houston.)

In an April 2005 exchange, BP's corrosion management team discussed three choices to meet budget cuts: stop pigging, stop the use of chemicals to control corrosion, or cut back inspections. These were the three practices widely accepted across the industry as the most important to maintaining an oil field and preventing a spill. "We have huge infrastructure that is hanging on with no margin for error," corrosion manager Kip Sprague wrote. Sprague noted that BP faced a maintenance backlog of more than 1,000 locations. "Bitch, bitch, bitch . . . I will try to wrestle down some middle ground between the reality of the situation and some feel-good placeholders." The spill was discovered eleven months later.

Cost-cutting decisions were not the only stress on the system. Even after years of warnings and numerous internal investigations, BP had grown ever more deaf to the warnings of its own workers. Since 2001, Jeanne Pascal had pressed for the company to elevate its Health, Safety and Environment leadership so that worker's complaints would register as an early warning of exactly the kind of accident that had now happened on the slope. But instead of getting better, BP's ability to receive signals from its front line of defense seemed to get worse.

The culture of impatience and of intolerance for interference with corporate momentum seemed to be growing stronger. The workers took their cues from the company's leaders, and while they preached safety and environmental responsibility, their actions were driven instead by quotas, budgets, and quarterly results. Those values, workers said, began to ricochet down through the ranks. Technicians and mechanics who were at risk in the oil fields were now more likely to cover their asses and collect their paychecks than risk their lives to meticulously examine the equipment that might blow up on them and that no one wanted to fix in the first place.

In many companies, Exxon in particular, this sort of erosion would have been exactly the sort of business-threatening red flag that executives would want their employees to step up and tell them about. But at BP's Prudhoe field in Alaska, workers who told their bosses about safety problems in the field were instead punished, harassed, and sometimes fired. One of them was a pipeline technician named Stuart Sneed. Sneed was, in many ways, a typical oil field worker. He lived in Manistee, Michigan, a small town on the eastern shoreline of Lake Michigan 120 miles north of Grand Rapids, on a modest salary earned on two- or three-week-long shifts in Prudhoe Bay. At home he worked on his truck and tended to his property. At work, he checked the pipelines and support struts and other infrastructure for Acuren, the contractor to which BP outsourced its inspection program. Sneed was known as an excellent technician—reliable, safe, accurate. He could also be known to rankle his co-workers. He was socially awkward—the kind of guy who always seemed to be standing too close or talking too loud—and was often described as an "odd duck." He had shoulder-length salt-and-pepper hair, narrow shoulders, and a short build. He was described as eccentric. But he was also honest and smart. "He's not politically correct, but he tells you what he thinks," said one co-worker in Alaska. "He crowds you a little bit. I guess that makes a couple people sort of uncomfortable."

Sneed was also known to be a stickler for the rules. A few months after the spill at Prudhoe Bay, Sneed was on-site near a high-pressure gas line being worked on by construction crews when he discovered a two-inch crack in one of the pipes. Nearby, contractors were doing metalwork, sending a fan of sparks shooting across the worksite. Sneed feared the sparks could ignite stray gases. "Every morning BP says it is your duty to stop any unsafe job," Sneed says. If there was ever a time to do it, this was it.

"The crack could have created a hellacious leaker with people grinding on it," he added. "Any inspector knows a crack in a service pipe is to be considered dangerous and treated with serious attention."

The welders weren't part of Sneed's crew, but he stopped all work on the line and called the problem in to his boss. "He was livid," Sneed said. "He tells me that it's none of my business to stop the job, and to just leave the workers alone."

Sneed knew it was dangerous to cross his managers over complaints in the field. A few years earlier he was working with an inspection team near Milne Point, a field thirty-three miles outside Deadhorse, checking what he called "the big chokes," or the branches of pipes where the oil comes out of the ground and gets routed off toward the transit lines. The men were divided into pairs and then split off, each assigned four locations. When Sneed finished his first inspection, he returned to the truck to find his partner for the day waiting in the heated cab. "He's sitting in the truck doing Sudoku puzzles while I'm out there doing all the hard work," Sneed says. Then he figured it out. "He was just going along out there writing them off, no change, no change. Same old shit." Sneed called it "pencil-whipping," meaning the lengthy draft inspecting reports were whipped into shape with a turn of the wrist rather than a long day's work. And he quickly found that the practice was widespread. When the crew gathered at the end of the day, they reported 2,500 completed inspections, a figure that Sneed knew would be impossible to achieve in a week. "They were signing off on entire pipelines, saying they hadn't corroded and hadn't deteriorated," he said.

He filed a complaint, but, despite his reputation for being meticulous, was reprimanded for minor safety violations a short time later and fired soon after. Sneed described the safety write-ups as harassment and challenged his firing in arbitration. He won, returning to work in the summer of 2006.

After the Prudhoe Bay spill, Sneed thought that BP management would be more amenable to hearing reports of safety problems. That was what BP told the news reporters and emphasized in its morning safety meetings. When he saw the pipeline crack, Sneed hadn't hesitated to stop the welding. It seemed he had misinterpreted the companies' priorities.

The next day, according to the accounts of multiple witnesses, Sneed's supervisor singled him out in the morning staff briefing and harassed him, poking fun at the overcautious man who was afraid to keep working. A couple of hours later, the supervisor sent emails to colleagues soliciting any complaints or safety concerns that could justify Sneed's firing. The Acuren manager collected a rap sheet of minor offenses—such as the time Sneed forgot to walk around his pickup truck and check the taillights before driving off. Such walk-arounds are mandated by company policy to make sure the vehicle is in safe condition to drive, but they are scarcely practiced. Two weeks after the welding episode, Sneed was out in the field and jumped a small stream on the tundra to take a shortcut back to his truck on the other side. That reckless behavior was all the ammunition his manager needed. Sneed was cited for a critical safety infraction; he was allegedly in violation of BP's rules for safe operations on the North Slope. After thirty-five years working in Prudhoe Bay, he was fired.

Sneed filed his wrongful termination complaint with an independent arbitrator BP used to handle worker complaints in Alaska, and after a multimonth investigation, according to confidential internal company materials, the group substantiated Sneed's concerns about the cracked pipe. The arbitrator also investigated Sneed's account of what happened when he reported the problem. Not only did the report confirm that he had been harassed and fired on trumped-up charges, but it determined that he was among the best at his job.

BP's internal investigators interviewed dozens of workers, and according to most of them Sneed "was likely to be the most careful technician on the Slope with respect to safety and quality of his inspections. If there was corrosion in existence . . . he would find it." The report exonerating Sneed was authored by environmental investigator Paul Flaherty and Washington, D.C., attorney Billie Garde—the same woman who had worked with both Chuck Hamel and Bob Malone over the years—and delivered to BP executives in late 2006.

So why would BP want to get rid of one of its most effective inspectors? The report echoed BP's internal investigations from 2001 and 2004, finding, once again, that BP pressured its contractors and employees in order to save money. "Many of the people interviewed indicate that they felt pressured for production ahead of safety and quality," the report stated.

Contractors received incentives to list large numbers of completed inspections, the report found, something Sneed repeatedly reported was leading workers to falsify their paperwork. Contractors also received a 25 percent bonus tied to BP's production numbers. With fewer delays, more oil would be pumped, and more cash would flow to companies executing the work under BP supervision. The message to workers was clear.

"They say it's your duty to come forward," said Sneed of BP's corporate policies and public statements, "but then when you do come forward, they screw you. They'll destroy your life. No one up there is ever going to say anything if there is something they see is unsafe. They are not going to say a word."

10

THE FIX-IT MAN

NEITHER THE ENVIRONMENTAL nor the human toll of the March disaster in Alaska compared to what had happened in Texas City. Yet in many ways, because of both its timing and its occurrence in the heart of the United States' oil production infrastructure, it was even more significant. Browne was right: problems *were* brewing, this time of the criminal sort. After the Texas City disaster, the federal government had launched a criminal investigation, still under way in the spring of 2006. It was likely that BP would face felony charges over the blast and its operation of the refinery. With the spill in Alaska, the Department of Justice had fresh cause to pursue the company, a move that would reengage Jeanne Pascal and the debarment office. Scott West, the EPA investigator, was a self-assured man with a healthy indignation for corporate polluters. He had launched the investigation in Alaska to determine whether BP had acted negligently and whether it had violated the federal Clean Water Act. Depending on the outcome of these investigations, BP potentially faced felony charges within the year. It also had to worry about being debarred and losing its lucrative federal contracts.

In the case of the spill, Browne dispatched a top aide from London, Bob Malone, to get to the bottom of what was happening in his troubled U.S. operations. Malone was promoted to head BP's North American operations, giving him unprecedented authority within the company to override production executives there and stop operations if he ever felt it was needed to improve safety and reliability. "He was appointed to try to bring some rationality, some maturity and operational knowledge and leadership," says Shell's Hofmeister, who worked frequently with Malone.

Malone, though, didn't necessarily want the job. He was fifty-four years old, and planning to retire. He hadn't aspired to lead BP, was never one of Browne's Turtles, and didn't have the deep financial experience to be the group CEO. He was never a company star like Manzoni, or even Hayward, but he had worked beside Browne for a long time. "Bob was somebody that was as loyal as the day is long," says Hofmeister. "He was calm, methodical, deliberate, and decisive." Malone also had a way with people: a congeniality that had a way of bridging chasms, as it had with Chuck Hamel years ago. That's what BP needed, and Malone, Browne hoped, would be his consummate fix-it man. "We needed to strengthen the BP America organization, appoint a great man as president," Browne said.

It was an awkward position for Malone, in part because the head of North American operations hadn't traditionally been a powerful position in the BP organization, and in part because his responsibilities overlapped ambiguously with those of other executives. If he were to be effective, he would need more authority than had been granted to BP America chiefs in the past. Traditionally, the Alaska division, for example, had been part of an operational chain of authority that led to London. BP Alaska's president reported to a group vice president for operations, who reported to a head of worldwide exploration and production, Tony Hayward. On the refining side, a similar ladder of command extended from direct plant management up to a national refining supervisor to an international refining vice president like Mike Hoffman and up to the global refining and marketing executive, John Manzoni.

The BP America leadership always occupied a powerless position in between, with greater responsibility for representing the company in U.S. political and regulatory affairs than actual operational decision making in the chain of command between London and the refineries or the oil fields. Now Malone was supposed to take over that position, with oversight over U.S. operations, but with a new level of authority

meant to give him more reach and influence in the corporate organization than BP America executives had been handed in the past. It could
work. But it also risked making the senior ranks of BP's corporate
business and lines of communication even more confused as a result.

In this case Hayward's job was to make sure the Gulf of Mexico
and the North Slope of Alaska kept producing oil and kept feeding the
belly of BP's business. Malone's job was not just to advise Hayward and
the other executives managing Alaska but to oversee safety in Alaska.
Meanwhile, he was also tasked with overseeing BP's relationship with
the U.S. and to pick up all the broken operational and legal pieces that
lay strewn across North America. With one hand he was to put them
back together again, while with the other, Browne seemed to hope,
Malone could pacify the government, BP's critics, and regulators. "I
had a pretty good feel for what I was walking into," Malone said. "I had
a lot of candid conversations with John Browne, and thought I could
make a difference."

Malone was the perfect man for the job. Like Browne, he took what
many described as a more cosmopolitan approach to management. He
was a gregarious, approachable consensus builder who took a forward-
looking and outward-reaching tack. While executives like Hayward
or Manzoni were more inclined to internalize big decisions, Malone
was inclined toward transparency and engagement with the public.
He liked to think of himself as a listener, and welcomed outside voices
that he thought could bring perspective to internal decisions. It didn't
hurt that he was politically connected. In 2000 Malone was a co-chair
for George W. Bush's presidential campaign in Alaska, and the two
were friendly. Bush, in Washington, was already sympathetic to the
oil industry, but BP had flirted so obviously with abuse of that sympa-
thy, making it difficult for Washington in 2006 to look the other way.
Maybe Malone could smooth things over.

He had scarcely begun when he was handed his first major setback.
On June 28, 2006, the U.S. Commodities and Futures Trading Commission filed a damning civil suit against BP alleging that the company's
trading desks had cornered and then illegally manipulated the market
price for propane in late 2003 and early 2004. BP owned more than
half the propane on the market and controlled the movement of a full
88 percent, according to the suit. To make matters worse, BP's traders

were taped at their desks, and the government had subpoenaed, and released, the recordings. They presented an embarrassing portrait of hubris and arrogance.

"How does it feel taking on the whole market, man?" Dennis Abbott, one of the traders, asked.

"Whew. It's pretty big, man," Cody Claborn responded.

"Dude, you're the entire fucking propane market," Abbott added.

"Here's my one fear," Mark Radley, the company's trading manager for natural gas liquids, chimed in. "And it's a significant fear. Everybody waits until the last fucking day to cover and then we get wound up in a bunch of fucking legal disputes."

The statements might have seemed like the actions of a few rogue financial hot shots, but it wasn't the first time such allegations had been made. In 2003 BP paid a record fine to the New York Mercantile Exchange to settle allegations of improper crude oil trading, according to reports in the *Wall Street Journal*. At the time, the company promised a stricter adherence to the rules. Now, faced with a similar case in the propane markets, the government alleged the manipulation happened "with the knowledge, advice, and consent of senior management." One of the traders pleaded guilty, and four more would later be indicted (their individual charges would eventually be dismissed, though charges against the company would proceed). It seemed to show yet again that in myriad facets of its operations, BP operated by its own rules.

Playing the role of fireman, Malone jumped from one smoldering pile to another, trying to stamp them out. "The trading issue, that really was about our values," he said. "Our values are very clear, and when I listen to the trader tapes there is no doubt in my mind, it certainly broke our values." Malone bemoaned the worst environmental accident on the slope as another breakdown of both values and discipline. By August, it began to seem as if he and Browne had gotten things under control. BP would later be indicted on felony charges in the propane trading scandal, and the case would take another three years to wend its way through the courts. But for the moment, the worst humiliation—having the scandal in the headlines and the bad news rippling across Wall Street—seemed to have passed.

In Alaska the oil had been cleaned up and Malone had committed to replacing sixteen miles of the oil transit line, at a cost of more than $150 million. A reinvigorated pipeline inspection program was under way, and a brilliant arctic summer had set in on the slope with all its warmth and optimism. Malone had a steady hand on the tiller of BP's operations there, and, despite everything that had happened, BP conveyed a sense of concern and a renewed commitment to safety.

On August 3, 2006, Browne and Malone flew to Alaska on a victory tour. In Anchorage Browne met with the governor, Tony Knowles. "On behalf of the BP group I apologize" for the spill, Browne said. He pledged a robust and careful corrosion and inspection process that would prevent anything like the spill from happening again in the future. It made sense. "If you are contemplating a really long-term investment in a really volatile market the last thing you need is unreasonable uncertainty about those things that can be controlled," he added, trying to allay the public's fears.

The next day the company's private jet touched down in Deadhorse, and Malone, Browne, and members of the Health, Safety and Environment team took a company bus out to the oil transit line that had leaked. It was a bluebird summer day, with young grasses shimmering a vibrant green. The sun alone made it seem as if everything that had gone wrong here had long ago been fixed. Browne wore a collared BP jacket over a pink dress shirt, a white hard hat, and large, clear safety goggles over his reading glasses. Together with a gaggle of reporters assembled for the junket, they stood on a dirt mound, with the pipeline running into a culvert beneath them. The worker who had discovered the leak on that very spot was there. So was Bill Hedges, BP's new head of corrosion management.

Hedges sought to assure the cameras, and his bosses, that BP's corrosion monitoring on the slope was now under control. The transit line spill, while regrettable, was an anomaly, he told them. "The other lines that we still have in operation today aren't showing this problem at all," Hedges said. "So we believe right now that the problem was limited to this specific segment of the line." Malone stood by Browne's side, his eyes shielded from the blinding light by mirrored lenses. He expressed contrition, reiterating that the reporters stood before a new BP. "The events that have occurred caused us to think that we need additional laser focus on the United States," he said.

Browne added a note of confidence. "The corrosion monitoring is very effective," he said. "Mind you that this is the only time that something has happened." His job done, Browne boarded the company's private jet and flew to Venice, where he would take a few days of rest in his vacation home there. Malone traveled to Daingerfield, Texas, in the northeastern corner of the state, where his boyhood friends were throwing him a party to celebrate his recent promotion to group vice president of BP. Forty-eight hours after posing in the bright arctic sun, he stood around a barbecue pit in the middle of nowhere, roasting alligator and catfish and being toasted for his success.

At about 1:30 p.m. Malone got a call on his cell phone from Steve Marshall, then the president of BP Alaska. Barely able to hear through the static, Malone walked away from the pit and climbed a cattle fence hoping to catch a stronger signal. Perched there, he strained to hear what Marshall was saying. Finally he got it: there was another oil leak in Prudhoe Bay.

Inspection crews checking the lines for corrosion had found another small hole, this time at the other end of the field, the eastern artery of Prudhoe Bay that gathered half the oil and sent it down the Trans Alaska pipeline. The leak was small, less than a thousand gallons, but inspectors reported that the pipeline was corroded along a length of sixteen miles. This time, records showed, the line hadn't been pigged since 1991—there were almost no recent inspection data showing how badly, or how quickly, it had corroded. They didn't know which part of it would spring a leak next, or when. Since this was the half of the system that had been considered reliable when the March spill had happened on the other side, the Alaska field managers' confidence was deeply shaken. They couldn't assure Marshall that other leaks weren't about to begin. Marshall wanted Malone to tell them what to do.

Malone, standing on the fence post in rural Texas, wasn't exactly sure. It was an operations decision. It should have been Tony Hayward's call. But Hayward was also on vacation, sailing his yacht somewhere. Company officials had been trying to reach him on the satellite phone he carried for just such emergencies, but Hayward didn't respond. The burden fell on Malone. "We had corrosion spots that exceeded our safety margin and . . . I couldn't be assured from talking to our experts,"

Malone said. "They looked at it and they said, 'We cannot assure you that we don't have similar problems in other transit lines on the north slope of Alaska.'" Malone didn't think the company had much of a choice. Department of Justice officials had been breathing down their necks ever since the first spill in March. How would they explain anything other than the most conservative decision? Under the pressure of the moment, he did what he thought was most prudent: he ordered the entire Prudhoe Bay field to shut down production.

Malone might as well have personally triggered an enormous earthquake, because the decision would ripple out into the media, the market, and even foreign governments, making the job he had reluctantly accepted at Browne's behest exponentially more difficult. Then he woke Browne up in Venice. "Bob, this is going to be big," Browne said.

"John, I know that," Malone replied.

"You're not asking for my approval, are you?"

"No, I think you delegated that to me, John."

"I'll back whatever decision you make. But think through the consequences and make sure you have a plan in place," Browne told him.

"Shutting down the whole oil field seemed a little extreme," Browne later wrote about that night. "I knew the repercussions would be massive."

At a moment when BP was still under intense scrutiny from its investors, the press, and regulators, this failure of its equipment was further evidence of a fundamental breakdown in the company's core control of quality. The oil transit line was not only one of the most important causeways to bring BP's product to market, but also a major piece of national security infrastructure. Roughly 8 percent of domestic oil flows out of Prudhoe Bay, half of that from the leaking line alone. That the spill came just five months after the last one in Alaska and sixteen months after the deadly accident in Texas City that threatened 3 percent of the nation's gasoline supply only exacerbated matters. If BP wasn't confident in the integrity of its own systems in Alaska, how could the world remain confident in BP?

"BP is in crisis mode," one television broadcast began. "BP apologized again this morning for their failure to keep the crucial commodity flowing," another program said.

It didn't take long for the questions to get more pointed. "Is the pipeline corrosion in Alaska just the latest example of bad luck for the company," a news anchor asked, "or are there serious management issues for BP?"

Hayward, according to executives inside the company, was furious when he found out about the shutdown and Malone's decision. As it turned out, much of the system could continue to run safely, and two days later, the company moderated its course. It restored half the flow of oil—about 200,000 barrels a day—and said that it would buy oil on the open market to shore up U.S. supply. But the damage was already done. "It was a rough week," Malone said at the time, explaining his actions. In his own defense, he noted that he had "been given the authority, the support and the resources to take action when I believe it is necessary."

The state of Alaska objected strenuously to the disruption; it counts on the royalties—$6.2 million—flowing daily into state coffers as each gallon of oil flows off to market. The U.S. Congress was equally furious—about gas prices, about security, and about the apparent chaos in its most valuable and productive drilling lands. Malone had to face Pascal and the EPA, conducting criminal investigations. Finally, the media, and the public had to be dealt with. Creative riffing on John Browne's forward-thinking slogan "Beyond Petroleum" had taken the form of rebranding BP with names like "Beyond Parody," "Barely Pumping," "Broken Pipelines," "Bloated Profits," and, in a particularly stinging but accurate headline from the company's hometown paper, "Battered Petroleum."

All the while, Hayward remained mysteriously quiet. While Malone was in the papers on a daily basis, Hayward was not only invisible as a public leader of a company in crisis, but he was scarcely quoted responding to the Alaska disaster. The board expected Browne to retire at the end of 2008, at sixty. Perhaps Hayward, a potential candidate to replace him, was wisely keeping his head down. Whatever the reason, Malone, who wasn't formally tasked with running BP Alaska, seemed to be calling the shots, a fact that only further confused the hierarchy of BP Alaska, effectively chaining its workers and its executives to two masters.

"I did not think things could get much worse," Browne wrote. His biggest fear was that the string of events BP had suffered would begin to look like a pattern. "Thunder Horse had already been wrongly linked to the Texas City explosion. They were totally unrelated, with completely different causes. And now the problems in Alaska would also be linked for good measure."

Malone, again, stepped up to defend the company, talking widely with the American press and preparing to address Congress. I don't at this time say that there is a systemic issue here," Malone said. But he also sounded less convinced, and for the first time in the company's era of troubles, he spoke about the need to change BP's culture. The issues were at the very "foundation" of operations, he said, and the company needed to learn from them, and then communicate its lessons widely across the entire corporation. "I've been asked both internally and externally, 'Is this just bad luck?' I don't believe in bad luck."

IF BP was going to get to the "foundation" of its issues in Alaska, the first step would be to get a grip on the true state of the company's pipelines. To do that, BP asked its inspection crews to do a blitz blanket assessment of the entire field. The idea was to identify every weak spot along the pipelines with the aim of quickly fixing and replacing them before a spill, like the two that had just occurred on the transit lines, could happen again. Acuren, one of the inspection and engineering companies contracted to carry out BP's corrosion program—the same company that Stuart Sneed had alleged was notorious for falsifying records and ignoring safety warnings—would oversee the job.

But this time, Acuren said it meant business. It asked a Kenai, Alaska–based veteran inspection engineer named Martin Anderson to supervise the inspection effort. Anderson had built a strong reputation training the oil companies' staffs on how to conduct what they call "nondestructive" technical testing of pipelines and facilities. He was a tough-minded technocrat, described by peers and colleagues as hypercompetent, with an exacting attention to detail. He had worked with Chevron and Shell and, before the BP acquisition, had headed up safety and inspections for ARCO in Prudhoe Bay.

Immediately after the leaks in Prudhoe Bay, the inspection program was in a state of chaos. BP's management was exerting extreme pressure on George Bryant, Acuren's executive in charge of the program, and on Acuren, to check every inch of pipe in the field. The checkups couldn't happen fast enough. "We go flying out there into the field," says Anderson. Everyone is tearing the insulation off the pipes to get to the metal. There aren't enough inspectors, so Acuren started flying off-duty workers in from Hawaii, and scrambling to hire anyone who said they were fit for work.

Significant worker safety issues came up almost immediately. In the midst of the mêlée, someone ran into Anderson's office one day early on and said that the inspectors out stripping the insulation were grinding away at some funny-looking coating on the pipe. It occurred to them that it might be asbestos. Anderson stopped the work.

"I pulled every inspector in and called a stand-down—no one leaves the room," Anderson said, once again testing John Browne's insistent rhetoric that every employee is empowered to stop work when they have a concern about safety. Rather than being rewarded, Anderson drew stern disapproval for his decision. Bryant, under pressure from BP and spitting mad, stormed into his office and ordered him to put the crews back to work unless Anderson could prove the lines were dangerous. While they talked, John Phillips, the BP manager oversee-ing Bryant, stood impatiently in Anderson's doorway, arms crossed, tapping his foot.

Challenging Anderson's authority, Bryant turned to the workers in the room and asked if anyone felt unsafe. "Everybody glances at each other uneasily and nobody says anything," Anderson recalls, disgusted at what he thought was blatant intimidation. Choosing to read their silence as an affirmation that the job was safe, Bryant tried to order them back to work himself. Anderson refused to allow it. "You put me in charge of these people, so it's my call whether people can go back to work," he told Bryant. "When the health and safety guy brings in a paper with a lab report—which is federal law—then we will go back to work."

That afternoon, the report came back showing that the coating was indeed asbestos, and a few days later, investigators from the EPA showed up to request copies of the records. If Anderson had let the workers back out knowing there was an asbestos risk, he could have been charged with a felony. Worse, Anderson says, "They would have been breathing those asbestos particles. I had friends working out there. There were people I knew for thirty years . . . sitting here in my office. I'm not going to take people I knew for three decades and their children and expose them to danger." Later, the state occupational safety board and the EPA would cite BP for mishandling the asbestos risk.

"They wanted to rush everybody out there and let the chips fall where they may instead of waiting for the proper procedures," Anderson said, referring to both the asbestos and the hasty hiring of inspectors. And when he resisted, BP and Acuren resorted to intimidation to keep their workers on the job.

The asbestos issue, as it turned out, was just the beginning of the problems Anderson would turn up in the oil field's inspection program. In the rush to bring in extra workers and to get the field assessment under way, no one had stopped to check for the certifications that inspectors are required to have, assuring that they are capable of accurately interpreting what they see on the pipeline; and Anderson had growing concerns about their competence.

Pipeline inspection and nondestructive testing are a technical specialization within the engineering profession. Inspectors handle ultrasonic and radioactive X-ray gear that can be dangerous, and the decisions they make in the field can determine the fate of an entire corporation and affect hundreds of people. When an inspector says a plant like Texas City or pipelines like the oil transit lines are safe to operate, people's lives depend on that assessment. To hold a nondestructive testing job requires hundreds of hours of experience and grueling exams to obtain various levels of certification. At least some of the people Anderson saw being sent out into the field clearly didn't meet that standard. "I've got one girl who has eight hours [of training on the books] when she is supposed to have eighty hours and she is doing ultrasonic testing on the oil transit line," Anderson says. "These people aren't even close to being qualified."

The fact that some of the inspectors Anderson came across didn't have their hours raised larger questions about how many other unqualified inspectors were out in the field. Anderson brought his concerns to Bryant, his boss, and says he was encouraged to look the other way. The contract just needs to get done, he was told. Anderson, though, couldn't let it go. If the problems he was seeing were systemic, what would that mean for the quality of data BP and Acuren were relying on to make decisions about which pipelines needed repair, and to prevent another spill? BP could take the results of its field inspection out to the world and say that its pipelines were found to be safe, but that might not mean that they truly were. Anderson kept pushing. He told Acuren's executives in the company's home office in Connecticut about the problems and then went to one of BP's corrosion managers directly. Finally, Acuren reluctantly agreed to undertake a broader assessment of its entire program.

In January 2007 Bryant asked Anderson, who was still working as an inspection supervisor, if Anderson would lead an in-depth quality assurance audit on the company. Anderson was skeptical of Bryant's commitment and had never meant to suggest that he should be the one hired to fix the problems. If Acuren wanted a whitewash, he worried, he was the wrong guy for the job. Moreover, he knew BP was one of Acuren's biggest clients, and he feared they weren't prepared for the truth. "Are you sure you want me to do this" Anderson asked Bryant. "If you put me in this position, I am going to do it. I'm going to bring the information to you and expect corrections, and it may not be pleasant. Are you sure I'm the guy you want?"

Bryant insisted that BP and Acuren now needed to know exactly what the state of its lines and its inspection program were, good or bad.

Things got off to a rocky start. "The first thing I did is say, 'Where are all your audits?'" says Anderson, referring to the quarterly statements the company is required to keep of its own inspection program and staff, which would show how many of them are certified and in which processes. "They stumbled around and then said they couldn't find them." Both BP and Acuren were required to keep regular records showing which employees had which certifications and when they expired. Acuren's files were poorly maintained and had large gaps. BP's recent audits didn't exist; the last time it had reported on Acuren's inspection program was in 2002. To complete his audit, Anderson would have to start from scratch, checking each employee's qualifications and reviewing the work they had done, entering thousands of points of raw data into the computer system and re-creating five years' worth of records.

To begin with, he asked Acuren to produce the human resources and certification files for each of its inspectors. It quickly became clear that Acuren possessed very few records to prove that its inspectors were qualified. "They say, 'Well, they just carry cards around to show they are a level two,'" Anderson says, referring to one of the tiers of certification. But the cards have to be backed up with files kept in the office, tied to the date of the inspectors' exams. When he raised the issue, he was told not to worry about it. "I can get the guy who cleans the bathroom to make up a card," Anderson told his boss, incredulous. "We need documentation. Some people had multiple cards with different expiration dates. They were obviously fake. How could you have a radiography card [a certification that allows an inspector to handle X-ray testing equipment regulated by the Nuclear Regulatory Commission] with four different expiration dates?"

When he investigated further, Anderson found an answer. In a crunch, Acuren management had asked a guy who was certified in high-level film interpretation to issue new certifications for workers, even though it wasn't normally his job. The employee got on the computer and printed them out. Many of the cards, Anderson said, had been printed in the weeks since he began to raise questions about the qualifications of the workers. But in his haste, the man who printed them didn't think to make sure the certification dates matched the company's other records. Anderson wasn't sure if anyone had intentionally ordered the certifications to be reprinted, but the issue raised serious questions. It was possible that some of the workers with missing documentation had the prerequisite experience—somewhere there was a record of their certification—but the system was disorganized. It was also possible that the certifications were given without the prerequisite hours of training, in which case they were forgeries and broke the law. "The worst problem is to be certified but not qualified, because that means the person did not meet the qualification standard but yet someone testified that they did," Anderson said. "To me, that's fraud and could be a criminal offense."

By the time he was finished, Anderson found scores of inspectors charged with documenting the conditions of BP's pipelines in Alaska who lacked the certifications required for their job or had never completed their training. In March 2007 Anderson put the details of his findings into several confidential reports that were scathing in their assessment of BP's inspection program and warned that he had little confidence in the consistency or accuracy of the data produced by the inspection teams about the condition of BP's pipelines. Of 146 Acuren inspectors working in the field, Anderson found, certification could not be verified—meaning documentation was lacking—for half of them. Deeper investigation found that 19 inspectors were not certified at all to do the tasks to which they were assigned. Another 19 had incomplete records in the company's files. In a few egregious cases, inspectors made errors that pointed to a total lack of understanding of their tasks. One time, Anderson recalls, an inspector was sent out to use a sophisticated piece of equipment that relies on radioactive material. After installing it backward, he couldn't get it to work. On at least two other occasions, inspectors went out into the field to do what they call "code" work: check to see if equipment is up to code and in compliance with regulatory statutes. But to do that, the inspectors have to know which codes to apply. The Department of Transportation regulated certain pipelines, and the Alaska Department of Environmental Conservation regulated others, each with different requirements. In the cases Anderson reviewed, the inspectors weren't sure which codes applied. They guessed, and they guessed wrong, resulting in a section of equipment being certified as legal when in fact it was not.

Anderson wondered how the lack of certifications and the hasty approval of inspected sites could be accidental. "I've had concerns," Anderson says. "Not being an attorney, I don't know what is breaking the law and what is not breaking the law, but I was very uncomfortable with the situation that they had."

The problems Anderson uncovered in the inspection group in 2007 were not isolated: there was a record of similar problems having arisen in the past. Internal company documents from 2002 show that another BP pipeline inspection company had been caught pencil-whipping inspection results. The report said that workers had falsified their inspection reports and that without good records and a system in place, the potential existed for inspectors to skip inspections altogether, and then complete the forms as if they hadn't found any problems. At the time, BP had investigated and prescribed a list of actions that needed to be addressed to restore the integrity of its program. BP went back to check its progress against that list in 2005 and found that 12 percent of the most urgent and high-risk action items from 2002 were still unresolved. Then again, in a separate case, Stuart Sneed had alleged that inspectors were pencil-whipping reports in 2006.

Now, in 2007, Anderson had found many of the same issues repeated yet again in the same place, under the same operating company, BP, albeit with a different contractor and a different staff, except this time it wasn't just a matter of a few problems. The problems were widespread. The findings raised immediate questions about more than 88,000 inspection points along the pipelines, a large portion of the work done to guarantee the pipelines' integrity. In short, none of those inspections could be counted on to be accurate. Unless something was done, not only did BP's inspection program violate regulations, but the Prudhoe Bay oil field remained very much at risk.

ANDERSON'S AUDIT was a highly confidential project, the details of which were known only to Acuren and some BP Alaska executives. While Anderson continued his assessment, Bob Malone, who knew little about Anderson's audit early on, was busy reframing BP's priorities, and its image, before the public. In Texas, he brought in a high-profile advisory committee for the ostensible purpose of helping the company get the Texas City refinery and the rest of its North American business back on track. The group included, among others, former Senate majority leader Tom Daschle; former EPA head Christine Todd Whitman; former Clinton White House chief of staff Leon Panetta; and former navy admiral and Nuclear Energy Institute director Frank "Skip" Bowman. It was a classic Malone play, undertaken partly to gather expert advice on the stricken plant, and meant to earn goodwill from deep in the ranks of American leadership. That was just as well, because in the fall of 2006, the U.S. House Energy and Commerce Committee summoned Malone and BP Alaska president Steve Marshall and BP's former corrosion manager for Alaska, Richard Woollam, to Washington to explain what had happened to the company in Texas and Alaska.

On September 6 the three lined up before the committee for an inquisition. "I suppose that this committee and Congress is expected to shrug our shoulders and say, well, now they get it. But the clever use of perfect hindsight to excuse consistent failure just doesn't cut it," said Joe Barton, the Republican congressman from Texas, an engineer and the chairman of the committee at the time. "If a company, one of the world's most successful oil companies, can't do simple, basic maintenance needed to keep the Prudhoe Bay field operating safely without interruption, maybe it shouldn't operate the pipeline. . . . this comes from a company that prides itself on their ads protecting the environment. Shame, shame, shame."

When it was his turn, Woollam stood before the committee and a row of television cameras and exercised his Fifth Amendment right not to incriminate himself. "I respectfully will not answer questions," he said. His lawyers explained that Woollam could be a subject of a criminal investigation.

Finally, Malone addressed the committee. He adopted a humble posture, head bowed as he read, seated, from a prepared statement. He was soft-spoken and conciliatory. "The public's faith in BP has been tested recently," he began. "We have fallen short of the high standards we hold for ourselves and the expectations that others have for us. . . . Some have questioned our environmental credentials while others have accused BP of profiteering at the expense of employee safety." He called the Texas City disaster "the greatest tragedy ever experienced by the BP Family" and said it would "never be forgotten," pledging that that accident and the others would forever change BP's approach to operations. "We are committed to attaining the highest levels of safety, reliability, and environmental performance." He addressed the close call on Thunder Horse, and the propane trading scandal, and said, in practiced talking points: "I don't believe in luck. We need to understand these issues and then translate the lessons we learn across all of our operations."

He said all of the right things. But Malone, never known for acting simply as a mouthpiece, seemed to genuinely believe what he said. He confessed to one of the sharpest accusations leveled at John Browne and BP's leadership: that it failed to listen to its workers and repeatedly was deaf to warnings coming from the field. "The problem has not been in workers raising concerns—sometimes it's been our responsiveness." Then, preemptively, he offered an olive branch to Congress. He announced that he was creating an ombudsman's office for BP North America that would act independently to hear workers' complaints. That way, he said, the safety complaints made on BP's front lines would find their way through the echo chamber of company politics all the way to the top.

The idea was somewhat revolutionary for a large, foreign-based corporation, and it was seeded back in the days of Malone's negotiations with Chuck Hamel over labor complaints on the Alyeska pipeline. The ombudsman would launch a full investigation into the worker complaints at BP Alaska since the Arco acquisition in 2000, airing, once again, the grievances of the Marc Kovacs and Stuart Sneeds of the company. Employees were expected to stop work on BP operations when they felt unsafe, and they had to feel comfortable with that privilege. "I expect this individual will call them as he sees them. This is critical. We encourage it," Malone told Congress.

To staff the new ombudsman office, Malone shrewdly reached out to the enemy's bench. Billie Garde, the woman who had represented Chuck Hamel during the Wackenhut scandal and who herself had led an anti-BP environmentalist group in Alaska in the 1990s, would be the lead investigator. The program would be run by Stanley Sporkin, a former federal judge, former director of enforcement for the Securities and Exchange Commission, and former general counsel for the CIA. It was probably not coincidental that he also happened to be the federal judge who ruled for Chuck Hamel when his lawsuit reached the courts in 1993.

As for the dots now splattered across BP's operational record, though, Malone continued to insist that they should not be connected. "Some policy makers and regulators have begun to question whether these operational problems at BP are symptoms of a systemic problem," he told Congress. "Clearly BP has had its share of issues. . . . I believe, overall, BP is a well-managed company with a solid long-term record. There has been a series of troubling problems that are unacceptable to us and contrary to our values. We want to understand why they have occurred and do whatever it takes to set them right."

For several hours after the remarks, the committee berated both

Malone and Steve Marshall. Marshall told the committee that in 2006 BP's inspection and corrosion mitigation budget had jumped to $74 million—15 percent higher than the previous year and an 80 percent increase over what BP was spending in 2001. "The buck stops with me," he told the committee. But he couldn't explain how, on his watch, BP had identified serious corrosion risks in its pipelines and then waited the better part of a decade before doing anything about it. Marshall's answers were deeply unsatisfying to the committee. Yet somehow, Malone's disarming assurances proved effective.

Before Congress could inflict its own punishment, Malone, just two months into the job, demonstrated BP's willingness to examine itself by establishing the corporate ombudsman. Faced with his plausible explanations, humble demeanor, and proactive solutions, Congress appeared ready to accept that BP had suffered a bout of awfully bad luck. Everything the members might suggest was already in motion: Browne had reorganized top executives, the company was paying tens of millions in fines, and Malone had announced a fix to the worker complaints in Alaska that seemed so aggressive and fair it could hardly be improved upon.

BEHIND THE SCENES, the cogs of BP's operations wouldn't mesh as smoothly as Malone promised. Anderson's audit struck at the core of what seemed to be wrong in Alaska, and his findings seemed to be exactly the kind Malone had pledged to act on. But for months after Anderson delivered his audit to Acuren executives, there was silence.

Frustrated, Anderson went over George Bryant's head, bringing his audit directly to BP's Alaska executives. Still, months passed with no response from BP. Anderson, bound by strict confidentiality agreements, couldn't tell anyone outside the company. And the government, though it was in the midst of a criminal investigation, never questioned BP's inspection workforce or checked whether BP had a handle on its programs to maintain the thousands of miles of pipeline running through the arctic fields.

Anderson's audit would remain a secret for nearly a year. The congressional committees subpoenaing BP records wouldn't learn about it until after their hearings on BP. The news media never reported it. For a long time, Scott West, Jeanne Pascal, and other criminal investigators watching what BP did in Alaska were also unaware of Anderson's findings. With five more audit segments left to go, according to his contract, Anderson was abruptly cut off from finishing his job. He would have trouble getting any more work in the Alaskan oil fields. The audit was buried, and no one seemed to care.

11

A TORRID AFFAIR

THE CASCADING SERIES of disasters that plagued BP in 2005–2006 were the sorts of events that could ruin a company. They could no longer be ignored or filed away in a list of unfortunate but isolated events. And they could no longer be explained away to investors and the public as sideshows in the great performance of a corporation steering toward a new energy economy. The disasters had become the story of BP.

Finally, it seemed, John Browne was paying attention. The relentless series of mishaps became his *Valdez* moment. The year 2006 was a turning point for him, and, perhaps, for BP. Was it too late?

The notion that BP was beyond petroleum—a responsible industry leader at a crucial moment in history—was in shambles. And within the company, differences of opinion about John Browne's choices and priorities were widening. Many inside the company, including Tony Hayward, had long thought that Browne was distracted by his pet issues of climate change and environmentalism, and by his flirtations with the public spotlight. They thought that he had been obsessed with branding the company and lowering its carbon footprint at the expense of BP's real business, producing and selling oil. Now, despite Browne's undeniable accomplishments, there was a sense that they had been proven right.

Browne was supposed to retire at the end of 2008, when he had reached the company's mandatory retirement threshold. Chatter about who might succeed him had spilled into the newspapers even before the accidents in Alaska the previous year. Browne's Turtles had been vying for the position. Eventually the list had boiled down to three: Robert Dudley, the man in charge of TNK-BP, the company's Russian joint venture; John Manzoni, the former refining executive; and Tony Hayward. Dudley, an American and a chemical engineer who had come to BP from Amoco in the 1998 merger, was still considered too outside the mold of BP's London culture. Manzoni, though he was widely seen as capable and brought the right experience, was tarnished by his link to the Texas City disaster. Hayward seemed to be the opposite of Manzoni—soft-spoken, almost cherubic, and easy to relate to. He had been a prince in Browne's operations ever since the early 1990s.

Browne groomed each of these men for the role that one of them would one day fill. At the same time, he was reluctant to go. With the death of his mother in 2000 BP had become his life. Any suggestion that Browne might stay on past the age of sixty, which he floated several times and which was reported in the press, rankled BP's chairman, Peter Sutherland, and other board members, who found the idea puzzling in the wake of the past two years. Turnover and change were good for the company, the board members thought, and they were already leaning toward Hayward as the company's next global chief. The question for them was when. By the end of 2006, as the board grew ever more impatient with Browne's blunders, it wasn't clear they could wait.

Then, on January 5, 2007, Browne got a phone call, while on vacation in Barbados, from the company's head of public affairs, Roddy Kennedy, with some disturbing news. London's *Mail on Sunday* was preparing to run a gossipy exposé about Browne's personal life. In addition to the private details about Browne's friendship with former prime minister Tony Blair and Browne's taste for $4,000 bottles of claret, they planned to write about Browne's affair with a male prostitute.

For four years John Browne had had a relationship with Jeff Chevalier, a Canadian thirty-four years his junior. Though he flaunted his lifestyle among his friends and in London's exclusive social circles, he had never publicly admitted that he was gay. The two men had met in 2002 through "Suited and Booted," a London escort service. According to Browne's later account, he had sought out Chevalier during a lonely period after his mother's death, and they grew close. Nine months later, Chevalier moved into Browne's extravagant Chelsea flat, and for the four years that followed, they traveled the world together, occasionally visiting Prudhoe Bay. When the relationship ended, Browne initially continued to support Chevalier financially. After some time, he stopped, ignoring Chevalier's emails and pleas for money.

Cut out of Browne's life, at twenty-five Chevalier sold his story to the paper. He told them about Browne's unreasonable fits over which first-class seat he was assigned to on a British Airways flight (he always requested the front row, except for the one time he found himself placed behind Mick Jagger), their dinners with royalty and movie stars, how the oil executive had lavished him with gifts, and details of private and sensitive discussions. The paper wanted a comment from Browne within hours. "I had been found out, I panicked," Browne wrote in his memoir. "What was in my mind is hard to say: confusion, anger, but most of all a sense of betrayal and affront. . . . I was desperate to protect my privacy and my secrets." He decided to seek a court injunction to stop the paper from printing the story. From Barbados, he hired a team of top lawyers, but in thus escalating the confrontation so quickly, he felt thrown off balance.

"I was ashamed and embarrassed, and had yet to confront the secret I had hidden in a dark corner all my life. I had never openly admitted to strangers that I was gay, and now I was talking to a lawyer whom I did not know, on a long distance phone call, with my Barbados host in earshot," Browne wrote. The lawyers asked him questions, and Browne, self-conscious about how he had met Chevalier, and how he sounded discussing it, lied. He used a story that he and Chevalier had prepared—that the two had met while jogging in Battersea Park. "I just could not bring myself to tell the truth."

The newspaper was forced to hold the story, granting Browne a brief reprieve. But within a little more than a week, he was again on the defensive, this time about a matter relating to BP business. On January 16, the Baker Panel, an independent commission that John Browne had set up to objectively examine safety culture and safety management at the company's U.S. refineries, led by former U.S. Secretary of State James Baker, released a scathing report about the disaster. Many had expected the panel to produce a BP-friendly version of the events.

Instead, it found not only that BP had allowed conditions at the Texas City refinery to deteriorate dangerously but that the company had created "a false sense of confidence," and that its problems were pervasive and present at all its refineries. "BP appears to have had a corporate blind spot relating to process safety," James Baker said, taking aim directly at John Browne: "Leadership from the top of the company . . . is essential. BP has not adequately established process safety as a core value. . . . While BP has an aspirational goal of 'no accidents, no harm to people,' BP has not provided effective leadership. . . . Significant process safety culture issues exist at all five U.S. refineries, not just Texas City."

Back in London, immediately following Baker's comments, a humbled but slightly defensive Browne held his own press conference, flanked by his top executives. At first he discussed the progress BP had made in terms of safety since 2005. Fewer people had died in vehicle accidents at BP properties, he said, for example. But then he got down to an admission: "BP gets it. And I get it too," he said. "This happened on my watch, and, as chief executive, I have a responsibility to learn from what has occurred. I recognize the need for improvement."

Those who knew him and who had worked on the report found him to be genuine. "At the beginning, right after when we were in the middle of writing our report, I had the feeling he didn't really get it," said Nancy Leveson, a member of the Baker Panel and a professor of aeronautics and astronautics at MIT. "But then they had this problem with the big spill in Alaska, and they had other problems. By the time we released our report, John Browne got it. I spent a lot of time talking to him and he truly wanted to do something about safety."

BP's board might have been able to tolerate Browne's personal scandal—after all, he had more than proven himself and had shepherded BP almost single-handedly through one of the greatest corporate recoveries of all time. But the Baker Panel report *was* about business, and, despite the shifting winds that people like Leveson detected in Browne's leadership, the report was enough to push the board's growing concerns about BP's direction over the edge. By mid-January the board had decided that Browne would turn over the reins of the company to Tony Hayward in July, eighteen months earlier than originally planned.

At about the same time, just before a January 23 hearing, Browne admitted to the judge in the case that he had lied under oath when he said that he had met Chevalier in Battersea Park. He attempted to retract his story, trying to correct, as he put it, a matter of conscience. But it was too late. In March, Browne lost his case and filed an appeal that would keep the court records sealed. Then, on May 1, 2007, the appeal also failed. The House of Lords, Britain's highest court, declined to take the case further. Justice David Eady released his decision in the case that morning. "I am not prepared to make allowances for a 'white lie,'" Justice Eady ruled, clearing the way for the *Mail* story to go to press. The ruling triggered the immediate release of court documents, and that afternoon, the public learned that Browne had met Chevalier at London's premier escort service and, more importantly, that he had lied about it.

There was little more his embattled company could do to protect him, even if it had wanted to. What had started out as a sex scandal, something the British public was accustomed to shrugging off, had ended with the chief executive of England's largest corporation per-juring himself. The same day, May 1, Browne resigned, effective imme-diately. After forty-one years with BP, Browne paid for a cluster of personal mistakes with his career.

"It's a sorry end for Lord Browne," said CNBC Europe commenta-tor Dan Mann on that evening's television news in London. "This is a man who has had the most incredible career at BP. Arguably he has taken them from a mid-playing oil company to one of the greatest. It's a little bit of a tragic end."

As sad as it was for John Browne, his departure would also prolong his company's cultural transformation, and may have even undone some of the progress the BP corporation had begun to make. "It's really a shame," Leveson says. "I think if he would have stayed, things would have changed faster at BP."

BP's TROUBLES wouldn't stop with John Browne's departure. They wouldn't even slow down to wait for him to make a smooth exit. On May 16, 2007, roughly two weeks after Tony Hayward took control of the company, the U.S. Congress summoned BP back to Capitol Hill for a second hearing before the Committee on Energy and Commerce's subcommittee on Oversight and Investigations. This time, members had done their own investigation into BP's oil fields in Alaska. They still had no idea about Marty Anderson's investigation into the qualifications of the pipeline inspectors there, but they had found enough to allege that a pattern of willful neglect existed in BP's pipeline maintenance programs. Among its findings was a damning copy of a critical 2002 Alaskan state report about BP called a compliance order by consent (COBC), which the committee believed BP should have delivered to Congress in response to its subpoena in 2006.

The newly uncovered report said that even in 2002, BP had been neglecting its pipelines, that corrosion was an escalating risk at the time, and that BP was delinquent in meeting its obligations under state law. "BPXA has not equipped the FACILITY [the oil transit lines in Prudhoe Bay] with the enhanced leak detection system to satisfy the requirement. . . . BPXA will not comply with EOA [Eastern Operating Area] plan condition of approval. . . . Since Dec. 7, 2000[,] BPXA has operated the facility in violation." According to the document, BP had been warned since the late 1990s that its lines were collecting sediment and risked severe corrosion and that an adequate leak detection system needed to be installed. The document also noted that the state of Alaska had ordered BP to pig its eastern lines (EOA) by June 2002 and its western lines by September 2002. The order corresponds to the same years in which Richard Woollam and the corrosion managers were limiting corrosion-related expenses in order to operate within the parameters of John Browne's budget. Neither set of lines was ever pigged.

When Congress discovered the previously withheld document in late 2006, even Joe Barton, known to be chummy with the oil industry, was perplexed by what looked like a blatant attempt by the company to mislead the committee. In the previous year's hearing, on September 7, 2006, Malone and BP Alaska president Steve Marshall had downplayed the role of cost cuts and told the committee—then chaired by Barton—that they had been caught off guard by the deteriorating condition of the pipelines. Now the uncovered compliance order clearly contradicted that testimony, and Barton wasn't buying it: "This compliance order shows that BPXA was aware in at least 2001 that these lines . . . should be pigged," he wrote to Malone upon discovering the document.

By the time of the 2007 congressional hearing, Congress had also gathered, with the help of Chuck Hamel and his sources in Prudhoe Bay, Richard Woollam's emails from the late 1990s in which he discussed cutting off the supply of the chemicals used to combat corrosion. In addition, Congress was given the 2005 emails in which the corrosion group debated ending the pigging program altogether, and lamented that on some lines pigging hadn't been done in years.

The internal emails suggested the extent to which BP had cut back its corrosion monitoring program in order to save money, and they again seemed to contradict what Malone and Marshall had told the congressional committee eight months earlier, when the two men had insisted that the oil transit line leaks were anomalies. Bob Malone had repeatedly professed his confidence in BP's corrosion management program and in the company's maintenance policies. Even as revelations about the extent to which cost cutting had allowed the Texas City refinery to deteriorate came out through the Baker Panel report, BP insisted that Alaska was different and that no such pressures were at play there. Now, with his company in shambles and London headquarters distracted by the messy transition between CEOs, Bob Malone once again traveled to Washington and stepped into the line of fire to answer the concerns of Congress.

In January Malone had demoted Steve Marshall. Marshall would be the first fall guy for what had happened on the pipelines, and the start of Malone's efforts to fix the safety culture and demonstrate progress. Marshall was never explicitly blamed, but the question of how BP's executives could have remained oblivious to the extent of the corrosion problems in Alaska, or not known about Alaska's compliance order until it surfaced in front of Congress, cast a pall over his departure as BP Alaska's president.

In Malone's view, the time for discussion and rehash was over. The change of management was less about consequences and more about the future. As one company insider put it, Marshall "could be blown over like a feather. BP Alaska needed a backbone." Malone didn't want talk. He wanted a man who could get things done. He wanted the pipelines replaced, the inspection program enhanced, and the company's systems tuned before another accident happened on his watch. To replace Marshall, he chose a headstrong field manager named Doug Suttles, an engineer trained in Austin, Texas, who had spent the past eight years with BP in Alaska, had a portfolio of international infrastructure experience, including at BP's Sakhalin Island projects in Russia's Far East, and had come to the company from Exxon years before. Efficient, authoritative, and decisive, he was also known for his fierce independence and stubborn pride, traits that could make him a difficult employee.

When Congress called BP executives back to testify, Malone kept Suttles on a leash. He was far too abrasive and arrogant to deftly navigate the lawmakers' barrage of questions. Malone also didn't want Marshall, who had taken a bruising in the first round of testimony, to represent the company. Thus it was Malone alone who came to answer for the company's troubles in Washington.

He sat in the center of the row of witness seats, stooping slightly to put his mouth to the microphone. Among the first questions, from Michigan representative Bart Stupak, the chairman of the subcommittee, was one meant to sting: "Will you agree with me that there is a pattern of cost-cutting pressure during a time of healthy profits?"

Malone's answer surprised the committee by its directness. "We recognize there were extreme budget pressures at Prudhoe Bay," Malone said, acknowledging in the most public forum yet that Browne's cutbacks had eroded the quality of operations. "Yes, sir."

Stupak continued: "Would you agree with me that this cost-cutting pressure could have contributed to a culture that disincentivized or discouraged preventative maintenance?"

Malone, who is known for his ability to defuse confrontational situations, took a tack of blunt honesty. He hadn't known about the consent order or the extent of the compromises unveiled by the Woollam emails, he told them, but in the past months, he had learned a lot about the budget pressures. "Mr. Chairman, not only could it, we believe it did," he said. Malone went on to assure the lawmakers that the company was now heavily investing in its facilities in Alaska. He promised, among other things, an investigation into what progress BP had made since the work done by Jeanne Pascal in the late 1990s and by Vinson & Elkins in 2004. In particular, he wanted to find answers to the following questions: Had the company's treatment of its employees improved? And what had happened to all the workers who had told BP's investigators in 2001 that they had been punished for voicing their concerns? In light of what the Baker Panel had written about Texas City, these were questions that were no longer just about BP Alaska, and Malone said as much. "There were similarities in what we found in these reports between Texas City and Alaska," he told the committee.

It was the start of a frank discussion with lawmakers about where BP stood and where it had gone wrong, and perhaps the truest start of BP's rehabilitation. Like an addict who can't begin to recover until he hits rock bottom, BP had sustained one tragedy after another, been made to face its lies, and been held accountable in the court of the public.

WEARY FROM the berating by Congress, Malone flew back to Houston and then made the short drive to Texas City. There, checking in to his waterfront hotel, he was greeted by a grateful Tony Hayward in the lobby. Malone had taken a bullet for the company, Hayward told him. Hayward was in the midst of his first tour of U.S. operations since becoming CEO, and the two would visit the refinery site the next morning.

Malone and Hayward had crossed paths professionally over the years—and both men served on BP's board, which had met just ten days earlier—but Malone didn't know what sort of man to expect. It was a few days before Hayward's fifty-first birthday, and his twenty-fifth year with the company. He struck Malone as competent but humble; soft-spoken but comfortable as a leader. Other colleagues described him as an organized thinker, with tremendous resolve but an unassuming touch, and the kind of confidence and down-to-earth traits that might come from being, as Hayward was, the first of seven children. "The eldest gets to do everything, takes care of everyone," Hayward once told BP's corporate magazine. "It requires you to be responsible quite early."

Hayward was raised in upscale Windsor, twenty-five miles west of London, in a household of such modest means that his family, which had enough money to send him to college, couldn't pay for him to finish. Hayward was more a football fan than an academic anyway; he was also keenly interested in rugby, cricket, sailing, and competing as a triathlete. He wound up in a geology program almost by accident, and when his studies finally began to interest him, he found a way to pay the remaining quarters of college tuition himself. A couple of years later, with a PhD from the University of Edinburgh and significant world travel behind him, Hayward landed his first job—at British Petroleum.

His first years with British Petroleum were spent as a rig geologist in Aberdeen, tough work among salty crews in the North Sea. "It was a great lesson in humility," he said once. It also gave him a thrilling taste of success. On a cold Christmas morning in 1982, his crew drilled into the top of the Miller reservoir, which would prove to be a three-hundred-million-barrel oil field.

After that, his career had moved in lockstep with John Browne and the revolution that Browne had begun in that 1989 meeting in Rockefeller Center. In 1990 Hayward asked Browne, then head of worldwide exploration and production, for an apprenticeship. He spent eighteen tough months shadowing Browne—earning, in experience, the equivalent of university degrees in finance and business. He worked his way into the role of treasurer and married a BP geophysicist. He and his wife had two children, one of whom was born while the couple was stationed in Colombia. In 2003, he was promoted to head of worldwide exploration himself.

Now, quite suddenly, Hayward found himself propelled out of Browne's shadow to stand in his place. Because he had learned much of what he knew from Browne, Hayward didn't have dramatically different values or a new philosophy about how to run the company. But he was a different sort of leader, a different kind of person, and it opened up a fresh opportunity for BP. "Hayward's shtick is that he's a bloke's bloke," says Matthew Gwyther, the editor of *Management Today*. "He knows about the business of getting oil out of the ground. He doesn't have airs and graces. He doesn't behave like Louis the Sixteenth or what have you. No expensive cigars, expensive wine, and all those sorts of things." Where Browne carried a sort of stodgy presidential air and hobnobbed with the elite, Hayward was more comfortable keeping a lower profile. Some in the company said he had a one-of-us kind of appeal that fit in with Hayward's desire to be seen as a team player and, for a change, a good listener.

His modesty seemed fitting, because the task ahead of Tony Hayward was far less glamorous than the opportunities that had unfolded before John Browne. He needed to rehabilitate his company's reputation, and to reorganize its value system and its operations to revolve around safety. It was something that Hayward had been thinking about for a long time—ever since Texas City and Thunder Horse. He began to boldly articulate his own vision for the company nearly two years before he became its chief executive, and long before the Baker Panel report and the other critical assessments of what had gone wrong in Texas City were finished. "This has been one hell of a year," he began, at a town hall meeting in mid-2005. "There is no place to start other than with Texas City. . . . This is about a fundamental lack of leadership and management in the area of safety, period." He pledged to undertake a substantive inventory and reanalysis of the company's risks. "I would say that this company is weak in the area of process safety. We have a lot of work to do there. . . . There have been a number of incidents this year, which you don't need me to recount, but that I hope make you realize that this is never done, and that we just need to stay absolutely focused on it."

Once he became CEO, much of that safety challenge amounted to housecleaning the mess left after Browne's party, and finishing the jobs already begun. In a sense, the mega-mergers BP had created in the 1990s with ARCO and Amoco still hadn't been completed. Integrating those companies remained the fundamental task facing BP. Hayward would also still have to figure out how to help the company grow in a postconsolidation age. Few big new oil fields were being discovered and global oil resources continued to decline. To his benefit, Hayward had a deep bench of leadership talent to draw on at the company. Iain Conn, his head of refining and marketing, had worked in just about every BP division. Andy Inglis was a trusted manager who had long worked under Hayward in exploration and ran the Gulf of Mexico fields. Hayward promoted him to head of worldwide exploration. Malone, who would continue in his role in the United States, seemed to be making fast progress in repairing the company's reputation there.

Perhaps most beneficial of all, Hayward had the opportunity to learn from John Browne's mistakes. For that, there was no better place to begin than with the ghosts of the past.

The morning of May 17, 2007, in Texas City, Malone and Hayward, along with a handful of refinery staff, walked across the barren concrete yard where the isomerization unit had once stood. There were no cameras or press conferences. This was a private visit. Ropes still cordoned off the area—they would until the Department of Justice finished is investigation. The wreckage of the JE Merit trailer was gone, but its ghost was marked by charred boundaries in an empty stretch of concrete. Burned and twisted metal still surrounded the site. It had been twenty-six months since the explosion, and it still looked bad. The discussion was somber. Hayward hadn't been a part of BP's refining group or borne the burden yet of what had gone wrong in Texas. Now, as the company's chief, he reflected privately on this legacy. After a while, Hayward wandered off apart from Malone and the others to a corner on the charred lot and stood there for a few moments in silence. When he turned to walk back, the back of his hand wiped across his eyes. Nothing more was said.

JEANNE PASCAL had watched the proceedings in Congress that week with a heavy dose of skepticism. She liked Bob Malone. She found him direct and honest and well intentioned. He seemed to her like a guy who believed that if he just tried hard enough, wished hard enough, he could steer what she increasingly saw as a *Titanic* of a company back in the right direction. But in her gut, she wondered if he was realistic about the momentum of the forces working against him. Nonetheless, she had high hopes that when Tony Hayward said that nothing would be as important to him as reforming the company's safety culture, the issues she had been peeling back in Alaska would earn a higher rank on his list of priorities.

She would give them time. But Pascal had known about Chuck Hamel's informants for more than six months before their stories and documents became public through the congressional hearings—and apparently before Malone himself had found out. She had seen those emails from Woollam's office, heard from the workers who found themselves out of a job—coincidentally—a few months after filing a complaint. And she had learned all about the sludge buildup in the pipelines that Alaskan officials wanted fixed years before they led to a spill. How was it that she could know about these issues and the company's own executives could tell Congress that they had not known anything about them?

Increasingly, Pascal thought that BP might not, in fact, be fit for the government contracts it was repeatedly rewarded with. That was her main concern in the matter. She had always believed strongly in the principle that whatever a corporation did wrong, the behavior had to far outweigh the benefits it offered to the American economy and to society before she would cut them off. The United States depended on BP to run its pipelines, to supply its fuel, even to manage some strategic international energy assets. But now she was concluding that it couldn't be trusted to protect its own workers or to abide by the law. And if a truly huge BP accident happened one day as a result, it might easily outweigh the benefits the company provided.

The EPA's criminal division was quietly laying the foundations of a case, and Pascal would watch, and wait, to see what they found. Mostly, she anticipated that Scott West, the Seattle investigator whom she had introduced to Chuck Hamel a few months back and who had been assigned the EPA's special agent in charge of the investigation, would dig up some answers.

West was a veteran agent who had investigated corporate environmental crimes for the EPA, working out of San Francisco for sixteen years. Before that he had been a U.S. Customs agent. In 2005 he was moved back to Seattle, where he worked with the EPA regional office. The BP case was his first investigation into the oil industry. West was exactly the kind of guy the government wanted on the job – bold, intimidating, purposeful, and fearless. He was six foot six, with a bushy beard and a head of flowing, wispy hair. In his driveway sat a Triumph Rocket III, one of the fastest and most powerful motorcycles ever made. West rode it hard, touring the Cascade Mountains and the countryside of the Pacific Northwest. When he was home he held practice bouts in fencing for fun. At work, he poured all that vigor into his investigations.

For months before the spill, West had been following up on the leads Pascal and Hamel had delivered to him. He had traveled the country interviewing BP employees, and each of Hamel's conspiratorial-sounding accusations had checked out. Even before March 2006, West had become convinced that BP management in Alaska clearly understood the risks they were taking in not maintaining the pipelines. But legally, there was nothing to prosecute and little he could do about it but wait. The morning of the oil spill, West got a call from a worker in Deadhorse before the sun rose. "It's happening," the worker told him. The news changed everything.

"When I received the phone call," West says, "I knew I had a criminal case right there. . . . The difference between an accident and a criminal case would be the knowledge that the officials had prior to the pipe rupture." He thought he had a head start in proving that knowledge existed.

Within hours, even as John Browne was ordering his management to "overreact," West had put an Anchorage-based EPA employee on a flight to Prudhoe Bay so the agency could observe every aspect of the spill response. Soon West was mapping out, under the Clean Water Act, what he believed could become one of the most significant criminal corporate cases in recent history.

The EPA was eager for such a case. The Criminal Investigation Division is relatively small, and tries to have a broad impact on corporate polluters even with its limited reach. Prosecution of a large, powerful corporation like BP would not only serve justice but would send a message to other corporations that the government regulators were watching, were effective, and, especially important to some of them during the presidency of George W. Bush, still cared. West was given a small staff to work with, and liaised with a team of U.S. Attorneys assigned by the Department of Justice.

It wasn't that the government suspected anyone at BP of intentionally pumping hundreds of thousands of gallons of oil onto the tundra. "But what is clear is that BP officials had knowledge from their own employees that this was of grave concern. And they chose to ignore it," West says. "That's negligence, at the very least." At most, if West could prove that BP managers knew about specific problems and covered them up—or, for example, that BP had relied on safety inspections it knew had been falsified—then the company could be looking at felony charges.

On the face of it, BP cooperated with the investigation. It gave West and the others access to the North Slope. And it opened up its facilities, including sleeping barracks and mess halls, to the government's staff. It would have been nearly impossible for the investigators to maintain a presence in such a remote area without BP's help. "But there was a subtle hindrance that was going on," West says. For one, the staff the investigators encountered in Alaska was afraid to talk. BP management, West says, didn't encourage its employees to cooperate or to tell the truth. Their silence was an effective threat to those who were inclined to talk to West's team. When he did get interviews with workers, they were apprehensive.

They'd say, "Look, we've got things to say. This is important. But, you know, we've got a family to feed," West says. They wanted to do their job and make their money and go home. They didn't want to end up dead or injured, they told West, and they were afraid that the conditions BP tolerated on the North Slope could kill them. Putting such concerns on the record was another thing. They'd seen friends and co-workers fired and blacklisted for far smaller offenses than talking to the feds, and they were intimidated. BP drives every aspect of the economy on the slope. Once a worker had fallen out of the company's graces, he or she would have a tough time getting work from any of the dozens of contractors, or even from competing oil companies like ConocoPhillips and Exxon.

To make headway, the Department of Justice convened a grand jury that could compel both the company's managers and its employees to testify. "Most of our witnesses needed to be brought in front of the grand jury for their own protection," West said. They also issued a surgical subpoena for BP's corporate communications and internal records. West expected that the subpoena would document the stories he heard from workers. In his thinking, the Clean Water Act case the government was pursuing against BP in Alaska could serve a purpose beyond the pipeline spill. In fact, the March pipeline spill turned out to have a limited environmental impact. However, it presented a moment of opportunity to address a broader environmental safety problem within BP and, West hoped, to prevent the next disaster from being worse. "If they were making these kinds of decisions for this one transit pipeline, they were likely making these kinds of decisions wholesale across the corporation," West says. The government was conducting a parallel criminal Clean Air Act probe into BP's accident in Texas, and West compared notes with the EPA's special agent in charge of that investigation in Houston. "He was finding identical sorts of scenarios as I was identifying. It wasn't just an isolated event in Alaska. It wasn't just an isolated event in Texas City, or a 'wink-wink, nod-nod, end-of-year bonus' encouragement," West says. "It was corporate-wide negligence that brought about these two disasters."

The next step was to prove it. And that would take time: both to depose his witnesses and to wade through the sea of internal BP documents. BP gave the EPA everything it wanted and more. The company's lawyers delivered records—the equivalent of boxes and boxes in a giant electronic database that gave each document a serial number and amounted to one of the largest catalogues of information the EPA's investigators had ever gathered. Almost instantly, it overwhelmed the government's staff. There was too much information to sift.

Where the government's subpoena might have requested all records pertaining to corrosion management in the month of July 2003 with Richard Woollam's name on it, it would receive every technical report, subcontractor license, chemical handling advisory, and so forth for the corrosion program for the entire year in response. BP delivered some sixty-two million pages of documents—to be viewed by an EPA staff of four. And while the deliveries were mostly electronic, they were programmed in a format that made them unsearchable.

"They were just burying us in information. We'd ask for one document and we'd get a file cabinet," West says. "They would say, 'Well, we just want to be sure you get what you want.' But we felt that they knew that they were burying us and knew that the government had limited resources, where they had fairly unlimited legal resources.

Pascal viewed the process with disdain. It was only a few months earlier that BP had kept the critical Alaskan state compliance order about pipeline maintenance secret from Congress's investigation, an omission that had drawn rebukes from lawmakers. And here the company was, portraying itself as thorough to a fault. It appeared to be only in the last couple of years that BP had adopted this strategy of obstructing investigations to cope with its critics. For eighteen years Ed Meggert was employed by the Alaska state Department of Environmental Conservation as the on-scene coordinator responding to spills on Alaska's North Slope. There were thousands of them, large and small, and they were somewhat routine, considering the large-scale industrial process that drilling for oil in Alaska represented. Part of Meggert's job was to inspect and investigate all of the oil companies, not just BP.

Meggert says that around 2001 his relationship with BP began to change from an amicable, easygoing one to tense and adversarial. He thought the change came from within the company, not the state. Early on, for example, when there was a small spill and BP's management knew Meggert had files to complete for the state, management would open their doors and let him do his job. Midway through the decade, the company began asking Meggert to get subpoenas for anything he needed, an approach that would cost the state money and delay an investigation for weeks. After the big spill in March 2006 and all the attention it brought, Meggert began getting unmanageably large responses to his subpoenas, where previously he had gotten exactly the document he was looking for. "We would get boxes and boxes of material that we had to sort through. From that point on it was always an antagonistic relationship," Meggert says. "So you wonder what they are hiding, and it isn't always easy to know the right questions to ask."

The EPA, though, planned to be patient and thorough. If its investigators had to read sixty-two million pages of documents to get to the bottom of things, they were prepared to do that, and they set in for a steady period of research. There was no rush. The statute of limitations provided five years within which to bring charges, and a typical corporate case like this one would last at least two or three years, anyway.

By the spring of 2007, West says, the case was progressing well. West's supervisor, in a rush of enthusiasm one day in Seattle, told him that the BP Alaska case was one of the top two or three cases the Department of Justice was pursuing anywhere in the country. They viewed it as clear-cut, and devoid of too much political baggage. Who, after all, would argue for not coming down heavy on an oil company after a big spill?

West and the U.S. Attorney's office in Alaska began to steer their investigation toward the individuals who made critical decisions at BP, not just the company itself. The grand jury records are sealed, but some documents obtained through Freedom of Information Act (FOIA) requests show that the government was interested in prosecuting the very highest levels of BP leadership. Steve Marshall, Richard Woollam, and Andy Ingles were all named in investigation documents. Even Tony Hayward, six weeks after he was elevated to chief executive, was named in the criminal probe. "I felt that very senior members of the BP Corporation all the way over to London could be tied to the decision and knowledge about the cost cutting that led to the rupture of the pipeline," West said.

At the U.S. Attorney's office in Alaska, investigators thought the case was evolving beyond the misdemeanor stage. The difference between a misdemeanor and a felony had to do with whether or not executives deliberately covered up information that could have prevented the spill—and the environmental crime that accompanied it. If they simply missed the warning signs, and were negligent, the lesser charge was appropriate. But if the government could prove "knowing," as the Department of Justice called it, then they might be able to send an executive to jail.

As the Alaska case progressed, so did an array of private and government cases against BP in Texas. The U.S. Chemical Safety and Hazard Investigation Board (CSB), the Occupational Safety and Health Administration, the EPA, and the Department of Justice all still had investigations under way. In an unusual twist, the work of each agency was at least partially intertwined with the myriad civil suits still under way, among them Eva Rowe's lawsuit over her parents' deaths.

When Eva Rowe rejected BP's settlement offer in the months after the March 2005 explosion, spurning an amount close to $20 million, she embarked on a personal and legal journey that seemed destined for heartache and frustration. She had lost both of the authority figures in her life, and her life direction along with them. It was in preparation for her lawsuit, however, that the hardest battles for transparency and justice seemed to have been fought, and from which the most influential testimony and evidence about how the company behaved was produced. Going up against a multinational oil corporation was difficult. For a while, Rowe was disoriented, says Brent Coon, her lawyer, who became a close friend and support figure. "You're talking about a twenty-year-old little girl from a very rural part of southwestern Louisiana. And she didn't have very many coping tools that she needed to get through this. She was very frail. She was very emotional, very upset." The grieving went in stages. The first was denial. "I felt like I was in the middle of some sort of movie. And I couldn't believe it," Rowe says, referring to her parents' death. "They worked away a lot. So it felt like they were just gonna come home, because they were always away. And, you know, they never did."

Then she grasped at the world—at her friends, and parties, and bars—looking for a handrail into the future. She fought depression, drank heavily, used drugs, and battled to overcome each. "I was tryin' to find a way to cope with my emotions that I didn't know how to process. . . . maybe I woulda killed myself had I not been on drugs to suppress my feelings. They could have really saved my life. It's kinda a bad situation. But it's a real situation."

Finally, the lawsuit gave her an anchor. It was a grounding force, and it changed her.

When BP issued its own findings about the disaster in the weeks after the explosion and blamed the accident on the incompetence of its workers, Rowe felt as if the company was desecrating her parents' memory. The more she and Coon built their case, the more plainly they saw a set of facts demonstrating that even while BP wrote its innocent narrative for the public, the company understood and discussed internally the systemic operational safety problems that had allowed such an accident to happen. It made their public explanations ring hollow. "It was patently false. It was a lie—a bold-faced lie," Coon said of BP's own findings about the disaster. "It was their attempt to whitewash . . . and to make those employees the scapegoats. We did want that reversed. Eva wanted that reversed."

A driving force for Rowe was getting the library of damning internal documents collected for the case and the sworn depositions of BP's executives out of the courtroom and into the public record. She wanted those records in the public sphere, where newspapers could

pore through them and federal investigators from the CSB and the
EPA could use them as evidence in criminal prosecution. Rowe felt
that she couldn't settle, at least not under the common conditions
where each side is sworn to secrecy. Any agreement BP put on the
table included sealing the case file.

"I took a stand. I wasn't going to settle. I wasn't going to just go
away," she says. "We needed to know what happened here. We needed
all their documents. And they all needed to be public."

For a long time, Rowe didn't realize how much her determined
stance had made her a target. She was a victim. But she was also the
last holdout among the families of those who had been killed in the
Texas City disaster. And the more she antagonized BP, the more she
established herself as a threat to the company. She told her compelling story to the press willfully and often. She became a crack in the
armor of a company bent as much on repairing its public image as it
was on repairing itself. Just as Chuck Hamel had provoked BP and Alyeska into spying on him in the early 1990s, Rowe began to draw BP's
fire and wrath in ways that reached far beyond the courtroom. "After
I really took that stand is when I noticed, you know, I wasn't comfortable anymore being places," she says. "I wouldn't be alone."

In the grocery store, in a parking lot, in a bar, even parked on the
street outside her home, Rowe would see people milling aimlessly
who didn't seem to fit in, and she suspected they were watching her.
"I was afraid. I wouldn't even sit in front of a window," says Rowe. "I
was afraid something terrible was going to happen to me. Everywhere
I went, there was somebody there following me."

Her worst fears were confirmed when she and Coon met with BP's
attorneys, who laid a stack of photographs on the table—of Rowe
partying in bars or leaving a restaurant, drunk, with friends. The
images seemed aimed at intimidating her, by making it clear that BP
was watching her every move, as much as portraying her as cavalier
and irresponsible. "Maybe we were out, having drinks, or something
of that sort," she says. "My parents had been killed. You know, when
you're twenty, how will you cope with that? So I drank and stuff. And
they tried to put it as I was a bad person."

The company went after her character, and it went into her history.
Under the pretense of establishing a thorough defense of its safety

operations at the Texas City refinery—proving that it was not culpable for the deaths of James and Linda Rowe—BP investigators hunted down anybody who had ever had anything to do with Eva Rowe. They showed up in Hornbeck, Louisiana, and called her old boyfriends. They unearthed a spotty history of legal troubles that Rowe had once gotten herself into. Once, she had been arrested, and when BP gathered the police reports, its investigators interviewed every person mentioned in them. "They went through every record of her existence," Coon said. Most of the information was inadmissible in court, but it wound its way onto the desks of newspaper reporters in Houston, who called Coon to say they had received anonymous brown bags full of records about Rowe's checkered past, including her brushes with the law. "I've handled a number of high-end, catastrophic-type cases before," said Coon. "I had never seen anything near the likes of this in terms of looking for dirt. It was leading them only to things that they could publicly embarrass her about."

One morning Rowe left her house and saw a truck parked outside. It seemed it was waiting for her to leave. A few minutes later the blue and white lights of a police car whirred in her rearview mirror and she pulled over. The officer told her he had a warrant for her arrest and was taking her to the local jail. "I was, like, 'Why am I being arrested?'" Rowe says. But she didn't get an answer. A call had simply come over the radio. "Nobody even checked it out. The police department must have got really excited about it." Half an hour later, with no explanation, they let her go. She is convinced that BP was behind the stunt. "I believe they were trying to intimidate me, you know, to scare me into settlement," she says.

The soap opera around Rowe's personal life threatened to distract from the substance of her case against BP. But Coon, who had already unearthed BP's email debate about paying for the blowdown drums and the Three Little Pigs risk analysis, was proceeding with dozens of depositions from BP employees and managers, assembling the most detailed portrait yet of the company's operations.

On the morning of September 8, 2006, he met with John Manzoni in a rented room at the Hilton at Chicago's O'Hare International Airport. Manzoni was the highest-level executive—one tier down from John Browne—that Coon had deposed under oath, and it was Coon's best chance yet to hold an individual responsible for what happened in Texas City. Manzoni, who earned a million-dollar salary, wore a gray suit and a light-colored tie and sat stiffly in front a plain backdrop hung for the video camera. He was patiently, stubbornly argumentative. How could BP compare its workers to the three pigs or coldly calculate that each one was worth ten million dollars? BP would never put a price on a human life, Manzoni said. He claimed to have never seen the internal documents that showed the company did just that. Manzoni said that he was never informed about the deterioration of the facilities at Texas City, either. He insisted that the company had not cut back on maintenance at the expense of safety.

Coon asked him about his time as a field manager in Prudhoe Bay, where he oversaw Richard Woollam and the corrosion inspection program there. Then Coon drew parallels between the budget cuts to the corrosion program in Alaska and what had happened to the maintenance program at Texas City as Don Parus tried to reinvest in the facility there. "We don't defer maintenance as a rule," Manzoni said. "Never, at least in my experience, have we refused expenditure for safety purposes. I'm saying we didn't do it then and we don't do it now."

At Texas City, Manzoni said that he was never aware that the facility was in disrepair. "We didn't know that risk existed," he said. "We simply didn't see it coming." The statement left Coon and another lawyer in the room, Tony Buzbee, incredulous. "When was the first time that you learned there were serious safety concerns at BP Texas City?" Buzbee asked him.

"The twenty-third of March 2005," Manzoni replied, referring to the day of the explosion.

"Before that you had no idea that there was a risk of catastrophic injury?"

"No," Manzoni said, his face calm and quizzical, as if he were also the victim of a baffling development, and clearly claiming that he had never been shown the reports that used that exact language to predict what would eventually happen in Texas City. "Had I been aware that we could have had a catastrophic failure, we would have taken action earlier, different action," he said.

Buzbee asked him how many people got injured at BP each year. Manzoni replied that the company didn't keep track of how many people had been hurt or what happened to them. Instead, it used an injury frequency rate, a formula, that factors injuries per two hundred thousand hours worked. By that calculation, he said, BP had an injury rate of 0.13. The explanation confirmed what other BP executives had said—that the company tended to translate even the most human issues into statistics—and it led to a notable exchange.

"You don't just try to figure out how many people you have hurt, and ruined their lives? You just try to figure out what the rate is?" asked Buzbee.

"I care about every single individual that we injure," Manzoni replied. "I care about all of our people."

"Tell me the names of some of the people that your company injured on March 23, 2005," Buzbee asked.

"No, I don't have that list."

"Can you name one of them?

"No."

"You can't name any of them that were killed?"

"No, I can't," Manzoni replied.

The exchange left Coon in disbelief. "Can't even name the name of the—*the*—person we were there about," Coon says. "I mean, Eva Rowe was known all over the place for losing both of her parents. He couldn't even come up with that name. If he'd read the paper he'd at least have known that name."

Almost all of the executive interviews had gone this way. Pat Gower, the number three at the plant whom Don Parus said he pleaded with to upgrade some of the facility's dangerous systems, denied being advised about the findings of Parus's Telos report. Mike Hoffman told Coon there were a few concerns, but BP was fixing them. Everything was under control.

Eventually, much later on, Coon would get to depose John Browne himself. Interviewed long after the Baker Panel report was released and after he had professed to "get it," Browne had a difficult time owning up to what had happened in Texas. Instead he suffered from an uncharacteristic failure of memory about the details of which reports warned of what and when—even when one scathing internal review recommended the dismissal of nearly his entire chain of command managing the Texas City plant. He said he hadn't known about the

Telos report prior to the blast; and, although he had ordered a 25 percent across-the-board spending cut, he said that he did not understand
that cost cuts were affecting the Texas City plant.

"Were you ever made aware of what BP Texas City did in response
to the budget reduction requests out of London?" Coon asked him, at
the beginning of the hour-long interview.

"No," Browne replied.

"Were you aware that the plant manager at Texas City initiated dozens of different cost-cutting measures after receipt of this request?"

"I wasn't aware of that," Browne said.

"When *were* you first personally made aware that there may be
some problems at Texas City?"

"I was never made aware directly," Browne said.

"Do you blame Mr. Manzoni for not bringing it to your attention?"
Coon asked him.

"Mr. Manzoni had delegated authority," Browne replied, effectively
deflecting the line of questioning.

The interviews left Coon with the company's word against a library
of documents that seemed to prove the contrary. "These are not dum-
mies," he said. "These are guys that are the key executives of a major
organization. They came in and basically professed ignorance—that
they were not aware of *any* of these problems." BP continued to refuse
to settle with Rowe on her terms. The company seemed to be bluffing
on the belief that what she really wanted was more money, and that
she didn't want the expense of arguing in court. Coon, however, was
confident that a jury would decide in her favor.

After months of motions and legal wrangling, on November 9,
2006, the parties were set to meet in a Houston courtroom to begin
selecting a jury. Win or lose, at this point, Coon relished the thought of
bringing each of his findings into the public record, one document at
a time, in front of the media, all day, every day, "in excruciating detail,"
until the trial ended. The next day, the unveiling of the documents
would begin.

But they never got there. Before jury selection could even begin,
BP suddenly settled the case, bringing an abrupt end to the public process of airing BP's record in court. The company would contribute $30
million to local schools and foundations, including $12.5 million to

the Process Safety Center at Texas A&M University, and $12.5 million to the University of Texas Medical Center in Galveston, where David Leining and so many other of the 180 who were injured were taken for treatment. Rowe received a large payment, the terms of which have never been disclosed, but which has been estimated to be in the range of $30 million. Most importantly, in a concession that would alter the historical record of the incident and aid the numerous government investigations under way, seven million pages of sealed corporate documents would be made public.

The documents, plus the sworn depositions of BP's management, led in part to the release, in March 2007, of the Chemical Safety and Hazard Investigation Board's report, a deeply analytical incrimination of BP at all levels. The report, completed in the model of the investigation into NASA after the *Columbia* space shuttle disaster, found that BP's "organizational culture and structure" had caused the Texas City refinery blast as much as any one condition. It found that "organizational and safety deficiencies" existed at all levels of the corporation, and said that the company's executives in London had failed to intervene to prevent the deadly disaster even though "warning signs of a possible disaster were present for several years." The report found that BP's cost cutting had clearly contributed to the disaster.

The U.S. Chemical Safety and Hazard Investigation Board had conducted its own detailed on-site investigation of the Texas City refinery blast, and produced the definitive moment-by-moment technical autopsy of what had gone wrong. CSB would not have gotten nearly as far without BP's decision to give in to Coon and Rowe and release the documents. "I think they decided, rather than the death of a thousand cuts . . . that it was better for them to just fold their tent and say, "Okay, y'all can have the documents. They can go to the public," says Coon. "We'd rather 'em go to the public in one big batch."

PART THREE

The Reformation

12

A CHANGING CULTURE

WHEN TONY HAYWARD took the helm at BP, he swore that everything would change. BP would be a new company, stripped of all that had led it down the perilous path of the past few years but still strong and profitable and growing. He was inclined to believe that the past was in the past, and in 2007, he was charting his own ambitious path for the company into the future.

The corporation Hayward had been handed operated in 100 countries, with more than $236 billion in assets and nearly 97,000 employees—33,000 of whom ran operations in the United States (not counting the many thousands more contractors there). For all of John Browne's remarkable successes in the twelve years he had run the company, Hayward took over at a time of lagging performance. Where BP had matched Shell's profits in 2005, by 2007 it was $8 billion behind. BP's U.S. refining business, which accounted for 86 percent of its revenues but only 29 percent of its profits, was stunted by maintenance problems and slowdowns at three of its biggest plants, in Ohio, Indiana, and Texas City, and the group was operating at just 50 percent of capacity. Hayward, with his background in exploration, was a firm believer that the Gulf of Mexico held most of the growth opportunity for BP, but Thunder Horse had brought costly delays, and another of BP's flagship new deepwater drilling rigs there, Atlantis, was also behind schedule.

One of Hayward's first steps was a candid, self-reflective declaration of how bad things had gotten. On September 19, five months after becoming CEO, he gathered a group of midlevel managers for a meeting in Houston. In his folksy and plainspoken style, he outlined his central criticisms of the company, both financial and organizational. BP's management was burdensome and overlayered. It failed to hear its employees and lacked accountability. It had somehow simultaneously become both blind to the consequences of risk and, in the recent crisis years, too risk-averse to make the smart plays that would move it forward. He calculated that those problems alone had cost the company some $2 billion a year. Then he added those faults to other, more tangible expenses, such as the ongoing Thunder Horse delay. "Due to all of these things I expect the third quarter to be absolutely dreadful," Hayward told the group.

Hayward may have intended his remarks to serve as a splash of ice water on the face of a drowsy company he hoped to startle back toward star performance. In 1989, Browne had said nearly the same thing, and it had kicked off one of the most remarkable eras in the oil business. But this time the statement went viral in the world's newspapers and trading rooms, further unsettling the New York and London stock markets' confidence in BP. The comments were read as a gaffe, the first of many as Hayward struggled to find a public voice sophisticated enough for the media but still candid enough to reflect his down-to-earth leadership style. "John was a wonderful spokesman for BP. He was articulate. He was thoughtful. He was an excellent public speaker," says Freeman. "Tony Hayward was none of those things." On the afternoon of his remarks, the company's stock dropped 3 percent on London's FTSE exchange: $6 billion had evaporated.

Unflagging, Hayward continued in a quest to make BP his own, in large part by laying a lot of blame at his predecessor's feet. He listed the aspects of BP he viewed as needing repair, summing up the worst that had been said about BP by its workers, its critics, and investigators over the past decade of John Browne's leadership. BP was an unfocused company, Hayward declared, distracted by a preoccupation with growth and by environmental do-gooders who had led the company away from its core business and allowed it to grow distant from its own workforce. The company would have to get back to its roots. Hayward articulated his thinking most lucidly in a speech he delivered at Stanford Graduate School of Business much later, in 2009.

"We diagnosed—in no particular order—the following: a company that was too top-down, too directive, and not good at listening," he said, recalling his thoughts at the time he became CEO. "There used to be a little joke about, you know, good news traveled instantly and bad news didn't travel at all. We failed to recognize we're an operating company. We had too many people that did not understand what it took to run operations. . . . We had too many shallow generalists. People who knew a lot about not very much. But not a lot about specific areas. . . . We had too many people that were working to save the world. We'd sort of lost track of the fact that our primary purpose in life is to create value for our shareholders. . . . You need to take care of the world. But our primary purpose in life was not to save the world."

Hayward set out to fix every one of the company's faults and said that management would be dramatically reorganized and resources reallocated to reflect the shift. Browne had left him a tangled mess. By Hayward's analysis, BP's myriad operations had something like ten thousand different organizational management groups, all trying to interact. BP operated with thirty-six distinct leadership models in various parts of the company—a working system that he believed was cumbersome, dangerous, and expensive. "It's not surprising: we assembled all these companies from all over the place," he said. "And they all had their different bits of heritage." Hayward's efforts rested on a recalibration of the company's approach to risk and safety, and he promised BP would maintain a "laser-like focus."

How separate could Hayward really be from the company Browne had constructed, though? After all, Hayward himself had been eager in 2005—before the pipeline failures in Alaska and the renewed criminal and congressional investigations there—to believe that BP's troubles had passed. "The only good thing I would say . . . is it's good to have it all behind you," he had said then, reflecting on Texas City and Thunder Horse during a town hall meeting with workers that year. He wasn't anticipating that the next accident would happen a few months later in his own division. To some who watched the company closely after he became CEO in 2007, his black-and-white differentiation of his own style of leadership from Browne's seemed forced. "The interesting thing about all these comments that Hayward made was that everybody swallowed hook, line, and sinker that, yes, BP was a bad company, but that that had nothing to do with Hayward," says Hoyos, who wrote about the transition for the *Financial Times*. "Excuse me? Hayward was running exploration and production at that point. He had the ear of John Browne and was his closest confidant. He managed to . . . shift this all into the past and almost extricate himself from that past. That's what people wanted to hear, and that's what he did. I said he was untested, and I think I was being diplomatic. In reality I thought that he may not be up to the job."

Ron Freeman, too, thought that Hayward's about-face was superficial. "Where was he when all these things were happening? It's this confession, this purging of the soul in very undiplomatic, blunt language," he says. "The 'save the world' comment was very much criticized as Tony's attack on John—gratuitous and unnecessary. Why did he have to do that?"

Purely motivated or not, Hayward would quickly discover that fixing what had gone wrong, and molding the company into his own vision, would be a lot harder than just firing a couple of levels of senior management—which he did. For all his simplistic idealism about more investment in safety and culture, Hayward would face the same relentless business pressures of any public company, and he would have to deal with them at a time of far less opportunity and flexibility than Browne had enjoyed when he took over in 1995.

Moreover, the challenges Hayward set for himself may have been premised more on conflicting trajectories than he could realize at the time. So much of the financial growth BP had enjoyed had been seeded by the very cuts that eventually led to accidents. Many of the extra layers and inefficiencies that Hayward targeted were originally implemented to improve safety and communication. To keep his promise, Hayward would not only have to unravel the intertwined relationship between cost cuts and profits but alter the outlook of the company's leadership and workforce to eradicate the deeply ingrained view that investing in safety wasn't worthwhile. The company had to adopt the philosophy that safety and risk management would stimulate value and growth. It was a fundamental difference in thinking. Hayward thought he was up to the task.

That year Hayward formulated plans for a system that would help standardize BP's approach to risk and operations in much the way Exxon had done after its *Valdez* disaster. In fact, the program, called the Operating Management System (OMS), closely mimicked Exxon's program in both name and intention. Then Hayward launched what he called an Operations Academy, a sort of higher-learning curriculum that would be run by MIT and teach BP managers how to identify risk and improve safety. In particular, it would teach them to focus on operations in a structured and rigorous way. Hayward himself would be among the program's first class of students.

"What I'm very certain about is that a culture of an organization is shaped by the leaders in it. People do what leaders do," Hayward said in the 2009 lecture at Stanford. "So this was about beginning to change the culture at BP. We never talked about it like that. We never used the words 'cultural change' or anything like that. But that's what we were doing. And we were creating the leadership basis on which that would happen."

He knew it would be a long haul. With sustained effort, he thought a cultural transformation might take root in management by sometime in 2010. It would take a few years longer before he expected it to trickle all the way down to the workers in the oil fields. Hayward's challenge would not only be achieving the shift but doing it faster than the pace of the government's criminal cases, and before safety problems led to another accident. The effort at transformation was like a race against an invisible opponent who could reach the finish line at any moment, except you could never see where that opponent was or, by extension, when the impending disaster might happen.

HAYWARD'S LEADERSHIP on safety seemed bold, but the changes he made in London and Houston wouldn't reach BP's Alaska business for a long time. There, in the latter half of 2007, the pipeline inspection program continued in an unaltered state of disarray, and Marty Anderson's allegations that BP relied on untrained, unlicensed technicians to inspect its lines was for a long time unaddressed.

Anderson's audit was still more or less a secret—not known beyond the inner management of BP's Alaska operations. Though it would begin to explain how the company's pipelines had deteriorated so far, so "quickly," the Acuren audit hadn't come up in the congressional hearings. Jeanne Pascal hadn't yet been informed of it. The EPA criminal investigators—Scott West and the Department of Justice team— had inexplicably skipped over Acuren and Anderson's group in their ongoing criminal investigation into the Prudhoe Bay spills.

In Alaska, Anderson's work had drawn a cool reception. The general preference, it seemed, was that deficiencies in the program be addressed quietly and informally. At one point, after more details from Anderson's audit were delivered to Acuren in April 2007, his manager, George Bryant, had pulled him into his office. "If you play well with this, you'll have a place at the table," Anderson recalls him saying. "I said, 'George, if the table is in federal prison, I don't want to be there,'" Anderson replied. Separately, an Acuren sister company had floated the idea of buying out Anderson's personal inspection business, a potentially lucrative offer for Anderson. Yet nobody did anything to address the core findings of his reports, even as Anderson's ongoing work uncovered more problems. Having found that the inspectors were questionable, he turned to the equipment they used in the field. He found that much of it was faulty, out of calibration, or just missing. In some cases, the wrong equipment was being used altogether. When Bryant did nothing, Anderson took his findings straight to BP, and BP, for a long time, also turned a blind eye. BP Alaska's president, Doug Suttles, "basically just denied everything," Anderson says. He dismissed the audit as "just documentation issues" and refused to meet Anderson in person.

BP had completed its own audit—its first in five years—and reached watered-down versions of Anderson's findings. It kept the same inspectors out in the field on the same jobs, stretching to meet the same sorts of quotas. The lack of action didn't make sense. How could a company plagued by one corrosion problem after another, one disaster after another, find out that the stopgap system meant to make sure its operations were safe in Alaska was faulty . . . and still do nothing? How could Hayward pledge a revamped focus on safety and insist that he now had his ear primed for the concerns of managers like Doug Suttles, and not do anything? One possibility was that Suttles wasn't communicating with the company's more senior executives about the challenges BP faced in Alaska, but even that failed to make sense to Anderson. Everybody was supposed to want the same thing: safety and reliability. And he had uncovered the key to rectifying one of BP's most significant safety and reliability lapses. The company should have been congratulating him, he thought. Instead, it seemed that BP was more intent on maintaining the status quo.

In the meantime, by the last months of 2007, Anderson had become something of a pariah. Acuren had begun to blame him for the problems in the inspection program, since Anderson, after all, was the supervisor when the problems were discovered. BP, watching the dynamic play out, condoned the revisionist approach, allowing Anderson to float in an employment purgatory. He wasn't fired, but he wasn't asked to do work. In BP's large worker cafeterias, he was left to eat by himself. Meetings were held without him ever being told. Most importantly, he couldn't get the staff or the resources to finish the sections of the audit that still needed to be done. Not sure where to turn, and having signed a nondisclosure agreement that prohibited him from telling anyone outside BP and Acuren about his work, he took his complaints to the ombudsman's office set up by Bob Malone. The ombudsman's office was meant to provide an oasis of objective, independent protection for workers in the swirling confusion of the company's safety-first mantras, reprisals, and harassment. The idea was to leapfrog over whatever links in the management chain were obstructing good communication between the workers and the executives about safety and the environment—right over the head of the president of BP Alaska, if necessary—and provide a channel straight to Bob Malone. It was an avenue for workers' complaints to be evaluated independently of the complicated politics and allegiances of staff on the slope.

From the start it was a strange arrangement, with its own set of potential conflicts. Stanley Sporkin, the former CIA lawyer and federal judge who had presided over Alyeska's multi-million-dollar settlement with Chuck Hamel, seemed to have solid credentials as a watchdog. Most of the power in his office seemed to lie with his lead attorney, Billie Garde, who had deep knowledge of the Alaskan oil fields and a soft spot for worker retaliation cases. Garde's interests were strangely intertwined with BP's, however. Ever since she had defended Chuck Hamel in court, she had built a career working not on behalf of labor but for Alyeska, and then for Bob Malone, representing the very clients she had once fought against.

In 2003 Garde was censured by the District of Columbia Bar Association for advising both a contract worker and his employer, representing both sides of the same conflict. She remained intertwined in both roles when, a few years later, she was again investigating worker concerns, but on behalf of BP. It was Garde who had helped write the scathing report that accused BP of blacklisting Stuart Sneed, one of its most capable inspectors; but it was never clear to the workers on the slope, who desperately wanted someone they could trust, where her allegiances lay. If the ombudsman's office was supposed to be objective, why were its attorneys so utterly entangled in past BP cases, with BP executives like Malone, and with the company's history? Nevertheless, the ombudsman's office was the next logical step for Anderson, and he brought to Garde and Sporkin his complaints about Acuren's inspection program, BP's whitewash of it, and his difficulty getting a job ever since.

"Marty Anderson's concerns were unusual," says Garde, who was to spend two and a half years investigating them. "They were programmatic and raised a lot of questions about the way the entire program was being managed. . . . they did have the potential for implications on the integrity of the pipe." The more Garde learned, the more she was appalled by what had taken place. Anderson's complaints were far more specific and yet broader-reaching than most of the hundreds of individual complaints she had received from workers on the slope. Rather than identifying one bad apple or abusive human resources issue, the types of concerns she most commonly dealt with, they pointed to system-wide failure and got at the heart of BP's approach to operations.

"He revealed a significant quality control breakdown in everything from the company's procedures . . . to inadequate record keeping . . . to having actually unqualified inspectors in the field performing inspections," Garde later wrote to BP's general counsel, describing the reach of the issues. "The concerns were serious, and although people try to downplay the significance of the issues, they reveal a complete breakdown."

Jeanne Pascal learned about Anderson's allegations after they were taken up by the ombudsman's office. To her, BP had condoned questionable—maybe fraudulent—behavior by its contractor. Then, given the opportunity, BP had done little to correct the situation. There were striking similarities to the Endicott Island dumping saga that had introduced her to BP nearly ten years earlier. Pascal was in a holding pattern, still waiting in the wings for the Department of Justice's criminal investigation of the 2006 Alaska spills to wrap up. The ombudsman's office had taken on Anderson's issues, and she sat back to watch how BP would respond to that situation, too. It was only after the ombudsman's office got wind of Anderson's audit, and after Billie Garde took the Acuren papers to BP's board in London, that BP finally started to react.

"The procedure did not move quickly enough or with enough rigor at the beginning both on our side and on Acuren's side," said an internal BP memo at the time. In October 2007—fourteen months after Malone shut down the oil field for fear of widespread corrosion, and seven months after Anderson first reported his findings—Doug Suttles hired an independent auditor and launched a three-part review of Acuren's inspection program that in February 2008 ultimately confirmed Anderson's claims. The review determined which locations along the pipeline had been inspected by unqualified workers and set out to amend their work. The Acuren inspectors weren't responsible for the exact sections of the line that had leaked in 2006, BP concluded, and many of them, once they were retrained or the legal paperwork was in order, turned out to be competent to perform their jobs.

However, Acuren, at BP's insistence, had to reinspect more than ten thousand locations along the pipelines and reassigned or fired its entire local management group, including George Bryant. Worse, it became apparent through the investigations that the computer database that BP relied on to track its maintenance progress on hundreds of thousands of pipeline maintenance points—the system that kept tabs on when a line was last inspected and when it would be expected to become unsafe—was itself compromised. For years Acuren had allowed its contractors' data supervisors and pipeline "integrity specialists" to go into the database and change their own records, with little verification of what was changed or why, and no trace of who changed what and when. The damage would take years to unravel. "So much data was incorrectly edited and invalidated that the permissions were eventually withdrawn," a BP corrosion manager wrote in an email to North Slope contractors much later, in mid-2009. "We are still setting right Slope-edited data." If the reliability of Acuren's staff was to be questioned, and now several audits in a row had confirmed that it was, then how much confidence could BP have that the database itself still portrayed an accurate picture of the state of maintenance across North Slope operations?

Once Anderson's case got under way, many of the problems with certification and training began to get fixed. Still, larger questions loomed, not just about the database but about how the system had been allowed to break down in the first place. BP is supposed to do its own vigilant audits of the program on a regular basis. Garde remained troubled that BP hadn't uncovered the problems that Anderson had found when BP did its own due diligence on Acuren and set up the contract. If BP had handled the pipeline inspection program so loosely, she wondered, what about everything else?

So much of BP's global business was being run by contractors—in Texas, the gulf, and Africa. They outnumbered BP employees and did the pigging, the drilling, the cementing, and the laying of pipe. The oil industry had always relied on an ecosystem of subcontracts, but Browne had turned to them more than most, in the hopes of slimming down his company and outsourcing some of the most technically demanding jobs—again, to save money. Hayward hadn't done much to change that trend during his first year. The contractors weren't liable for meeting BP's standards, or reporting to the state and federal regulators. Only BP was, and yet here the company hadn't taken the simplest steps to protect its own interests. "It would be a rare occasion to have another Marty Anderson in other contracts, and you can't rely upon that," Garde said. "BP has oversight responsibility of all of its contractors, and it should have identified these issues without the need for a worker to come forward and speak about them."

BP's reliance on contractors also had the effect of severing BP management from the implementation of some of its most sensitive and dangerous work. A contracting company dependent on BP's lucrative projects to stay in business is less able to communicate candidly with BP management and more vulnerable to the judgment-bending temptation to make BP, its client, happy at any cost. Contractors' first allegiance isn't to the integrity of BP's projects, it's to clearing a profit and getting another contract next time. The incentive is to swallow criticism and make the project work no matter what it takes. "Where the rubber meets the road is at the individual contract supervisor level," says Garde, who saw a pattern in the complaints she received from workers. "It's at that level that the decisions are made on how to use the resources that you've got, and sometimes that's a balance between safety and production."

The poor relationship cut both ways. Not only did contractors not always feel accountable to BP for safety issues, but BP itself became less accountable for the actions of its contractors. When close calls—or real accidents—were almost always blamed on the contractor's not following BP's written rules, or on poor communication with BP management, BP, Garde thought, maintained plausible deniability about problems and tended to shrug off responsibility. It thus risked losing control of how its own contractors operated. One important way to mitigate that risk was to listen to workers like Anderson, who spent their days at the front lines of the operations. That, however, wasn't going well, either. By late 2008, nine years and four internal BP investigations after Marc Kovac and his union colleagues first wrote John Browne with complaints about staffing issues and harassment for raising safety questions at BP, workers were still routinely punished, banished, or blacklisted. Malone, John Browne, and Tony Hayward had each personally assured Congress, the public, and BP's own staff that harassment of workers wouldn't be tolerated. Their promises, it turned out, were mere window dressing.

One worker after another anonymously told Garde and Stanley Sporkin that they wouldn't report a corroded pipeline or a breaking valve because they were afraid fixing it would stop work. Stopping work meant slower results, which in turn jacked up the costs and ultimately meant someone had to take the heat for running over budget or missing deadline. The blacklists ran deep. Anderson lost his work with Acuren after the audit. Once the review by the ombudsman's office began, Doug Suttles grudgingly gave Anderson a contract, guaranteeing him work as a trainer of inspectors for three years. Even with the contract and the paycheck that came with it, in 2008, Anderson wasn't getting booked for jobs. Instead, BP managers bad-mouthed him in front of their crews, attacked his credibility, and spread rumors that he had made technical mistakes. BP paid him, while he sat at home without any work assignments to fulfill. Worse, when Anderson applied for jobs with separate companies on the slope, word often got back to him that BP had intervened to keep him from getting the job. Nobody wanted to talk to him. His work life in Alaska had come to a screeching halt.

"Marty became the subject of both overt and subtle retaliation by Acuren and BPXA personnel," Garde wrote to BP's legal staff. "There is no question that there remains a high degree of hostility toward Marty by Acuren for 'getting them in trouble.'" The message was heard loud and clear among the contractors still working on the slope: don't snitch. "This is what happens when you go up against BP on the slope. They are vindictive," Anderson says.

Their vindictiveness enraged Pascal. She watched how BP tried to manage this problem. BP was supposed to be reforming after its Endicott Island felony conviction and living up to Browne and Hayward's promises to change. Yet the company's failure to evolve in its approach to worker safety complaints pointed to a larger failure. Pascal was losing hope that BP was a company that could live up to its promises. Given the stakes, the reports, the professions made before Congress, BP seemed to be displaying an institutional inability to learn from its mistakes.

The worst part was that every day that change wasn't happening, work conditions in Alaska grew more dangerous. While Hayward sat in reflection in London and criminal teams probed records in Prudhoe Bay, teams of welders and operators like Don Shugak and Marc Kovac were still reporting to their early-morning shifts and walking the same dangerous pipelines that could explode at any moment. For them, the threat was real, and the clock was ticking. Pascal bided her time. She expected imminent resolution of the criminal investigations in both Texas and Alaska, and she expected that once charges were filed, her authority and formal role in the debarment process would be restored. Then, she would move as quickly as possible to bring the force of the debarment program into play, hoping that the threat of grave financial consequences might get BP back on track.

THE CRIMINAL CASE in Alaska, according to its lead investigator, Scott West, was going extremely well throughout the first half of 2007. West was more confident by the day that not only would the government get a conviction on the spill, but a case could be made to hold some of the most senior executives in BP management accountable, possibly including Tony Hayward.

Then, on August 26, 2007, West got a call to come to Anchorage for a status meeting on the case at the U.S. Attorney's office. It was an abrupt request, but it had been a few months since all the agencies involved had touched base. West gathered his notes and material and caught the next flight north from Seattle. "It's not uncommon to bring all the different participants together on a large case and say, 'Okay, what have we got? Where are we? Where do we need to go? What are we missing?'" West says. So that is what he was expecting.

At the meeting, about twenty people sat around a large oval conference table: a couple of FBI officers, the criminal investigators from the Alaska Department of Environmental Conservation, the Department of Justice, and the EPA's CID team. Karen Loeffler, then the chief of the criminal division at the U.S. Attorney's office, led off. "If we had to go to trial today," she asked the group, "what could we prove?"

West was surprised. Based on his sixteen years as a criminal investigator, he didn't think this was a "status meeting" sort of question. It was a question usually asked when investigators had exhausted most of their options and were trying to assess what remained. It had only been seventeen months since the spill. The team was working its way through a very long list of witnesses and had mounds of paperwork to sort through from BP. Some of the best leads had just come in. West thought he would soon be able to link the spill to what John Browne and others had said and had done and had known in London. "We were only just beginning."

The group explored the question of what they could charge right away. Based on the information gathered into evidence by that moment, there was a rock-solid case for negligence, but nothing more. His team, West explained, had taken a steady, deliberate pace and had yet to work through the millions of documents BP had given them in response to the subpoena. They thought they had time. Negligence, in this case, was only a misdemeanor charge. It was the least aggressive position the Department of Justice could take, next to not filing any charges at all. West expected Loeffler to take the information presented at the meeting and map out a path forward. If felony charges against BP leaders was the goal, how would the team get there, which individuals should it focus on first, what evidence did it expect it would need, and what should it do next?

Instead, he ran into a wall.

"Well, then, that's what we have," Loeffler said about the misdemeanor, according to West's recollection. "And we're going to work towards that plea."

West felt his limbs go numb as a mixture of rage and disbelief swept over him. Was the government going to cut off his case when it had barely begun? He'd focused the last two years of his life on this, catching up to Jeanne Pascal and Chuck Hamel and committing to carry their concerns forward. Moreover, he, too, had come to believe that without some sort of severe penalty for what had happened in Alaska, another accident—perhaps deadly—was bound to occur. Two months earlier he had been told his investigation was one of the most promising and high-profile efforts of the Department of Justice. Now some arbitrary deadline was being thrust upon him with no warning. Why the rush? Why would anyone else at the table go along with this? He was in shock that a case of this magnitude and this early in the investigation was going to be shut down.

In fact, a review of thousands of pages of documents obtained from the Department of Justice through the Freedom of Information Act supports West's recollection and shows that the case had strong momentum heading into that summer. In April 2007 federal investigators arranged for BP to provide a consultant to help them interpret BP's internal database, MIMIR, for tracking the pipeline inspection program—the very database that Anderson had determined was fundamentally flawed.

Then, on June 6, Justice staff met with BP's attorney, Carol Dinkins, and asked BP to deliver ten years' worth of performance measures and salary bonus information for Tony Hayward and three other BP executives who had managerial responsibility over Alaska at the time of the spill. The officials also asked for BP's strategy documents, as well as a report from Billie Garde about inspection falsification. The FOIA records did not show that any of this information had been delivered to the government by August.

On June 12, Andrea Steward, the assistant U.S. Attorney in Anchorage and the chief prosecutor on the case, wrote a memo to colleagues summarizing her progress in optimistic terms. "Other parts of BP's organization besides the corrosion team knew that there was sediment in the line. So perhaps a corporate collective knowledge would get us to knowing," she wrote, referring to the prosecutorial term for having known a crime was occurring. "What makes this criminal? BP has said that they changed their attitude of aggressive cost cutting in 2005 and that they were changing how they did things . . . that they were trying to do the right thing but they just didn't do it quickly enough," she wrote. "It was all, however, a little too late."

The documents show that BP was often late in delivering material responsive to the government's subpoenas, but that some of the most important internal BP documents may have been given to the Department of Justice just as West's meeting was being called in Anchorage. On August 27, 2007, BP's attorneys released several DVDs full of documents that it had previously withheld from the government's subpoenas based on claims of attorney-client privilege. Having been challenged on that determination, BP was now releasing the material. It was a potential gold mine. And it would be ignored.

"What the hell is going on here?" West demanded, his temper flaring.

The government had three criminal cases open against BP: the Alaska spill case under the Clean Water Act; a Clean Air Act case in Texas City still being investigated by the FBI and the EPA; and a separate investigation into the propane trading scandal from 2005. BP's lawyers, West says he was told, wanted to wrap all three cases into a bundle of plea agreements. If the government would essentially quit pursuing the company, BP proposed to plead guilty to each of the cases. From the Department of Justice's perspective, it was an opportunity to free up staff resources and save money while getting some sort of a conviction. It was "win-win-win."

Ideally, for the company at least, such a deal could be struck before BP's quarterly results were announced at the end of October

2007. "They wanted to report that this was all behind them," West says, describing a public relations philosophy similar to what BP pursued in its last-minute settlement of Eva Rowe's lawsuit. "Having all three cases wrapped up together was one day of bad news—a one-day hit instead of three different days spread out over a period of time."

For West, the thought that the government would back down on the strength of its case and shut down an investigation just because BP asked it to defied logic. "Since when do we care what a serious environmental criminal wants to do?" West asked the group, looking around the conference table at the U.S. Attorney's office in Anchorage. "Why is that our concern? We're not done. We think we've got much bigger targets here, and much more significant targets. Why in the world would we want to accept this deal? Just give me one more year." He was told there wasn't time. "Well, then give me six months." Again, the answer was no. "Give me three months."

"We're done," Loeffler told him, folding her briefcase, standing, and walking out of the room.

West, distraught and visibly shaken, remained at the table for a few moments. It's one thing if a case agent has investigated a case for a number of years, turned over all the rocks and followed every lead, and won't let go because he got too personally invested in it, West thought. In that case a good prosecutor will say, "Look, you've done everything you can, but we're done. We have to move on." That can be difficult but appropriate.

"But I'd never, *ever* seen where a special agent in charge was sitting there in front of the Department of Justice and saying, 'I am not done with my investigation.' It is ridiculous that the Justice Department would just ignore those sorts of concerns," he said. "It's unprecedented."

In the hallway after the meeting, West says that Loeffler pulled him aside and told him that the decision to kill the case had been made on high, by Alberto Gonzales's assistant attorney general of the environment and natural resources division, Ron Tempest, in Washington. "Look, I know how you feel," West recalls Loeffler telling him. "This is difficult. But it's not me. It's not this office. You need to understand that." Loeffler, who was soon appointed a U.S. Attorney for the District of Alaska, would later deny that conversation happened, and says that West's recollection was clouded by his frustration.

Much later, the Department of Justice also issued a statement refuting West's assertion that the case was prematurely closed. "The allegations by Mr. West that the Department improperly handled the case are not based in fact and are simply not true," the department stated in a November 2008 press release, after West had told his story to the *Seattle Times*. "No further investigation was likely to find evidence that would shed any new light on the essential facts of the case."

However the events had transpired in August 2007, West's investigation into BP was finished, and so were the government's criminal investigations into the trading scandal and the Texas City disaster. The Bush administration's Justice Department would not pursue Tony Hayward, John Browne, John Manzoni, or any of the other executives in charge of BP's divisions during the time when critical miscalculations were made. Bob Malone, as the fix-it man brought in to repair BP's image and its relationship with the government, had pulled off a masterstroke.

On October 25, 2007, BP pleaded guilty to a single misdemeanor charge under the federal Water Pollution Control Act, acknowledging that its corrosion and pipeline maintenance program in Alaska hadn't addressed the risks of operating there and that the company had failed to take action to prevent a spill. The state of Alaska also relinquished the right to bring charges against the company. In exchange, BP agreed to three years of probation and to pay roughly $20 million—$12 million in a federal fine, $4 million to the state of Alaska, and another $4 million to the U.S. Department of Fish and Wildlife, to support research. The amount was roughly $40 million less than West and his team had recommended the Department of Justice seek in the plea negotiations that fall, and a fraction of the $672 million he says the Department of Justice once estimated it would seek in the case.

"This leak, and the spill that resulted from it, revealed a significant gap in our corrosion management program—a gap that existed because our approach to assessing and managing corrosion risk in these lines was not robust or systematic enough," Malone said in a statement after the plea, and he reiterated that BP had replaced the entire sixteen-mile-long transit line, at a cost of $150 million.

BP admitted it fixed propane prices, and, for another $303 million in fines and a slew of good-management requirements, the Department of Justice agreed to defer its prosecution in the propane trading case for three years, and to dismiss the case if BP was operating satisfactorily then. (Though one of the traders pled guilty, a judge would later dismiss the criminal case against the others.)

In the Texas City case, BP pleaded guilty to felony charges for not having maintained instructions and documentation for the startup procedures at the isomerization unit, and for not evacuating the JE Merit workers from the poorly sited work trailers on the isomerization lot. For that conviction, the company agreed to pay $50 million in fines, accept another three years of probation, and finally replace each of its remaining blowdown drums with modern flares, an upgrade that would cost $250 million.

There was nothing in the settlements recognizing that BP management had ignored years of explicit warnings that a disaster was imminent at both sites, and no investigation to attempt to reconcile the contradictory denials offered by Browne and Manzoni and others in their court depositions about the case that Brent Coon had found so implausible. After all, those executives had stated that they had no knowledge of any mounting risk at the refinery, and then the public record came to show that the Telos and other reports had predicted the disaster.

Malone, as usual, seemed contrite and repentant. And those qualities, for the time being, were welcomed by a forgiving government and public. "These agreements are an admission that, in these instances, our operations failed to meet our own standards and the requirements of the law. For that, we apologize," Malone said in a statement. "They represent an absolute commitment to work with the government as we continue our efforts to prevent another tragedy like Texas City, to make our Prudhoe Bay pipeline corrosion program more responsive to changing operating conditions and to ensure that our participation in the nation's energy markets is always appropriate.

"In the months and years since these violations occurred, we have made real progress in the areas of process safety performance and risk management. Oversight of our trading operations has also been greatly enhanced. However, there is more to do and we are committed to doing it."

In all, when OSHA fines were included, these three cases and their settlements cost BP nearly $1 billion. It seemed like an extraordinary and consequential sum, but many questioned whether it would be enough to influence BP's long-term planning and decision making. BP earned $284 billion in 2007. In total, its fines amounted to a little more than one day's worth of revenue.

West says no amount of money was more important than the message that would have been sent by the indictment of a BP executive. Holding an individual accountable is rare in U.S. environmental prosecutions of corporations. West believed it would have been one of the few ways to guarantee a change in behavior.

Out of frustration, West resigned from the EPA a few months later. "We had the potential to go way high. It was very significant. And we were foolish to stop," he says. "It's not what the American public, in my opinion, was paying me to do—to turn my back on this."

Malone had accomplished exactly what John Browne had originally asked of him. He got rid of every major bit of legal and government baggage from BP's disaster years except for one: Jeanne Pascal and the threat of a ban on U.S. federal contracts. That fight would continue.

13

OFF THE HOOK

THE CONVICTIONS, however faulted in West's view, put Pascal officially back on her beat. Under debarment law, the deferred trading conviction counted as a crime. In Alaska the misdemeanor was enough to once again require a compliance settlement with the EPA. The felony conviction in Texas was also an automatic trigger. In each case, the local facilities—the Prudhoe Bay pumping stations and the Texas City refinery—were automatically prohibited from receiving any money from the U.S. government until the government could decide what to do with the company as a whole.

BP would have to reach a broader debarment settlement with the EPA, as it had in 1999, to avoid losing its oil leases and being banned from government contracts, including its drilling leases and its fuel sales. Having become the most knowledgeable government employee on BP conduct outside of the criminal teams, Pascal was put in charge of the national negotiations. By her count, BP now had four criminal convictions, more than any other of the seven hundred or more companies she had dealt with in her twenty-six years at the agency. She was still displeased that BP had gotten off without fully complying with the agreement after Endicott Island. The company was becoming, in her words, "a serial environmental criminal."

Still, Pascal wasn't inclined to take the extraordinary step toward a full government ban. There were the obvious issues of justice and environmental protection to be looked after. But she remained concerned that BP's role in U.S. foreign policy decisions might be more important than what it did to the environment in Alaska or Texas. "The question is, Does the environmental damage outweigh the government's need for and reliance on BP's oil and gas?" she said.

The conflict between this practical take on the importance of the company's function globally and her own moral outrage about how the company operated globally left her torn. Even if she wasn't confident debarment would be the best solution, though, she continued to pursue the company. Her job was to insist on reform and guarantee that it happened. Prompted by Tony Hayward's new position and new priorities, those reforms were under way. Her expectations for the company were clear: a strong safety and environmental program, an open line of communication for worker complaints, and heavy investment to fix the known dangers from the dilapidated equipment remaining in Alaska and the company's refineries. All of this seemed in line with what Hayward himself had demanded. Pascal would patiently wait to see how Hayward's leadership panned out.

Hayward did begin to make immediate changes that he intended as measures to improve safety, but more of them were short-term, and even seemed superficial given the deep operational challenges the company faced. He believed that if he made safety issues a prominent part of every workday, the culture of the company would become more safety-oriented. Core strengthening in safety on an individual level became a daily ritual and a constant message at all of BP's facilities. Signs went up everywhere warning workers to hang onto handrails. Outside of the Texas City plant, large LED message boards warned employees to stay hydrated in the Texas heat and to fasten their seatbelts. In Alaska, employees were forbidden to run in icy conditions, and they would be reprimanded if, for example, they hurried across a parking lot. Meetings everywhere began with safety sermons. Each time a BP Alaska employee parked a pickup truck, he had to place an inflatable yellow tray under the drive train in case a drop of oil fell from the gearbox.

The efforts produced statistical results that created the appearance of success. The number of recordable safety incidents and lost hours began to dip downward in 2008; fewer people were getting injured on the job. The number of environmental spills dropped, too, even as BP's profits increased. If one were to evaluate BP's progress on safety based on the statistical measures the company summarized in its annual reports, it would appear that the message was getting through. "They had achieved very good records for worker safety, they had at the same time achieved extremely good records for profitability and company growth," said Robert Bea, an industry veteran and engineering professor at the University of California, Berkeley. But individual safety, though it may be hard to argue against, didn't address the kind of systemic risk that had caused the Texas City explosion or Don Shugak's well fire or any of the other big accidents BP had endured. Those were caused by widespread failings by the company to build and maintain a safe and predictable place to work or, in industry parlance, to maintain operational and process safety. U.S. Air Force regulations, for example, define operational safety as "the condition of having acceptable risk to life, health, property, or environment caused by a system or subsystem in an operational environment." BP itself provided one of the best explanations of process safety in a presentation the company made in Trinidad and Tobago in 2008. It defined it as "a disciplined framework for managing the integrity of hazardous operating systems and processes by applying good design principles, engineering and operating practices."

BP under Hayward, for all its improvements, wasn't focused on the most important issues facing the company, the issues that would prevent another catastrophe. It preferred to focus on things like holding onto the handrail when you go down the stairs. "They spent an enormous amount of money on stuff like that, rather than . . . fix the stuff that, day to day, could kill people," said Kris Dye, a BP mechanic and the local union president in Prudhoe Bay.

Hayward's laser seemed to be focused on the wrong things. "Everything was around lost workdays, or recordables," said one former senior executive. "That was what the board wanted." BP put all of its attention on what industry safety experts call "slips, trips and falls," and the consequence was that not enough attention was being paid to what Bea calls the "low-probability, high-consequence systems failures lurking in the background"—the Black Swan events.

James Baker had demanded a focus on process safety issues that could result in rare and unexpected catastrophes when he said that a lack of operational safety was BP's missing ingredient, and it was also what the Chemical Safety and Hazard Investigation Board found lacking in Texas and what virtually every critic of the company, from Exxon's executives to Pascal, found was needed at BP. The superficial safety improvements might have been an important place to begin, but a safety transformation wasn't supposed to stop there. The fact that the process safety improvements were vastly more expensive than individual safety improvements only made it seem, again, that BP was unwilling to put its money behind its promises. "Wearing spikes out on the ice, or holding the handrail—that's cheap," Dye says. "But to replace a fire and gas detection system, that's money."

Hayward did have his Operating Management System, which focused on operational safety and was being put in place in a handful of test locations around the world. It hadn't been universally applied across the company. That would take years. Even where they were applied, it was becoming increasingly clear that the practices and policies within OMS weren't necessarily new. "There was nothing in there that was actually a game-changing standard that was going to drive BP management to a higher level," said one former company HSE manager. "They were just repacking it under a different wrapper." What BP needed to do most to achieve operational and process safety was to invest a huge chunk of cash to quickly upgrade its industrial facilities and create a predictable environment where workers felt they, as operators, were trusted by their management and in control of their actions.

This is where Exxon is said by many to excel, and where a reliance on low-level workers to engage unreservedly with management is the key to long-term safety. It's a mechanic like Kovac or Dye or an ultrasonic tester like Stuart Sneed who sees what could go wrong out in the field, far from executives making budget decisions in London. As Karlene Roberts, a process safety expert at the University of California, Berkeley's Haas School of Business, who worked as a consultant with BP, put it, the slips and trips statistics are a distraction. The real work in transforming a safety culture has to go on every day, it is expensive, and it never stops. "I think BP just stopped," she said. "It created its handbook, it gave it to all its managers, it implored its managers to pay attention to safety, and then it just stopped. Apparently it never realized that training isn't implementation."

A company can know that its philosophy has been implemented when its employees are confident enough in their leaders' commitment to disrupt work to protect safety. Roberts cites an example from the U.S. Navy in which a young recruit on the aircraft carrier USS *Carl Vinson* stopped flight operations in the middle of the night—while planes were in the air—because he had lost a tool on the ship. "And a tool ingested into a jet engine can make for a very bad day," she says. When the incident was over, the ship's commander came over the PA system and called the recruit up to the control tower. The recruit comes up, shaking, and stands before the commander, expecting to be berated. "Good job," he's told, instead. "We want you to do that all of the time."

"What you want is a company that is open enough so that low-level people will report things that can really turn into damage," Roberts says.

Texas City was a prime example of management's relying on slips and trips statistics while ignoring workers' warnings, said Don Holmstrom, who headed the CSB investigation. In the months before the refinery blast BP had achieved an excellent safety record as measured by recordable injuries and lost hours. But that didn't reflect the lurking dangers at the plant and it didn't prevent the disaster. After the explosion, and after "safety" became the company's staple refrain, the dangers at Texas City persisted. At least three more workers had died in accidents there since 2005.

In Alaska, too, many of the same system-wide maintenance issues that Marc Kovac and others had drawn attention to in 2001 remained unaddressed. If the safety statistics touted in annual reports were mostly window dressing, then the maintenance and reinvestment in the operational performance of BP's facilities were the structural studs holding up the business. BP had begun to invest in those systems. In Alaska, internal records show that hundreds of millions of dollars had been spent on maintenance and equipment upgrades on the North Slope since the 2006 oil spills. By 2007, the maintenance budget there had jumped to nearly $195 million, four times what it was in 2004; and more was invested in 2008.

Yet it wasn't enough. In the decades of austerity imposed on Alaska's operations, the infrastructure had begun to break down at a rate that seemed to far exceed what Hayward and Malone were willing to do to rehabilitate it. Hundreds of millions of dollars might seem like big money, but it was a tiny fraction compared to the value of the equipment the company maintained, and the revenues that it produced. It was as if BP's management had left a car sitting out in an open field for ten winters and then was surprised when an oil change and new tires didn't make it safe to drive. The condition of the pipelines—even though the main transit line had been replaced in 2006—remained as much a concern to Sneed and other workers as it had been before the Prudhoe Bay spill. "It's kind of a catch-up thing now. You know, they slacked off on inspections for so long," says Mike Theurich, a pipeline inspector for Mistras, another of BP's contractors in Prudhoe Bay.

At the end of 2007 a BP safety team in Alaska decided to follow up on the scathing operational integrity report that Malone had ordered six years earlier. That report had found that the company wasn't maintaining safety equipment and faced "a fundamental lack of trust" among its workers in Alaska. Leaked internal BP documents show that when the issues were revisited, the company had done little to fix the problems, even while breathlessly claiming to prioritize safety and maintenance.

More than four hundred BP workers and contractors across the Prudhoe Bay drilling fields were surveyed for the follow-up, and three out of four of them said that BP's maintenance program was still not aligned with BP's business priorities, meaning they were still being pushed to cut back on important work in order to preserve the revenues flowing from Alaska to London. The workers said that while BP had chipped away at some of the problems it had communicating with staff and training them (it had improved "listening"), it hadn't reduced lengthy maintenance backlogs on some of the most important and most dangerous equipment. "We found that 50 percent of everything that was originally brought up was not fixed, it was ignored," says Marc Kovac, who participated in the follow-up report and had also been a part of the 2001 operational integrity review team. "BP plays the time game. People forget and they know that. So as long as they file reports and do investigations and produce paperwork, they know that people will eventually go on with their business."

All of this was supposed to be changing across the company, since, as Hayward had put it, all the disasters were "behind us." But in Alaska the mood was much more like what workers in Texas City had been telling Don Parus and their management there in the lead-up to the refinery blast in 2005: we're afraid to go to work; you are ignoring us; someone is going to get killed.

IN ALASKA, as in Texas, the dangers boiled down to technical specifics in some of the most arcane equipment, and to how those components worked together in the giant interdependent system. On the North Slope, for example, BP runs some 120 turbines inside its plants, some for generating power, some for pumping oil, and some for compressing gas into the pipelines and for injection back underground. They are giant engines, some as large as thirty feet long and twelve feet tall. The largest turbines were bought from GE around 1980 and by 2008 were on the equivalent of life support. According to the mechanics who work on them, as the demands and size of the Alaskan oil field grew, the turbines were modified to run at higher stress levels and higher temperatures than GE originally designed them for. Workers described the machines vibrating severely when pushed to such limits. Gradually, their old parts failed, and so many new ones were creatively machined and slapped on in their place that the turbines sometimes bore little resemblance to their original design. "When you make a complaint about it, rather than fix it right they come up with another Band-Aid," said Dye. "It's very frustrating."

While the turbines themselves are vulnerable to failure, they are just a part of a complicated interconnected chain of processes that shapes and transports the oil and gas across Alaska and to points south. The rough oil harvested from the wells comes out of the ground as a messy mixture of water, crude oil, and gas. It's not until the first processing sites, or gathering centers, that the streams are separated. There, the turbines run giant compressors that pump the separated gas back into the oil field to be injected underground, and send the purified oil off toward the Trans Alaska Pipeline. The turbines and compressors that do the work are lined up, and they are side by side, each one with its own skid, or sledlike rails that make the machinery portable. A wall of sheet metal and foam separates them into quasi-contained facilities, but the entire system remains connected by a tangle of thousands of pipelines and hoses and valves. It makes for a fragile setup, because each of those lines handles some sort of toxic or flammable substance; and set in the middle of them is a vibrating, dilapidated tractor-trailer–sized turbine running full throttle. If oil is spilled from one of the lines, it might cause an environmental calamity. If gas piping is broken apart, it can lead to a huge combustible cloud and, if there is a fire, start a domino effect, blowing up one unit after another.

BP relies on a critical layer of safety protection designed to prevent such an explosion: the gas and fire detection system that dumps a cloud of halon gas to suffocate a fire before it can spread, and to interfere with the chemical reaction that allows an explosion. The fire and gas systems are used not just in the drilling fields in Prudhoe Bay but in the refineries and barracks and even out on the open waters of the Gulf of Mexico, in the engine rooms of the big platforms.

In Alaska, however, many of the fire and gas detection systems hadn't been updated or replaced since the 1970s. They relied on old technology that was obsolete—the manufacturers that made the sensors and systems are shuttered—so replacement parts were hard to come by, says Kovac. By 2008, BP technicians had taken to resoldering old circuit boards to try to repair the system's electronics. Halon, toxic to people and a potent ozone-destroying gas, was eventually outlawed and labeled as dangerous. An exception in federal law allowed BP and other companies to get a waiver to continue using it if their fire systems depended on it. Workers in Alaska had feared for years that the sensors wouldn't work and that the system would fail to prevent an explosion. In 2001, the operational review stated that oil field technicians were "very concerned about continuing degradation of system reliability, and the ability of these systems to protect the workforce."

More importantly, the fire and gas detection systems are incompatible with the newer ultrasonic radiographic and X-ray testing machines that crews like Stuart Sneed's and Anderson's used to scan and examine the pipelines for corrosion and leaks. The modern UV and radiation waves created by the corrosion equipment have been known to trigger the fire detector's ultraviolet sensors and set off a halon release. False triggers are not uncommon, unnecessarily releasing huge amounts of the polluting gas into the atmosphere. The two most important safety systems BP uses to prevent an accident are completely incompatible.

Since those corrosion testing techniques are used to test a wide array of equipment inside large facilities like the gathering centers, not just the pipelines out in the field, every time testing is under way, a significant portion of the fire systems in those facilities have to be shut down. There is almost always some portion of equipment being tested at any given time.

In 2007, BP technicians on the North Slope were warning their own managers that the detectors at some facilities were shut down nearly a third of the time; the workers also sent letters to Chuck Hamel and Jeanne Pascal to this effect. The shutdowns meant that huge industrial facilities processing explosive materials around the clock had no fire alarm or warning system in place for an average of eight hours a day. To adjust for the gaps, BP assigned "human fire detectors": a foot patrol that looks out for spilled flammable materials and listens for the whistle of broken pipes—to patrol the sites. "You look for a vapor cloud," said one oil worker. "And if it's a small leak it sounds like a high-pitched hissing noise." If they find gas, and there is time, they are to run to the halon control box, manually set off the alarm, and try to get out of the building before the halon itself poisons them.

In August 2007, a turbine mechanic named Joe Good was patrolling Gathering Center 1, a sprawling plant extending from a sixteen-story-tall khaki-colored windowless cube that stands out along the barren tundra a short ways from the Beaufort Sea. Like the five other gathering centers in the Prudhoe Bay field, this one processes and separates the oil and relies on turbines to move the materials off into their respective pipelines.

Good smelled a hint of smoke as he was checking one of the facility's large engines. Within moments, he thought he had found the cause. A hydraulic oil line that supplies lubricant to the turbine's jet was jury-rigged across the bottom of the turbine engine. As he crouched underneath the machine to get another look, the hydraulic line, under 500 pounds of pressure and running fluids at 150 degrees Fahrenheit, frayed and burst, spraying lubricating oil across the engine. "It sounded like a gunshot going off, then a fan of hot oil passed about 6 inches in front of my face," he said. In an instant, the turbine burst into flames, but the fire alarms and the halon—disabled—weren't triggered. Good jumped up and sprinted for a small hatch meant as an emergency exit. He crashed through that door and kept going, a cloud of black smoke behind him.

The danger was not just to the one turbine unit. Volatile gas vapors were common inside the facility because of small leaks in the systems. If the fire spread rapidly through the facility's HVAC ductwork, it would reach the turbine unit next door, risking a larger fire and a violent explosion. As Good ran, he passed a manual lever to trigger the halon extinguisher, but there was no time. He could stop and arm the fire and gas system, or save his own life. He hurled himself through the second exit. Then he radioed for help. From a remote location, a field manager was able to power up the fire system and put out the flames.

The turbine fire was potentially serious not only because no alarms were sounded but because the turbine engines operate near high-pressure gas and oil pipelines that could be detonated by an uncontrolled fire. "If there was a gas cloud, a fuel cloud inside, he would have died and the facility would have been blown up," Kovac says. The GC-1 incident, as it was called, was classified by BP Alaska's then-president Doug Suttles as a "high-potential" event, and news of the incident was distributed around the BP organization globally as a precaution.

IT IS EASY to look at such examples and think such a rich company could afford to fix dangerous and essential equipment. But one of the things standing in Tony Hayward's way was the persistent mandate to grow the company and its profits even while rehabilitating it. It was the curse that accompanied the financial benefits of being a publicly traded company; shareholders always demanded short-term growth. BP was never as strong at selling the notion that their investments in safety were part of a long-term growth strategy as Lee Raymond and then Rex Tillerson had honed the message at Exxon. For Hayward, growing profits, once again, would mean reducing expenses. He would do that by carefully moderating the budgets for maintenance, even if they were increasing, and by focusing on the elimination of what he saw as layers of redundancy in BP management. He said there was excess fat in BP's operations, and he meant to lose it.

There were, to be sure, some easy opportunities to improve efficiency and cut costs. In the gulf there was pressure to get new platforms online and slash the expenses that came from their delays. In the refineries, excessive downtime for repairs presented ample opportunity for change. But in Alaska, although the fields were operating at their full capability, oil production and revenues were in consistent decline, and there was little anyone could do to reverse this. Increasing revenues there was like expecting to find a greater volume of water while wading into the shallower end of the pool. Once again, the company's management pursued a paradox: boosting investment in safety while somehow continuing to cut costs.

For budgetary reasons, Hayward set out to eliminate more than five thousand jobs worldwide and save BP at least $2 billion a year. In November 2008, he announced quarterly profits nearly double what they were in 2007. By the end of his first full year as CEO, BP's revenues increased by 27 percent and profits were still up, even after making up for a dismal start to that year. A surge in oil prices helped, too. Using a common oil industry measure that figures in replacement costs for oil reserves, BP's profits jumped 39 percent. Hayward became an instant darling of Wall Street.

Some of his changes, though, seemed to contradict his pledges to improve operations and continued to erode safety rather than improve it. While he had at first said that BP needed a stronger approach to risk, Hayward raised blunt questions about the very philosophy and structure of risk management that BP operators had in place, suggesting not that they were insufficient but that that were too slow-moving and too expensive. In a seemingly paradoxical move, he took aim at what the company calls "assurance." These are the layers of checks, balances, and systems meant to ensure that decisions aren't made hastily; that workers' concerns are communicated to management; and that regulations guaranteeing safety aren't abused for the sake of expediency. In his view there were too many protective layers. Forethought and safety had become bureaucracy, and excessive cautiousness was paralyzing. For Hayward, assurance equaled waste.

"Assurance is killing BP today," Hayward told the town hall gathering in Houston the same day he shocked the markets by characterizing his own company's performance as "dreadful." "Right now we have multiple layers of assurance, too many layers. I don't think that having all these layers of assurance reduce[s] risk, and it can actually increase it. The best way to reduce risk is to have deep technical competence where we need it. Individuals need to be accountable for risk, and to manage it."

Philosophically, Hayward's remarks harked back to the British preference for management based on strong principles and a disdain and impatience for the more American style of strict prescriptive rules and procedures. Hayward seemed to think that lessons having now been learned from the company's string of disasters, a little bit of loosening up, and creative leadership would encourage a healthy appetite for the kind of risk that can allow a company to progress and get rid of excessive bureaucracy within the organization.

His ideas appeared to be headed in the exact opposite direction as Bob Malone's efforts in the United States. Where Malone was still constructing layer after layer of outside review panels and professional advisory committees and the ombudsman's office, Hayward was targeting those very layers as standing in the way of BP's future.

In Alaska, there was no more significant layer of assurance in place than the Health, Safety and Environment division. Long before Hayward had himself diagnosed that the company had difficulty listening to its workers, Pascal and Chuck Hamel and others, including Malone, had insisted that management needed a mechanism that channeled important issues straight to the leaders of operational groups like BP Alaska. That's why in 2000 the company had agreed that the HSE group be elevated to a vice-presidential level at BP Alaska and that its manager would report directly to the president of the organization. This, Pascal said, would ensure that safety and environmental issues got the ear of staff with seniority to handle and address them.

The HSE group is where Marc Kovac and the union would bring their complaints about patchwork repairs and pipeline integrity. It's where Glen Trimmer, the Gathering Center 3 operator, raised fears about the dangerous turbines and the absence of fire and gas detectors when he went to work. And it was the management group that oversaw both the 2001 operational integrity review and the 2007 followup that kept the pressure on BP management to continue emphasizing safety because not enough progress had been made.

The group was meant to be an antidote to the difficulty BP has routinely had in ensuring that field-level dangers are communicated to top management. It was meant as an answer to upper management in Alaska and Texas City who claimed after each serious accident that they had never been informed of the risk. That was what Browne and Manzoni had told Brent Coon and Eva Rowe after the refinery blast killed Rowe's parents. Claiming to have never been informed was also what trapped Bob Malone when he first told members of Congress there was no way that cost cutting had interfered with safety in Alaska. Malone looked foolish when he was called back a few months later and admitted he was unaware how severe the cost cutting that had led to the spill in Alaska had been. The HSE group's elevated importance in the BP group architecture was supposed to be the fix. It was supposed to be in everybody's best interest: Hayward's, the government's, Malone's, and the workers'.

It came as a surprise, then, to Malone, Pascal, and others—but perhaps not to Hayward—that in late 1998 Doug Suttles, the president of BP Alaska, decided to move the Health, Safety and Environment director from a vice-presidential position reporting directly to him and drop it a tier further down in the management hierarchy, effectively deemphasizing safety and communication in the BP organization there. BP's spokespeople described the move as an efficient consolidation that addressed some of the company's "assurance" redundancies in Alaska, and insisted that it didn't mean safety and environmental management were less important. HSE wouldn't be dissolved, they said, but it would be put into what the company calls a "technical directorate"—a group tasked with corrosion management and balancing maintenance against the company's budget priorities.

To Pascal, that was as good as taking a decade of effort to contain BP's sprawling weaknesses and undoing whatever progress she had made, progress that others, including Browne and Hayward, had pledged to recognize. Some BP managers confessed in private that the move created a conflict because now the person responsible for raising profits was also responsible for deciding how much to invest in safety. Pascal felt that what was left of the HSE function now lacked its own independent voice to defend against such a conflict. "When you have environment and health and safety reporting to a business unit, what do you think gets the first attention?" she asked. "Business."

A spokesman for BP in Alaska insisted that the reorganization was meant to clarify leadership authority at the top of the organization, improve efficiency, and emphasize safety rather than diminish it. "For someone to look at a line on an org chart and determine that we had devalued the importance of HSE—that would just be wrongheaded," Steve Rinehart, a former reporter with the *Anchorage Daily News* turned company representative, said. "I don't think that anybody could spend much time working around BP Alaska and not see pretty clearly how focused that organization is on safety and HSE."

But the explanation rang hollow. At the same time that BP's corporate message machine was in high gear soliciting the workers' trust and promising that worker safety was paramount, Suttles's HSE reorganization sent a conflicting message. To employees in Alaska, it said that no matter what was preached on paper and in morning meetings, in practice, safety was less important. "They brought it in-house to a place where the workers have nowhere to go but to their direct supervisor. BP wanted it contained, in-house, and they wanted it quiet," Kovac said.

One former BP executive who followed the development there said that demoting HSE relieved lower-level managers of their accountability to that unit and eliminated consequences for ignoring safety. He put the matter in the simplest terms: "Symbolism's important. The big stick's gone."

WITH BP's OFFICIAL downgrading of HSE, Pascal felt that she was backtracking. Suddenly the most important component of the agreement she was negotiating with BP over debarment became the inclusion of the clause that she had already gotten the company to agree to eight years earlier. In late 2008 she and Carson Hodges, of the EPA, sent a letter to BP's attorney, Carol Dinkins (the same lawyer who had represented BP in 1999, and against the DOJ in 2006), in which they laid out the government's conditions for the company. They pointed out that not only had the HSE group been reorganized multiple times—

a direct affront to the government's position over the years—but that Pascal had tried to warn BP management that the pipeline corrosion issues would lead to a spill long before they actually did in 2006. "That information was communicated by Jeanne to BPXA's management who denied and ignored it. In retrospect, BPXA's management was wrong, and the informational and oversight processes used by BPXA's management at that time were deficient.

"As a result," the letter continued, "the current agreement needs to operate differently in order to be effective. Working with someone who is trustworthy is key in settling debarment exposure."

Most of the terms the government sought were similar to those it had fought for in 1999, but two terms were underscored as the most important in the letter. Number one: Suttles had to put HSE back at the top of BP Alaska's hierarchy. Number two: the EPA wanted to designate who BP assigned to work with them to make sure the company complied with an eventual debarment agreement—the closest possible thing to a guarantee to Pascal that she wouldn't be duped again.

"HSE will NOT be restructured without EPA SDD [Suspension and Debarment Department)'s concurrence during the term of the agreement," the letter stated. The "conditions listed above are prerequisites for EPA SDD to enter into a settlement agreement with BPXA or with BP. . . . If we are not in agreement . . . settlement negotiations between us will terminate."

Those close to Suttles say the demands irked him. He showed little interest in negotiating with the EPA. "He said, 'I'm not going to let some EPA bitch tell me how to run my company,'" Pascal says she was told.

In fact, Suttles didn't like to be told what to do by anyone. He and Malone knocked heads routinely, and the two had become famously at odds within the company. Now Malone wanted an agreement. He thought BP should continue to do whatever it needed to get its legal house in order and finally lay the specter of the past few years to rest. Suttles wasn't oblivious to the importance of safety and integrity issues. He had a reputation for cutting through belabored decision making and getting things done. He had replaced the oil transit line. That was partly why Malone had made him president in the first place.

Suttles's weakness was that he didn't handle criticism well—it provoked a childish obstinacy that tended to bring any negotiations to a halt. Marty Anderson and Stuart Sneed's harassment claims were prime examples—the more Suttles heard them complain about retaliation and blacklisting, no matter how legitimately, the less he wanted them to work for BP ever again. And the ombudsman's office, which had successfully mediated hundreds of serious worker complaints by then, was an equally intolerable affront to his seniority. Suttles wanted the whole office gone.

Suttles's inflexibility and stubbornness were becoming less and less tolerable for Malone, too, as they were clearly beginning to interfere with BP's recovery. Yet as long as Suttles was running BP's Alaska division, he would rebuff the government's demands. It began to look like a stalemate.

"BP was very recalcitrant," Pascal said. "It was turning into a major impasse."

14

RUN TO FAILURE

Even after the 2006 Alaska oil spills brought international scrutiny to BP's corrosion program, forcing the company to revamp its efforts to care for its oil lines, much of the rest of the pipeline system remained neglected. Hundreds of pipelines carrying gas, wastewater, and other toxic or dangerous mixtures still weren't being pigged or monitored for decay. No set of lines was of greater concern to the workers than the high-pressure gas lines that traverse each of the fields in the Greater Prudhoe Bay area.

After the gas and some water are separated out of the oil at one of the gathering centers, the gas lines, powered and compressed by the turbines, return the gas to the fields, where it is injected back underground to artificially repressurize the geology and push out more oil. But because these pipes aren't part of the primary oil transport system, and because there are so many miles of them, they tended to get overlooked in an inspection program already stretched beyond its capabilities. At best, the inspection program handled problems on a spot-check or a case-by-case basis. Finding corrosion was a matter of chance. "Our plan would say—'This line, this line, and this line, you're going to do five inspections on it this year.' And it might be miles and miles long," says Mike Theurich, the pipeline inspector. "It's kind of like a crapshoot, as far as, Are you going to find some damage or not?"

It was a high-pressure gas line that Stuart Sneed, the Michigan-based inspector who got fired for hopping frozen puddles, had been trying to bring attention to when he complained that corrosion was going unnoticed by field inspectors. Sneed thought it would eventually be one of those gas lines, not another oil leak, that would be the undoing of BP in Prudhoe Bay. "That gas line," Sneed says, referring to an eighteen-inch pipeline under more than five thousand pounds of pressure. "That line went right behind all those camps up there. It would make Texas City look like a backyard barbecue up there if that thing went off."

The thing about the gas lines is that they don't drip silently and slowly into the snow. When they blow, it happens all of a sudden, on a tremendous scale, and it comes out of nowhere. A shiny silver-sheathed pipeline might look sturdy one moment, but suppose it has a weak spot, its nearly half-inch-thick wall worn down to just a few thousandths of an inch thick. As the corrosive chemical transformation continues, another thousandth of an inch is dissolved away, until the pipe wall gets too thin to contain the thousands of pounds of pressure, and it gives way violently.

The weak spots are invisible, but they can by anywhere. And the pipelines—those sleeping time bombs—are everywhere. To the workers on the slope, guys like Kovac and Trimmer and Dye, who understand the danger, a journey through the field is like running a sniper alley in a war-torn city. Four or six pipelines run alongside most roads; a crew working the field in a pickup truck has them constantly in sight. The lines run behind mess halls and office trailers and the sleeping barracks. "I tell the new employees every day: 'Listen, you could be driving next to these lines, it's nice and peaceful and quiet,'" Kovac says. "'But these explosions can happen in a fraction of a second without any indication that anything is going to happen, and you need to know exactly what to do to save yourself.'"

The field's veterans have their survival tricks. Years of experience and accidents have taught them to keep their eyes open. No fiddling with the radio or digging through papers on the passenger seat. Never, ever rush in to fight a small fire or investigate a separation in a pipeline. If you're in trouble, run upwind. And when you park your truck, it becomes a getaway vehicle. Always back it in and nose it out, ready to "get the hell out with God's speed."

That constant danger of explosion on an incomprehensible scale is why the man who pulled Don Shugak out of the fire by his collar at A Pad was considered so selfless and heroic. Fear of an explosion is a constant that eats away at the nerves of otherwise unemotional, hardened men who have spent their lives on big equipment in difficult places. Each time Kovac, or Anderson, or any of the others flies up to Deadhorse, he says good-bye to his family with the knowledge that there is always a chance he won't come home. And each year they've worked in Deadhorse, the chances of being killed have gotten slightly greater. "I go to work every day and I know that something could blow out and I probably wouldn't live through it," says Kris Dye. "I know, as union president here, that probably at some point I'm gonna have to bury some members. And that scares me to death."

Some risk is acceptable. It goes with the job. But what burns people like Dye and Kovac up is the fact that their managers know how to make it safer but time and again choose not to.

Drilling is a carefully regulated business, taking place in some of the most developed countries in the world, and it's supposed to rely on state-of-the-art technology. Yet there are calculated decisions about risk that management makes every day—and that workers accept because they feel they have no choice. Workers are ordered to go on shift and walk the gangplank out onto a factory floor as a human fire detector because management chose to shut down the safety systems. They are assigned, as Don Shugak was, to go and start up wellheads without being issued equipment to test the pressure behind the cap. They are sent out, day after day, to walk along high-pressure gas lines when a professional member of the team has already warned management that he thinks the corrosion is so bad that the line is about to blow up. These are rolls of the dice that increasingly seemed guaranteed to result in losses.

"BP puts everything on a risk matrix and it's signed off on at an executive level," says Patrick O'Farrell, a project manager for BP. "Does a risk matrix cover a one-in-a-million incident? Probably not, but what do you do when you drive to work? You take risks. Companies are no different from individuals. There is no such thing as zero risk. Operators are very informed about what the risks are. If an individual is uncomfortable, [he has] the right to stop the work."

By late 2008, it had been eight years since the union crews on the North Slope had begun accusing BP of running their oil field to failure. Records show that after the 2006 pipeline spills, BP finally began investing more money in maintaining its pipelines and other facilities. The company said that it had been investing $50 million a year into its fire and gas detection system—and it had, since 2006. That example, however, proves how slow the rehabilitation process in BP's Alaska fields had become. The list of those facilities still awaiting upgrades was so long that BP's O'Farrell estimated it would cost at least $1 billion. At $50 million a year, it wouldn't be until 2026 that the overhauls were completed, in the best case. Only then would all the facilities run with modern safety systems. "So you are saying it is taking BP almost twenty years to address worker concerns about the fire and gas integrity?" another BP Alaska manager, incredulous, said in an interview. Almost no one expected Prudhoe Bay to be producing more than a trickle of oil by 2026 And the twenty-year maintenance schedule assumed that $50 million a year would be invested in fire and gas systems until then, with no delays or cutbacks. The same thing would have to happen with the high-pressure gas lines.

As the state of Alaska began to head into the winter of 2008, Doug Suttles began to pursue a different agenda. The nation's economy was falling off a cliff. Oil prices had once again slackened. Prudhoe Bay's output was dropping by 8 percent each year. By 2020 Suttles thought Alyeska would be pumping just two hundred thousand barrels of oil a day toward the lower 48, nearly one-tenth what it was when Malone was in charge of the pipeline in the early 1990s and less oil than the Thunder Horse platform alone—which had finally begun operating that June—produced in the gulf.

Hayward was straining to answer shareholders' demands and boost profits on a global scale. Suttles's job was more defensive: just don't make Hayward's task any harder. Keeping BP Alaska's head above water, though, meant once again trimming back at a time when Alaska's facilities needed attention most. Suttles announced the delay of $120 million in investment in the Prudhoe field, mainly for a new drilling project, and said the company would cut back oil production by 10 percent over the next year. It didn't look as if he would be able to fix up the high-pressure gas lines anytime soon.

On September 29, 2008, Karl Massera was part of a four-man crew assigned to Y Pad, or "Yankee," as some of the workers tended to call it over the radio. The pad has about seventy wells on it, each housed in a metal shack. Some of the wells are for oil production and some are to inject gas to stimulate that oil production. The gas injection wells are connected by a series of pipes that run like branches to a larger limblike header pipe at the edge of the pad, and then get routed into a nine-inch-wide main line, or trunk of the system, which runs many miles back to the Gathering Center 1. Several drilling pads are served by the same main high-pressure gas line.

At Yankee Pad, the gas line ran a couple dozen feet behind a manifold building—where the production is controlled and the oil tested for its water-gas-oil ratio—on the way to the wells. Three mechanics were inside, and Massera was walking the lines, outside. The layers of insulation wrapped around the main gas line had become waterlogged. Instead of protecting the pipe, the insulation held the moisture against it, and over time, rust had slowly eaten away at the metal, from the outside in. That particular section of the high-pressure gas line, one of the lowest priorities for inspection in the entire oil field, hadn't been checked for nearly fourteen years. In 2003, it had come to the top of the lengthy list of pipes due for inspection, but it was scheduled for midwinter. Workers arrived at the pipeline to find it buried deep in drifts of snow and unreachable unless they dug it out. They skipped the inspection—and never returned.

The sun was up, drenching the vast, open tundra with that Alaskan light that is so glaring it can seem almost bleak, like an overexposed photograph. There were no human sounds except for Massera's footsteps. The stillness was broken only by the sound of the wind blowing through the stiff tufts of grass and, when it gusted, whistling through the pipelines and their fittings.

Suddenly, the high-pressure gas line, seventy feet from Massera, blew apart. Shards of steel hurtled through the air and thudded into the moist soil around him. One piece splashed in a small lake several hundred feet away, and another, a twenty-eight-foot-long section of steel, soared nine hundred feet. Thousands of pounds of pressure had found the weakest spot in the pipe and cracked it open like an eggshell.

Breaking free of the stilts and metal bands that shackled it to the ground, the pipeline rose up like a snake and began whipping violently through the air. Massera dove to the ground, covered his head, and expected to die. Then he reached for his radio. His biggest fear was that the men in the manifold house already knew that the line had blown. If they knew, they might shut down power. Killing the power could lead to a spark, and one spark would ignite the cloud of gas that now enveloped Yankee Pad. An electrical spark had once set off an explosion in a similar incident and burned several facilities to the ground.

Kovac was working a few miles away when the radio call came over his monitor. He had trouble hearing Massera over the roaring of gas. It sounded as if he was standing underneath a waterfall. "You could tell he was scared," Kovac says. "He was trying to say there was an emergency and he didn't know where to shut this thing down. And he needed help." If any shard had landed on the pipeline itself, or on a rock, it would have ignited the gas like flint on steel. Even a burst of static electricity from Massera's hair in the dry Alaska air would do it.

In a frenzy, the operators tried to find the valves to shut off the gas, but no one knew the equipment. The leak went unchecked until the pipeline, whipping through the air, folded over on itself. Eventually, the crews got Y Pad under control without an explosion. But thirty minutes after Massera radioed for help, another, unrelated gas pipeline leak was reported a couple of miles away. "You have hundreds of miles of this pipeline and you never know where it's going to break," Kovac says.

THE CLOSE CALL at Yankee Pad served as a low-grade wake-up call to BP management. Over the past twelve months such accidents had happened with increasing frequency. After the turbine fire at the compressor plant, three more fires had rocked the oil field. Then came the Y Pad gas line blowout. Meanwhile, Marty Anderson's file, with all the allegations about the competency of the pipeline inspection program, sat like a canon ball on Bob Malone's desk, a telling insight into the field's fundamental problems that inexplicably had yet to lead to action. Stuart Sneed's similar complaints had percolated up through the ombudsman's office, and it was known that he had warned of exactly the kind of risk that led to the crisis on Y Pad. His warning had gone unheeded.

Some of BP's critics began to blame Doug Suttles. Suttles, of course, had only been on the job in Alaska since 2007 and couldn't be blamed for the long-term neglect that plagued the facilities. But as the man in charge he wasn't doing enough to fix it, either. Pascal found him nearly impossible to work with. "He's an arrogant son of a bitch," she says. "His response to her was always, 'Screw you, I'll do what I want.'" The ombudsman's office had so much trouble dealing with him that at one point an investigator there told Malone that Suttles wasn't a viable partner for their efforts. "He is self-promoting, arrogant, doesn't care about the people who work for him," said one person involved in the ombudsman issues. BP itself liked Suttles's work but didn't want him to represent the company in front of Congress. He had, as one of his executive colleagues put it, "very little respect for having to take the time to go before people in Congress who don't know what a screw-driver looked like."

The series of increasingly serious incidents in Alaska, including Marty Anderson's allegations that the entire inspection program was faulted, seemed to say that for all Suttles's diligence in carrying out a rehabilitation of the oil transit lines, his self-confidence may have gotten in the way of BP's larger goal of fixing its operating culture. The Sneed and Anderson cases weren't the first time Malone had heard from a third party that Suttles had either ignored warnings or wasn't aggressively addressing problems. After the Gathering Center fire in 2007, Suttles told the Anchorage press that it was a small flash fire, and he blamed the worker, Joe Good, for recklessness. Chuck Hamel, with testimony from workers on the slope, went to Congress complaining that the incident was far worse: workers nearly died and the fire was a hairbreadth from starting a chain reaction that would have detonated all the nearby facilities. When Malone found out about Hamel's version of events, he summoned Suttles to Washington and the group—Malone, Suttles, Hamel, and another *Valdez* man turned mediator named Stan Stephens—sat down over breakfast at the Holiday Inn in Alexandria, Virginia, to hear what Hamel had learned. Malone wanted Suttles to listen to Hamel's concerns, even if he disagreed with them, but Suttles was too stubborn. "He said that he was educating me, that I'm not well-informed," Hamel says about Suttles's reaction. "He said the workers exaggerated. It was just a fire. He's a bald-faced liar."

What Suttles didn't know is that Hamel had been leaked BP's own incident log for the fire, explaining in excruciating detail how a larger disaster had been averted. That meeting was at the end of 2007. Now, a year later, the Anderson case had come along and Malone was again faced with questions about Suttles's actions. Anderson was widely seen as a reputable expert, and he was raising serious concerns about the integrity of BP's pipelines. Instead of reacting to those concerns, it seemed as if Suttles was instead exploring everything wrong with Marty Anderson. It was becoming clear that Suttles had to go. The question was how. Malone couldn't just dump him. For all his detractors, Suttles was smart, a strong leader, who played a valued role at BP and was closely aligned with Hayward.

By the middle of October 2008, barely twenty-two months after he took the head job in BP Alaska, Doug Suttles was promoted to a new role in North American operations with executive authority. He would be the chief operating officer for North American exploration and production. Instead of patching gas lines, he would have an influential role in the company's most promising new oil field, in the Gulf of Mexico. Perhaps an environment based more on building for the future rather than repairing and mitigating the past would better suit Suttles's strengths.

The change was transparent to those close to Alaskan operations. "You guys remind me of the Catholic Church," said one consultant who worked with Suttles on behalf of the ombudsman's office. "You moved a guy to another Parrish and called it a promotion and you expect me to believe you?" Suttles was replaced by the head of BP's operations in Indonesia, John Minge. Before heading south, he made a presentation to the Resource Development Council for Alaska, a nonprofit group of business leaders focused on economic development. He didn't discuss the string of problems and near-misses his group had endured in recent months. Instead, he used his speech to push for a new natural gas pipeline to be built across Alaska, pinning the company's hopes for growth on the harvest of a relatively underutilized resource, as opposed to the one everyone knew was in decline.

In his first PowerPoint slide, Suttles projected a quote from George Bernard Shaw. It was supposed to be in the context of the inevitable drop of oil prices, even after a period when it looked as if they would only climb. However, in the context of BP Alaska's troubled history, his own departure from the state, and the risks that Kovac and the work crews insisted were about to get worse, the quote seemed to bear a different message: "We learn from history that we learn nothing from history."

PASCAL HAD BEEN planning to retire in 2009. She had spent twenty-six years with the EPA, and she was sixty years old. She and Dallas had moved into a new home that they built outside the small town of Monroe. The property sat perched on a shallow lake, tucked in to a wooded fold in the rolling farm fields, with views of the Cascades. The couple enjoyed their new house, and they wanted to travel, but Pascal put off the decision to retire.

How could she not see this one case, the most prominent project in her career, and something that had dragged on for nine years, through to the end? It seemed as if it was almost done. Her office had drafted a template for an agreement with BP, and BP said it supported everything she asked for. All the EPA had to do was nail down the details and get BP to sign the agreement. Once they did, she would quit for good.

But the turnover in BP Alaska management slowed Pascal's investigation and the debarment process. She would have to adjust to Minge's leadership and wait for him to get in gear. BP had also hired a new general counsel, Jack Lynch, and Pascal had to navigate that transition as well. Correspondence was slow, and people's schedules were difficult to coordinate. Months could pass between meetings or waiting for an email reply, eating up the calendar.

Then, in January 2009, in the midst of all the turnover, Bob Malone abruptly announced his own retirement. He was fifty-six, arguably at the peak of his career. "It seemed early, it surprised me. It surprised a lot of people," said Shell's Hofmeister. "He just suddenly one day announced his retirement." Malone said that he pined for his personal pursuits, perhaps a run for political office. Hayward said that Malone had "made an extraordinary difference during his tenure at BP America," and demonstrated an "unflagging commitment to safe operations." In reality, with little warmth between Malone and Hayward, Malone seemed to no longer have a niche in management. While the rumor was never confirmed, and always denied by Malone himself, colleagues speculated that Malone had been pushed out, one of the last casualties as Hayward made BP his own. "There have been a lot of purges since Tony came on that trade solid experience and skills . . . for compliant personalities," said one person close to management decisions.

For Pascal, Malone's departure was another loss. In her experience, he had often been a voice of reason in her dealings with BP. He practiced what he preached more than the others and had sought a debarment agreement as a capstone resolution to the crises of 2005 and 2006 that he had been brought in to clean up. In Malone's absence, the debarment process slowed to a crawl.

Time ticked away for Pascal as the decks continued to get shuffled. Her boss, Bob Meunier, the former EPA official who had written the debarment law in 1981, had retired, too, having been replaced by a man friendly with BP's own attorney on the debarment issue. Pascal worried that if she left, no one would push the case any further.

At the same time, BP had become even more recalcitrant about the specific demands Pascal had put on the table for a debarment agreement, and progress in the negotiations began to slip. Its lawyers answered the EPA's written demands with a firm rebuff. BP would not allow Pascal or anyone else to choose who the company put in charge of government compliance, and it didn't much like Pascal telling them how to structure the HSE division, either. "BP does not agree with your pre-conditions for negotiations," Fred Levy, BP's point attorney for the debarment issue, wrote her. If Pascal wanted to abandon her demands, the company was ready to sit down and sign an agreement. If not, Levy wrote, the company would go over her head. It wanted a meeting with Pascal's new boss, Richard Pelletier, Levy's longtime associate from the American Bar Association.

Pascal found the move "arrogant" and born of misplaced confidence. It was as if BP executives believed the company was so indispensable to U.S. interests that the government would never dare to debar it, and so they would continue to act with impunity. "BP told me multiple times that they had direct access to the White House and they would go there," she says.

The challenge placed her in politically treacherous territory. Barack Obama was now president, a fact that might have been expected to make her job easier than it had been during the past eight business-friendly years of the Bush administration. But with Pelletier at the head of her division, Pascal was no longer confident she had the unwavering support of the government. BP knew it, and its lawyers dragged their feet, waiting her out and knowing soon their case would fall into the hands of people like Carson Hodges, a younger employee with a long career ahead of him, who might be less committed to seeing such a sensitive case through. In the politics of the moment, her leverage was evaporating.

Pascal understood that the burden of proof had just been increased. To support a debarment decision—a consequential move that would test the Obama administration's willingness to hold corporations accountable—she would have to make her case bulletproof. She was ready then to debar BP, but the reality of the moment demanded that she find the patience to give the company one more chance, and do everything she could to get BP's lawyers to the table. In a last-ditch effort, Pascal decided to tackle BP's arrogance head-on and call the company's bluff. If BP thought the Defense Department needed it so badly it would never allow debarment, Pascal would show them they were wrong.

In the spring of 2009 she called a meeting with BP's new general counsel, Jack Lynch, at the Fairmont in Seattle to show him an email her office had received from the Defense Department. In it, an official with the Defense Logistics Agency, the division responsible for BP's fuel contracts, stated its unconditional support for debarment. "You could do anything you wanted to BP and we could deal with it," the official, Normand Lussier, wrote. The next move was BP's.

LIKE A STEADY, somber bass beat, 2009 yielded one near-disaster after another in BP's Alaska facilities. Some would rise to the top of the heap, alarming management and workers because they could easily have become catastrophic, or because they resembled so closely what had happened in the past, and what BP had been warned about in reports and investigations and court settlements so many times before. It was a volatile combination of failing equipment and poor decision making.

On January 15, just two weeks after Minge had taken over as president of the division, a cleaning pig got lodged in a thirty-four-inch-wide oil transit line near Pump Station 1, the giant compression facility outside Deadhorse that marks the start of the Trans Alaska Pipeline. The cleaning pig looks like a bullet ribbed with bright orange plastic rings that slip snugly inside the pipeline. The diameter of the rings is slightly larger than that of the pipeline; the plastic scrapes and clears the metal of sediment and debris like a circular squeegee.

Normally the pig is pushed through the pipeline by a liquid mixture, but this time, for reasons that remain unclear, BP's operators had filled the line with pressurized gas. When the pig got stuck, gas continued to seep around the edges of the lodged plastic rings. The warning systems on the line failed to sound as the gas spilled out into the main arteries of the pump station, mixing with the oil, and stalling the pumps that send oil into the Trans Alaska Pipeline. With the system down, pressure built up in holding tanks until a relief valve opened, releasing a mist of gas and oil into the environment that was detected half a mile away. By chance, the mist never reached the nearby steady flame of a lit flare. "If the wind was blowing in the right direction it would have blown everything up," says Kovac. "Forty workers were in the plant, and workers were driving, in the course of their normal routine, through the cloud that enveloped nearby roads. We were just very lucky that gas plume didn't ignite. If it did, all of the workers would have been killed." When the operators finally realized what was happening, they shut down the entire Trans Alaska Pipeline.

Nine months later, a staging valve meant to route excess gas to a flare stuck closed at the Central Compressor Plant, the facility that injects gas back underground in Prudhoe Bay. Gas backed up behind the valve, sending a monstrous volume of it back into the system, looking for a way out.

Normally, when gas spills out at a facility like the compressor plant, the overflow is routed to a second emergency flare, so it can burn off without building up and risking an explosion. The flares that had been

278   RUN TO FAILURE

installed at the plant weren't lit that day and didn't function. A closed-circuit camera with a view of the plant is wired to a monitor, and operators in the control center can watch for trouble. This was the third critical safety backup, but it also didn't function. The camera, it turns out, was pointed off in an odd angle, showing a close-up of a wall.

It was like Texas City all over again—a series of relatively minor malfunctions and errors of judgment that piled on top of one another, seemingly in slow motion, until the net effect was a volatile potential disaster. With neither the safety flares nor the manual monitoring device working, the gas built up and spread outward around the plant, snaking along the ground and billowing up in a cloud.

Because of its central location, and its high volume of compressed volatile gases, a blast at the Central Compressor Plant had the potential to cause great destruction. Offices were located nearby. Twenty workers might be on the site at any given time. If the cloud were ignited, says Robert Bea, the Berkeley professor and former industry consultant, a blast zone could reach three hundred feet and leave a crater ninety feet wide. "It's hard to describe these explosions in terms that people can understand," Bea said. "It would rival the biggest ones that we have ever had in the history of the oil and gas industry." In 1988, a similar gas valve error caused a massive explosion in the North Sea of an Occidental Petroleum rig called *Piper Alpha*, killing 167 workers. But in Alaska in 2009, there was no spark. "Let's just call them lucky," Bea said.

Just seven weeks later, BP Alaska would test its luck again, this time outside the Lisburne Production Center (LPC), where maintenance issues had also been ignored. Workers had a list of concerns. An air compressor that circulated fresh air throughout the industrial facility wasn't working; seal failures on several pumps used to empty tanks of hazardous fluids were rampant; a high-temperature alarm was malfunctioning and hadn't been reset for months; and a waste line that led to a flare was blocked with ice. "We are basically running a broken plant with too few people to address the problems in a timely and safe manner," a mechanic at the facility would later explain in a complaint to his manager.

Keeping the plant running, the workers said, was like playing an arcade game: you get a hammer and race to hit the thing that pops up.

You are always chasing after that, oblivious to whatever else might go wrong next.

BP management did nothing to fix the list of problems there. Then, on November 29, 2009, a frozen, twenty-five-year-old pipeline split open, dumping nearly 46,000 gallons of crude oil, toxic wastewater, and natural gas onto the frozen ground. After the spill, a mechanic sent an email to the facility's manager complaining that BP still wasn't dealing with Lisburne's disrepair. An investigation found that management had relied on a temperature sensor to warn of freezing conditions in the pipeline but had placed the sensor inside a heated facility. It found that the managers knew the ruptured pipeline had ice in it before the spill but ignored the problem, and the alarms it triggered, for 165 days because they didn't need to use the line at the time. The findings triggered an investigation by the FBI into BP's conduct at Lisburne, and a fresh Department of Justice examination of the company's compliance with its 2007 settlement.

"The facility was not being maintained to an acceptable standard," Phil Dziubinski, BP's compliance and ethics manager on the slope at the time, would later write to federal investigators in Anchorage. Dziubinski had been warning senior management that staff were overworked and reporting that the company hadn't fixed fire and gas systems or addressed other safety concerns when the spill occurred at Lisburne. (A few months later, Dziubinski would be laid off by BP, would lose a wrongful termination complaint he filed with OSHA, and then would reach a confidential settlement with BP.) "They did not have the resources to fix the fourteen items presented—or to address the more systemic issues where they needed more maintenance. It was just clear and convincing evidence that BP lacks the capability to maintain the integrity of the North Slope production facilities."

AFTER EACH MISHAP, Pascal launched an inquiry into the cause, but she could barely get through one case before another began. She began to ask for proof of what was changing in the oil fields and to demand that BP agree to a set of rigid checks in order to fend off a ban on government contracts. She wanted detailed progress reports on BP's maintenance projects, not just memos and summaries. She demanded receipts. "I was no longer willing to accept their word," she said. "Show me, what did you maintain? I want to see what you paid, who you paid. What did you replace? I wanted the details."

"They did not like that at all," she adds.

Two and a half years had passed since Hayward had become CEO, and BP still claimed to be pumping tens of millions of dollars into improving its most tired operations. At the very moment when operations should have begun to show signs of improvement, the accidents were happening so fast and so consistently that the company seemed on the verge of spinning out of control. It wasn't just the occasional headlines that made BP look bad. Statistically, the picture Pascal saw was stark and ugly. Between 2000 and late 2009 in Alaska, BP had suffered more than 350 large spills, more than three times as many as its closest competitor, ConocoPhillips. BP produces nearly twice as much oil in Alaska as ConocoPhillips, but it spilled four and a half times as much volume. Other, smaller Alaskan oil companies—Unocal, for example—had twenty spills or fewer over the same period. If small spills were counted, Alaskan officials had cited BP for more than 3,000 incidents, and ConocoPhillips for just 744 since 2000.

At times managers at BP would explain away some of these environmental accidents as the consequence of being the largest operator in the large, old, and geographically challenging oil field that the greater Prudhoe Bay area was. In the 2006 congressional hearings, for example, Malone said, "We had a huge infrastructure, a very expensive infrastructure, built for an arctic environment, and as the production level dropped so did we need to define the facilities to match that production level."

BP also spilled more oil in the Gulf of Mexico—with its state-of-the-art oil field, utilizing BP's most advanced technology and its best minds—than any other company. Since 2000 the U.S. government had tallied more than eight thousand barrels of oil spilled in gulf waters by BP, 65 percent more than Shell, which actually produced more oil there, and two and a half times as much as Chevron, the gulf's third largest producer.

The company's safety statistics were no better. In Alaska, since 1990, BP had fifty-two serious safety violations recorded by the Alaska Occupational Safety and Health Department (AKOSH). ConocoPhillips had just seven. When the whole country was taken into account, BP was by far the leader in violations. The federal Occupational Safety and Health Administration recorded 518 violations in the United States from BP at the company's refineries. That was more than twice the number of violations recorded by Chevron, the second most egregious actor in terms of safety, and nearly five times as many violations as Exxon.

Experts estimate the death toll at the company would compare similarly, but there is no way to know for sure. Government records only calculate worker fatalities for their direct employer—in this case, the hundreds of contracting companies. Relying on contractors to perform some of the oil fields' most dangerous work makes it difficult to tie the most serious risks statistically to the owners of the sites at which they happened.

In his speech at the Stanford Graduate School of Business, delivered in May 2009, Hayward seemed to congratulate himself on having fixed the company's safety problems just by daring to talk about them openly. He shared a well-worn anecdote that he often liked to repeat from his early days in the Venezuelan oil fields in the 1990s, in which a young worker was killed. Hayward went to the young man's funeral. "The mother, his mother, came up to me and beat me on the chest and said, "Why did you let it happen to him? Why did you let it happen?" Hayward recounted. "That was a real wake-up to me." Then he said, referring to his success in amending BP's more recent record, and the business and safety pressures that drove it, "We used that as the rallying cry behind this big change that we have subsequently been driving through BP."

Just because two years had gone by without a major incident—and he didn't seem to be counting all the minor ones—it looked as if BP was off scot-free. Hayward didn't claim his job was finished, but he relished the progress. "Is it working? I would say we're making progress. We're not there yet."

Shell, Exxon, and other partners who invested in joint projects with BP in Alaska, in Asia, and in the gulf had begun to wonder, though, whether BP's standards were strong enough to protect the joint ventures' financial interests. When they financed a BP-led project, Shell or Exxon would embed a full-time staff person on-site as a sort of minder to babysit BP and, as Shell's Hofmeister put it, "to make sure that Shell's interest was being respected, and frankly to look over their shoulder because BP's operating reputation left something to be desired. That was through the lessons of experience." It wasn't normal practice. "When you have a lead partner, you want them to carry the load," he says.

One Exxon manager who worked closely with the company's BP partnerships suggested that Hayward might not have the endurance needed to address safety issues. "If someone thinks that they can change the fundamental outlook on overall integrity of operations, including safety—if you think you can fundamentally change it in a worldwide organization in two to three years—you don't understand the problem," he said. "It requires a twenty-four-hour-a-day, three-hundred-sixty-five-days-a year commitment. . . . It is never going to go away."

Members of Congress watched what was unfolding within BP in 2009 with growing alarm. Each fire, explosion, or leak amplified questions about whether BP was a reliable choice as the government's partner in supplying the country's oil. Congressmen like Henry Waxman, chairman of the House Energy and Commerce Committee, openly questioned whether BP could protect American interests. Waxman's unease was focused on Alaska, but it suggested broader concerns. If BP continued to be one of the most active and significant oil companies operating across the United States, and continued expanding aggressively in the waters of the Gulf of Mexico, was it inevitable that their sloppiness would lead to an accident there, too?

For decades BP had answered such questions with suave public relations campaigns. The pattern was to publicly embrace rather than deny large problems: "Apologize and open their wallets," as one executive put it. BP would pledge to reorganize the company's management structure, launch new programs like the ombudsman's office, and appear to take swift action. It would launch investigations, like the 2001 operational integrity review, leading to verbose reports that appeared proactive and responsive.

History, though, had shown that BP often stopped short of following through. Some within BP's own ranks had begun to question whether the company was losing control. "You have to wonder about the significant events of 2009. Are they just indicators of something bad that is going to happen? I think the big accident is likely," said one Alaska-based manager who took a lesson from previous investigations into catastrophic accidents and thinks they help predict what will happen next. "Whenever you have significant events—a fatality or this type of thing—you always find underlying it less significant events cascading down that were indicators of things going wrong."

THEN, for the first time, complaints about safety began coming from BP's advanced drilling operations in the gulf. In early 2009 a senior-level offshore rig engineer named Ken Abbott had come to BP's ombudsman's office alleging that BP was skipping over critical design steps meant to guarantee safe operations on the huge new deepwater drilling platform Atlantis, which was almost as large as Thunder Horse, and capable of producing more than 200,000 barrels of oil a day from the ocean floor.

As Atlantis was about to be put into service the previous year, Abbott, a thirty-year industry veteran who had worked for companies like Shell and General Electric, discovered that BP did not keep final design manuals, called "as-built" drawings, which prove that a piece of equipment—say, a shutoff valve or an engine winch—was built properly, and thus serve as a final check of safety.

Missing design documents not only prove that equipment was assembled properly but are the instruction manuals workers rely on in emergencies. If there is a fire on deck or a blowout, for example, operators under extreme stress and danger can use the design drawings to find the hidden kill lever that can shut an engine down before it explodes.

This was not the first time missing design documents had been raised as a safety concern for BP. When BP had conducted its own internal operational integrity investigation in Alaska in 2001, the company had concluded that missing design drawings presented a risk. Back then, updating the records was one of the compliance conditions BP had to meet to avoid debarment. Abbott's allegations, eight years later, essentially repeated those earlier complaints.

On Atlantis, Abbott says that as-built documents had been issued for only 274 of more than 7,100 pieces of equipment, and that it was the equivalent of constructing a house without having an architect or engineer sign off on the blueprint. Among the infrastructure without documentation were the wellheads themselves, and the subsea risers—the pipelines and hoses deep underwater that serve as a conduit for moving materials from the bottom of the ocean to the rig. If this was an indicator of how BP managed its other rigs, its offshore drilling operations could also be in trouble.

Abbott, a contractor, alerted BP's senior project engineers to the problems, but he was ignored. "I hit a lot of resistance from the lead engineers," Abbott says. "They got really angry with me. They wanted to shortcut the system and not do the reviews, because they cut short the man-hours. There seemed to be a big emphasis to push the contractors to get things done, and that was always at the forefront of the operation." Abbott estimated that BP saved $2 million to $3 million by streamlining the document process.

After he complained to his managers about the documentation, his contract was cut short, in February 2009, and suddenly Abbott couldn't find any more work in the gulf. He took his story to BP's ombudsman's office, which is where Pascal learned about it. He also filed two lawsuits against the U.S. government—one to force regulators to tighten oversight of the Atlantis before an accident happened, and another that could earn him a cash settlement.

THE LONGER this seemingly endless cycle of repeat offenses went on, the more Jeanne Pascal became convinced that soon the only way to make the company improve would be to take the dramatic step that for so many years she had viewed only as a last resort: ban the entire corporation from government work in the United States. By the end of 2009, BP had three criminal convictions—in Endicott Bay, Texas City, and Prudhoe Bay—and a deferred criminal conviction in the price-fixing scandal. (In September 2009 a judge dismissed price fixing charges against BP's individual traders, but the company had already agreed to a plea, which, for debarment purposes, counts as a conviction.) In just the time that Pascal had been on the BP case, at least twenty-six workers had been killed in accidents in its North American business alone. BP documents show at least 108 of its workers had been killed worldwide since 2002, but it's unclear how many international contractors are included in those statistics, since they are not counted in BP's reports. Who knew what was happening in Egypt, Azerbaijan, and all the other places BP had business?

BP management had come to view Pascal as a zealot out for its scalp. Pascal felt that she had given BP every conceivable benefit of the doubt. When the company violated its agreement and lied to her in 2005, she still found a way to work within the debarment process. When BP blatantly disregarded one law after another, she convinced herself that the services the oil company provided to the United States in wartime were more important than holding the company accountable for environmental crimes. "It doesn't make sense to cripple the government because a company violated the Clean Water Act," she said. Throughout the years, even after Scott West went public with his story about the flubbed criminal investigation, Pascal had never gone to the press and never jumped her chain of command. She respected the government process, and she would try almost to the bitter end.

Debarment is most appropriate, the statute says, when a company doesn't just break the law a couple of times but demonstrates what debarment officials call a "corporate culture of non-compliance." John Browne had once said that the most telling detail would not be how BP performed but how it responded to a crisis. Bob Malone had famously asked Congress to judge BP not for what it said but for what it did. Now BP's record was speaking for itself. "How many times can a debarring official grant a resolution to an agreement if it looks like no matter how many times they agree to fix something it keeps manifesting itself as a problem?" asks Bob Meunier.

Pascal was getting close to answering that question. "There comes a point where the events conspire to . . . show federal regulators that a particular company, for whatever reason, has no intent of complying with U.S. law and regulations," she said. In January 2010, Pascal was shown an email from the deputy ombudsman, Billie Garde, to BP Alaska's president John Minge that made it clear that after more than twenty-four months of wrangling, Marty Anderson's complaints were still unresolved. The pipeline inspection still had faults waiting to be addressed, and Anderson remained out of work. "Marty became the subject of both overt and subtle retaliation," Garde wrote. "The current managers still have their noses out of joint about him." Here Pascal was, working out a final agreement that pivoted around open communication between workers and their managers, and the company appeared to be punishing the man who had raised a flag about one of its worst spills in a decade.

In a burst of anger, on January 19, 2010, she wrote a lengthy email to Minge and to BP America's chief attorney, Jack Lynch. It was part diatribe—an expression of frustration with the company's resistance to agreeing to her terms—and part shrill, final warning:

> I have been told that ever since he brought information to BP, his employer and BP have tried their best to get rid of Marty and marginalize him. His request for help has not been resolved, and although many people in BP are aware of this situation, nothing has been done in TWO YEARS. The retaliation is now spreading to other people who supported Marty. This is a bad situation that is getting worse and it has been handled poorly by BP.
>
> Why [has] neither of you gotten involved in this matter sufficiently to stop/curtail what is going on or resolve this? You say you want our trust to operate the employee complaint program, but this is a current and graphic example of why EPA does not trust BP to do that appropriately. I have also heard that the persons who retaliated against Marty are from the senior BP employee ranks. Again, it appears that BP, regardless of its code of conduct and statements to the government[,] will do whatever is necessary to cover up the improper actions of its senior managers—which means you have a code of conduct you force employees to follow, and one, unwritten and unspoken code (or lack of a code) for senior managers who appear not to be bound by company policy. This promotes intimidation, retaliation, blackballing and unethical behavior in the management ranks, and a culture of fear and a lack of ethics in the employee ranks.
>
> It sends a message to your work force that BP does not mean what it says, it will not enforce its policies against its senior staff and that workers don't matter. BP will never get better until it enforces its policies and the law equally against all its employees—from CEOs to roughnecks.

The next day, Pascal had final debarment papers against BP drafted. There would be one more meeting with BP. Should the company still resist an agreement, she would send the debarment papers up the flagpole for a final signature from Pelletier, her new boss.

Congress had also sent Minge a letter, on January 14, 2010, warning that further cost cutting could imperil safety at BP facilities and demanding assurances from BP. The letter expressed doubt that BP could be trusted to safely run the Alyeska Pipeline and demanded that the company answer a spate of questions. It seemed to Pascal that a government consensus was building, and that Pelletier would be hard-pressed not to sign the debarment papers, but a strange twist of fate would get in her way. Two days later, on January 21, Pascal parked her car in the basement garage of the EPA's downtown Seattle office building and headed inside, the debarment papers tucked under her arm. On her calendar were discussions about her decision on BP. It was just after 6:00 a.m. She was late and in a hurry.

The elevator bell rang, and the doors slid open. As Pascal stepped inside, her foot caught a lip at the floor, sending her sprawling forward. She reached for the handrail, but the momentum of her fall brought her down even as she hung on. Her face clipped the wall on her way down, and her arm twisted behind her, yanking her shoulder out of its socket. She lay there for a few minutes before help and then an ambulance arrived. Her meetings, canceled, would never get rescheduled.

For a few weeks after the accident, she tried to work from home, but an MRI showed that she had torn her rotator cuff. She would need surgery to reattach the ligaments in her shoulder, followed by physical therapy and months of recovery. Her arm in a sling, Pascal couldn't type. She couldn't drive, couldn't travel. She could barely write, let alone work. It took her a few weeks to arrive at the most difficult decision of her career.

On March 1, 2010, Jeanne Pascal submitted her retirement papers, leaving the BP case she had worked on for nearly twelve years unresolved.

15

A DELICATE BALANCE

THROUGHOUT JANUARY 2010, much of BP's focus was on getting back to a partially drilled hole that it had abandoned deep beneath the surface of the Gulf of Mexico. The well, called the Macondo, was one of the company's great new prospects for a big find of oil. Geologists expected to strike a reservoir with more than fifty million barrels. But the Macondo, a capped hole 49 miles from the Louisiana coast, and under 4,992 feet of water in the unexplored trenches near what hydrogeographers called Mississippi Canyon, was also one of the company's deepest, most expensive, and most complicated offshore wells yet. The previous November, a hurricane had interrupted BP's drilling. Now the company was returning to try again. Finishing the job would severely test the BP organization.

BP had leased the rights to drill in this particular section of Mississippi Canyon, called Block 252, in 2008, for $34 million. From the shoreline, a shallow continental shelf extends into the gulf, ringing the coastline from the Florida Keys past New Orleans and around to Cancún and the tip of the Yucatán Peninsula in a near-complete circle. Farther from shore the shelf drops precipitously thousands of feet into a deep underwater expanse, like a high Utah mesa eroding to a valley far below. The canyon itself is a prominent jagged underwater geographic breach in that shallow shelf. Extending to the east of it, for nearly two hundred miles, a group of undersea real estate lots had been doled out by the United States government for some of the nation's most productive—and experimental—drilling. Parts of the Mississippi Canyon region had been drilled extensively, both by BP on Thunder Horse and by most of the other big companies that produced in the gulf. That spring Shell was fast on its way to a huge discovery of oil in 7,200 feet of water, a little farther out.

Macondo was closer to shore, and to the steep underwater escarpment of the shelf, tucked between a series of mountainous underwater domes in a flat seafloor valley. Like treacherous mountain valleys, each area can present its own surprises. Block 252, where the Macondo prospect lay, had never been explored by BP. And it presented unique geological challenges, even in the context of the gulf's notoriously difficult drilling.

The oil lay buried deep beneath layers of sediment that had washed out of the Mississippi River drainage over a million and a half years ago. Underneath this sandstone, salt was wedged into the slope of the escarpment, and it stretched over the folds of rock, disguising what lay beneath it and confounding scientists who examined it. The salt caused so many shifts of the seafloor over time that nothing was where it was expected to be, including oil. When geologists used seismic and sonic waves to pierce the earth and map the layers of stone they planned to drill through, the salt reflected and interfered with the signal. BP's vice president of gulf exploration, David Rainey, described it as presenting "the same barrier to our seismic imaging capability that a pane of frosted glass presents to our eyes." The barrier, like a veil over the unknown, increased uncertainty and frustration about what oil lay beneath the crust and where, exactly, it would be.

Perhaps that is why BP named the well Macondo, after the troubled town in Gabriel García Márquez's novel *One Hundred Years of Solitude*. Marquez's description is full of foreboding: "It was as if God had decided to put to the test every capacity for surprise and was keeping the inhabitants of Macondo in a permanent alternation between excitement and disappointment, doubt and revelation, to such an extreme that no one knew for certain where the limits of reality lay."

BP first began to drill an exploratory stab into Block 252 in the fall of 2009, in the first of what was originally planned to be two wells. It contracted Transocean, the world's largest offshore drilling rig operator, and brought the Marianas, another of the industry's giant semisubmersible drilling rigs, to a spot over the target. By its nature, an exploratory well is dangerous because it deals with the unknown. Beneath the shield of salt BP could encounter anything—a huge reservoir of overheated oil ready to burst out of the ground, or no oil at all. If they did strike oil or gas, it was expected to be under enormous pressure, weighed down by the miles of solid rock and water that lay on top of it and heated by the earth's core. The underground pressure, combined with the lack of a reliable image of the geology in the region, presented the greatest uncertainty for BP. For that reason, an exploration well is rigorously designed and constructed to be a safe bet—an experiment. If a standard production well is a passenger car, an exploration well is an Abrams tank, outfitted with extra precautionary equipment and design redundancies to prepare it for anything. "You don't know what you are going to encounter until you encounter it, so it's a heftier well, a stronger casing program, a thicker casing program," says Michael Norton, a veteran well designer who has designed hundreds of wells for Mobil, ARCO, and other companies around the world. The process, too, Norton says, will go slower. At each stage in an exploration well, every available test will be done to assure that things are going according to plan and to try to shed more light on the mysteries of the earth at that particular location.

The Macondo well was designed to reach down to 19,650 feet, and it would allow BP to collect data about the rock layers and accurately map the salt wedge—information the company could use to more routinely develop the area later on. Yet when BP filed its application to drill with the U.S. government, it expressed an extraordinary confidence in the project, and even a sense of complacency about its challenges— as if it weren't experimental at all. It defined the Macondo A and Macondo B wells as exploration wells but downplayed the uncertainties. The company's spill response plan, drafted March 10, 2009, said that "in the event of an unanticipated blowout resulting in an oil spill . . . no significant adverse impacts are expected."

The plan, it turns out, had been cobbled together without, it seemed, much thought for the specific challenges of the Macondo site or the increasingly severe risks BP faced as it waded deeper and deeper into the frontier of drilling. A number of pages, for example, had been copied from the website of the National Oceanic and Atmospheric Administration (NOAA) and promised to protect wildlife that many third-grade students knew did not live in the warm southern waters of the gulf, including sea lions and walruses. BP's plan also named a marine biologist at Florida Atlantic University, Peter Lutz, to guide the company's cleanup in the event of a spill. But Lutz had died in 2005. No matter what happened at Macondo, he wasn't going to be providing much guidance.

The U.S. government, which allowed BP to rely on a somewhat generic response plan—overlooking its regulatory requirement to submit details specific to the Macondo well site—has had a cozy relationship with drillers that has at times been problematic. The Minerals and Management Service, which regulated offshore drilling at the time, also operated under a conflicting mandate to generate revenues from drilling while aggressively regulating that drilling. Finally, BP downplayed how much oil could possibly be spilled at the Macondo site, claiming a worst-case blowout might spill 162,000 barrels of oil—less than half the 500,000 barrels BP claimed it was prepared to handle.

By November 2009 the Macondo was drilled to four thousand feet below the seabed, nearly one-third of the way to the depths where BP expected to strike oil. People close to the company say that right away BP had difficulty controlling kicks of gas from the well. But before much could be done to fix it, on November 9, Hurricane Ida struck— the first real bit of bad luck on the project. The Marianas rig was battered by 90-mph winds and badly damaged. Drilling on the Macondo was stopped.

In early 2010, BP had returned to finish the job.

DEEPWATER offshore drilling had become the true frontier of the oil industry. It was where almost all of the opportunity and most of the experimentation and risk lay. In 1995, when John Browne became CEO of BP, nearly 2.4 million barrels of oil a day were being produced from the Gulf of Mexico, but almost all of it was from water less than a thousand feet deep, and there were just a handful of wells in deeper water. Gradually, the industry, led in large part by BP and Shell, ventured deeper. Between 2001 and 2004 alone, eleven new oil fields were discovered in the gulf in waters deeper than seven thousand feet. Drilling in four thousand to six thousand feet of water, once considered extreme, had become less unusual. By 2010 roughly 60 percent of gulf production came from deep water, where 60 installed oil platforms had drilled some 3,600 wells. The United States was believed to hold 18 percent of global deepwater reserves of oil.

Around the world, from the coast of Angola to Brazil to the Arctic, exploration was moving away from land and into the oceans, where vast topography had yet to be explored. But in the United States, exploration was limited. In 1990 President George H. W. Bush had placed a temporary moratorium on new offshore drilling in U.S. waters almost anywhere but in the central gulf, expressly prohibiting drilling off the East and West coasts. In 1998, President Bill Clinton extended that ban for another fourteen years, adding several marine sanctuaries that would remain off-limits indefinitely. The effect was to concentrate drilling in the places where it was already allowed, places like Mississippi Canyon and the rest of the western and central gulf, an area that extends roughly from the Texas coast to just east of Mobile, Alabama. There seemed to be plenty of oil there to be had. Geologists began to believe that deepwater parts of the gulf alone could yield as much as forty-five billion barrels of oil—far more than all the nation's known onshore and shallow-water drilling combined, and amounting to the sort of elephant that John Browne had set out to hunt two decades earlier. Drilling in the gulf could establish a consistent and secure domestic supply of oil.

BP alone had at least two billion barrels of reserves in the gulf. In September 2009 it announced a huge discovery in what it called the Tiber prospect, a field that could contain as much as six billion barrels and was one of the largest U.S. discoveries ever. It had just drilled the world's deepest oil well there, in a place called Keathley Canyon, in 4,000 feet of water—reaching a depth of 35,055 feet. Thunder Horse, in 2010, was pumping more oil each day than BP executives predicted would be routed through the entire Trans Alaska Pipeline from all of Prudhoe Bay within a few years. Gulf oil already amounted to about one-third of the nation's domestic oil production and 8 percent of U.S. supply, and it was only expected to increase, as companies ventured farther offshore. While BP prepared the Macondo well, it was also invested, with Shell and Chevron, to begin drilling at Perdido spar, in 8,000 feet of water—the world's deepest offshore venture.

Other energy supplies were being rapidly explored and expanded at the same time that deepwater drilling evolved. Renewable power production, despite all the naysayers who claimed that it was too impractical and too expensive, was booming. Globally in 2010, installed wind energy capacity, representing the potential for electrical generation, overtook nuclear energy, supplying close to a fifth of the world's electrical power, according to the Worldwatch Institute. What the oil industry calls "unconventional" hydrocarbon resources were also being developed at a fast pace. In Canada, sand rich in bitumen was being dug out of open-pit mines so big they were visible from space. Though mining and producing oil from the tar sands, as they are called, was taking a devastating toll on water and forest resources, the tar sands produced one and a half million barrels of oil a day in 2009. In the United States, natural gas development in deeply buried shale deposits was also booming—more than 35,000 wells were being drilled a year, and the American Petroleum Institute estimated that with gas making up about 22 percent of the nation's energy supply, the United States had enough gas reserves to last a century.

The predominant source of global energy, however, is still oil. Oil alone provides roughly 35 percent of energy needs in the United States and around the world. Together, oil and gas (which usually come from the same wells) provide more than 60 percent of global energy needs. No matter how necessary a broader portfolio of fuels was to political and environmental sustainability, the role of oil production wasn't going to be eliminated anytime soon, and the future of U.S. energy production lay in harvesting the oil cradled by the coasts of Louisiana, Florida, and Texas.

The question, rather, was what risks the nation and the industry were willing to take to get it, and whether those risks could be mitigated so that the rewards would outweigh them, not just financially in the form of profits for the oil industry but for society as a whole.

The nation had scarcely begun to contemplate these issues, and only a very few people—Jeanne Pascal, Scott West, and Chuck Hamel among them—had thought them through sufficiently to question whether BP should be the company entrusted to take on this responsibility. Could BP take its decade's worth of commitments to reformed corporate safety and convert those words into action when it came to development in the world's riskiest and most technically demanding ventures? Or would it also run its offshore program to failure, slipping into the same old grooves of rushed decisions, hubris, and a haphazard assessment of risk? The question mattered, because as the United States reached farther and farther into the gulf for oil, BP held the majority of the leases there and could be expected to do the majority of the drilling.

On January 31, 2010, a little more than a week after Jeanne Pascal's career-ending accident in Seattle, BP returned to the Macondo well site. This time it had a giant semisubmersible rig called the Deepwater Horizon in tow to finish the job. The Deepwater Horizon was one of Transocean's largest and most capable rigs. It was the rig that drilled BP's record-setting well in the Tiber field's Keathley Canyon. Now it was being maneuvered over Block 252, where BP would continue drilling into the well it had begun in November. But by then, BP was already behind schedule and over budget.

The Deepwater Horizon, the company hoped, might be able to make up for lost time. It was a remarkable rig, like a miniature industrial city perched atop four legs that sank into the sea, connecting 130 feet underwater to pontoons that kept the ship afloat. The Deepwater Horizon could sail itself into place, and then remain above its target using thrusters directed by satellite positioning devices and sonar "anchors" on the seafloor, constantly readjusting its position to stay precisely centered over the target well hole no matter what the wind and the weather brought. The rig was capable of drilling in deeper water than Thunder Horse—in up to ten thousand feet—but unlike Thunder Horse it was only designed to drill, not to produce, the oil. Once a well was completed the Deepwater Horizon would temporarily abandon it, and BP would seal the well and come back later with a producing platform.

The Deepwater Horizon was slightly smaller than Thunder Horse, weighing 32,500 tons and measuring 396 feet long. On the lowest deck were the mud pits—large holding bins for drilling fluids going into and out of the well—and enough berths for the rig's round-the-clock crew of 126 people. The second deck housed the engine control rooms, the ship's six turbines, and four large lifeboats as well as a movie theater and the galley. The drilling operations happened mostly on the main deck above that—a large open platform with a driller's shack and equipment yard—and then on a smaller elevated deck in the center of the rig called the drill floor. The drill floor, where some of the most dangerous work took place, surrounded the drill pipe and sat squarely underneath the tower of the 270-foot-tall derrick that guided the pipe into the well.

The Deepwater Horizon rig, of course, floated atop the water, and the Macondo well sat at the bottom of the gulf. Between them a mile-long connection called a riser pipe ran from the very top of the rig's derrick, down through the drill floor and the middle of the rig, past the lower decks, and into the water, all the way to the seafloor. Only then, after the riser passed through a large safety valve device called a blowout preventer, did it reach the top of the Macondo well. By design, the well would be drilled from that point nearly three miles farther into the earth in search of oil. To begin drilling a deepwater well like Macondo, the crew first dangles a mile-long string of drill pipe into the ocean to drop what they call a jet pipe—a 36-inch-diameter, three-quarter-inch-thick heavy section of steel pipe—like a dart into the silty ocean floor. The pipe, under the force of its own weight, sinks three hundred feet into the mud, creating a starter wellbore in which the drilling can safely begin without the soft mud walls collapsing in on themselves. Once the jet pipe has hit solid rock, the drill string coming from the rig's derrick, with a drill bit at the end and driven by the torque of the engines way above on the floating platform, starts to burrow into the earth.

From here, a well is drilled in stages. First, a 36-inch-wide hole is drilled for several thousand feet, and lined with a 36-inch pipe, called a conductor casing. To fix the casing in place, cement is pumped down into the well through the drill string into the bottom, where it is forced out the sides and squeezed back upward, or circulated, into the small space left between the raw dirt wall of the wellbore and the conductor casing, sealing it in place against the earth. Then the process is repeated with incrementally smaller sections of pipe the deeper the well is drilled. In the Macondo, BP would run a 28-inch casing to 6,200 feet, then a 22-inch casing to 7,900 feet, and so on, until the last section of the well, which would wind up calling for a narrow, 7-inch-wide pipe. The encased hole becomes the architectural structure of the well, allowing another narrower string of pipe, called production string, to be run from top to bottom, on the inside, to ferry the oil. In between those telescoping casing layers and the production string is a long open space—the well's main annulus.

One of the toughest parts of drilling a well in the Gulf of Mexico is balancing the awesome difference in what is called hydrostatic pressure between the inside of the well and the outside. This is where many wells can go wrong. Far beneath the waters of the gulf and under the immense weight of miles of rock piled on top, the natural pressure from the earth constantly threatens to collapse the well, or force water, oil, or gas trapped in pores in the rock into the wellbore. If hydrocarbons under pressure hit the well—and if they find their way up through either the drill pipe or the long open annulus—they are likely to rush out toward the top in a violent kick, risking a blowout. To control that dynamic, drilling companies use a heavy mud—a dirty mixture of viscous synthetic fluids, polymers, oil, and chemicals with a lead-like heft—to balance that pressure inside the well. The idea is to make sure the outward pressure exerted by the mud constantly matches the inward pressure exerted by the geologic formation. As long as the two remain equal, there is balance and stability and the walls hold up. The mud can be twice as dense as water, and twice the weight. It is constantly circulated down the drill pipe, out of the drill bit, and then flows back up the annular space between the drill pipe and the casing, cooling the machinery, clearing away debris, and, most importantly, maintaining the well's delicate balance of pressure.

But the earth, too, can be fragile. If the drilling mud gets too heavy, the force of its weight can fracture the rock inside the well, risking a collapse, or allowing the mud to seep out into the cracks it creates. Since every drop of fluid that is pumped down into a well is circulated back up through the annulus toward the surface, its volume is strictly accounted for. When fluids are lost in a weakened well, the result is a loss of circulation: a crack exists in the wellbore structure so significant that some of the drilling mud has drained out. If that happens, the well can become unstable, again risking a blowout, or the loss of the well. For a process relying on brute force and immense machinery, it's an extraordinarily delicate balance that ultimately decides the fate of a deepwater well.

When BP returned to the Macondo well in 2010, the jet pipe had already been laid and the conductor casing already inserted to nearly four thousand feet by the Marianas rig. All the Deepwater Horizon had to do to begin drilling again was put in place the last critical link between the well and the platform floating on the water's surface: the blowout preventer. The BOP, as it's called, is a steel stack of emergency shut-off devices that jut like branches from a main pipe stem, and it sits latched to the top of the wellhead on the ocean floor. The topmost valves are a set of two donut-shaped rubber seals called annular preventers that can cinch tight around a drill pipe and close off the annular space around it. Below that is the queen of safety backups, a last resort called a blind shear ram, which provides some peace of mind in a worst-case scenario. If the oil well is out of control, the ram's powerful hydraulic pincers slice through the well pipe, like wire cutters through a cable, shutting off the flow of oil and gas altogether. It's the kind of thing that should never need to be used but has to be in place. Below that, closer to the seafloor, is a set of devices called variable bore rams that also have pincers that could close in an instant around the drill pipe, but do not cut it, instead sealing off the annular space around without interfering with the main flow. In all, the Deepwater Horizon's BOP had seven redundant mechanisms that would shut off the flow of oil or gas in case of an emergency. By February 10 it was installed, and, within a few days, BP began drilling the Macondo anew—its second attempt to strike oil in Block 252.

That same month, BP management called a closely guarded three-day meeting of some North American managers at the Egan Conference Center in Anchorage. Beginning on February 22, the company ran an intensive media relations training session to coach its midlevel executives in how to communicate with the public and the press in the event of a catastrophic accident or spill. In particular, the group discussed the hypothetical scenario of a large offshore spill. One message, according to a person in the room that day, was hammered home: when questioned by a reporter, talk about safety improvements and reliability in every answer. Media training for executives is not unusual, but the serious tone and disaster-specific focus of this one seemed odd. Perhaps management was losing some of the confidence—even complacency—that the company had shown when BP had first filed its application to drill the Macondo well.

If they were uneasy, there was good cause. Drilling in deep water presented technical difficulties that challenged every bit of engineering experience at any company, and the processes were inherently unpredictable and unsafe—far more so than the public, or the government, tended to believe. Famously, in 1979, Pemex's Ixtoc platform dumped more than three million barrels of oil into the gulf off the coast of Mexico, swamping a seventeen-mile stretch of Texas beach with black oil. In that case, the unthinkable happened. The drillers lost circulation of their drilling fluids into cracks in the well and the earth, leading to a massive blowout. When the crews triggered the blowout preventer, it failed. The blind shear ram meant to slice through the pipe couldn't cut all the way through because it was positioned at a spot where the well pipe was extra thick. The spill went on for more than nine months.

Then, in 1988, Occidental Petroleum's Piper Alpha rig exploded off the coast of Britain, killing 167 workers on board. More recently, in August 2009, the Montara rig blew out in the Timor Sea off the coast of Australia. In that case it took more than two months to control and "shut in" the well, a term for closing it up and leaving it in storage.

These headlining catastrophic cases were punctuated by lots of less noticed but consequential accidents as well, especially off the coast of the United States. There had been more than 110 serious oil spills in the Gulf of Mexico over the previous decade, from which records show at least thirty thousand barrels of oil were spilled. BP had had its own share of accidents in the gulf—almost one every year between 2000 and 2010, including the fires in 2002 and 2003, and Thunder Horse's near-sinking in 2005.

There was also considerable natural environmental risk to undertaking exploratory technical ventures on the open waters of the Gulf of Mexico. Hurricanes regularly battered the gulf's small city of drilling and production platforms. In 2002 Hurricane Lili swept across Cuba before strengthening to a Category 4 storm over the prime drilling region. In 2004, Ivan, a Category 5 storm, ripped across the water

south of New Orleans and sent rigs floating off their moorings, drag-
ging loose a dozen pipelines running along the gulf's bottom. In 2005,
Katrina, on its way to New Orleans, destroyed 51 platforms and drilling rigs and seriously damaged another 29. Then, just a month later,
Hurricane Rita destroyed 70 more platforms and rigs and damaged
another 42. Each time, the oil wells attached to the rigs were put in
jeopardy. During Hurricane Rita, Chevron's Typhoon platform cap-
sized, and between Katrina and Rita, that summer alone 70 ships and
nearly 130 oil and gas pipelines were damaged.

The vast majority of these accidents were on wells or older platforms that had been installed years ago on the gulf's shallow shelf,
where the drilling was more concentrated. As the drilling went deeper
into the gulf, the equipment was more sophisticated and more dura-
ble but also more expensive, and the risk and the unknowns were far
greater. Yet drilling in the gulf had become so critical to U.S. oil supplies, and such an irreplaceable part of the nation's energy strategy,
that the government also seemed to grow complacent about the risks.

On March 31, at Andrews Air Force Base, President Obama stood
at a podium, carefully staged in front of a biofuel-powered F/A-18
"Green Hornet" fighter jet, to announce that offshore drilling on
American coasts would be greatly expanded. "This is not a decision
that I've made lightly," he said. For the first time in twenty years, and in
a departure from the policies of the past three presidents, he proposed
allowing drilling exploration off the coast of Virginia, in the eastern
Gulf of Mexico near Florida, and farther out from Prudhoe Bay into
Alaska's Beaufort Sea.

The announcement demonstrated Obama's eagerness to display
political support for the oil industry and appear moderate in the eyes of
voters critical of his plans to support renewable energy. "We'll employ
new technologies that reduce the impact of oil exploration. We'll protect areas that are vital to tourism, the environment, and our national
security. And we'll be guided not by political ideology, but by scientific
evidence," he said.

BP's record, in particular, might have been cause for concern
to Obama. Not only was the company the subject of both EPA and
Department of Justice interest in early 2010, as it had not yet resolved
its contentious negotiations over debarment, but both Republican and

Democratic members of Congress were voicing concerns over BP's reliability as a partner in U.S. energy policy. As the largest leaseholder and most active driller in the Gulf of Mexico, BP could be expected to be a major player in developing whatever new areas the Obama administration opened to drilling. In just the past couple of years, BP had had serious trouble on both its Atlantis and Thunder Horse rigs. A modest inquiry might have turned up the fact that a few months earlier, BP's senior vice president for drilling operations in the gulf, Kevin Lacy, had resigned from the company because he said BP was not committed to process safety there. Yet the White House says that discussions about BP never came up, and the company's track record was not considered as part of the decision to open up offshore drilling.

Carol Browner, a former EPA administrator and then President Obama's chief adviser on energy and climate issues, believed that there was no reason for the administration to leave its comfort zone on drilling. "What we knew [was that] the safety records were quite significant," Browner would later say in an interview. "There was this really impressive track record of safety." She said that BP's record was never mentioned in the White House's discussions about drilling policy. "Should a lease be granted to a particular company?" she asked. That's "something that the Department of Interior decides. That's their responsibility. It's not part of the broader policy decision, which is, Should we enhance and increase the amount of domestic oil production?"

Browner essentially punted responsibility to a lower rung on Obama's ladder. The Department of the Interior, when asked, was no more attentive to the specific concerns that a glance at BP's rap sheet might have raised. Asked whether it is ever appropriate to consider a single company's safety record—BP's four criminal convictions, for example—in deciding whether it should be a major player in the gulf, the Department of the Interior's deputy secretary, David Hayes, was pensive but unclear. "Well, it's a good question," he said. "The enforcement philosophy that we have . . . is we expect every applicant to come in and provide the demonstration required to show that they can do the activities they're being requested to do.

"BP as a company had some issues, to be sure. The Texas City refining issue being the most obvious one. But in terms of deepwater performance, I'm not aware that BP was—would be singled out for special attention." The momentum toward finding new sources of energy may simply have been too great to allow for such scrutiny.

Americans relentlessly demand more energy, and we demand that our oil companies go out and get it and supply it as inexpensively as possible, even while demanding that they do it without incident or environmental risk. The gulf coast states, for example, though they have suffered the pollution of numerous gulf spills and refinery blasts over the years, continue to be among the nation's largest consumers of oil, and the slowest in terms of seeking out renewable or alternative substitutes for oil. "The only reason the oil companies are invited to be in the Gulf of Mexico is because the U.S. customers want a steady stream of oil," says Derek Brower, the editor of *Petroleum Economist*. "How on earth do you do that if you are not going to keep drilling ever deeper and further out?"

The contradiction represents a political quagmire for U.S. presidents and also presents a widening chasm of understanding about the risks inherent in powering the American lifestyle. On the one hand, there is BP, which, its record shows, has difficulty acknowledging that catastrophic accidents are possible, or that they will happen to BP in particular. "BP thinks of itself as the teenager of the oil industry, invincible," says one consultant who worked closely with the company to address its safety concerns over the years. "It has the best of intentions, but a real blind spot about how decisions get made that affect risk. It thinks fast and furious won't kill them." On the other hand, there is a citizen population that assumes that their government has in place the regulations to guarantee their safety, protect their fisheries, and keep their air clean, no matter what.

"It's an inherently dangerous and dirty business and people get killed doing it. I think people forget that," says Matthew Gwyther, the editor of *Management Today*. "Getting that stuff out of the ground isn't like developing software or growing fruit." Yet people appear to expect that, even while they drive farther and fly more often and buy more products made of plastic (an amount equal to more than half of the total gulf oil production, or 4.6 percent of U.S. oil production, goes to manufacture plastics), drilling should be perfectly safe. The demand, Brower says, created political pressure for global oil companies like BP to come and get more oil in the United States. "You combine that with the fact that the Gulf of Mexico is known to be an expensive place to operate, and so one way to attract investment is to make it a convenient place to do business," he says. "And convenient means low regulations and low oversight." This means that the demand is directly correlated with eroding safety.

It doesn't have to be that way. To begin with, any company is capable of establishing a safety baseline akin to Exxon's since the hard lessons of the *Valdez*. At a minimum, it is imperative to focus on process and operational safety, and then to enact best practices that may extend beyond what regulators demand into the realm of common sense and technological capability. Accessible best practices are safer and cleaner and more reliable but often cost more and take more time to implement. Wells can be constructed with multiple redundant barriers in the annulus to make a blowout unlikely, for example. Their cement casing can be tested to make sure it won't leak. Some companies follow these practices, and many do not, instead adhering to the lowest common denominator of standards. Government regulations, too, often tend toward less stringent requirements. This makes for plentiful opportunities to improve the safety and reliability of drilling and maintaining oil fields and at least tempers its inherent risk. BP recognized the aspirational potential of best practices in 2001, when John Browne set ambitious goals for his company to reduce greenhouse gas emissions—and then met them by aggressively capturing stray methane emissions from its gas fields in the Southwest. Nearly a decade later, the company had been unable to consistently apply best operational practices and reshape its culture. "I never quite believed the rhetoric reflected the underlying reality," says John Hofmeister, Shell's former CEO. "There was a hyperbole about the accomplishments that was inconsistent with on-the-ground working knowledge that people across the industry actually witnessed.

"I never really saw the steps of an integrated process to bring it all together. If you don't have an overriding safety management system, [and if] you haven't taken the time to build in the rules and regulations into an auditable process, and at the same time captured the hearts and minds of the employees who need to follow that process, [then] you haven't done your job."

By filing a gulf spill response plan to protect the walruses and by promising that a large spill was impossible, BP not only once again shirked its own responsibility to assess risk, but it fed the public misperception about the dangers of its industry. It told the country what it wanted to hear. It wasn't looking out for itself or for its industry peers. Thus, by early 2010, there was a sort of willful dishonesty on the part of both the public and the energy industry about how real the risks of drilling in the Gulf of Mexico were, and about how capable BP, in particular, was of handling them.

BY THE END of the first week of April 2010, the drill bit on the Macondo well was closing in on eighteen thousand feet, approaching its targeted depth.

It hadn't gotten that far without incident. Almost from the beginning, according to the men working on the rig, there was an underlying impatience with the process. One day, the well operator came onto the drilling deck. "Let's pump it up," he said, according to Mike Williams, an engineer on the rig, meaning run the drill bit a little harder, and faster, into the hole. BP was in a rush.

It didn't take long before the fluids started seeping out of the bottom of the well. "We lost circulation almost immediately," Williams said. "We blew the bottom out of the well." A short time later the senior subsea engineer, Mark Hay, came into Williams's office with a double handful of rubber chunks that looked like they came from somewhere inside the well. "What the hell is that?" Williams asked him, alarmed.

"Oh, no big deal. That's normal," Hay replied. A minor burp of pressure in the well had apparently broken off parts of one of the rubber seals of the annular preventer inside the BOP—a sign that an annular preventer may no longer be able to make a good seal. Williams and others didn't think it was normal at all.

On March 8, with the well bit at 13,305 feet, an upset in the hydrostatic balance of the well had allowed a flood of natural fluids from the geologic formation to rush into the wellbore—like a loss of circulation, but in reverse. The well's operators hadn't noticed the problem for thirty-three minutes, and by the time they had, it was too late. Their drill pipe and all the well-logging tools attached to it had gotten stuck deep in the wellbore, permanently blocking the Macondo's progress.

BP had had to back off the well, abandoning and sealing off the lowest portion of the hole and instead rerouting the wellbore several thousand feet up in a slightly different direction.

Then, on April 9, BP's contractors once again lost circulation of their mud in the well. Its weight fractured the walls of the Macondo hole, seeping out into the earth. The engineers dumped more than seven thousand gallons of viscous fluid called a "lost circulation pill" inside, hoping to gum up the well and fix it. But that, too, disappeared into the hole. The more they worked the well, the more it kicked back burps of gas and the more it vexed them. "The situation had become delicate," a government investigator would later say.

In fact, the drillers faced an impossible situation. The Macondo well was so fragile that the drillers didn't think they could maintain a balance of pressure inside at all, meaning it was at constant risk of collapsing in on itself. In a little more than a month, the Macondo had become, as one rig worker put it in an email, "a nightmare well."

The crew was spooked. When Shane Roshto, a roughneck on the Deepwater Horizon, went ashore to visit his wife, Natalie, a week later, he described a cursed project. "Baby, the earth is—it's like blowing up a red balloon and taking a pin and just pushing it and pushing it and pushing it as far as it could go and it['s] just blowing," he told her. Roshto wasn't exactly soft about the trials of drilling. He was a big, muscular guy, and he loved his job. Still, something seemed wrong. "Mother Nature just doesn't want to be drilled here."

"From day one," Natalie Roshto said, "he deemed this hole a well from hell."

Tentatively, the company pushed the drill bits a little bit farther, testing fate. They could slightly adjust the weight of the mud, but BP's margin for error had evaporated. The Macondo had reached to 18,193 feet, and there was still more than 1,900 feet to go. That was the target zone the company had identified as being most likely to hold a trapped reservoir of oil, given the images that their geologists were able to create of the deep formations within the earth, using sonar and other tests. The drillers made it another 167 feet into the well and stopped. "Well integrity and safety" concerns, BP told its two investors on the project, Anadarko and MOEX, would keep them from going any deeper.

For five days, experts analyzed the hole, deciding what to do next.

Should it be abandoned? Or could the delicate well still be cased and cemented and made to produce oil? And even if it could, had it *reached* any oil? A contracted testing crew analyzed the well and found that it had indeed crossed two zones containing hydrocarbons. BP decided to proceed.

The most delicate part of constructing an oil well, though, isn't drilling a hole in the ground, the process that BP had just completed. Rather, it is the transition from drilling to producing oil that presents some of the toughest technical challenges, and the greatest risk. The well needs to be stabilized—its construction finished so that it is certifiably leakproof and strong enough to withstand the natural pressures of the earth—and prepared to be shut in.

From the moment they stopped drilling, BP's crews, along with the Transocean and Halliburton contractors working for them, would face a rapid-fire succession of critical decisions that would draw heavily on the judgment and depth of experience of their management. Almost every one of the decisions that team would make would turn out to be wrong.

16

SOS

WHEN BP STOPPED drilling the Macondo well, the bottom portion of the hole still wasn't lined with casing or cement. The hole was simply an eight-inch-wide unlined raw wellbore, and it cut into the most sensitive layers of rock—the ones that were under intense pressure and would eventually yield oil and gas. If there were ever to be a substantial leak or kick out of the Macondo, this is where it would come from. This was, after all, the portion of the well that had eaten up BP's circulation fluids and was so fragile it had kept the company from drilling into it farther.

The next step in construction would be to insert one more liner—the seven-inch production casing that would extend from this bottom section of the wellbore all the way to the top of the wellhead. Then the small annulus at the bottom of the well between the seven-inch casing and the earth would need to be sealed off with cement so that there was no way for fluids, gas, or oil to seep out into the hole, and into the larger internal annulus space above where the wellbore and casings became wider.

A two-dimensional design drawing of the Macondo well shows the structure as a long, stretched V—wider at the top with the 36-inch casing, getting narrower in a stepped progression. The mouth of the V is capped, with the narrow pipe leading up to the blowout preventer centered directly over the bottom of the well thirteen thousand feet below. A final casing string hangs in a straight line from that opening at the top, leaving an open annulus on the sides, from the widest part of the V all the way to the bottom. The final cement job at the bottom of the well aimed to fill the bottom of the V around the sides of the production casing. In this way, the bottom of the well, which was the part known to be unstable and delicate, would be separated entirely from the rest of the annulus space all the way back up to the wellhead.

Macondo's casing and the cementing were designed for BP by a Halliburton engineer in Houston named Jesse Gagliano. Gagliano used Halliburton's complex proprietary software to model exactly what materials and what design would make the well work, based on everything from the pressure gradient inside the well to the temperature. He met daily with BP and Transocean's senior management on the project and, since February, had run some forty models testing different scenarios for how to safely case and cement the well.

BP faced two choices for casing the Macondo: a "single string" or long continuous steel pipe could be hung thirteen thousand feet, from the wellhead on the gulf floor all the way to the bottom of the well. This would leave the full length of the annular space open and uninhibited, from the cement layer at the bottom to the wellhead at the top. Any burst of gas into the annulus would run directly to the top of the well at full force. Alternatively, BP could install a more conservative option, called a liner and tieback. The liner is like a funnel inserted into the bottom portion of the well, which is then capped and connected farther up to a long production string that hangs from the wellhead. Where the liner and production string meet, a tieback anchors the components to the side of the well, bisecting the long annular space and effectively dividing it into confined segments. From the start, BP had planned to use the single string.

A single string wasn't best practice, though it wasn't unheard of in a deepwater exploratory well. A single string was more risky because it had few barriers—just the cement at the bottom and the cap at the top—to block off the inner annulus, whereas a liner system had the tieback, like a plug, inserted in the annulus midway. The liner method offers better protection against a blowout but takes longer to install and is considered less reliable over time. That only matters if the intention is to create a producing well that will operate for many years. In a

presentation about well design, a senior offshore design engineer from
Shell, Joe Leimkuhler, explained that Shell would never use a single
string because it left the single pathway for a blowout all the way to
the top of the well, and that the liner method provides three barriers
against a blowout. "That's our best practice," he said, "design your well
so that you don't have to rely on blowout preventers for well control."

Given the circulation problems BP had already had with the
mud—Macondo had lost circulation at least three times—and the
extraordinary delicacy of the well, its engineers began to reconsider
whether the single string casing would work. "They had terrible losses
throughout the well," Gagliano said. "They were banking everything
on if they could get the cement job in place." To do so, the cement
would be injected down into the bottom of the well through the drill
pipe and forced out and back up the sides of the annulus space, just
as it had been in other, more routine casing installations. But if mud
couldn't circulate without being lost, the cement might also seep out
into the rock formation. The cement job itself was also riskier with a
single string. When cement is circulated up, it needs a consistent open
space in the annulus in order to fill it uniformly. As it was, there would
only be a thin annulus space to fill between the seven-inch pipe and
the eight-inch hole. A single string was likely to bend and turn slightly
inside the bottom section of the well, running up against the sides in
places instead of staying centered in the middle. Where the casing
leans up against the rock, it can block the cement, leaving a bubble or
channel of uncemented space, like a river leaves an eddy behind a boulder. If the cement doesn't fill the annulus void consistently, then there
is no effective barrier to control the pressure balance in the well and,
ultimately, to stop a blowout. Gagliano's models showed that the single
long string option in the Macondo well could not be cemented reliably.

At the last minute, BP's managers reconsidered. "Rich, there's a
chance we could run a production liner on the Macondo instead of the
planned long string," Brian Morel, the BP well engineer stationed on
the Horizon, wrote to Richard Miller, a drilling engineer with BP. "We
could be running it in 2–3 days, so need a relative quick response. Sorry
for the late notice, this has been a nightmare well which has everyone
all over the place."

The switch made Miller uncomfortable. "We [had] flipped design parameters around to the point I got nervous," he wrote. Mark Hafle, a BP engineer who was copied on the email, also chimed in: "This has been a crazy well for sure."

The liner system, though, would cost BP $7 million to $10 million more, nearly 10 percent of the well's $96 million budget, according to another internal email. It would also take longer to install, adding as much as thirty-seven hours to the job. The Macondo well was almost six weeks behind schedule and more than $58 million over budget. John Guide, the well's team leader, who had more than seven years' experience on deepwater wells, including in Mississippi Canyon, pushed back against the change of plan and, on April 14, reverted to the single string design.

To address the risk of channeling and make a long single string casing safe, it has to be held in place using hardware called centralizers. The centralizers are rings—in this case sized to fit around the seven-inch pipe—that look like an artery stent, with bulging flanges that brace against the outer well wall and hold the casing string in the middle so that the cement can fill in the space around it.

If it was going with the ill-advised long single string, BP had to figure out how many centralizers it would need and where to put them to make it safe. One problem, Morel had figured out a few weeks earlier, was that BP only had six centralizers in stock on the Deepwater Horizon. Gagliano kept running his models. On April 15, he saw a trend he didn't like. Six centralizers wouldn't be nearly enough to allow a cement job that would keep stray gas from flowing up the annulus of the well. If that's all BP used, it would be risking a bad cement job, which, if not fixed, could very well lead to a blowout.

Gagliano snatched the results off the printer in his office in Houston and took them to show his counterparts at BP. In the hallway, he ran into Hafle. "Hey, I think we have a potential problem here," he said, showing him the model. To Gagliano, the picture was clear as day. "I'm showing channeling."

Over the next couple of hours, senior BP and Halliburton managers on the project engaged in a discussion about what to do. To BP, it was far from a clear choice. Morel, from the Deepwater Horizon, sent an email that afternoon to Gagliano, Hafle, Brett Cocales, BP's drilling operations engineer team leader in Houston, and Gregg Walz,

BP's senior drilling team engineer, also based in Houston, expressing frustration with the possibility of a change. "We have six centralizers," Morel wrote. "We can run them in a row, spread out, or any combination of the two. It's a vertical hole. So hopefully the pipe stays centralized due to gravity. As far as changes, it's too late to get any more product to the rig. Our only option is to rearrange placement of these centralizers."

That evening, though, Gagliano, Cocales, and Walz stayed late to discuss their options further. Gagliano went back to the computer. By his count, BP would have to use at least twenty-one centralizers, more than three times as many as it wanted, to sustain a single string casing. "I didn't just jump to the twenty-one centralizers. I went through a number of scenarios and slowly added until I felt we were comfortable with the output," he said. With just six, the model showed that the risk of gas flow out of the well annulus was "severe." "They clearly understood that," Gagliano said.

By the end of the night Walz, the most senior in the group, had been persuaded that more centralizers would be needed before the production string could be hung in place. Early the next morning he called Weatherford, the drilling services company that manufactured the centralizers, and arranged for fifteen more to be flown by helicopter out to the Deepwater Horizon in time for the casing string to be installed. The operations, Walz wrote to his staff of engineers that morning, need "to honor the . . . modeling to be consistent with our previous decisions to go with the long string."

Morel, Guide, and Cocales all resisted the change, though not for the same reasons. Morel thought the Macondo well was vertical and straight enough that the production casing would hang naturally in the center without extra centralizers. "I don't understand Jesse's centralizer requirements," he wrote in an email the morning of April 16.

Guide was concerned, in part, about the cost. The string was ready to go. Installing the extra centralizers would take up to ten hours, considerable time on a rig that was costing BP a million dollars a day to lease and operate. Guide also worried that the centralizers themselves could cause problems; it had happened during an emergency on the Atlantis rig. He also had little faith in Halliburton's software. "It's a model, it's a simulation," he later would explain. "From past experiences sometimes it's right and sometimes it's wrong. It's not, you know, the real thing."

Cocales seemed persuaded by the model but was impatient. "Even if the hole is perfectly straight, a straight piece of pipe, even in tension, will not seek the perfect center of the hole unless it has something to centralize it," he wrote the group. "But who cares. It's done. End of story. We'll probably be fine and we'll get a good cement job."

Gagliano never heard another word about the final plan—not, that is, until a colleague at Halliburton told him he heard BP was going ahead with the six-centralizer design. Gagliano fired off an email to the BP management group. "Can you also confirm if we are running the additional centralizers or not? I heard from the rig that we were not going to run them."

Guide, Cocales, Hafle, and Morel never replied. On April 18, even though the additional fifteen centralizers had been flown to the Deepwater Horizon, BP began to install a long single string casing, using the six original parts. Gagliano, in Houston, tried to tweak some of the parameters in his models and ran the models again, hoping he could get a result that would justify the six centralizers. He did not.

That night Gagliano emailed the group a final data report with the models. Inside, the Halliburton document warned of "a SEVERE gas flow problem." Guide got the email at 9:00 p.m. but didn't open it. "I was in bed," he says. "I looked at the email the next day. The casing was already run, by the way. So it was a little bit late." Guide would later say that he rarely read the gas flow sections of the Halliburton reports anyway.

BP was racing ahead now, trying to get the Macondo well back on schedule. The next step, after the casing was hung, was to cement the bottom of the well annulus, one of the most critical safety steps in any oil and gas well. The cement would be circulated just like the mud— pumped down through the middle of the well so that it could then be squeezed out into the annulus and pushed back up from the bottom. The exact quantity of fluids—whether mud or cement—in the well is known at any given time, and, barring a loss of circulation, what goes in must come out. The volume of cement necessary to fill the annular space is carefully calculated, and then a load of cement is poured into the well and is pushed down to circulate through the annulus by the mud on top of it, often with a spacer in between. When the cement reaches its designated height in the annulus, the process is stopped. But the entire well, ahead of and behind the cement, is filled with fluid at all times in order to maintain hydrostatic pressure.

When a well is finished and the heavy mud is finally removed to make way for oil, it's the cement barrier that ultimately maintains that critical pressure balance so that the well doesn't collapse on itself or blow out. But all it takes is a crack or a gap in the final cement job to upset that delicate balance. According to an MMS report, nearly half of all blowouts in the gulf are ultimately traced back to faulty cementing.

"The number one risk," as John Guide put it, is that the cement doesn't circulate all the way around, and instead escapes into fractures in the earth, much the way the well had already, from time to time, lost circulation. The Macondo was especially susceptible to this risk, because the walls of the well had already proven so fragile and delicate. In fact, BP was afraid it would lose circulation in the cementing of the Macondo, so much so that it dramatically altered the normal, accepted cementing routine, again stepping away from its own best practices.

Usually, before the cement is run through the well, a turbulent cycle of fresh drilling mud is pushed through ahead of it. This is called a "bottoms-up" circulation, and it is designed to scrub and flush out the well, removing whatever junk and debris might be trapped down in the hole so that the cement, when it follows, can set in against a clean surface. When the fresh mud resurfaces at the top of the annulus, the drillers know that the well has been completely cycled through, and, importantly, that the annulus did not leak.

BP had little faith in the condition of the Macondo. It feared that circulating so much turbulent mud in the fragile bottom of the well would only increase the chance of a fracture in the bore, and the loss of circulation. It sent only 350 barrels of mud into the well hole ahead of the cement, about one-eighth of what was necessary to complete a bottoms-up circulation and not enough to be sure the well was cleared of debris.

Then, when it began pumping the cement down, it used a lighter-weight nitrogen-cement mixture that was also unusual in a gulf well and that Gagliano had also determined was unstable. Again, BP was afraid that the well wasn't strong enough to handle the weight of normal cement. Then BP had Halliburton inject the cement mixture gently, slower than is normal. Cement flowing at slow speeds was less likely to do damage, but it was also more likely to harden along the way, leave gaps, or collect bubbles.

After that, BP made one more critical compromise. Still concerned that the well couldn't sustain anything but the most gingerly touch, BP significantly cut the designed height of the cement level in the annulus. BP's own standards require that the cement extend a thousand feet above the uppermost layer of rock that can contain oil or gas, to be sure that a barrier extends well into the next solid layer of rock. It is recognized across the industry as a best practice.

The cement in the well column weighs a lot, however, and once again, engineers feared that the excess burden was more likely to damage the fragile well than protect it. So they made another exception, running the cement to just five hundred feet above the hydrocarbon-bearing layer—enough to meet the minimum government requirement. BP's engineers, the government would later say, "recognized it would provide very little margin for error."

BP finished cementing the Macondo well at 12:36 a.m. on April 20. The returns—the mud displaced by the cement and pushed back up to the top of the well showing that it had circulated all the way around—looked good. At 5:45 a.m., one of Halliburton's crew on the Deepwater Horizon sent Gagliano an email: "We have completed the job and it went well."

That conclusion, however, would have been based only on appearances. Almost always, a well's cement job needs to be tested. Standard practice in the drilling industry, whether for an onshore well or an offshore well, oil or gas, is to run an acoustical exam called a cement bond log to test the consistency of the barrier in the annulus. Like sonar, waves are sent into the well casing to measure for channels, bubbles, or inconsistencies in the cement. If problems are found, drillers are capable of sending a device back down the hole to perforate the casing wall with explosives and then inject more cement through the holes to the space behind the annulus. BP had always planned to do the test. It hired a crew from Schlumberger, the global drilling services company, to perform it, and flew them to the rig. The Schlumberger technicians were waiting that morning on the drill deck for clearance to begin testing the well.

After a 7:30 a.m. safety meeting held by the project's top management, including Guide, Walz, Morel, and Hafle, BP instead decided to send the Schlumberger team home. "Everyone involved with the job on the rig site was completely satisfied with the job," said Guide, explaining why the bond log wasn't needed. "You had full returns running the casing, full returns cementing the casing . . . really all the indicators you could possibly get."

Though Guide was content with the returns and other technical details of the cementing process, the indicators he relied on only tell a part of the story. The full returns, a government expert would later say, "provided, at best, limited or no information about the precise location where cement had ended up, whether channeling had occurred, whether the cement had been contaminated or whether the foam cement had remained stable."

Each of the major decisions BP had made in the construction of the well so far ran against the industry's best practices or BP's own experience and instincts. The Macondo well had already proved troublesome and lost circulation several times. Then BP ran with a cheaper steel casing liner against advice. It used far fewer centralizers than recommended, knowing that that would make it difficult to get a reliable cement job. BP used half as much cement as recommended, in a mixture that had been found to be unreliable, and injected it at slower than normal speeds. Now the company was declining to test, using a cement bond log, whether the scheme had worked. Given the fact that this had begun as an exploratory well, and given the gambles BP had already made, it might have decided that a cement log on Macondo was far more crucial than usual.

Instead the company doubled down, siding with momentum, cost savings, and expediency over prudence. It just wanted to get the job done and start producing oil.

There are conflicting reports about what happened next. Several accounts have it that the Schlumberger crew was so concerned about how BP was constructing its well that an argument ensued. They didn't think it was safe to remain on the Deepwater Horizon, and if BP didn't fly them to shore, the story goes, they would call a chopper themselves.

Those reports are unconfirmed. At a minimum, BP simply decided not to have Schlumberger complete the job it was contracted to do. This was exceedingly rare. In the previous thirty months Schlumberger had been contracted to perform seventy-four cement bond logs on Gulf of Mexico wells. Schlumberger had only been sent home three times— twice by BP.

What is clear is this: the cement bond log would have cost BP $128,000 and taken twelve hours, time that would cost at least another half a million dollars on top. The Schlumberger crew flew back to the mainland on an 11:15 a.m. helicopter on April 20. Guide said that the decision to send Schlumberger home was only made after evidence showed how well the cement job had gone, and he denied that cost cutting played any role in the decision. Guide and the operators on the rig didn't learn that the cementing process had gone well until around 8 a.m. on the twentieth. But the Deepwater Horizon's departing flight manifests have to be approved the day before, meaning the Schlumberger crew was listed and approved by BP management to fly home sometime in the afternoon of April 19.

AS THE SCHLUMBERGER TEAM departed, BP and Transocean's crews began a final sequence of steps on the Deepwater Horizon to prepare the Macondo well for what the drillers call temporary abandonment. Transocean would lift its blowout preventer and riser pipe off the top of the Macondo well and sail away. The Macondo well would be left capped on the bottom of the seafloor until BP could bring in a new production platform at a cheaper contract rate than the Deepwater Horizon to produce the oil.

But first the well itself needed to be made secure enough to leave unattended. According to federal regulations, BP would have to plug the well by inserting a three-hundred-foot-long cement stopper three thousand feet below the wellhead, effectively sealing off the wellbore. (BP would have to drill through it again when it returned to produce oil from the well.) Above that, the long column of heavy mud that still filled the well and riser would be removed and replaced with seawater, a change that would immediately upset the hydrostatic balance that had been so carefully maintained, and put the cementing and casing jobs to their ultimate test. A cap, called a lockdown sleeve, would be placed across the top of the well, fastening the long string casing to the wellhead, and also providing the topmost seal on the long annulus space that ran up the inside of the well. Finally, a set of critical pressure tests needed to be done to ensure that the well structure could hold itself together and wouldn't leak.

Since BP had bypassed the cement bond log, the pressure tests were the next most important step in evaluating the success of the cementing job. The first, called a positive test, was straightforward. The mud inside the well would be pressurized to see if it leaked and to make sure the well could contain its contents. The second and more important test, for negative pressure, did the opposite. Because the rock layers buried far beneath the gulf were under great pressure, it was essential to make sure that once the mud was removed from the well, the well would be strong enough to hold back gas from seeping in from the outside. If the gas got in, it would rocket to the surface and threaten a blowout.

For days, there had been general confusion about the order in which these steps would be taken. BP's plans for this sequence of tasks had changed at least three times in the previous week, records show, once on April 12, then again on April 14, and most recently on the sixteenth. None of the changes had been reviewed through a formal process or subjected to a risk assessment, and little about them had been communicated to workers on the rig in time to be useful to their planning. At about noon on April 20, with the cement job only just finished and the crews on the Deepwater Horizon already beginning the positive pressure test, a meeting took place on the main deck of the Horizon. Three people—Jimmy Harrell, Transocean's senior installation manager; Miles "Randy" Ezell, the senior toolpusher constructing the well; and Dewey Revette, a driller—met with BP's company man, or most senior man on the rig, Robert Kaluza, to discuss Transocean's next steps. "We've got some changes," Kaluza said. Harrell listened to his orders but didn't hear mention of a plan to perform the negative pressure test on the well, which is the more critical one because it is the only part of the process that emphasizes the cement barrier in the bottom of the well. Harrell wanted the test done. "The plan that I seen did not have a negative test to be performed before displacing with seawater," he said.

The discussion erupted into a shouting match over what to do after the pressure tests, said Doug Brown, the rig's chief mechanic, who was within earshot. The BP manager wanted to displace all the heavy mud in the Macondo well with seawater right away, putting the well under immediate stress. Others thought that the lockdown sleeve, which would cap and contain the annulus from the top and secure the production casing in the event that there was a kick large enough to dislodge it, should be put in place first. BP overruled. "This is the way it's going to be," Brown recalls the BP man saying.

"Well, I guess that's what we have those pincers for," Brown heard Harrell mutter as he walked away, referring to the ultimate backup plan, the blowout preventer sitting on the bottom of the gulf.

At about 11:00 a.m. crews had begun the positive pressure test. The pressure inside the well was pumped up to 2,500 pounds per inch, like air into an inner tube, to check for leaks. It was left for thirty minutes to see if it held. It did. "Things looked good with the positive test," remarked Pat O'Bryan, BP's vice president for deepwater drilling and completions in the gulf, when he visited the Deepwater Horizon platform later that day. (O'Bryan was among several executives who had convened—while the well was still being built—to celebrate seven years without an accident on the Deepwater Horizon.)

Next came the negative pressure test. To do it, the crews first had to displace 3,300 feet of mud from the wellbore with seawater in order to replicate the conditions under which the well would eventually be left. A spacer fluid and then the water were injected into the well through the drill pipe, filling the well from the bottom and pushing the heavy mud upward until it passed through the BOP and into the riser pipe. The fluids would look almost like Guinness and Harp in a black-and-tan beer, with the spacer working like a barrier between the light and dark bands, and allowing the top band to move all at once without mixing. Then one of the BOP's annular preventers was closed, in order to hold the mud in place outside of the well.

Here, once again, an inexplicable departure was made from normal procedure. An exemption in the federal Resource and Conservation Recovery Act, the law governing disposal of toxic industrial wastes, states that any waste used inside the well, as opposed to in related processes, does not count as waste and therefore isn't regulated. Anything pumped down into the well, even temporarily, would become exempt. This is how drillers in Endicott Bay in Alaska tried to pass off their dumping back in 1993. On the Deepwater Horizon, large pools of spent drilling mud and other toxic material had been collected and were waiting to be shipped back to shore for treatment.

For the pressure tests, a liquid spacer is normally inserted into the well. That day, someone on the rig tried to make the drilling waste eligible for the regulatory loophole by using it as the spacer. The problem was that the normal spacer fluid is meticulously engineered, and the waste mixture had never been used for this purpose before. The switch put BP's final and most important test into the realm of the experimental.

At first, the negative pressure test went according to routine. With the wellbore isolated from the weight of the mud in the riser pipe, the drillers were free to manipulate the pressure of the lightweight sea- water in the well. The idea was to allow the pressure inside the well to decline until it was less than the natural pressure of the rock forma- tions around it. If the underpressurized well held steady, then it meant that the cement job at the bottom of the well, and the casing farther up, were airtight. But if fluids spurted out of the well during the test, or if the pressure increased, it would signal that somewhere gas was leaking from the earth through the cement and into the well, building pressure in the wellbore where there should be none.

From the drilling deck, the drill pipe was inserted into the wellbore and then opened to release the pressure in the well and reduce it to zero. It should have taken just a few minutes, but the crew couldn't get the pressure to bleed all the way down. It dropped as far as 266 psi, meaning that the water in the wellbore still exerted that much out- ward pressure. But as soon as the drillers sealed off the drill pipe—the straw piercing down through the spacer into the well—the pressure jumped again, to 1,262 psi. It was as big a red flag as one could wave: a clear sign of a significant vulnerability in the well that was allowing gas to seep in from outside.

BP could have stopped there. The negative pressure test had done exactly what it was supposed to do: it unambiguously warned of a severe problem in the well. But they were so close. This was almost the last step, and they were just hours from certifying the first successful new well on

Mississippi Canyon Block 252. So instead of accepting the test result, they began seeking explanations for how it could be wrong. Right away, the drillers noticed an oddity in the mile-long riser pipe holding back the mud and the spacer solution: the level of the spacer fluid inside the well was dropping. It meant that the spacer, and perhaps the mud, too, were somehow leaking past the rubber annular seal and down into the wellbore. Some of the drillers began to think that if the mud had infiltrated the seawater, its weight could be responsible for driving up the pressure in the well test. If that were the case, the poor pressure test result wouldn't reflect a leak in the cement casing but rather a leak between the riser and the wellbore, a technicality that could be addressed. The engineers shut the annular preventer tighter, hoping to isolate the problem, and twice more measured the pressure. The next reading dropped to zero but then the pressure rose again—to 773 psi. The last reading jumped to 1,400 psi as soon as the drill pipe was shut. For a successful test, the pressure needed to hold at zero for thirty minutes.

An astute and experienced well technician would have known at this point that the Macondo well was seriously compromised. A senior BP manager later described the pressure test results as "a very large abnormality."

Inexplicably, BP's well site leader continued to search for an explanation that would justify continuing the process. On the drill floor of the Deepwater Horizon, the Transocean crew and the BP managers met to discuss their options. Jason Anderson, an experienced toolpusher managing the tests, told the group that he thought something called "bladder effect"—the weight of all the mud sitting above the isolated well—might be causing the pressure on the pipe and giving a false reading.

It made sense, at least theoretically, so they carried out a fourth test. This time they measured the pressure not on the well itself but on a kill line, one of several separate three-inch pipes that run from the drill rig down to the bottom of the blowout preventer as a way to access the wellbore when the BOP is closed. The kill line is used to inject fluids or pressure into the well, and, theoretically, the pressure on the kill line would match the pressure of the well itself. What the crew didn't know was that somewhere down below, the kill line was blocked altogether, and it wasn't really flowing into the wellbore at all.

The fourth test gave the engineers what they were looking for. The pressure in the kill line was bled to zero and the top of the line was left open for thirty minutes, with no change. Strangely, the readings in the drill pipe itself remained at 1,400 psi, however, showing that there was still pressure in the well. But the difference between the kill line and the main well, for unknown reasons, was never reconciled. Perhaps choosing to believe Anderson's bladder effect explanation, at 8:00 p.m. BP's well site leaders declared the fourth test a success. Despite three failed tests in a row, the Macondo well's integrity, both BP and the Transocean crew decided, had been confirmed.

THERE ARE ASPECTS of deepwater drilling that are experimental and rest on the cusp of what is technologically feasible. But these last steps taken to finish the Macondo well were neither experimental nor unpracticed. Cementing, casing, testing the cement integrity—all are basic, well-known, and intimately understood parts of the drilling process, carried out more or less the same way for any well, oil or gas, onshore or offshore. Forty-five thousand wells are drilled each year in the United States. Many undergo casing and cementing and then pressure tests and integrity tests. The tests exist for a reason: as checks meant to balance the known risks of drilling. They are done in search of exactly the warning signs BP got that day in the gulf.

That the Macondo was an exploratory well did not mean that these basic rules of practice were any different, or that BP did not know how to drill the well. It meant, rather, that they should have taken extraordinary precautions and placed unusual importance on each of the tests that could warn the company it was about to make a mistake. "A lot of people run single strings, but they don't run a single string with everything else that is going on," says Michael Norton, the former well designer. "You may say, 'Okay, if I do this I'm going to centralize it, I'm going to cement it and I'm going to run a cement bond log.' They are not going to cut all the steps out. But of ten steps, BP did nine differently." BP followed almost none of the well-established protocols accepted by the industry.

It skipped or willfully ignored the best information available at every opportunity, often overriding it with spontaneous and unevaluated decisions by individual managers on the deck of the rig. BP hadn't even put its best managers in place that week. Ronald Sepulvado, the veteran BP well site leader who had run operations on the Deepwater Horizon for the past seven years, had been replaced on April 16—in the midst of all the final preparations—by Robert Kaluza. Kaluza had been a well site leader on BP's Thunder Horse but had never set foot on the Deepwater Horizon before. He was assigned at the last minute to the Deepwater Horizon—ironically, so that Sepulvado could go to "well control" school, where he would practice steps to prevent a blowout.

Over the years, BP's chief executives—first John Browne and then Tony Hayward—had articulated what BP needed to do to improve each time it got itself into trouble. One of those key things was to cultivate expertise within the company and then rely on it. Now, on one of its most important projects, the company was once again ignoring its own best advice.

AT 8:02 P.M. on April 20, BP began the next to final step in shutting in the well, and one of the most controversial ones: removing the full burden of drilling mud from the riser pipe. The pressure on the Macondo well would be released for good as lower-density seawater was injected. This would leave the well permanently "underbalanced" and at the mercy of the several hundred feet of cement lining at the bottom. It was like the negative pressure test, but for real, and permanent.

On the deck of the Deepwater Horizon, Dewey Revette sat down on his chair in the driller's shack in the center of the drill floor beneath the towering scaffolds of the derrick to watch the process. He scanned for signs of a kick in the well, a bubble of gas that expands exponentially as it rises and the enormous weight of the ocean is released. A single gallon of gas can become a hundred gallons by the time it reaches the surface. That is why a blowout—which is more or less a very large, sustained kick—can quickly become so powerful and so dangerous.

The crews diligently watched the volume, the well pressure, and the rate of flow of fluids into and out of the well. Any changes, however slight, can be an early indicator that a kick, somewhere deep down the pipe, has begun. For almost an hour, the pressure steadily decreased, as it would be expected to do as the seawater slowly replaced the heavy contents of the well. The data were indicated by fluctuating needles on a paper graph and visible in real time to both the engineers on the rig and those sitting at their monitors in the BP control center in Houston—except that, on that night, there was nobody in Houston paying attention to these crucial last processes on the Deepwater Horizon. "Everybody had gone home," said Fred Bartlit, a lawyer who would later analyze the events for the government.

Just after 9:00 p.m. the line of ink on the pressure-reading graph began to rise. Over the next seven minutes it crept upward, from 1,250 psi to 1,350 psi. The magnitude of change was subtle. But the fact that the trend switched directions—that a downward-sloping line had bottomed out and made a V—was not. It was the first signal of an impending crisis. At 9:18, a pressure relief valve on one of the pumps blew, and Revette sent a group down to the pump room to fix it: Roy Wyatt Kemp, Shane Roshto, and Adam Weise. It was a hiccup, but not one that the crew couldn't handle, and they proceeded with the routine of replacing the mud in the well with seawater. At 9:20 Randy Ezell, the senior toolpusher, called the rig floor to ask Anderson how the negative pressure test had gone. "It went good," Anderson told him. "We bled it off. We watched it for thirty minutes and we had no flow." Then Ezell asked how the seawater displacement process was going. "It's going fine," Anderson told him confidently. "I've got this. Go to bed."

Ezell trusted Anderson. He had worked with him for more than eight years. Anderson probably had more experience watching for kicks and shutting in a well than anyone else on the rig that night. "Jason was very acute on what he did and that made me feel comfortable," Ezell said. "When you know somebody that well you can even tell by their body language if something's wrong. He was just like a brother. So, I had no doubt that if he had any indication of any problem or had any difficulty at all he would have called me." Ezell retired to his cabin, just across the narrow hallway from the toolpusher's office. He called his wife. Then he switched off the light, leaving only the blue glow of the television as he flipped through the channels.

At about 9:30 p.m., the crew on the drilling floor had noticed a difference in pressure between the kill line and the drill pipe, and they stopped the work to investigate. As soon as the pumps were turned off, the pressure inside the well jumped, this time by 550 psi in just five minutes. Revette dispatched a crew member, Caleb Holloway, to bleed off the pipe. Nine minutes later, the gauges showed a decrease in pressure, but it wasn't the relief Revette had expected. Most likely, miles beneath the lapping waves of the gulf, lighter-weight hydrocarbons had slipped into the wellbore and were now shoving the heavier-weight mud on top of them out of the way and moving up the production casing, past the drill pipe.

At 9:38 p.m., well data show that the first hydrocarbons passed through the blowout preventer at the seafloor and began rushing up the riser pipe, with five thousand feet to go before they would reach the decks of the Deepwater Horizon rig, expanding as they went. It was as if a shot had been fired, and the bullet was racing toward the crew of the rig up the long barrel of a gun.

Everything that happened next seemed to unfold in a paradoxical swirl of slow motion and breathtaking speed. One by one, the warning signs of a blowout appeared, each distinctly evident and etched permanently in the memories of the men working that night. There was no blur. Yet the signs couldn't be interpreted quickly enough to get ahead of the process.

Drilling mud began spewing out of the top of the derrick. As from an overflowing toilet, the material backed up out of the well and filled a catchment, called a crown, before spilling down across the main deck of the Deepwater Horizon.

First, the crew tried to shut the annular preventer around the drill pipe. But that was probably the device that had shown up in rubber shards in Mike Williams's office weeks earlier. Now, when it needed to, it didn't work. Besides, the gas was already above the blowout preventer and was racing toward the surface.

The mud came at high pressure, splattering across the walls on the drill floor and rushing against the door to the drill shack, dripping down the steel steps toward the main deck. Below, crew members saw a waterfall of dirty fluid pouring off the steps of the derrick and the drill floor above them. At 9:46 p.m., crews first tried to activate the rams on the Deepwater Horizon's blowout preventer. The variable bore ram, the second line of defense to seal the annular space without severing the drill pipe, also didn't respond. By 9:49, the giant, expanding bubble of gas was reaching the top of the drill pipe, turning the mud being pushed ahead of it into a frothy aerated mixture. The kick rose out of the ocean waters, racing up the pipe, passing one deck after another on the Horizon like "a five-hundred-fifty-ton freight train," according to one Transocean worker. Then, he said, "a jet engine's worth of gas" came spewing out the top of the well. Workers heard a deafening bang, like a "blown tire times 100."

EZELL WAS still watching TV when his phone rang, startling him. He slapped the light on his alarm clock: 9:50 p.m. Steve Curtis, the rig's assistant driller, was on the other end of the line. "We have a situation," he said, describing the heavy flow of mud cresting the crown of the Macondo. "The well is blown out."

Ezell was horrified. "Do y'all have it shut in?" He asked. Anderson was working on that, he was told: Anderson, who always had his crew under control. But this time it sounded different. There was no confidence in Curtis's voice.

"Randy, we need your help," he said.

Ezell hopped out of bed, grabbed his overalls from a hook by the door, and tugged them on. He put on socks, but his boots and hard hat were across the hall. When he opened the door, men were standing around in the hallway. But Ezell had adrenaline-driven blinders on now. This was bad. He made a beeline for the door to the toolpusher's office.

ON THE SECOND DECK, Mike Williams was chatting on the phone with his wife when a beeping alarm sounded in his office, the electronics shop adjacent to the engine control room. On either side of his office, about a hundred feet away, the rig's diesel engines whirred away, providing electrical power and stability for the rig. Before taking this job six months earlier, Williams had been an avionics technician in the Marine Corps. Now he had to maintain the fire and gas system and the electronic systems on the Deepwater Horizon, and he sat in front of a large panel of monitors and lights and switches.

The beeping indicated rising levels of gas in the mud flowing out of the well. But to Williams it was routine—alarms and beeps happened almost constantly, especially with the Macondo, because gas had seemed to be trickling out of the well for weeks now. He'd gotten to the point where he barely heard the warnings anymore. His wife asked if he needed to get off the phone. "No," Williams told her.

Then he heard an odd thump and a hissing sound and reconsidered. "Hey, I need to go check this out and see what's going on," he said, and hung up. Through the ventilation shaft he could hear alarms in another office. "I'm hearing the beep, beep, beep, beep, beep, beep, beep. It's continuous," Williams says. "And I'm thinking to myself, Okay, what's going on?

A sweet odor filled his office, and Williams recognized it as gas. In the engine room, the tempo of the diesel pistons picked it up, too. "I could hear Engine Number 3 start to rev up, and its normal operating rpm rose to way above what I ever heard it run before," he said. Like the pickup truck parked beside the isom at Texas City, the engines sucked fuel out of the air. Gas detectors—like the ones Kovac and the Alaskan workers had been complaining about for years—should have sensed the vapors on the Deepwater Horizon and shut off the air vents to the engine rooms. But they didn't. "It's continuously, steadily rising, and I knew then that we were—we were having a problem."

On his control panel, the tiny bulbs grew brighter, straining under a surge of power. The room lights flared, bathing the shack in a bright, naked glow. The incessant alarms were drowned out by the whine of the engines now. It all happened in seconds. As Williams pushed his chair back to go check out the engines, the bulbs began to pop, one by one, in tiny explosions. His computer monitors followed, their screens bursting into shards of flying glass. "I thought then that we just had an engine run away," he says. In blackness now, Williams dashed for the control room, grabbing the handrail, spinning around it, and reaching for the door.

The door to the engine shack is steel and three inches thick, a fire-rated slab of armor hung onto its frame by six stainless steel hinges. Behind it, Williams could hear an eerie hissing and the whine of the engines increasing in pitch. It's "higher than I can even describe it. It's spinning so fast that it just—it stopped spinning."

A huge explosion ripped the door off its hinges, slamming into Williams and tossing him across the room. He blacked out, probably for only a second. When he came to, he couldn't breathe, his left arm wasn't moving, and a fire suppression system that emits carbon dioxide was going off. He needed air. "I remember thinking this is it, I'm going to die right here, no one is going to be able to find me." He stuck a flashlight in his mouth and crawled back toward the door. A second explosion threw him back against the wall and he started the slow crawl all over again. He still couldn't see. He made it out of the shack, stumbling over the bodies of two men along the way. He tried to wipe whatever was in his eyes away. "I didn't know if it was blood, if it was brains, if it was flesh. I just knew that I was hurting."

Instinctively, Williams turned into the wind—any person who works around fire knows to walk into it to get out of the smoke, not downwind of it. As he did, the air cleared and he found himself teetering on a precipice where the stairway should have been. The waters of the gulf lapped below him, maybe seventy feet away. Off the stern of the Deepwater Horizon, where the engines jutted out from the main structure, there was nothing. The entire Engine No. 3 was gone. The exhaust stacks, the guardrail, the catwalk, "they were completely blown off the back of the rig."

In disbelief, Williams turned around. The bridge, where the captain and the rig's command would be, was about four hundred feet away, up to the main deck and up again toward the helipad. When he got to the main deck, he found the entire rig in "a raging inferno." The derrick disappeared in billowing balls of fire. Debris flew through the air. There was an announcement on the public address system telling the men that this was not a drill: "All hands on deck."

Now I know there are other people alive—I just need to find them, Williams thought.

Ezell hadn't yet made it into the toolpusher's room—ten feet from his bunk—when he heard a tremendous explosion, and a ball of fire ripped down the corridor, coming straight at him. "It blew me probably twenty feet against a bulkhead," he says. "Then the lights went out. I could hear everything. Deathly calm." He was covered in debris, and he couldn't move. "I told myself, Either you get up or you're going to lay here and die." His right leg was pinned, but he tore at it until it came free. He tried to stand up, and when he did, he found himself in a dark curtain of smoke. Ezell dropped to his hands and knees and began to crawl, but he was disoriented and didn't know where to go. "I remember just sitting there and just trying to think, Which way is it?"

JIMMY HARRELL, Transocean's most senior man on the ship, was in the shower when the first explosion hit. He heard it, and he smelled gas. A strong backdraft sucked the air from his cabin, and within three seconds or so there was another devastating blast. Above him the ceiling tiles crashed down. Debris, perhaps fiberglass, flew in his eyes. Harrell, blinded, managed to grab his pants and put them on. Over the loudspeaker a voice blared: "This is not a drill, this is not a drill, this is not a drill. Report to secondary muster stations, do not go outside."

No shit it wasn't a drill, Harrell thought. "I managed to get debris out of the way and crawl and walk up towards the bridge," he said. Harrell didn't have details, but the fact that a massive blowout was under way was obvious. One explosion after another rocked the Deepwater Horizon. In the bunk rooms, walls were obliterated and equipment crashed down. Giant fireballs rose into the night sky. Down below, scared and injured crew leapt from the deck into the dark water and hurled themselves into lifeboats.

Harrell knew that if the Deepwater Horizon was to be saved—if they were going to survive—they somehow had to stop the flow of gas still shooting out of the Macondo well. This meant cutting off the physical tether between the floating rig and the well altogether. If they couldn't do it, they were doomed. "I knew we needed to get away," he said. But he, too, had to make it to the main control room.

WILLIAMS GOT THERE first. On the bridge he found eighteen to twenty people and utter chaos. No one knew, at that point, how many were dead. People down below the bridge were running toward the lifeboats, and many were injured or bleeding. It was difficult to tell who was who. But to anyone who stopped to think about it, it was the crews closest to the drill pipe who were the most at risk. Jason Anderson, Steve Curtis, Don Clark, and Dewey Revette had all been on the drill floor closest to the blowout, working desperately to contain the shooting gas, and none of them had been seen since the initial explosion. All four had likely been killed instantly. Someone had seen Dale Burkeen, the crane operator, blown by the blast wave off of a catwalk on the starboard crane. He had fallen to his death. Six others had also died, but that wouldn't be clear until later.

Williams was just trying to make sense of the activity in the control room. People and alarms were screaming. Radio chatter echoed: "We've lost propulsion! We've lost power! Man overboard on the starboard forward deck." Williams was frantic as he tried to convey to the ship's captain, Curt Kuchta, the extent of the damage to the engines. No. 3, he said, had been blown off the deck.

Kuchta, stunned, gave Williams a blank look. Williams continued: the consoles were all gone. Without power there was no way to control the position of the Deepwater Horizon in the gulf. There were no lights. There was no water with which to fight the fire. "I was pretty emphatic telling the captain it's time for us to go, we should abandon ship now," Williams said. "I was told to shut up and calm down."

At the console desk, Andrea Fleytas surveyed the scene on the deck while her managers debated what to do. Normally, Fleytas was charged with driving the rig, keeping it positioned accurately on its GPS target, and sounding alarms. When the blast occurred, she felt a jolt, and a series of alarms that warn of combustible levels of gas across the rig went off. On the closed-circuit cameras, she could see mud flowing over the deck on the starboard side of the ship. Now those same decks and planks were enshrouded in black-and-red fireballs.

Beside her, someone brought Williams a roll of toilet paper to wipe the blood from his eyes and then wrapped his head in it. It was the only bandage available. Someone else was screaming, "We need to disconnect from the well." At the control panel, the subsea night adviser, Christopher Pleasant, refused to disconnect without first obtaining permission from Jimmy Harrell, who wasn't there yet. Cutting the line to the well meant abandoning the entire Macondo project. Valuable seconds ticked away in hesitation.

Then Harrell arrived, coughing and vomiting, insulation still stinging his eyes. Someone grabbed him by the shoulders. "Jimmy, we've got to disconnect."

Finally, they opened the panel from which a series of buttons would initiate the emergency disconnect. A disconnect meant activating the blowout preventer's blind shear ram, the last line of defense. Once the pipe is sheared, the upper section of the riser pipe would drift free, and the Deepwater Horizon would not only be cut off from the gas still fueling the fire but free to drift away from the Macondo well site. Harrell hit the button to activate the ram, but nothing happened. The panel before them lit up in a dazzling array. But if the blowout preventer had worked, the raging flow of gas fueling the fire would have been cut off, and the blaze should have died in seconds. "I looked outside and saw the fuel to the fire wasn't going down," Kuchta said. "Something had gone wrong."

"I felt really disgusted at that point," said Williams. "All these things that are supposed to protect us are failing, and nothing is going right."

Even if hydraulics and the electricity were cut as a result of damage from the blast, there was another backup, a deadman switch. Harrell and Pleasant did not know—no one on the rig did—that one of the power pods that ran the deadman far beneath the water's surface had faulty electrical valves, and the battery power of the other was nearly dead. That switch, too, failed to respond. The last and final backup in such an improbably linked set of scenarios, when one backup after another fails, is to use an acoustical control switch, a remote-control activation of the blowout preventer that can be triggered from off the Deepwater Horizon. But BP and Transocean had never installed such a switch on the Deepwater Horizon rig, even though it had become standard safety equipment for legal drilling in other parts of the world, such as in Brazil.

Only seven or eight crew members were still on the bridge. The rest had escaped in lifeboats or jumped overboard into the oil-filled waters of the gulf to escape the balls of fire that consumed the rig. Ezell had fought his way out of the toolpusher's shack and helped carry an injured colleague toward the lifeboats. Then he, too, got in, and slowly rowed away from the burning rig. On the bridge, Fleytas leaned into the microphone, sending the last message she ever thought she would send over the radios to Houston, to the U.S. Coast Guard, to whoever was listening: "Mayday, Mayday."

Postscript

The Deepwater Horizon burned for eighteen hours as crew members made their way to a nearby freighter, the *Damon B. Bankston*, in lifeboats or hurled themselves overboard. Eleven people died: Karl Kleppinger Jr., Keith Blair Manuel, Shane Roshto, Gordon Jones, Roy Wyatt Kemp, Jason Anderson, Donald Clark, Stephen Curtis, Dewey Revette, Adam Weise, and Dale Burkeen. Seventeen more were seriously injured.

At 10:22 a.m. on April 22, the Deepwater Horizon listed, dipped underwater, and sank to the bottom of the gulf, finally extinguishing the flames that had burned since the blowout began. As the thirty-two-thousand-ton platform fell through nearly a mile of water, it twisted and kinked the long riser pipe that tethered the floating platform to the Macondo wellhead on the ocean floor, breaking the pipe open and sending its contents, pressurized by the natural conditions of the deep rock layers that had been tapped, gushing into the Gulf of Mexico. None of the multiple rams built into the blowout preventer, and meant to sever the rig from the well and control a spill, had worked.

For eighty-six days, the oil flowed freely, as BP and the government repeatedly tried, and failed, to stop it. Working underneath a mile of water with remote-control submarines was a new kind of emergency response that quickly came to demand equipment and technology that did not exist. Neither oil workers nor the federal government knew exactly what to do to stem the flow of oil. At one point, BP shoved golf balls and old tires into the hole, hoping to plug it with what they called a "junk shot." BP built a sort of upside-down funnel of steel from scratch, and then hung it above the well, hoping to capture the free-flowing oil rising into the gulf. The company sprayed millions of gallons of toxic dispersants into the water to break up the oil and make it disappear, despite fears that the dispersants themselves would make people sick and pollute the waters more.

In May, Doug Suttles, who had become BP's public face in the response, said repeatedly that BP had found itself at the technological limits of what was possible a mile beneath the gulf despite the company's oil spill response plan, which promised that the company had "proven equipment and technology" to deal with a spill. Months later, in an interview with the BBC, Tony Hayward himself would confirm that BP was "making it up day to day."

In the first few weeks that the oil gushed, BP claimed that the spill rate was moderate—just a thousand barrels a day—even as the public grew outraged that the company was grossly underestimating the amount of oil in the gulf. When government estimates finally put the spill rate at closer to thirty-five thousand barrels a day, Suttles said that estimating the flow rate was a diversion and explained, "We didn't think it was relevant."

As the oil continued to spill unabated and Americans feared that the company was doing little to stop one of the worst environmental catastrophes in recent industrial times, Tony Hayward summed up the decades of BP's irreverence in ten syllables: "No one wants this over more than I do." He added, with a bitter twist of anger directed toward his critics, "I'd like my life back."

By mid-July, when BP finally stopped the spill, scientists had again doubled their estimates for the amount of oil in the water, determining that some two hundred million gallons of crude—more than six times the size of the *Exxon Valdez* spill—had washed into the fisheries of the gulf, spreading across hundreds of square miles in a sheen. Fishing was banned. Tourism faltered. The oil began to come ashore along the beaches of Florida, Louisiana, Texas, and the rest of the gulf coast.

The Obama administration struggled to respond. It unleashed a confusing bureaucracy of agencies that, together with BP, mobilized one of the largest environmental cleanup efforts in history. It forced BP to set aside $20 billion in an escrow fund to pay for the damage, and BP not only began paying claims to gulf residents out of work but employed many of them to skim and rake and otherwise try to capture the oil. The process was Sisyphean, and much of the oil could never be cleaned up.

What was clear from early on, even before the precise chain of events that led to the blowout were known, is that oil companies, like most of big industry, for that matter, could not be trusted to police themselves and balance the public good against their own profits. The Minerals and Management Service, the agency regulating offshore drilling at the time of the spill, quickly acknowledged that better regulations and stricter oversight might have prevented the disaster and would be necessary to avoid another one in the future. "What we need as a society is not just to say we trust you, big oil companies. But to regulate with a different set of incentives—that is, do a serious job at regulating," said Joseph Pratt, the historian and professor at the University of Houston. "In retrospect, when we look at MMS, what we see is a model where one regulatory agency was created to both promote and regulate. And in a capitalist system, the promotional role will almost always trump the regulatory one. But sooner or later, we're going to have to pay for the regulation we deserve and need."

Indeed, after a brief period of soul-searching, the administration broke apart the Minerals and Management Service, acknowledging that regulators had been far too cozy with BP and other drillers to provide effective supervision over the exploration process. Only a few years earlier that agency had been embroiled in scandal over revelations that its agents had partied, shared cocaine, and had sex with the oil industry employees they were regulating. The newly created agency, the Bureau of Ocean and Energy Management, Regulation and Enforcement (BOEMRE), cleaved the MMS in two in order to separate the conflicting mandates of gathering oil revenues from policing drilling behavior. Shortly after the creation of BOEMRE, regulations governing offshore drilling that would have directly affected what happened on the Deepwater Horizon were put in place. In many situations, a liner and tieback casing, which would have isolated the Macondo's annulus into segments, is now mandatory. Rig operators need government approval for their cementing plans, and they can no longer displace mud with seawater without regulators' approval. The lockdown sleeve is now required to be put in place earlier in the drilling process. Finally, the Department of the Interior's offshore regulatory agency, having already been renamed BOEMRE, was further divided into an arm focused on permitting new wells and one devoted exclusively to safety and the environment.

Less clear was how BP had allowed one of its most significant and valuable projects to go so wrong, and whether the company was any different from its peers in the oil industry. Dozens of congressional and government hearings teased out the details of what had transpired on the decks of the Deepwater Horizon and pieced together the specific steps that had brought about the disaster. Few people, however, wondered whether there was a larger pattern of BP misconduct that invited closer scrutiny into how the company operated in the United States.

In what would seem like déjà vu for Jeanne Pascal and Chuck Hamel, the public heard testimony about one process after another that had been skipped to save time or money, in some cases as little as $128,000. They heard that the blowout preventer had a dead battery and hadn't been tested. They learned that BP's contractors at Transocean had warned in the months before the Macondo blowout that Transocean's working environment was unsafe, and that they were flirting with disaster. They heard that BP rushed into the casing and cementing process knowing that Macondo was "a nightmare well" presenting unique risks.

On June 17, 2010, Tony Hayward flew to Washington and sat before the House Energy and Commerce Committee at a broad wooden table before a mob of cameras and lights and reporters in the Rayburn House Office Building to answer for his company's actions. He said that a new BP culture revolving around safety was at the core of the company, and expressed frustration and bewilderment that, in spite of his efforts, this disaster had happened. "One of the reasons that I am so distraught is that . . . we have focused like a laser on safe and reliable operations," Hayward told the committee. "That is a fact, every day." He was at a loss to explain how that focus had failed to take root in the field.

Hayward was a petroleum geologist who started his thirty-year career on offshore rigs in the North Sea, had run BP's global exploration and production units since the mid-1990s, and had led the company's charge into gulf drilling. Yet he claimed to have been out of the loop about how the Macondo well was drilled or what had taken place on the Deepwater Horizon. This despite its being one of BP's most important projects globally. "The only knowledge I had of the Macondo well was in April, when I was told that we had made a discovery," he testified. He denied that he was told of the repeated kicks from the well or the urgency to get the well online faster. "I had no prior knowledge."

"But you are the CEO of the company," said Michael Burgess, a normally oil-friendly Republican from Texas.

"With respect, sir, we draw hundreds of wells around the world each year," Hayward told him.

"Yeah, I know," Burgess said. "That's what scares me."

Hayward was accused of stonewalling the government by members of Congress and was pilloried in the press after his appearance. The testimony, says Ron Freeman, the former Salomon banker, "was really embarrassing." Added Freeman: "He said he wasn't part of the decision-making process. Outlandish. You're *supposed* to know."

In the aftermath, BP's board deposed Hayward and sent him— literally—toward Siberia, where he would take a nonexecutive role in the joint venture TNK-BP. Later, Hayward would leave to start a multi-billion-dollar energy-oriented private equity firm. He was replaced as CEO by Robert Dudley, the American of Amoco corporate heritage who had once been on John Browne's short list of Turtles and had recently run TNK-BP himself.

Dudley again rejiggered the corporation to focus on safety. He declared that safety and risk management were BP's "most urgent priority," and that the gulf disaster held "lessons for us relating to the way we operate, the way we organize our company and the way we manage risk." Establishing a company-wide division devoted exclusively to safety and operational oversight, he promised that it would have the authority to intervene anywhere it needed to. He fired Andy Inglis, BP's head of drilling, and Doug Suttles retired.

Yet there were signs that little would change in how the company operated. BP's September 2010 report from its own investigation into the gulf spill fed a hunger for information, but for those who had followed BP's accidents in the past, it also fit neatly into a pattern of deflecting blame. The report broke down the rig's failures into eight specific key findings that might explain the accident and said that BP was only directly involved in one of them. The others were the fault of contractors.

Halliburton was blamed for the poor cement job and Transocean for the negative pressure test, the faulty blowout preventer, and other things. BP never acknowledged that, as the operator of the project, its company men directed nearly everything that happened on the rig. BP also never investigated the root causes of the disaster—the culture and management pressures and communication protocol failures that had allowed it to happen in the first place.

The government's initial report was far more scathing, but it also sounded like an echo of the reports released after Texas City, underscoring not only how many errors BP had made on the Deepwater Horizon, but how little the company had progressed since its catastrophe at Texas City in 2005. President Obama's National Commission on the BP Deepwater Horizon Oil Spill and Offshore Drilling said the blowout occurred because of "systemic failures" in industry management. BP, it said, had not evaluated or addressed the risk inherent in its operations, hadn't communicated proper procedures, and had made a string of consistently poor decisions that all led to "chaos."

"The blowout was not the product of a series of aberrational decisions made by rogue industry or government officials that could not have been anticipated or expected to occur again. Rather, the root causes are systemic and, absent significant reform in both industry practices and government policies, might well recur," the report stated. "Most of the mistakes and oversights at Macondo can be traced back to a single overarching failure—a failure of management. . . . A blowout in deep water was not a statistical inevitability."

Even that supposedly final word allowed for ambiguity. The commission said it found no evidence that the company had skipped steps in order to save money. The report was tough in the details and message of its conclusions but failed to hold any of the managers or executives, whether at BP or among its contractors, responsible for the decisions they had made.

According to people close to the review process, a decision had been made early on not to attempt to address the cultural genesis of the problem that eroded BP's operations: that for fifteen years John Browne had cut BP to the bone, and then Tony Hayward had fallen into the same pattern. That would remain outside the scope of analysis.

After taking a financial loss in 2010, BP announced in April 2011 that it had earned more than $7 billion in first-quarter profits, a 17 percent increase over the same period the year before. Transocean, in an SEC filing disclosing bonuses paid to its executives for 2010, said that despite the deaths in the gulf and the explosion of its largest rig, it had "recorded the best year in safety performance in our company's history." Like BP, it calculates its safety record using a statistical formula.

President Obama, who had initially placed a moratorium on new drilling permits in the gulf so that the accident could be understood, quickly changed his tune. After strengthening some regulations for offshore drilling, by March 2011 his administration was once again issuing permits to drill in the Gulf of Mexico; by June, fifteen had been granted. In October, BP's first new drilling plan for the gulf was approved. The deputy director of the government permitting agency said that BP's record did not warrant any special consideration.

Obama also announced a vast expansion of oil drilling on the North Slope, proposing to open Alaska's National Petroleum Reserve lands to the west of Prudhoe Bay and ANWR, where BP would again be expected to play a significant role.

The EPA has not made a decision about whether to ban BP from U.S. government contracts. In May 2011, the government reached a $25 million civil settlement with BP over the 2006 Alaska spill. As of late 2011, however, the debarment settlement talks over BP's 2005 and 2006 criminal convictions still hadn't been concluded, and no individual employee of BP, past or present, has been charged with a crime or held accountable for the decisions made within the company. "That's what bothers me most in this whole scenario," says Dave Senko, who has retired from the oil industry and continues to suffer emotional and psychological stress he says is related to the disaster in Texas City. Senko sued BP, Don Parus, and Jacobs Engineering for negligence and intentionally inflicting emotional distress. In 2007 the court found in BP's favor, and in 2009 Senko failed in his appeal. "Here we are, five-plus years after the blast, and there has been zero accountability so far."

After leaving BP, John Browne took a job as managing director of Riverstone Holdings, an energy-oriented investment house affiliated with the Carlyle Group, where former secretary of state James Baker was senior counsel until 2005. More recently, Browne was hired by Britain's conservative government as an "efficiency tsar," with the idea that his expertise in cutting expenses might help the government trim its own budgets.

Robert Malone, retired, lives on his ranch outside of Sonora, Texas, and works as the chief executive of a local bank, the First National Bank of Sonora. After Texas City, John Manzoni went on to become the chief executive of Talisman Energy, a Canadian oil company with a close relationship to BP.

The generation of critics who took on BP for so many years is itself fading, leaving the company to operate free of the weight of its own history. Chuck Hamel, eighty-four and in poor health, declared bankruptcy after Exxon sued him in a separate business suit. He ceased whistle-blowing long ago. Jeanne Pascal had several rounds of shoulder surgery and, while she regrets not banning BP from contracts while she had the chance, looks forward to a peaceful retirement. Stuart Sneed lost his labor case against BP and has not returned to work. Mark Kovac, long the standard-bearer on issues of safety and maintenance, may retire sometime in the near future.

Since Marty Anderson broke the oil industry's code of silence over BP's handling of its inspection program, he has continued to battle an industry-wide blacklisting. BP and Acuren never hired him again. After his story was told by this author on national television, Chevron, a steady client of Anderson's in Alaska, canceled his contracts despite internal company emails praising his work. In spring 2011, Anderson was forced to shutter his consulting business, and he feared that someone sympathetic to the oil industry in Alaska and angry over the damage he had done to BP's reputation might track him down. "I just beefed up my security system at my house," he said. "We have two dogs. . . . I'm sitting here right now with a nine millimeter in my lap, so bring it."

In the Alaskan oil fields, conditions continue to worsen. A leaked company memo from late 2010 showed that BP had given 148 sections of its pipelines on Alaska's North Slope an F rank, meaning that at least

80 percent of the walls of those pipelines has corroded and couldn't be relied on for normal operations. The maintenance inventory shows that in more than 350 "hot spots" the metal walls of the F-ranked pipes are worn to within a few thousandths of an inch of bursting, risking an explosion or spills. BP's leadership said the rankings were not as damning as they looked. "An item can be an F rank and can stay that way for some period of time as long as the situation is stabilized," says BP Alaska spokesman Steve Rinehart. He says the company has options: a pipe can be patched, shut down, or de-rated to handle less material. "It's a big job and we're all over it."

Anderson says that's not the case. "It means the pipe wall is corroded to the point where it has to be retired," he said simply.

Four decades after its construction, and after two decades of debate about how long the dilapidated field could be strung out, there were few signs that operations in Alaska would wind down. Instead, all signs, including President Obama's endorsement of new drilling, pointed to a further prolonging of its lifespan with minimal additional investment. Opening the petroleum reserves was only practical because a network of Alaskan pipelines was already in place to move the oil. Meanwhile, another competitive oil frontier was opening up beyond the outer continental shelf in the Arctic. The waters north of Prudhoe Bay, all the way to the North Pole, were likely to be the locus of new drilling for decades to come.

BP has shown signs that it might sell its remaining stake in North Slope operations, but it hasn't done so. If it did, it would likely continue to operate the fields under contract and would also be a major player in the expansion of Arctic offshore drilling. At the start of 2011, the company was preparing its newest and largest rig, the Liberty. Liberty would drill a short ways underground and then turn its wellbore horizontally, enabling it to reach as far as six miles out under the Beaufort Sea and access a broad swathe of territory without having direct access above the well hole. Liberty would press against the boundaries of drilling technology yet again.

The farther BP and the rest of the oil industry go into the Arctic Ocean, the greater the environmental risks, and the more important it is for the drilling companies to be the safest and most reliable industrial operators in the world. A spill offshore in the Arctic would be devastating. Experts expect oil would remain trapped under sheets of ice for years. It would be difficult, if not impossible, to navigate the frozen waters or to clean up contaminants that have already proved to be such a challenge in the open waters of the gulf. Yet by early 2011, neither BP nor the government appeared to be prepared for an Arctic spill. They essentially count on a spill not happening in the first place.

In Alaska, oil spill response is managed by Alaska Clean Seas, an industry-organized nonprofit agency set up to handle cleanup in the event of an accident on the North Slope. BP, like the other oil companies operating there, is a partner in the program. In a 2010 interview in Deadhorse, a senior manager of Alaska Clean Seas said the group was only capable of responding to a five-thousand-barrel-a-day spill. The lessons of the gulf demonstrated that a blowout could produce more than six times that much oil, and Alaska's own oil and gas commissioner, Dan Seamount, said in an interview that the Beaufort Sea wells contained enough pressure to produce forty thousand barrels a day. "It would be a concern," Seamount said. "I would think . . . that someone would have to be prepared to take care of that, to handle it."

When the federal government pursues more oil in Alaska, it relies on Alaskan environmental officials and the state's oil commissioners, including Seamount, to make sure drilling is carried out safely. Seamount, it appears, relies at least in part on Alaska Clean Seas, which is only as good as its own members.

Many things, it seems, haven't changed at all.

Acknowledgments

Writing this book was like assembling a large puzzle, and a great many of the pieces were gathered by a team of colleagues to whom I am forever indebted. In particular, Martin Smith, with whom I worked to report the PBS *Frontline* episode "The Spill," conducted a number of important interviews used in these pages. His partner at Rain Media, Marcela Gaviria, and their talented staff also provided reporting, perspective, archival research, and personal encouragement that enriched this story. Thank you to Rebecca Thomas and Carola Mamberto. And thank you to Raney Aronson-Roth and David Fanning at *Frontline*, and Ryan Knutson, who at both *Frontline* and *ProPublica* conducted vigorous reporting and then backed me up by making sure my work was accurate.

I am grateful for the support of my editors at *ProPublica*: Paul Steiger and Stephen Engelberg generously allowed me many months of reporting and then cheered me on when the project took on a truly long form, even at the expense of other work. Susan White was unwavering in her encouragement and incisive in her editing through some of the toughest and most competitive deadlines. Later, she volunteered her time to critically read this manuscript. Thank you also to Nick Kusnetz, Marian Wang, Sasha Chavkin, Richard Tofel, Lisa Schwartz, Sydney Lupkin, and Sheelagh McNeill, all of whom contributed to our collective reporting on BP. Thank you also to David Baez and Riley Blanton.

Thank you to my friends and family who provided invaluable feedback, including Alex Grabcheski, who both read the manuscript and provided me a quiet place in the country to write. Thank you also to my agent, P. J. Mark, who once again coached me through this process while deftly handling the business of publishing.

At W. W. Norton, my editor, Starling Lawrence, pushed me to write clearly and to bring so many complicated and technical explanations in these pages down to earth. Janet Byrne was forever patient and worked tirelessly to bring the manuscript into its final form. Melody Conroy guided the production, as did the many other talented professionals at W. W. Norton.

Finally, the story would not be a story if it were not for the individuals who selflessly shared their experiences—often at some personal risk—in these pages. Mark Kovac, who still faces the unmitigated dangers at work every day, has spent a decade spreading word about the chances BP takes in Alaska. Martin Anderson could have been a rich man endlessly employed by the Alaskan oil industry if he had simply played by their rules. Instead he took a stand based on a belief that honesty and transparency would prevent more accidents and would eventually save lives. Jeanne Pascal felt loyal to the government she had served and had kept the EPA's efforts to police BP confidential. Only after the gulf spill did she decide that breaking her silence could do more good than harm. Others contributed equally, including Scott West, Chuck Hamel, Stuart Sneed, and many more who have chosen to remain anonymous and cannot be thanked here by name. In particular, several present and past employees of BP bravely shared their own experiences working within the BP organization, knowing that doing so would be seen as disloyal and consequential to their careers. I am grateful for their commitment to truth.

Author's Note

Much of this book was written without the cooperation of BP and its executives. Throughout 2010, BP was informed about my reporting direction and asked to respond to the information I uncovered. The company repeatedly declined to offer its executives for interviews or to allow me or my colleagues tours of its facilities. In October 2010, after requesting—and receiving—dozens of pages of detailed questions in writing, BP provided a one-paragraph response. In a public statement, BP's new CEO, Robert Dudley, denied that BP has an enduring problem managing safety and warned that my forthcoming report, first published and aired in October 2010, would be unflattering.

John Browne, Tony Hayward, Doug Suttles, Robert Malone, Don Parus, Richard Woollam, John Manzoni, Mike Hoffman, and Karen Loeffler all declined repeated requests to speak about themselves or the company for these pages. Acuren, one of BP's contracting companies in Alaska, owned by Rockwood Service Corporation, also declined repeated requests for interviews.

Notes

Some of the interviews for this book were carried out by my colleagues at PBS Frontline, *Martin Smith and Ryan Knutson, hereinafter referred to as MS and RK.*

PROLOGUE

xiv **The state of Alaska was suing**: *The State of Alaska v. BP Exploration (Alaska) Inc.*, State Superior Court, Anchorage, Alaska.

CHAPTER 1: THE RISE OF THE SUN KING

4 **gathered in a private meeting:** Nick Butler (former BP Group policy adviser and chief of staff to John Browne), in an email discussion with the author, December 2010.

4 **"This is dreadful":** John Browne, quoted by Tom Bower, *Oil: Money, Politics, and Power in the 21st Century* (New York: Grand Central Publishing, 2010), 80.

4 **"What was said in those press releases":** Tom Hamilton (BP's former global chief of exploration), in an interview with the author, December 2010.

4 **"There were some improvements":** Nick Butler, in an email exchange with the author, December 2010.

5 **"I knew that BP controlled":** John Browne, *Beyond Business* (London: Orion Publishing, 2010), Kindle edition, loc. 1174.

7 **"It's a matter of convincing people":** William Glaberson, "B.P. America's 'Hatchet Gentleman:' Robert B. Horton; Cost-Cutter with a Soft Touch," *New York Times*, January 10, 1988, http://www.nytimes.com/1988/01/10/business/bp-america-s-hatchet-gentleman-robert-b-horton-cost-cutter-with-a-soft-touch.html?pagewanted=all&src=pm.

7 **"If it was a secret"**: Tom Hamilton, in an interview with the author, December 2010.

7 **"an enormously powerful company"**: Steven Prokesch, "Now It's Bob Horton's Turn at BP," *New York Times*, September 17, 1989.

7 **"It was a very hidebound company"**: Ronald Freeman (former general partner, Salomon Brothers), in an interview with MS, August 2010.

8 **American entrepreneurship**: Tom Bower, *Oil: Money, Politics, and Power in the 21st Century* (New York: Grand Central Publishing, 2010), 88.

9 **"British agents began conspiring"**: Stephen Kinzer, *All the Shah's Men, An American Coup and the Roots of Middle East Terror* (New York: John Wiley & Sons, 2003), Kindle edition, loc. 85.

9 **"BP was the number one oil company"**: James Bamberg (historian), in interview with MS, August 2010.

11 **"The whole philosophy"**: *Platts Oilgram News,* "BP's Browne Urges North Sea Producers to Revise Business Philosophy, Cut Costs," September 6, 1989.

12 **Hamilton was asked to come up with:** Tom Hamilton, in an interview with the author, December 2010.

12 **"there are no sacred cows"**: Prokesch, "Now It's Bob Horton's Turn at BP."

13 **the Great Oil Depression:** Matthew Simmons, "What a Difference 20 Years Makes in Crude Oil Prices," oilcrash.com, http://www.oilcrash.com/articles/simmons1.htm.

13 **"free fall"**: George H. W. Bush, quoted by Timothy J. McNulty, "White House: Oil-Price Policy Firm," *Chicago Tribune*, April 3, 1986.

13 **"The danger arises"**: Prokesch, "Now It's Bob Horton's Turn at BP."

17 **"He came to a company which was large"**: James Bamberg, in an interview with MS, August 2010.

17 **"inextricably linked"**: Browne, *Beyond Business,* Kindle edition, loc. 1549.

18 **"We were very aware"**: Browne, *Beyond Business,* Kindle edition, loc. 1560.

18 **"the most important single issue"**: David Brierley, "Striding Up to the Giants," *Sunday (London) Times*, October 15, 1989.

18 **"We must plan prudently"**: John Browne, "BP Exploration Embarks on New Worldwide Strategy," PR Newswire, September 14, 1989.

19 **"I had forty-two offices"**: Tom Hamilton, in an interview with the author, December 2010.

20 **"shocking for its boldness"**: Cotton Timberlake, "BP Announces Restructuring; Cutting More Than 1,700 Jobs," Associated Press, September 14, 1989.

21 **"The rapid growth"**: John Browne, "BP Exploration to Be Reshaped and Slimmed, British Jobs to Go," PR Newswire, September 14, 1989.

21 **"Performance this year"**: Walter Andrews, "'Disappearance' of $900 Million Drove BP sale," United Press International, October 20, 1989.

21 **"In essence we are significantly re-directing"**: Browne, "BP Exploration to Be Reshaped and Slimmed."

22 **"We are reducing our scattergun approach"**: Brierley, "Striding Up to the Giants."

22 **"He wanted to pull them into the big leagues"**: Ronald Freeman, in an interview with MS, August 2010.

22 **"It is vital that we explore"**: Browne, "BP Exploration Embarks on New Worldwide Strategy."

23 **"Cash and management resources"**: Brierley, "Striding Up to the Giants."

CHAPTER 2: THE WHISTLE-BLOWER

26 **Then, just before midnight:** Alaska Oil Spill Commission, *Spill: The Wreck of the Exxon Valdez*, final report, February 1990.

26 **"no one seems to be doing anything"**: Browne, *Beyond Business*, Kindle edition, loc. 783.

27 **Response from Alyeska:** Alaska Oil Spill Commission, *Spill: The Wreck of the Exxon Valdez*.

28 **waging a righteous war:** Chuck Hamel (businessman and whistle-blower targeted by oil companies), in interviews with the author, July and November 2010.

29 **"They denied the truth"**: Chuck Hamel, in testimony before U.S. House Committee on Interior and Insular Affairs, November 4, 1991.

30 **"They knew there were problems"**: Rick Steiner (marine advisory board member, University of Alaska, Fairbanks), in interviews about Hamel aired in *The Whistleblower*, Court TV, 2004.

31 **"I was treated as a kook"**: Chuck Hamel, in interviews with the author, November 2010.

32 **"I joked to Rick that I was too old"**: Ibid.

32 **"I still don't understand"**: Chuck Hamel, audiotapes collected by Congress, aired in *The Whistleblower*.

33 **He darted to Hamel's office:** description from video of event collected by Congress, aired in *The Whistleblower*.

34 **"I was so scared"**: Ricki Jacobson (private investigator hired to spy on Hamel), in congressional testimony aired in *The Whistleblower*.

34 **"Black told Ricki"**: Michael Lozoff (Jacobson's attorney), in an interview for *The Whistleblower*.

34 **in a test project with Chevron:** U.S. Department of the Interior, *Oil and*

Gas Development on Alaska's North Slope: Past and Future Prospects, report, March 1991.

35 **"we had a right and an obligation"**: Pat Wellington (Alyeska Pipeline's director of security), in an interview for *The Whistleblower*.

36 **"almost a keystone cops"**: Linda Chase (chief counsel, House Natural Resources Committee), in an interview for *The Whistleblower*.

36 **"I have some spending money here"**: Wayne Black (director of Wackenhut special investigation division who spied on Hamel), from video of event collected by Congress, aired in *The Whistleblower*.

37 **the wire Rich wore**: Sherree Rich, in testimony before the U.S. House Committee on Interior and Insular Affairs, Rayburn Office Building, Washington, D.C., November 4–5, 1991.

38 **"He had no conscience at all"**: Anna Contreras (Wackenhut employee), in congressional testimony aired in *The Whistleblower*.

38 **"Gus was terrified"**: Kathy Hamel, in an interview with the author, November 2010.

38 **"We became more and more aware"**: Linda Chase, in an interview for *The Whistleblower*.

38 **Scott was immediately fired**: Kim Fararo, "Alyeska Fired Whistleblower over Personnel's Objections," *Anchorage Daily News*, April 1, 1992.

39 **"Within two hours we vanished"**: Wayne Jenkins (Wackenhut investigator), in an interview for *The Whistleblower*.

CHAPTER 3: THE FIRST OFFENSE

45 **started getting rid of it on their own:** *United States of America v. BP Exploration (Alaska) Inc.*, Criminal Complaint no. A99-549-CV.

46 **started illegally injecting:** Ibid.

47 **the Doyon crew dumped the waste:** *United States of America v. BP Exploration (Alaska) Inc.*, Stipulation of Settlement and Order.

49 **"In many ways he wasn't a Texas oilman":** Carola Hoyos (*Financial Times* journalist who wrote about Browne and BP), in an interview with MS, August 2010.

49 **"John called me up":** Ronald Freeman, in an interview with MS, August 2010.

50 **"completely devoted to that company":** Matthew Gwyther (editor of *Management Today* magazine), in an interview with MS, August 2010.

50 **"The teacher would say"**: Tobias Buck and David Buchan, "Sun King of the Oil Industry," *Financial Times*, January 12, 2007 (originally published July 2002).

50 **"I asked people to challenge the status quo"**: Browne, *Beyond Business*, Kindle edition, loc. 1303.

51 **"There had been a yearning desire for leadership"**: Ibid., loc. 120.

51 **"BP was stuck"**: Ibid., loc. 1347.

51 **"big fat greedy guy"**: Bower, *Oil: Money, Politics, and Power in the 21st Century*, 143.

51 **"The industry was now measured"**: Browne, *Beyond Business*, Kindle edition, loc. 797.

52 **"We had to ensure that there were no deviations"**: Ibid.

52 **"No amount of argument"**: Ibid.

53 **"I would be at the helm"**: Ibid., loc. 109.

53 **"Oil companies have two choices"**: Ronald Freeman, in an interview with MS, August 2010.

54 **"The time to consider the policy"**: John Browne, in a speech on climate delivered at Stanford University, May 19, 1997, http://www.gsb.stanford.edu/community/bmag/sbsm0997/feature_ranks.html.

54 **"He wanted to identify himself"**: Ronald Freeman, in an interview with MS, August 2010.

54 **"The American Petroleum Institute said"**: John Browne, *The Charlie Rose Show*, April 10, 2002.

55 **"The whole thing about climate change"**: Derek Brower (oil analyst and editor of *Petroleum Economist*), in an interview with the author, September 2010.

59 **"The potential impacts . . . are major"**: Bruce Botelho (former attorney general of Alaska), in testimony delivered before the U.S. Senate Committee on Energy and Natural Resources, June 24, 1999.

59 **"We can only do this"**: James Palmer (former BP Alaska head of external affairs), in testimony before Alaska State Legislative Council, June 30, 1999.

59 **"Clearly this acquisition"**: Kevin Meyers (president, ARCO Alaska), in testimony before Alaska State Legislative Council, June 30, 1999.

59 **"Downsizing will result"**: Kay Brown (director of the Alaska Conservation Alliance), in testimony before Alaska State Legislative Council, June 30, 1999.

61 **Besides the leases**: Inventory of annual Department of Defense contracts with BP, obtained through Freedom of Information Act, September 2010.

61 **Sometime soon after the call**: Jeanne Pascal (former EPA debarment attorney handling BP cases), in interviews with the author, June, July, September 2010.

64 **As expected**: *United States of America v. BP Exploration (Alaska) Inc.*, Stipulation of Settlement and Order.

66 **In exchange for not being debarred**: *The Compliance Agreement of BP Exploration (Alaska) Inc.*, EPA case no. 99-0139-00.

CHAPTER 4: A SLIPPERY SLOPE

70 **"We devised a new decentralized organization"**: Browne, *Beyond Business*, Kindle edition, loc. 1274.

70 **Kovac was beginning to see**: Marc Kovac (BP mechanic and Pace Union representative in Alaska), in interviews with the author, July, September 2010.

72 **"The North Slope was vast"**: Browne, *Beyond Business*, Kindle edition, loc. 559.

73 **"I saw people fishing"**: Ibid., loc. 639.

75 **Instead, Crannis says**: Crannis is a pseudonym for a BP employee working on the North Slope who did not want to be identified for fear of losing work. The information is from interviews with the author, July 2010.

77 **"The main concern is"**: Email from Richard Woollam to Prudhoe Bay field operations manager, "Re: Smart pigging of oil transit line," July 27, 1997, 2:15 p.m.

78 **"We will not be getting any relief"**: Email from Richard Woollam to the Prudhoe Bay corrosion team leaders, "Re: Draft-Budget Review 1-Pager," June 2, 1999, 5:05 p.m.

78 **Two days later**: Email from corrosion team manager John Todd et al. to Richard Woollam and staff, "PW inhibitor at GC2 and GC3," June 4, 1999, 11:42 a.m.

78 **"Here's one for our HSE files"**: BP internal email, sender and recipients redacted by U.S. House Energy and Commerce Committee, "Fw: PW inhibitor at GC2 and GC3," June 4, 1999, 6:46 p.m.

79 **"much of the system is in poor condition"**: Email from Dominic Paisley to Richard Woollam, "Re: MOC for discontinuation of EC1081A," June 8, 1999, 4:06 p.m.

79 **"Thanks for the warning"**: Email from Prudhoe Bay operations manager to corrosion team and Richard Woollam, "Re: PW inhibitor at GC2 and GC3," June 9, 1999, 2:08 a.m.

80 **"Dear sir"**: Letter sent to Sir John Browne, from "Concerned Prudhoe Bay operators and maintenance personnel," obtained by the author, January 14, 1999.

81 **"We're using equipment"**: Marc Kovac, in interviews with the author, July 2010.

CHAPTER 5: SAVING THE WORLD

82 **"greatly strengthen the sense of identity"**: John Browne, in BP statement "BP Amoco Unveils New Global Brand to Drive Growth," July 24, 2000.

82 **"They have nailed their colors"**: Patrick Barrow (Public Relations Consultants Association), in an interview with the author about BP's rebranding, October 2005.

83 **"a company that was really moving"**: Joseph Pratt, in an interview with MS, August 2010.

84 **"they created something that hadn't existed yet"**: John Hofmeister (former CEO, Shell) in an interview with the author, May 2011.

84 **"Between breadth and depth"**: Ronald Freeman, in an interview with MS, August 2010.

85 **"Our workplace environment"**: Letter from concerned operating technicians on the North Slope to Charles Hamel, January 10, 2001.

85 **grease up the safety valves**: Chuck Hamel, in an interview with the author, July 2010.

86 **nine out of thirty valves failed**: Jim Carlton, "Oil and Ice: In Alaskan Wilderness, 'Friendlier Technology' Gets a Cold Reception—BP Amoco Workers Question Safety of Drilling Systems Bush Touts for Refuge—Firm Defends Pioneering Rigs," *Wall Street Journal*, April 13, 2001.

86 **"anomalous"**: Ibid.

86 **"I was more interested"**: Jeanne Pascal, in an interview with the author, July 2010.

87 **"Theirs is an odd relationship"**: Tony Hopfinger, "Chuck Hamel Pulls All Strings to Keep Oil Giant BP Honest," *Anchorage Daily News*, March 24, 2002.

88 **robust, independent team**: *Review of Operational Integrity Concerns at Greater Prudhoe Bay*, confidential internal report obtained by the author, October 2001.

88 **riddled with "unacceptable" lapses**: Ibid.

88 **"These reported deficiencies"**: Ibid.

89 **overzealous cost cutting**: Ibid.

89 **"fundamental lack of trust"**: Ibid.

91 **Two weeks earlier**: *Investigation of Explosion and Fire at Prudhoe Bay Well A-22 North Slope, Alaska*, an investigative report by the Alaska state Oil and Gas Conservation Commission, August 2002.

92 **Shugak went back to the well**: Wesley Loy, "Don Shugak Recalls the Wellhead Explosion That Nearly Killed Him," *Anchorage Daily News*, November 3, 2002.

93 **"I started crawling"**: Ibid.

93 **"I didn't even feel like I was hurt"**: Ibid.

94 **"We are quite prepared"**: *Platts Oilgram News*, "BP Prepared to Increase Debt Ratio if Acquisition Opportunities Develop," March 29, 1988.

94 **"at least 10 percentage points"**: Fadel Gheit (oil industry analyst at Oppenheimer), in an interview with RK, October 2010.

95 **"BP was promising its shareholders"**: Derek Brower, in an interview with the author, September 2010.

95 **"He made promises"**: John Hofmeister, in an interview with the author, May 2011.

95 **"BP had to restate its production targets"**: Carola Hoyos, in an interview with MS, August 2010.

CHAPTER 6: A WAKE-UP CALL

100 **Ernesta Ballard, charged**: Wesley Loy, "BP Hasn't Lived Up to Spill Agreement, DEC Chief Charges," *Anchorage Daily News*, January 14, 2004.

100 **behavior on the slope was reckless:** Jeanne Pascal, in interviews with the author, July 2010.

100 **listed a couple of examples:** Wesley Loy, "No Fine for BP in Past Spill," *Anchorage Daily News*, April 11, 2006.

102 **"It was a floodgate":** Jeanne Pascal, in interviews with the author, July 2010.

102 **Had BP violated the terms:** *The Compliance Agreement of BP Exploration (Alaska) Inc.*, EPA Case no. 99-0139-00.

102 **"It is often chemotherapy":** Robert Meunier (former senior EPA debarment official and author of regulations), in interviews with the author, May and June 2010.

103 **Exxon confronted a string of serious problems:** *New York Times,* "More Trouble with Oiled Waters," January 14, 1990.

104 **"Exxon answered very aggressively":** Joseph Pratt (history professor at University of Houston and former Amoco employee), in an interview with MS, August 2010.

104 **"full-scale, top-to-bottom review":** Rex Tillerson (CEO, ExxonMobil), in testimony before the U.S. House Subcommittee on Energy and Environment, June 15, 2010.

104 **"It is our common global language":** Ibid.

105 **"I have not had an employee":** Robert Malone (former BP executive and president of BP America), in an interview with the author, August 2006.

105 **"The question before BP":** Joseph Pratt, in an interview with MS, August 2010.

108 **had been accused then:** John C. Roper, "Vinson & Elkins Settles with Enron for $30 million," *Houston Chronicle*, June 2, 2006.

109 **the lawyers established:** *Report for BPXA Concerning Allegations of Workplace Harassment from Raising HSE issues and Corrosion Data Falsification*, BP internal review conducted by Vinson & Elkins, October 20, 2004.

109 **ordered BP's contractor to cut:** Ibid.

110 **"I'm sure Richard":** *Report for BPXA Concerning Allegations of Workplace Harassment*, 20.

110 **" 'NO!' or even 'HELL, NO!' ":** Email from Richard Woollam to Daniel Wuthrich et al., "Re: APC Requests for Additional Manpower," December 6, 2001, 9:17 a.m.

110 **"I will make any changes":** *Report for BPXA Concerning Allegations of Workplace Harassment*, 22.

110 **"We need to get commitment":** Email from corrosion team leader to Richard Woollam and Rick Felix, "Re: CIC MOC," March 22, 2003.

110 **"We need the very best":** Email from Richard Woollam to BP Alaska corrosion team "Re: FYI: Maureen's Slope Trip Next Week," March 30, 2004.

111 **"run to failure":** Internal BP safety complaint filed by Marc Kovac, reproduced in *Report for BPXA Concerning Allegations of Workplace Harassment*, 25.

111 **"Dan wants somebody fired":** *Report for BPXA Concerning Allegations of Workplace Harrassment from Raising HSE issues and Corrosion Data Falsification*, 22.

111 **"unintended chilling effect":** Ibid., 39.

111 **"King Richard":** Ibid., 17.

111 **"We found evidence":** Ibid., 39.

112 **"Our investigation did not uncover":** Ibid., 7.

112 **"We are not technically qualified":** Ibid., 36.

113 **"What do I think?":** Jeanne Pascal, in interviews with the author, July 2010.

114 **was given forty-eight hours to cut:** Email from Greater Prudhoe Bay Operations Support manager to Richard Woollam et al., "Re: ACTION; 2003 August LE's and Field OVERVIEW," September 8, 2003, 7:01 p.m.

114 **several options to win back the money:** Email from Richard Woollam to Rick Felix, "Re: ACTION; 2003 August LE's and Field OVERVIEW," September 9, 2003, 7:11 p.m.

114 **A budget document:** Internal BP budget document, *CIC Group 2002 Budget Challenge—$1 million Opportunities.*

114 **not unanimously:** Email from corrosion team leader to Richard Woollam, "Re: ACTION; 2003 August LE's and Field OVERVIEW," September 10, 2003, 2:43 p.m.

115 **"discretionary spend on materials":** Internal BP budget document, *Greater Prudhoe Bay/Field Lifting Cost Challenge (LCC) Maintenance and Reliability*, April 15, 2004.

115 **The division's special agent in charge:** Jeanne Pascal, in interviews with the author, July 2010.

116 **nearly 80 percent of the critical war-support:** Jeanne Pascal, in interviews with the author, October 2010.

117 **"Our laws don't create any barriers":** David Uhlmann (former head of the

environmental crimes division at the Department of Justice), in an interview with the author, September 2010.

CHAPTER 7: DANGER AT THE PLANT

122 **The office trailers weren't supposed to be there**: U.S. Chemical Safety and Hazard Investigation Board, *Investigation Report, Refinery Explosion and Fire, BP, Texas City, March 23, 2005,* March 2007, 126.

125 **"We're not using those anymore"**: TJ Aulds (editor of *Galveston Daily News*), in interviews with the author and with MS, August 2010.

126 **"They knew exactly what they were buying"**: Carola Hoyos, in an interview with MS, August 2010.

127 **"the only major opportunity to capture advantage"**: BP internal document, *BP Texas City Business Unit Business Strategy*, October 1999.

127 **"continually and aggressively drive costs out of the system"**: Ibid.

128 **Eliminating safety calendars saved $40,000**: BP internal document, *TCBU (Texas City Business Unit) Reduced External Supplier and Materials Usage*, 1999.

128 **"thought a bit more of themselves"**: Tom Hamilton, in an interview with the author, December 2010.

128 **"We need to decide if we want to spend"**: Email from BP employee David Arnett to Gary Scoggin et al., "Re: Line Size for NDU flare," January 8, 2002, 3:14 p.m.

129 **"Bank $150k savings now"**: Email from BP employee Walt Wundrow to Arnett and Scoggin, "Re: Line Size for NDU flare," January 9, 2002, 10:58 a.m.

129 **"Bank the savings in 99.999% of cases"**: Email from George Carter to Wundrow, Arnett, Scoggin, and others, "Re: Line Size for NDU flare," January 9, 2002, 4:13 p.m.

129 **The refinery appeared "run down" and "decayed"**: Interview with Don Parus, conducted by Jud Starr's office, Washington, D.C., for BP's internal incident review, known as the Bonse Report, October 12, 2006.

129 **"serious concerns about the potential"**: BP internal document, *Good Practice Sharing Assessment*, BP South Houston, Final Report, August 2002.

130 **"clearly linked to the reduction in maintenance"**: BP internal document, *Texas City Refinery Retrospective Analysis*, October 28, 2002.

130 **"Cost cutting efforts have intervened"**: U.S. Chemical Safety and Hazard Investigation Board video, *Anatomy of a Disaster,* March 2007.

130 **"checkbook mentality"**: Ibid., 161.

130 **"widespread tolerance"**: Ibid., 166.

130 scathing investigation reports: Report from Scottish Environmental Pro-

tection Agency, *Major Incident Investigation Report, BP Grangemouth, May 29, 2000–June 10, 2000*, August 18, 2003.

130   **"is NOT delivering on profitability vs. % of capital investment"**: Email from BP employee Dennis Link to GJ Anderson et al., "Fw: Update—Texas City repositioning project," November 14, 2003, 11:56 p.m.

131   **"accountabilities were unclear"**: Interview with Don Parus, conducted by Jud Starr's office, October 12, 2006.

131   **"is concerned that the top level in London"**: Email from James Hay to David Pierpoline, "Re: S. Houston," August 16, 2002, 11:16 a.m.

131   **"There were a number of reports coming up"**: Don Holmstrom (lead investigator at the U.S. Chemical Safety and Hazard Investigation Board), in an interview with MS, August 2010.

131   **"had a set of principles"**: Interview with Don Parus, conducted by Jud Starr's office, October 12, 2006.

132   **"BP is decentralized"**: Ibid.

133   **"The incentives used"**: U.S. Chemical Safety and Hazard Investigation Board video, *Anatomy of a Disaster,* March 2007, 164.

133   **"It was typical for them to experience a fire every week"**: Mike Sawyer (consultant and process safety expert), in an interview with the author, August 2010.

133   **in thirty years, twenty-three workers had been killed**: U.S. Chemical Safety and Hazard Investigation Board, *Investigation Report, Refinery Explosion and Fire,* 306.

133   **"I recall a guy slipping"**: David Leining (BP Texas City worker), in an interview with the author, August 2010.

134   **"Texas City is not a safe place to work"**: PowerPoint presentation made by Don Parus, internal BP document identifier: "BPtSOME13409138."

134   **"portrayed to them"**: Interview with Don Parus, conducted by Jud Starr's office, October 12, 2006.

135   **"the refinery was not in prime shape"**: David Senko (JE Merit manager), in interviews with the author, August 2010.

136   **"Something's really wrong"**: *BP Texas City Site Report of Findings: Texas City's Protection Performance, Behaviors, Culture, Management and Leadership,* a report compiled by the Telos Group, January 21, 2005, 36.

136   **"What does it take for us"**: Ibid., 53.

137   **"We tell them what goes down in the trenches"**: Ibid., 23.

138   **Hoffman didn't read the report:** Interview with Don Parus, conducted by Jud Starr's office, October 12, 2006.

138   **"I exhausted every avenue"**: Ibid.

139   **"kills someone in the next"**: U.S. Chemical Safety and Hazard Investigation Board, *Investigation Report, Refinery Explosion and Fire*, 177.

141 **more than an hour late**: U.S. Chemical Safety and Hazard Investigation Board video, *Anatomy of a Disaster,* March 2007, 51.

143 **"We, the project team"**: David Senko, in interviews with the author, August 2010.

CHAPTER 8: A TRAGEDY

146 **"It was just a real steady, steady constant"**: David Leining, in an interview with the author, August 2010.

147 **"Texas City 9-11"**: Original recording used in *The Spill*, PBS *Frontline*, October 24, 2010.

147 **"A plant just blew up"**: Ibid.

147 **"It's the isom!"**: Ibid.

147 **Eva Rowe was in a gas station**: Eva Rowe (daughter of Texas City explosion victims), in an interview with the author, August 2010.

148 **"that one of the fire trucks"**: *Galveston County Daily News*, "Scariest Thing I've Ever Seen," March 24, 2005.

149 **"This is Dave Leining"**: David Leining, in an interview with the author, August 2010.

150 **"They had been sending us reports that showed 99 percent compliance"**: Joseph Panasiti (lawyer with the South Coast Air Quality Management District, which sued BP), in an interview with RK, June 2010.

151 **"the worst construction workplace"**: David Senko, in interviews with the author, August 2010.

154 **"at the cost of a precious day of my leave"**: Email from John Manzoni to Mark Linder, according to transcript of Manzoni deposition given to Brent Coon and Tony Buzbee, September 8, 2006; also according to Mark Linder interview with RK.

155 **"Mr. Browne has spent the morning"**: Video footage of BP press conference at City Hall in Texas City, March 24, 2005.

155 **"Yesterday was a dark day"**: Ibid.

159 **"The core issue here"**: Anne Belli, "BP Blames Staff for Deadly Texas City Blast," *Houston Chronicle*, May 18, 2005.

160 **"Failure to take emergency action"**: *Fatal Accident Investigation Report; Isomerization Unit Explosion Final Report* (known as the Mogford report, to which it will hereinafter be referred), December 9, 2005, 3.

160 **"They tried to put the blame"**: Anne Belli, "The BP Explosion: BP Says Its Initial Findings Misstated—Employee Error Only Partly to Blame, Company Officials Now Say," *Houston Chronicle*, May 25, 2005.

161 **"A for effort, F for a grade"**: Loren Steffy, "BP Makes a Doubtful Run at

Taking Responsibility," *Houston Chronicle*, May 22, 2005, http://www.chron .com/CDA/archives/archive.mpl?id=2005_3872567.

161 **"There is no stone left unturned"**: John Browne, video footage of BP press conference at City Hall in Texas City, March 24, 2005.

162 **"The working environment had eroded"**: Mogford report, 4.

162 **A *Houston Chronicle* investigation**: Lise Olsen, "BP Leads Nation in Refinery Fatalities," *Houston Chronicle*, May 15, 2005, http://www.chron.com/disp/ story.mpl/special/05/blast/3182510.html.

162 **"They should've learned some major lessons"**: Jordan Barab (deputy assistant secretary of labor at OSHA), in an interview with the author, September 2010.

163 **reported injuries and safety concerns**: *BP Texas City Site Report of Findings: Texas City's Protection Performance, Behaviors, Culture, Management and Leadership*, 62.

163 **"If a catastrophe has to occur"**: Email from Jeanne Pascal to Marc Kovac, "Re: How the heck are you?," August 5, 2005, 5:58 p.m.

164 **"It appears they are taking their moral standards"**: Anne Belli, "BP Expects Blast Won't Sink Profits," *Houston Chronicle*, July 1, 2005, http://www .chron.com/disp/story.mpl/special/05/blast/3250203.html#ixzz1 No3wJtCe.

165 **"The big bad wolf blows"**: BP internal document, *BP Group HSE Standard; Major Accident Risk Awareness Training*, October 17, 2002.

165 **the company knew exactly what sorts of consequences**: BP internal report, *Fire and Explosion Risks for Selected Refining Processes—A Generic Risk Ranking*, November 22, 2000.

166 **"BP embraced the principle"**: Email from Robert Mancini to BP staff, "Re: Risk Management and Assessment," March 4, 1999, 8:45 p.m.

166 **"Dear Ms. Rowe"**: Letter from Paula Sharp, BP's director of human resources at the Texas City refinery, to Eva Rowe, April 29, 2005.

167 **"Call it a two-for-one deal"**: Eva Rowe, in an interview with the author, August 2010.

CHAPTER 9: CODE BLACK

169 **"There were many technology gaps"**: *Aberdeen Press and Journal*, "Thunder Horse Project Galloping Along in GOM," May 2, 2005.

170 **"It was a marvelous time"**: Daniel Cusick, "OIL AND GAS: Deepwater Drilling Promises Big Rewards—and Risks," *Greenwire*, May 6, 2005.

170 **"an exciting year for exploration"**: Foster Natural Gas Report, "Interior Calls 2004 'Exciting Year' for Exploring in the Deep Water Gulf of Mexico," May 5, 2005.

172 **"Blowouts can occur during any phase"**: United States Minerals and Management Service, *Site Specific Environmental Assessment, Shell Deepwater Development Inc., Development Operations Coordination Document*, May 9, 2000.

172 **"If we've learned anything"**: Cusick, "OIL AND GAS."

172 **"We find ourselves developing systems"**: *International Oil Daily*, "BP Pushed Depths of Deepwater Exploration in the U.S. Gulf," May 9, 2005.

173 **"leaning tower"**: Ray Massey, "Leaning Tower of BP," *Daily Mail*, July 14, 2005.

173 **"there does not appear to be any structural damage"**: *Platts Gas Market Report*, "Thunder Horse Unlikely to Begin Gas, Oil Production by Fourth Quarter: BP," July 29, 2005.

174 **"It was not storm-related"**: *International Oil Daily*, "BP Challenged on Thunder Horse Accident," October 31, 2005.

174 **Thunder Horse was the victim of a series of straightforward assembly errors**: United States Minerals and Management Service, Accident Investigation Report, BP Exploration and Production, July 8, 2005.

175 **"Having always seemed so competent"**: Harry Wallop, "Stand by Those Pumps, BP Is Positively Oozing with Mileage," *Daily Telegraph*, October 29, 2005.

176 **had already shown some signs of wear**: *GC-2 Transit Line Spill Incident Investigation Report*, April 14, 2006.

176 **"We've got a leak"**: Browne, *Beyond Business*, Kindle edition, loc. 4170.

177 **"I could see problems brewing"**: Browne, *Beyond Business*, Kindle edition, loc. 4183.

177 **"We had a lake of oil out there"**: Marc Kovac, in interviews with the author, July 2010.

178 **No alarms sounded at all**: *GC-2 Transit Line Spill Incident Investigation Report*, April 14, 2006.

178 **"two hundred thousand gallons is nothing to be sneezed at"**: Scott West (EPA criminal investigator), in an interview with the author, July 2010.

178 **"Why did our system not detect"**: Browne, *Beyond Business*, Kindle edition, loc. 4175.

179 **"We have huge infrastructure that is hanging on"**: Email from Kip Sprague to North Slope corrosion team, "Re: Emailing CIC-MR Capex AFE Tracker 2006," April 10, 2005, 5:03 p.m.

180 **"Every morning BP"**: Stuart Sneed (whistle-blower and former BP-contracted pipeline inspector), in an interview with the author, June 2010.

182 **after a multimonth investigation**: Billie Garde and Paul Flaherty, "Report Documenting the Result of an Independent Investigation into Two FAST Concerns," internal BP document, May 2007.

182 **"they felt pressured for production ahead of safety"**: Ibid.

CHAPTER 10: THE FIX-IT MAN

185 **"He was appointed"**: John Hofmeister, in an interview with the author, May 2011.

185 **"We needed to strengthen the BP"**: John Browne, video footage of press conference, Prudhoe Bay, Alaska, August 4, 2006.

186 **"I had a pretty good feel"**: Robert Malone (former president, BP America), in an interview with the author, August 2006.

186 **his first major setback**: *U.S. Commodity Futures Trading Commission v. BP Products North America*, United States District Court for the Northern District of Illinois, Eastern Division, Civil Action 06C 03503, June 28, 2006.

187 **"How does it feel taking on"**: Audio recordings used in *The Spill*, PBS *Frontline*.

187 **"Whew. It's pretty big, man"**: Ibid.

187 **"with the knowledge, advice and consent"**: Ibid. See also http://www .cftc.gov/pressroom/pressreleases/pr5193-06.html.

187 **"The trading issue, that really was about our values"**: Robert Malone, in an interview with the author, August 2006.

188 **"On behalf of the BP Group"**: John Browne, video footage of press conference, Anchorage, Alaska, August 3, 2006.

188 **"The other lines that we still have"**: Bill Hedges, video footage of press conference, Prudhoe Bay, Alaska, August 4, 2006.

188 **"The events that have"**: Robert Malone, in an interview with the author, August 2006.

189 **"this is the only time"**: Browne, *Beyond Business*, Kindle edition, loc. 4183.

189 **"We had corrosion spots"**: Robert Malone, in an interview with the author, August 2006.

190 **"Shutting down the whole oilfield"**: Browne, *Beyond Business*, Kindle edition, loc. 4200.

191 **"It was a rough week"**: Robert Malone, in an interview with the author, August 2006.

191 **"Battered Petroleum"**: *Sunday (London) Times*, "Focus: Battered Petroleum," December 24, 2006, http://business.timesonline.co.uk/tol/business/ law/article1264161.ece.

191 **"I did not think things"**: Browne, *Beyond Business*, Kindle edition, loc. 4200.

194 **encouraged to look the other way**: Martin Anderson, (pipeline inspection program supervisor and auditor for Acuren, a BP contractor), in interviews with the author, July 2010.

195 **he feared they weren't prepared**: Ibid.

196 **Acuren possessed very few records**: Internal BP and Acuren documents, *Acuren Inspection Quality Audit*, March 26, 2007–February 4, 2008.

197 **several confidential reports that were scathing:** Ibid.

197 **In a few egregious cases:** Martin Anderson, in interviews with the author, July 2010.

199 **"I suppose that this committee":** Congressman Joe Barton (R-TX, then chairman of the House Energy and Commerce Committee), in U.S. House Committee on Energy and Commerce hearings, September 7, 2006.

199 **"I respectfully will not answer":** Richard Woollam, in U.S. House Committee on Energy and Commerce hearings, September 7, 2006.

199 **"The public's faith in BP":** Robert Malone, in testimony to the U.S. House Committee on Energy and Commerce, September 7, 2006.

199 **He confessed to one:** Ibid.

CHAPTER 11: A TORRID AFFAIR

204 **Browne got a phone call:** Browne, *Beyond Business*, Kindle edition, loc. 4353.

204 **$4,000 bottles of claret:** Dennis Rice, "The TRUE Story about Lord Browne by ex-Rent Boy Lover," *Daily Mail,* May 6, 2007, http://www.daily mail.co.uk/news/article-452983/The-TRUE-story-Lord-Browne--ex-rent-boy-lover.html.

204 **"I had been found out":** Browne, *Beyond Business*, Kindle edition, loc. 4357.

206 **"a false sense of confidence":** BP-commissioned, publicly available document, "The Report of BP U.S. Refineries Independent Safety Review Panel" (known as the Baker Panel report), January 2007.

206 **"BP gets it":** John Browne, video footage of BP press conference, London, January 16, 2007.

206 **"he didn't really get it":** Nancy Leveson (MIT professor, Baker Panel member, and an author of the Baker Panel report), in an interview with RK, June 2010.

207 **"I am not prepared to make allowances":** Chip Cummins, Carrick Mollenkamp, Aaron O. Patrick, and Guy Chazan, "Scandal, Crises Hasten Exit For British Icon—BP Chief's Tenure Was Increasingly Rocky; Then He Lied to Court—Hiding an Escort Service," *Wall Street Journal*, May 2, 2007.

207 **"It's a sorry end":** Daniel Mann, CNBC broadcast, May 1, 2007.

208 **"BPXA has not equipped the FACILITY":** *State of Alaska, Department of Environmental Conservation v. BP Exploration (Alaska) Inc.,* Compliance Order by Consent, June 3, 2002.

208 **"This compliance order shows":** Letter from Congressman Joe Barton to Alaska commissioner for the Department of Environmental Conservation Kurt Fredriksson and BP America president Robert Malone, October 6, 2006.

210 **"Will you agree with me":** Bart Stupak (D-MI), U.S. House Energy and Commerce Committee testimony transcript, May 16, 2007.

210 **"there were extreme budget pressures"**: Robert Malone, U.S. House Energy and Commerce Committee testimony transcript, May 16, 2007.

211 **"The eldest gets to do everything"**: Judi Bevan, "An Interview with Tony Hayward," *BP Magazine*, http://www.bp.com/liveassets/bp_internet/global bp/STAGING/global_assets/downloads/B/BPM_04one_P19-22_Pro file.pdf.

212 **"It was a great lesson"**: Ibid.

212 **"Hayward's shtick"**: Matthew Gwyther, in an interview with MS, September 2010.

213 **"This has been one hell of a year"**: Tony Hayward as chief of exploration and production, video of BP internal meeting, 2005.

216 **"When I received the phone call"**: Scott West (EPA criminal division, special agent in charge of the BP Alaska investigation), in an interview with the author, July 2010.

218 **"corporate-wide negligence"**: Ibid.

219 **"We would get boxes and boxes"**: Ed Meggert (former Alaska Department of Environmental Conservation inspector in Prudhoe Bay), in an interview with the author, July 2010.

220 **very highest levels of BP leadership**: Letter from assistant U.S. Attorney Andrea Steward to Carol Dinkins, Vinson & Elkins LLP, June 22, 2007, "Re: Meeting of June 6, 2007," in which Steward specifies Tony Hayward, Andy Inglis, and two other executives as subject of file request; and Scott West, in interviews with the author, July and August 2010.

220 **When Eva Rowe rejected**: Eva Rowe, in an interview with the author, August 2010.

221 **"You're talking about a twenty-year-old"**: Brent Coon (attorney who represented Eva Rowe against BP), in an interview with the author, August 2010.

222 **"I took a stand"**: Eva Rowe, in an interview with the author, August 2010.

224 **He claimed to have never seen**: John Manzoni, transcript of deposition given to Brent Coon and Tony Buzbee, September 8, 2006.

224 **"We don't defer maintenance as a rule"**: Ibid.

224 **"When was the first time that you learned"**: Tony Buzbee, transcript of deposition given to Brent Coon and Tony Buzbee, September 8, 2006.

225 **"Can't even name the name"**: Brent Coon, in an interview with the author, August 2010.

225 **an uncharacteristic failure of memory**: John Browne, transcript of oral deposition given to Brent Coon, April 4, 2008.

226 **"Were you ever made aware"**: Ibid.

227 **"organizational culture and structure"**: U.S. Chemical Safety and Hazard Investigation Board, *Investigation Report, Refinery Explosion and Fire*, 18.

CHAPTER 12: A CHANGING CULTURE

232 **BP's management was burdensome**: Tony Hayward, in Houston town hall presentation, according to internal BP documents, with notes taken by Laurie Beppler, "BP CONFIDENTIAL Notes from Tony Hayward's Town Hall Meeting," September 19, 2007.

232 **"Due to all of these things"**: Ibid

232 **"John was a wonderful spokesman"**: Ronald Freeman, in an interview with MS, August 2010.

233 **"a company that was too top-down"**: Tony Hayward, in a speech at Stanford University, May 12, 2009, video recording last viewed 6/26/11, http://www.youtube.com/watch?v=FwQMooclxgM&feature=player_profilepage (hereinafter Hayward, Stanford University speech).

233 **ten thousand different organizational management groups**: Hayward, with notes taken by Beppler, "BP CONFIDENTIAL Notes from Tony Hayward's Town Hall Meeting."

233 **"It's not surprising"**: Hayward, Stanford University speech.

233 **"laser-like focus"**: Russell Hotten, "BP Shifts Focus to Safety, Not Big Deals," *Daily Telegraph*, February 7, 2007.

233 **"The interesting thing"**: Carola Hoyos, in an interview with MS, August 2010.

235 **"What I'm very certain about"**: Hayward, Stanford University speech.

236 **"If you play well with this"**: Martin Anderson, in an interview with the author, July 2010.

238 **"Marty Anderson's concerns were unusual"**: Billie Garde (attorney and deputy BP ombudsman), in an interview with the author, October 2010.

238 **"He revealed a significant quality control breakdown"**: Email from Billie Garde to Jack Lynch, BP America's general counsel, September 25, 2009, 12:18 p.m.

239 **"So much data was incorrectly"**: Email from Lee Wheaton (program manager for CSI, contractor, in Alaska) to BP, Acuren, and other company management overseeing corrosion program, "Re: 2009 Internal Inspection Program Status & Recovery Plan," October 6, 2009, 5:21 p.m.

240 **"It would be a rare occasion"**: Email from Billie Garde to Jack Lynch, BP America's general counsel, September 25, 2009, 12:18 p.m.

241 **"Where the rubber meets the road"**: Billie Garde, in an interview with the author, October 2010.

242 **"Marty became the subject"**: Email from Billie Garde to Jack Lynch, BP America's general counsel, September 25, 2009, 12:18 p.m.

243 **"If we had to go to trial today"**: statement by U.S. Attorney Karen Loeffler

as recalled by Scott West (former EPA investigator), in an interview with the author, July 2010.

245 **"Other parts of BP's organization"**: Email from Aunnie (Andrea) Steward to "chrisjemail@aol.com," "daniel_cheyette@law.state.ak.us," Matt Goers, and others, "Re: BP theory of the Case," June 12, 2007, 11:23 a.m. Accessed 9/11/11 on the website for Public Employees for Environmental Responsibility, http://www.peer.org/docs/ak/08_11_11_us_attorney_memo_on_bp_case.pdf.

245 **"What the hell is going on"**: Scott West, in an interview with the author, July 2010.

247 **deny that conversation happened**: Jim Carlton, "Ex-EPA Official Faults Probe of BP Alaska Oil Spill," *Wall Street Journal*, November 19, 2008.

247 **"The allegations by Mr. West"**: Public statement released by the Department of Justice, November 3, 2008, http://www.peer.org/docs/ak/08_11_11_doj_and_epa_official_responses.pdf.

247 **"This leak, and the spill that resulted"**: Robert Malone, in a statement released by BP, October 25, 2007.

248 **"These agreements are an admission"**: Ibid.

CHAPTER 13: OFF THE HOOK

250 **"a serial environmental criminal"**: Jeanne Pascal, in interviews with the author, June, July, and September 2010.

252 **"They had achieved very good records"**: Robert Bea (engineering professor at University of California, Berkeley, and former consultant for BP, Shell, and other oil companies), in interview with the author, June 2010.

252 **"the condition of having"**: *U.S. Air Force Technical Manual TO 00-35D-54*, May 2007.

252 **"a disciplined framework"**: BP.com, http://www.bp.com/sectiongeneric article.do?categoryId=9023275&contentId=7043216.

252 **"They spent an enormous amount"**: Kristjan Dye, BP mechanic and union president, in an interview with the author, July 2010.

253 **"I think BP just stopped"**: Karlene Roberts (management professor at University of California, Berkeley, and former BP process safety consultant), in an interview with the author, September 2010.

255 **"It's kind of a catch-up thing"**: Mike Theurich (inspection team member for Mistras, a BP contractor in Alaska), in an interview with the author, July 2010.

255 **"a fundamental lack of trust"**: *Review of Operational Integrity Concerns at Greater Prudhoe Bay*, confidential internal report obtained by the author, October 2001, 5.

255 **it hadn't reduced lengthy maintenance:** *ORT Progress Report Questionnaire Results*, internal BP document obtained by the author, http://www.pro publica.org/documents/item/2007-bp-ort-review#document/p4.

257 **"very concerned about continuing degradation":** *Review of Operational Integrity Concerns at Greater Prudhoe Bay*, confidential internal report obtained by the author, October 2001.

258 **"It sounded like a gunshot":** Email from Fritz Guenther to Doug Suttles, "Re: reponse to DNR Press Conference," September 21, 2007, 10:11 a.m.

260 **"Assurance is killing BP today":** Tony Hayward, Houston town hall presentation, September 19, 2007.

263 **"For someone to look at a line":** Steve Rinehart (BP Alaska public affairs), in an interview with the author, October 2010.

264 **"That information was communicated":** Email from Jeanne Pascal to Tony Brock and Bob Batch at BP, and to Carol Dinkins at Vinson & Elkins, among others, "Subject: 10/21/08 Meeting recap," October 22, 2008, 3:31 p.m.

CHAPTER 14: RUN TO FAILURE

266 **"Our plan would say":** Mike Theurich, in an interview with the author, July 2010.

267 **"I tell the new employees":** Marc Kovac, in an interview with the author, July 2010.

268 **"BP puts everything on a risk matrix":** Patrick O'Farrell (BP Alaska project manager), in an interview with the author, July 2010.

270 **they skipped the inspection:** Letter from Alaska Department of Natural Resources to Tony Brock, BP Alaska's senior vice president and technical director, "Re: Status Report—PSIO Investigation of September 29, 2008 Y-pad Artificial Lift Gas Pipeline Rupture," February 20, 2009.

274 **In his first PowerPoint slide:** PowerPoint presentation of Doug Suttles (president, BP Exploration [Alaska]), "Resource Development Council Annual Meeting November 19, 2008," http://www.akrdc.org/membership/events/conference/2008/presentations/suttles.pdf.

274 **"made an extraordinary difference":** BP Press Release, "Lamar McKay to Lead BP America," January 6, 2009, http://www.bp.com/genericarticle.do?categoryId=7106&contentId=7050700.

275 **"BP does not agree with your pre-conditions":** Email from Fred Levy (BP's attorney for debarment) to Jeanne Pascal et al., "Re: Phone Call recap," April 9, 2009, 5:50 a.m.

277 **gas continued to seep around the edges:** letter to BP Exploration (Alaska) president John Minge from U.S. Congressmen Henry Waxman (D-CA) and

Bart Stupak (D-MI) and the House Energy and Commerce Committee, January 14, 2010.

278 **the third critical safety backup**: Ibid.

278 **"It's hard to describe these explosions"**: Robert Bea, in interview with the author, June 2010.

279 **An investigation found**: A petition to revoke probation for BP Exploration (Alaska), filed in U.S. District Court for the District of Alaska by Mary Frances Barnes (probation officer), November 17, 2010, http://www.contrac tormisconduct.org/ass/contractors/61/cases/829/2124/bp-amoco-ak-pipe line-leaks_nov-2010-update_petition.pdf.

280 **Between 2000 and late 2009**: Spill statistics compiled from records at the Alaska Department of Environmental Conservation, the Occupational Safety and Health Administration, and the U.S. Department of the Interior. Actual numbers referenced in a chart published at propublica.org, http:// www.propublica.org/article/bp-accidents-past-and-present.

280 **"We had a huge infrastructure"**: Robert Malone, in testimony to the U.S. House Committee on Energy and Commerce, September 7, 2006.

280 **BP also spilled more oil in the gulf**: Spill statistics compiled from records at the Alaska Department of Environmental Conservation, the Occupational Safety and Health Administration, and the U.S. Department of the Interior. Actual numbers referenced in a chart published at propublica.org, http://www.propublica.org/article/bp-accidents-past-and-present.

280 **safety statistics were no better**: Ibid.

281 **"Why did you let it happen to him"**: Hayward, Stanford University speech.

282 **openly questioned whether BP could protect American interests**: Letter to BP Exploration (Alaska) president John Minge from Waxman and Stupak and the House Energy and Commerce Committee, January 14, 2010.

283 **as-built documents had been issued**: Letter from U.S. Congressman Edward Markey (D-MA), Barney Frank (D-MA), and others to Minerals and Management Service director Elizabeth Birnbaum regarding concerns about Atlantis, February 10, 2010.

284 **"I hit a lot of resistance"**: Ken Abbott (BP contractor and supervisor on Atlantis offshore rig project), in an interview with the author, May 2010.

285 **after more than twenty-four months of wrangling**: Email from Billie Garde to Jack Lynch, BP America's general counsel, September 25, 2009, 12:18 p.m.

286 **In a burst of anger**: Email from Jeanne Pascal and Carson Hodges to BP attorney John (Jack) Lynch and BP Alaska President John Minge, "Fw: Problems from Jeanne and Carson," January 19, 2010, 11:28 a.m.

CHAPTER 15: A DELICATE BALANCE

289 **"the same barrier to our seismic":** Statement of David Rainey (vice president, Gulf of Mexico Exploration), in a hearing before the Senate Energy and Natural Resources Committee, November 19, 2009.

289 **"It was as if god":** Gabriel García Márquez, *100 Years of Solitude* (Cambridge, UK: Cambridge University Press), 58.

290 **"You don't know what you are going to encounter":** Michael Norton (offshore oil well designer), in an interview with the author, September 2010.

290 **"in the event of an unanticipated blowout":** *Gulf of Mexico Regional Oil Spill Response Plan,* June 30, 2009.

298 **serious oil spills:** Spill statistics compiled from records at the Alaska Department of Environmental Conservation, the Occupational Safety and Health Administration, and the U.S. Department of Interior. Actual numbers referenced in a chart published at propublica.org, http://www.pro publica.org/article/bp-accidents-past-and-present.

299 **"This is not a decision that I've made lightly":** President Barack Obama, in remarks at Andrews Air Force Base, March 31, 2010, http://www.white house.gov/the-press-office/remarks-president-energy-security-andrews-air-force-base-3312010.

300 **"What we knew [was that] the safety records":** Carol Browner (Barack Obama's chief adviser on energy and climate), in interview with MS, July 2010.

300 **"Well, it's a good question":** David Hayes, deputy secretary of the U.S. Department of Interior, in interview with MS, July 2010.

301 **"The only reason the oil companies":** Derek Brower, in an interview with the author, September 2010.

301 **"It's an inherently dangerous":** Matthew Gwyther, in an interview with MS, August 2010.

302 **"I never quite believed the rhetoric":** John Hofmeister, in an interview with the author, May 2011.

303 **"Let's pump it up":** Mike Williams, Transocean chief electronics technician on Deepwater Horizon rig, in testimony before the Joint United States Coast Guard/The Bureau of Ocean Energy Management, Regulation and Enforcement Investigation, New Orleans, July 23, 2010.

303 **"We blew the bottom out of the well":** Ibid.

303 **"Oh, no big deal":** Ibid.

304 **Its weight fractured the walls:** *Deep Water: The Gulf Oil Disaster and the Future of Offshore Drilling,* Report to the President from the National Commission on the Deepwater Horizon Oil Spill and Offshore Drilling, January 2011, 110.

304 **"The situation had become delicate":** Ibid., 94.

304 **"a nightmare well"**: Email from Brian Morel to Richard Miller and Mark Hafle, "Subject: Macondo APB," April 14, 2010, 1:31 p.m.

304 **"it's like blowing up a red balloon"**: Natalie Roshto, wife of Transocean rig hand Shane Roshto, in testimony before the Joint United States Coast Guard/The Bureau of Ocean Energy Management, Regulation and Enforcement Investigation, New Orleans, July 22, 2010.

304 **"Well integrity and safety"**: *Deep Water: The Gulf Oil Disaster and the Future of Offshore Drilling*, 94.

CHAPTER 16: SOS

307 **From the start, BP had planned**: *Deep Water: The Gulf Oil Disaster and the Future of Offshore Drilling*, 111.

308 **"That's our best practice"**: Joe Leimkuhler (offshore well delivery manager, Shell), in a presentation to the Aspen Ideas Festival, July 2010.

308 **"They had terrible losses throughout the well"**: Jesse Gagliano (technical sales adviser for Halliburton, employed as contractor on the Deepwater Horizon project), in testimony before the Joint United States Coast Guard/The Bureau of Ocean Energy Management, Regulation and Enforcement Investigation, New Orleans, August 24, 2010.

308 **"there's a chance we could run a production liner"**: Email from Brian Morel to Richard Miller, "Subject: Macondo APB," April 14, 2010, 1:31 p.m.

308 **"We [had] flipped design parameters"**: Email from Richard Miller to Brian Morel et al., "Re: Macondo APB," April 14, 2010.

309 **"This has been a crazy well"**: Email from Mark Hafle to Richard Miller, "Re: Macondo APB," April 14, 2010, 11:09 p.m.

309 **more than $58 million over budget**: *Deep Water: The Gulf Oil Disaster and the Future of Offshore Drilling*, 2.

309 **he saw a trend he didn't like**: *Deepwater Horizon Accident Investigation Report* (Bly report), internal analysis by BP, September 10, 2010, 22.

309 **"I'm showing channeling"**: Jesse Gagliano (technical sales adviser for Halliburton, employed as contractor on the Deepwater Horizon project), in testimony before the Joint United States Coast Guard/The Bureau of Ocean Energy Management, Regulation and Enforcement Investigation, New Orleans, August 24, 2010.

310 **"We have six centralizers"**: Email from Brian Morel to Jessie Gagliano, Greg Walz, Brett Cocales, and Mark Hafle, April 15, 2010, 4:00 p.m.

310 **"I didn't just jump to twenty-one"**: Jesse Gagliano, in testimony before the Joint United States Coast Guard/The Bureau of Ocean Energy Management, Regulation and Enforcement Investigation, New Orleans, August 24, 2010.

310 **"be consistent with our previous decisions"**: *Deep Water: The Gulf Oil Disaster and the Future of Offshore Drilling*, 97.

310 **"I don't understand"**: Email from Brian Morel to Brett Cocales, "Fw: Macondo STK Geodetic," April 16, 2010, 4:04 p.m.

311 **"It's not, you know, the real thing"**: John Guide (BP's wells team leader), in testimony before the Joint United States Coast Guard/The Bureau of Ocean Energy Management, Regulation and Enforcement Investigation, Kenner, Louisiana, July 22, 2010.

311 **"But who cares. It's done. End of story"**: Email from Brett Cocales to Brian Morel, "Fw: Macondo STK Geodetic," April 16, 2010, 4:15 p.m.

311 **"Can you also confirm"**: Jesse Gagliano, in testimony before the Joint United States Coast Guard/The Bureau of Ocean Energy Management, Regulation and Enforcement Investigation, New Orleans, August 24, 2010.

311 **"a SEVERE gas flow problem"**: Ibid.

311 **"I was in bed"**: John Guide, in testimony before the Joint United States Coast Guard/The Bureau of Ocean Energy Management, Regulation and Enforcement Investigation, Kenner, Louisiana, July 22, 2010.

312 **"The number one risk"**: *Deep Water: The Gulf Oil Disaster and the Future of Offshore Drilling*, 99.

312 **unusual in a gulf well**: Ibid., 16.

313 **"recognized it would provide"**: Ibid., 100.

313 **"completed the job"**: Ibid., 102.

314 **"Everyone involved with the job"**: John Guide, in testimony before the Joint United States Coast Guard/The Bureau of Ocean Energy Management, Regulation and Enforcement Investigation, Kenner, Louisiana, July 22, 2010.

314 **"limited or no information"**: *Deep Water: The Gulf Oil Disaster and the Future of Offshore Drilling*, 99.

316 **None of the changes had been reviewed**: Ibid., 20.

316 **"We've got some changes"**: Recollection of Doug Brown (Transocean chief mechanic, Deepwater Horizon) about statement by Robert Kaluza, according to recorded interview with Anderson Cooper, AC360, June 11, 2010, http://transcripts.cnn.com/TRANSCRIPTS/1006/11/acd.02.html.

316 **"This is the way it's going to be"**: Ibid.

316 **"I guess that's what we have those pinchers for"**: Douglas Browne, in testimony before The Joint United States Coast Guard Minerals Management Service hearing, Kenner, Louisiana, May 26, 2010

317 **"Things looked good"**: *Deep Water: The Gulf Oil Disaster and the Future of Offshore Drilling*, 104.

319 **"a very large abnormality"**: Memorandum from Congressman Henry Waxman to House Subcommittee on Oversight and Investigations, "Re:

Key Questions Arising from Inquiry into the Deepwater Horizon Gulf of Mexico Oil Spill," May 25, 2010.

320 **"they don't run a single string with everything else"**: Michael Norton (drilling engineer and consultant), in an interview with the author, September 2010.

322 **"Everybody had gone home"**: Fred Bartlit (member of the National Commission on the BP Deepwater Horizon Oil Spill and Offshore Drilling), in a deposition delivered in a regular meeting, November 8, 2010, Washington, D.C.

322 **"It went good"**: *Deep Water: The Gulf Oil Disaster and the Future of Offshore Drilling*, 112.

324 **"We have a situation"**: Ibid., 24.

325 **"I need to go check this out"**: Mike Williams (Transocean electronics technician on Deepwater Horizon rig), in testimony before the Joint United States Coast Guard/The Bureau of Ocean Energy Management, Regulation and Enforcement, Kenner, Louisiana, July 23, 2010.

325 **"higher than I can"**: Mike Williams, in testimony before the Joint United States Coast Guard/The Bureau of Ocean Energy Management, Regulation and Enforcement, Kenner, Louisiana, July 23, 2010.

326 **"I didn't know if it was blood"**: Mike Williams, *60 Minutes*, May 20, 2010.

326 **"It blew me probably twenty feet"**: Randy Ezell, in testimony before the Joint United States Coast Guard/The Bureau of Ocean Energy Management, Regulation and Enforcement, Kenner, Louisiana, May 28, 2010.

327 **"I knew we needed to get away"**: Jimmy Harrell (senior Transocean manager), in testimony before the Joint United States Coast Guard/The Bureau of Ocean Energy Management, Regulation and Enforcement Investigation, Kenner, Louisiana, July 22, 2010, and May 27, 2010.

328 **we should abandon ship**: Mike Williams, in testimony before the Joint United States Coast Guard/The Bureau of Ocean Energy Management, Regulation and Enforcement Investigation, New Orleans, July 23, 2010.

329 **"I looked outside and saw the fuel"**: Kurt Kuchta (captain, Deepwater Horizon), in testimony before the Joint United States Coast Guard/The Bureau of Ocean Energy Management, Regulation and Enforcement Investigation, Kenner, Louisiana, May 27, 2010, July 22, 2010.

POSTSCRIPT

332 **"proven equipment and technology"**: *Gulf of Mexico Regional Oil Spill Response Plan*, June 30, 2009.

332 **"making it up day to day"**: Tony Hayward, in an interview with the BBC, November 8, 2010, http://www.bbc.co.uk/news/business-11709027.

332 **"We didn't think it was relevant"**: David Hammer, "BP's Doug Suttles Says Company 'Threw Everything' at Gushing Oil Well," *Times-Picayune,* June 25, 2010, http://www.nola.com/news/gulf-oil-spill/index.ssf/2010/06/bps_doug_suttles_says_company.html.

332 **"No one wants this over more than I do"**: Tony Hayward, in a statement to the press, June 1, 2010, http://www.huffingtonpost.com/2010/06/01/bp-ceo-tony-hayward-video_n_595906.html.

333 **"What we need as a society"**: Pratt, in an interview with MS, August 2010.

334 **"One of the reasons that I am so distraught"**: Tony Hayward, in testimony before the U.S. House Committee on Energy and Commerce, Subcommittee on Oversight and Investigations, June 17, 2010.

334 **"But you are the CEO of the company"**: Congressman Michael Burgess (R-TX), in hearing of the U.S. House Committee on Energy and Commerce, June 17, 2010.

335 **accused of stonewalling**: Hearing before the U.S. House Committee on Energy and Commerce, June 17, 2010.

335 **"lessons for us relating to the way we operate"**: Robert Dudley, in a statement posted on BP's website, http://www.bp.com/sectiongenericarticle800.do?categoryId=9036210&contentId=7066976.

336 **"systemic failures"**: *Deep Water: The Gulf Oil Disaster and the Future of Offshore Drilling,* 122.

337 **"recorded the best year"**: Dan Berman, "Transocean Celebrates 'Best Year in Safety,'" *Politico,* April 4, 2011.

339 **"An item can be an F rank"**: Steve Rinehart, in an interview with the author, October 2010.

340 **"It would be a concern"**: Dan Seamount, commissioner, Alaska Oil and Gas Conservation Commission, in an interview with the author, July 2010.

Index